MARTIN BUBER'S LIFE AND WORK

MARTIN BUBER'S

LIFE AND WORK

The Middle Years, 1923-1945

Maurice Friedman

Wayne State University Press   Detroit   1988

92   91   90   89   88   5   4   3   2   1

Library of Congress Cataloging-in-Publication Data

Friedman, Maurice S.
    Martin Buber's life and work.

    Originally published: New York: Dutton, c1981–c1983.
    Includes bibliographies and indexes.
    Contents: [1] The early years, 1878–1923 — [2] The middle years, 1923–1945 — [3] The later years, 1945–1965.
    1. Buber, Martin, 1878–1965. 2. Philosophers, Jewish —Germany—Biography. 3. Philosophers—Germany— Biography. 4. Zionists—Germany—Biography. 5. Jews— Germany—Biography. 6. Jews, German—Israel—Biography. I. Title.
B3213.B84F727   1988   296.3′092′4   87–25415
ISBN 0–8143–1945–9 (pbk. : v. 2 : alk. paper)

For David and Dvora

"Bundled together, men march without Thou *and without* I *, those of the left who want to abolish memory, and those of the right who want to regulate it: hostile and separated hosts, they march into the common abyss.*

"Modern collectivism is the last barrier raised by man against a meeting with himself.

"On the far side of the subjective, on this side of the objective, on the narrow ridge, where I *and* Thou *meet, there is the realm of 'between.'*

"When the man who has become solitary can no longer say 'Thou' to the 'dead' known God, everything depends on whether he can still say it to the living unknown God by saying 'Thou' with all his being to another living and known man. If he can no longer do this either, then there certainly remains for him the sublime illusion of detached thought that he is a self-contained self; as man he is lost."

—MARTIN BUBER, *Between Man and Man*

Contents

CONTENTS

Preface

Martin Buber's Life and Work attempts to show Buber's thought and work as his active personal response to the events and meetings of his life. Even Buber's translation of the Hebrew Bible and his retelling of Hasidic tales grew out of his response to situations, and it is this response that forms the real matrix of his philosophy. The first volume of *Martin Buber's Life and Work* is *The Early Years 1878–1923.* Buber's loss of his mother as a child; the threat of the infinite he experienced at fourteen; his activity in cultural and political Zionism; his encounter with mysticism and discovery of Hasidism; his breakthrough to dialogue from the impact of the First World War; his "speeches on Judaism" and his editorship of *Der Jude;* his work in postwar education and politics; and his maturing from the "easy word" to the "hard word" —all these were necessary steps toward Buber's depth understanding of the philosophy of dialogue and the life of dialogue.

Martin Buber's Life and Work: The Middle Years 1923–1945 shows Buber's application of his philosophy of dialogue to many spheres of life and his continuing "encounter on the narrow ridge" in the face of the cruel demands of the hour that he encountered in Nazi Germany, prewar Palestine, and the Second World War.

In this second volume, as in the first and the third, I have myself translated all the material from the German except that already existing in reliable published translation. In this volume too I have almost entirely avoided footnotes. In several cases I have referred to notes inserted in the Sources for particular chapters at the back or to longer Notes also set in the back. In this way the reader who wants to comprehend the whole is not impeded by unnecessary detail; yet material of concern to scholars is preserved. A case in point is my exposition of the principles and methods underlying the Buber-Rosenzweig translation of the Hebrew Bible into German, which many readers would find too technical but which is important to retain for scholars.

MAURICE FRIEDMAN

Solana Beach, California
Spring, 1983

Acknowledgments

I AM INDEBTED to my former wife, Eugenia Friedman, who read through the manuscript of this second volume of *Martin Buber's Life and Work* and made many helpful suggestions. I am also indebted to my friend Virginia Shabatay who has spent untold hours in helping me edit and, where possible, cut the second volume. I also wish to express my gratitude to my friend and longtime editor Richard Huett for his invaluable assistance in making the second volume accessible to a wider audience. He brought to my attention countless places that needed clarification or retranslation. "In twenty years of editing I cannot recall a book that occupied me so intensively," Huett wrote me. I am also grateful to my friend and student Judith Stoup (now Laurel Mannen), who accomplished the difficult task of bringing the manuscript of the second volume into finished form. I also wish to mention here again my friend Susan Richards, who in many ways made it practically possible for me to write the second volume.

I wish to acknowledge here the generosity of the Leo Baeck Institute,

New York City; the Martin Buber Archives of the Jewish and National University Library of Jerusalem, Israel (Arc. MS Var. 350); Rafael Buber, Martin Buber's son and heir; and Ernst Simon, Buber's literary executor, in giving me permission to reproduce here some of the photographs of Buber and a number of Buber's letters to Franz Rosenzweig. I am also indebted to Schocken Books and to Professor Nahum N. Glatzer, author of *Franz Rosenzweig's Life and Thought,* for permission to reproduce here two pictures of Rosenzweig and the picture of Rosenzweig's death mask which appeared originally in that book.

I dedicated *Martin Buber's Life and Work: The Early Years* to Dr. Grete Schaeder of Göttingen, Germany, because of her immense labor of love in editing the three volumes of *Martin Buber: Briefwechsel aus sieben Jahrzehnten* which have been of such enormous service to me in bringing my own three volumes of *Martin Buber's Life and Work* into final shape. Here I must go beyond this acknowledgment to point to a dialogue and cooperation between us unique in my experience. In addition to the letters, which I have used as a foundation for my "dialography," the most impressive form of this dialogue has been the immense task that she has taken on of reading the manuscript of the second volume and sending me detailed suggestions and criticisms, showing a mastery not only of Buber's letters but of the entire range of his corpus. She has caught repetitions from one volume to the next of which I have been unaware, has corrected errors in dates and facts, has suggested the retranslation of unclear passages and has put in her own words the meaning of several passages from the letters that were unclear to me. Much of the form and some of the content of the first pages of Chapter 8—"Hermann Gerson and the 'Work Folk' " I owe directly to her suggestions. The second volume has been greatly improved through her help.

Yet I must say more. After my fifteen years of close work with Buber himself, what I have continued to do on him since his death has often been a lonely and isolated task. In Grete Schaeder I have found confirmation—both understanding and critical—that has mitigated that loneliness and given me fresh resources for work. She shares with me the conviction that some of us who knew Buber well are called to preserve their understanding of him as a person and not just as a thinker.

PART I

The Weimar Republic

(1923–1933)

CHAPTER 1

Zionism in the Twenties

HEBREW UNIVERSITY AND PALESTINE FOLK SCHOOL

AN IMPORTANT CONCERN for Buber during the years of the Weimar Republic was the shape that the Hebrew University, now at last becoming a reality, should take when it was founded in Jerusalem. To Buber the choice was essentially between the traditional European university and a *Volkshochschule,* a folk school after the model of Grundtvig in nineteenth-century Denmark. The committee in Jerusalem had, since 1923 and earlier, thought of creating a faculty in the human studies after the European model. One part of the problem was how to combine knowledge of the latest scientific methods with a grounding in Jewish knowledge and Jewish cultural life undisturbed by alien methods and disciplines. Another was how to provide the satisfaction of the deep spiritual and intellectual needs of the new pioneer workers in the Jewish settlement (Yishuv). There was also a Hebrew University com-

mittee in London. This committee invited Buber to come to a conference there in 1924. "Your cooperation could be a decisive significance
for the foundation of the conceptual structure of our university," they
wrote Buber. Despite conditions which at first made it seem impossible, he managed to get to London and won a partial victory. The
Executive of the Zionist organization, after hearing a presentation by
Buber, resolved to establish a land-folk school within the structure of
the Jerusalem university. The school would have the task of educating
and satisfying by unified methods the cultural needs of the maturing
generation of the Yishuv, thus supplementing the work of the already
established and still to be established scientific institutes. At the invitation of the Executive, Buber declared himself ready to draw up a public
presentation of the folk-school plan, for which purpose he would make
a study tour of Palestine the coming year.

Buber had prepared for this victory by a long letter sent to the
Executive in London in January 1924. In this letter he pointed out the
need of Jewish cultural continuity and of developing a Jewish science
of knowing which could include but not be swallowed up by Western
methods of knowing (as the so-called *Wissenschaft des Judentums* in the
nineteenth century had been swallowed up). He also proposed a seminar for labor leaders within the framework of the university which
would send out traveling teachers and students into the individual
colonies and *kvutzot* (collective settlements) to teach *and* to learn the
needs of the young settlers.

Buber kept in touch with Paula from London and shared with her
those parts of his experiences that he thought would interest her. The
Parthenon frieze in the British Museum made a great but melancholy
impression on him. "The whole collection has something oppressive
about it, it is so enormous," Buber added. "Here, better than in Italy,
one can understand the people who want to destroy all museums.
. . . The cameo room with its famous Portland vase (which a madman
once smashed) had for me something especially woeful." The most
remarkable thing about London to Buber was the fact that everything
in it was so public. "The people really live on the streets—entirely
otherwise than in Italy but no less so. . . . One sees on the streets, one
after the other, the most wonderful rituals and the most wonderful
spectacles."

Chaim Weizmann invited Buber to be in Palestine for the opening
of the Hebrew University on April 1, 1925, but Buber had to postpone
the study tour he had planned for that year and thus could not be

present at the opening. Writing Rosenzweig about the Zionist Executive Committee's action on the issue of the folk-school versus the university, Buber said, "My youthful years return again with force, if without song." Folk-school homes seemed to Buber the institutional ties binding the generations in which alone the human types that are needed could be educated. Such folk-school homes could be bound with centers in the Diaspora. But in Palestine there should be a close connection between the homes on the land, the teaching houses in the cities, and the traveling courses. For this purpose the new research institutes should not too quickly develop into a university in the European sense. "We must create what the real interest of the Palestinian settlement demands and in the measure in which this interest demands it."

BUBER'S VISIT TO PALESTINE

In the spring of 1927 Buber finally succeeded in making his study trip to Palestine along with Paula. "I have in this month experienced more than in any earlier one," Buber wrote Rosenzweig, "and I shall gradually tell you about it when we return home." What that visit meant to the Jews in Palestine Hugo Bergmann expressed in a short article in a Prague Jewish journal:

> The man who has done more than any one else for the deepening of Zionist thought, who has bound the thought of the building up of Palestine with the deepest meaning of Jewish history, on the one side, and with the highest ideas of mankind, on the other, the man who dreamed of a renewal of the life of the people out of the life of the commune or group . . . , this man comes to us now as a tourist and at the end of the third Aliyah [Jewish immigration to Palestine] which is rooted in his work. A whole new epoch has begun. Economic concerns, concerns about the material existence of those few communes that were created by that Aliyah, the difficult fight against unemployment all fill our world. Who is there to hear the voice of this guest?

What lay closest to Buber's heart, the question of the folk school, has been forgotten, Bergmann reported, or in the circles of the organization has not even found an echo. Not until Buber himself established schools for the teachers of the new immigrants in 1949 and the rise of educational work among the kibbutzim themselves during the last decade of his life was his dream to approach fulfillment. A paradigm of the educator of character whom Buber had in mind was Siegfried Lehmann, who directed the Volksheim for Eastern European Jews in Berlin during the First World War and who founded the Jewish Youth Village Ben Shemen near Lydda in Palestine in 1927. Gustav Landauer and Buber both had been influential in establishing and advising the Volksheim, and Albert Einstein and Buber were important sources of encouragement for the founding and continuation of Ben Shemen. In theory and in practice, Lehmann was dedicated to the establishment of a genuine "community of otherness" both within Ben Shemen and between it and the neighboring Arab villages by which it was sur-rounded. He explored methods of living together justly and working the land just as the kibbutzim and moshavim (cooperative settlements of privately owned farms) were doing. Lehmann, like his spiritual guide Martin Buber, was a cultural and spiritual Zionist who believed that Judaism would be regenerated in the National Home that was being built in Palestine.

Like the German-Jewish youth from Berlin seven years later, the Lithuanian Jewish youth who came to Ben Shemen under Lehmann's guidance had been frustrated in their native country and turned with eager yearning to the prospect of building a better society in Palestine, where they were free to develop both their socialist and their national ideals. Lehmann's conception of education of the youth in the Land of Israel envisaged their preparation for rural life in a village. As Norman Bentwich, Ben Shemen's historian, has put it: "They were to be a conscious community and foster a communal life, children citizens of a commonwealth, which included diverse national and religious elements, and, notably, a large majority of Arabs. They were to be inspired from their childhood by the great teachers of the humanities, and the great artists of all nations." To achieve this, a children's village and a farm-school were set up, followed by an open-air theater, chil-dren's homes, and a library. Lehmann's philosophy of education, which he had formulated even before he came to Ben Shemen, em-braced Jewish culture—Hebrew language, Judaism, and the achieve-ment in Israel—education for work on the soil and for cooperative living in a village, emphasis on the nonrational elements of education, such as religion, music, and the arts, and the inculcation of social justice and international understanding. Coeducation of boys and girls of all ages in the village, and the combination of academic lessons in the primary and secondary schools with manual work in the field and workshop, facilitated the carrying out of these goals. Lehmann placed particular emphasis from the beginning on understanding the Arab world, its history, religious tradition, language, and art, meetings of the community with neighboring Arab villages, invitation of Arab elders and boys to the feasts in Ben Shemen, recognition of the strength of Arab nationalism, identification with the whole life of the country, including the majority Arab population, the study of Arabic, and the search for a synthesis of the Oriental and the Western. Above all the Jewish youth at Ben Shemen had to get rid of the notion they were European colonists, alien to the root culture of the Asiatic environment.

By 1931, Ben Shemen was firmly settled and could claim to be the largest youth village in the world. The exodus of Jewish youth from Germany, Austria, and Czechoslovakia following the Nazi persecution caused the youth village to grow quickly, so that by 1939 it accommodated six hundred children and a hundred adult workers—teachers, youth leaders, and agricultural instructors. Ben Shemen was the precursor of that movement of child regeneration known as Youth Aliyah, which was to become the nursery of agricultural settlement in the National Home. Henrietta Szold, director of Youth Aliyah, was in complete accord with the fundamentals of Lehmann's program for Ben Shemen: education for a community in small groups, division of the school day into lessons in general education and work in the field, self-government of the children's groups guided by a youth leader, and education for life in a village, although the children of Youth Aliyah were not trained in a separate youth village but in a kibbutz or moshav. Ben Shemen quickly became, and remained, one of the principal places of training for the children's villages of Youth Aliyah. "Graduates of Ben Shemen were chosen to be educators of the groups that continued to arrive, and some of its veteran teachers became directors of new villages and institutes." During the years of Arab revolt against the British administration (1936–1939), Jewish settlements were constantly subject to attack. Yet no attack was ever made on Ben Shemen, owing to the friendship Siegfried Lehmann had established with surrounding Arab villages.

Lehmann also followed Buber's narrow ridge in his approach to religion. He managed, on the one hand, to make the Sabbath and other Jewish holidays a central part of the life of Ben Shemen, and, on the other, to preserve a complete openness and freedom of opinion that eschewed any attempt to impose religious beliefs or any form of orthodoxy on the youth, many of whom were not only socialist but strongly antireligious in their orientation. This too is a tribute to Lehmann, since for years the Yishuv knew only total secularism or total orthodoxy.

In 1927 Buber met and came into close contact with the great fighter for Zion and for peace, Judah Leib Magnes, a rabbi and conscientious objector in America during the First World War, the founder of the Jewish National Fund, the founder of Hebrew University when it opened in Jerusalem in 1925 and its first president and, for the rest of his life, chancellor. From that time on, there were continual correspondence and efforts on the part of Magnes, Gershom Scholem, and many others to bring Buber to Hebrew University if a position could be found for him which would be approved by the faculty and Board of Governors. The first form which this attempt took was a plan for an Institute of the History of Religions which Buber would direct at Hebrew University. Buber himself was most amenable to this.

ZIONISM, SOCIALISM, AND COMMUNITY

Buber also maintained an active interest in the political life of Palestine during this period.

During the First World War the British openly proclaimed the Balfour Doctrine that promised the Jews a homeland in Palestine but secretly wooed the Arabs in and outside of Palestine. When the League of Nations officially gave Great Britain the Mandate for Palestine after the War, this mandate included the Balfour Doctrine. But the familiar British policy of "divide and conquer" predictably led to strife between the Arabs and the Jews who had settled in Palestine, all the more since the growing Jewish settlement (the Yishuv) already seemed to many Arab leaders to pose a threat to Arab interests. When the Arab masses were incited to riot during the Jewish Passover in 1920, the Russian-born Zionist writer and leader Vladimir Jabotinsky (1880–1940) organized the Haganah (a Jewish defense army) and led them to confront the rioting Arabs. Jabotinsky and the other Haganah leaders were arrested by the British military government, but there was such an outcry from Jew and Christian alike that by July amnesty was announced. After the Mandate government quashed the whole military proceedings in March 1921, Jabotinsky was released from prison and was immediately proclaimed a hero. Jabotinsky used his advantageous position to press for the establishment of a Jewish Legion, and in 1925 he founded the Zionist Revisionist group whose goal was the "revision" of the British White Book of 1922, according to which Trans-Jordan was to be excluded from the realm of the Jewish Homeland that the Balfour Declaration envisaged. The Revisionists became a right-wing nationalist party among the Zionists which worked for a Jewish state on both sides of the Jordan and the foundation of a Jewish army (the Legion). In 1933 the Revisionists seceded from the Zionist World Organization, and their tradition was carried on by the Herut ("Freedom") party, of which Menachem Begin became the leader after the death of Jabotinsky.

During the 1920s and 1930s Buber and his circle fought a behind the scenes battle against the Revisionists and their demand for a Jewish Legion, but it was a battle that was not often successful. Robert Weltsch, Buber's old friend from the Bar Kochba circle who took over the editorship of the *Jüdische Rundschau* in 1919, wrote Buber in 1923 that Chaim Weizmann himself wished to appear "hand in hand" with the Arabs at the next Zionist conference, that he had a great desire to travel to Palestine in order to deal with the Arabs directly, and that he held that at this moment there was great promise of success in such an undertaking. But he knew well that he did not have the majority of the Zionist organization behind him, and that made his situation very difficult. It seemed to Weltsch that one of the most important tasks was to win over the Zionist circles in all countries to a politics of understanding with the Arabs. He quoted the editor of *Davar,* the most important Hebrew newspaper, as saying that it was characteristic of this time that the Zionist Revisionist Jabotinsky was succeeding in his propaganda, which was not true of anyone from the Buber circle. "In this reproach there is a kernel of truth," Weltsch concluded.

Buber himself no longer looked to Zionist majority politics to further his goals but instead joined forces with Brit Shalom, or Covenant of Peace, a group characterized by its concern for Jewish-Arab understanding in Palestine and by its advocacy of a binational state with population parity. Of the three philosophers of Zionism who were particularly concerned with the Arab problem—Ahad Ha'am, Ahron David Gordon, and Martin Buber—only Buber actually preached binationalism, and only he lived long enough to take an active part in Zionist politics focusing on this question. Brit Shalom was founded in 1925 on the initiative of Dr. Arthur Ruppin, head of the Palestine Land Development Company, one of the tasks of which was buying land from the Arabs. The persons who were predominant in Brit Shalom until the 1929 disturbances were men who had immigrated into Palestine before the First World War, and two of these remained central in the years to come—the agronomist Chaim Kalvarisky (1868–1947) and the religious socialist Zionist Rabbi Binyamin (the pen name of Yehoshua Radler-Feldman (1880–1957). The second group, which became predominant after 1929, were intellectuals of a Central European liberal background, three of whom in particular, Hugo Bergmann, Hans Kohn, and Robert Weltsch, had all been Bar Kochbans in Prague and were all disciples of Martin Buber. There were also Ernst Simon and Gershom Scholem and a group of pacifists, such as Nathan Hofshi, the non-Zionist Werner Senator, and Orientalists. Lord Edwin Samuel, son of the first high commissioner to Palestine, and Norman Bentwich, attorney general during this period, were both sympathetic to Brit Shalom, as was Judah Magnes, who did not belong to it because of his position as chancellor of Hebrew University but who was in many ways a leading spirit of the group, as of later groups of a similar nature. *"Brit Shalom* had no ideology," writes Susan Hattis in her perceptive study of the binational idea in Palestine.

> Bi-nationalism, they said, is not the ideal but the reality, and if this reality is not grasped Zionism will fail. They were not defeatists who were willing to make any concession for the achievement of peace, they simply realized that the Arabs were justified in fearing a Zionism which spoke in terms of a Jewish majority and a Jewish state. Their belief was that one need not be a maximalist, i.e., demand mass immigration and a state, to be a faithful Zionist. . . . What was vital was a recognition that both nations were in Palestine as of right.

After concerted study of the Arab problem and a number of attempts at setting up a joint Jewish-Arab effort in administration, economics, education, medicine, culture, politics, and labor, Brit Shalom faded out of existence in 1933, partly because of the rise of Nazism and the growing preoccupation with the situation of the Jews in Europe. Hugo Bergmann explained their lack of greater influence in Zionism: they represented "the last flicker of the humanist nationalist flame, at a historical moment when nationalism became amongst all the nations an anti-humanist movement. After 1933 the Zionist Associations in Central Europe lost all significant influence." Brit Shalom was lambasted in the Hebrew press in Palestine by dozens of hostile articles, and Professor Joseph Klausner on the outside and R'Binyamin within pointed out that one of their own spiritual fathers, Ahad Ha'am, had called for an eventual Jewish majority in Palestine. Magnes, on the other hand, maintained in his pamphlet "Like All the Nations" (1929) that the living Jewish people did not need a Jewish State either to maintain its very existence or to "perform its great ethical mission as a national-international entity."

What is not recognized today, even by most people in Israel, is that the binational idea was a specific response to a specific moment in history prior to the existence of a Jewish State, rather than some treasonous anti-Zionism. Still less is it recognized how widespread the idea of binationalism was at that time. Hapoël Hatzaïr the left-wing Zionist group that joined with Achdut Haavoda (United Workers) in 1930 to become the dominant Mapai party, counted quite a number of Brit Shalom members and supporters in its ranks, including Buber, Kohn, Weltsch, Bergmann, Hofshi—and even many of its other members were not opposed to the binationalist principle, such as Joseph Sprinzak, one of the leaders of the party. Chaim Weizmann, president of the Zionist Organization and first President of the State of Israel, was a staunch and unswerving supporter of binationalism, or "parity," as he preferred calling it, even when this position made him most unpopular. In 1931, he met with British Prime Minister Ramsay Mac-Donald and secured his agreement in principle to the idea of parity. In July 1931, at the Basel Congress, Weizmann said in his opening speech:

> The Arabs must be made to feel, must be convinced, by deed as well as word, that, whatever the future numerical relationship of the two nations in Palestine, we, on our part, contemplate no political domination. Provided that the Mandate is both recognized and respected, we would welcome an agreement between the two kindred races on the basis of political parity. It is our duty to explain our aims and ideals clearly and without ambiguity to the Arab peoples, and to neglect no opportunity of coming into touch with them and no channel of communication which may help towards a mutual understanding. . . . Only in this way shall we succeed in cooperating with the Arab peoples, who themselves are struggling toward the light and now, after many centuries, are reentering the political arena of the world.

Partly because of his approach to the Arab question, Weizmann received a no-confidence vote at the Congress, and he resigned from the presidency of the Zionist Organization. Even after his decision to resign, Weizmann remained firm in his stand. In an interview he said: "I have no sympathy or understanding for the demand of a Jewish majority. . . . The world will construe this demand only in one sense, that we want to acquire a majority in order to drive out the Arabs." In a further speech to the Congress, Weizmann reiterated that a numerical majority in itself was no adequate guarantee for the security of the Jewish National Home but only "far reaching political guarantees and friendly behaviour towards the non-Jewish world about us in Palestine," and again he called for "complete parity between both peoples irrespective of their numerical strength."

Moshe Shartok (Sharett), the future prime minister, was also strongly in favor of parity, and even David Ben-Gurion, who moved to the fore in the Mapai party, seriously put forward the cantonization of Palestine and parity in 1930, 1932, and 1934, without mentioning, in these proposed constitutions for Palestine, the desire or necessity for a Jewish majority. This was, to be sure, an attempt at compromise arising out of the effect on him of the 1929 riots and his disappointment in the way the British authorities had handled the disturbances. But it was, by the same token, a clear indication that the ideas of binationalism and parity were not the product of a small group of idealistic and unrealistic intellectuals, as is commonly thought today.

When Brit Shalom was founded, Buber identified himself with its principles, for they were identical with the ones he had himself espoused for many years. The third part of *Kampf um Israel* (Fight for Israel, 1932) was devoted to Arab-Jewish problems in Palestine and was dedicated to the "friends from Brit Shalom." From 1929 on, Buber retired from participation in official Zionist policy, despairing of influencing it directly, but he strengthened his ties with all the organizations concerned with rapprochement and peace between the Arab and Jewish nations in Palestine. Even after the 1929 riots and the British restriction of immigration and settlement, official Zionist attempts to deal with the Arab problem were only fragmentary and intermittent without a comprehensive and consistent political, economic, and cultural plan. In the wake of the great and justified anger at Arab deeds of horror, Buber was one of the few who dared to remove the emotional and verbal veneer from the roots of the phenomenon and expose them to the Jewish public. Then and later such actions on his part evoked hostility that affected and obscured the significance of much of his other activity.

In 1926 he carried on behind the scenes in committees a secret fight against the plan for a Jewish legion of Vladimir Jabotinsky, the leader of the militant wing of the Yishuv. Although the majority of the Congress was not anti-Arab, they simply failed to see through the plan for a Jewish legion and its consequences. A colonization that wishes to build a motherland, rather than start out from one, can be accomplished only through passion, Buber wrote in 1926, and that passion is not manifested only in the isolated moments of the revolutionary act but, more importantly, in the hidden, anonymous perseverance in constant daily activities. The Jews are not merely stateless, Buber declared, but also unprotected by the states in which they live (a fact which most of us have long denied knowing). But this protection cannot come about through turning the tables around and becoming the majority in Palestine who might then treat the Arab minority as they had been treated (even if more humanely). Buber feared that "Zion" might turn out to be "the great Galut-Hotel," the comfortably fixed-up replication of the exile. "It belongs to the signature of our splendid and humane age that the dreams of mankind are fulfilled in it—in caricature."

In August 1929 a quarrel over the conditions under which the Jews might pray at the Wailing Wall in Jerusalem—a quarrel in which England stood unequivocally on the side of the Arabs—released an Arab unrest and violence against the Jews in Palestine that was unprecedented in its fury. In these conditions Ernst Simon wrote Buber asking him to intervene with Chaim Weizmann to impress upon him the need of building good-neighborliness between the Jews and Arabs. Buber appealed to Weizmann, who answered that the situation was not so simple, given the enmity of the Arabs and their feelings of victory, strengthened by many Englishmen, by the anti-Semites, the Catholics, and perhaps even Moscow, while revisionist and chauvinist Jews acted without really knowing what they were doing. Later Buber wrote Weizmann again to lament the fact that the Political Committee of the Zionist organization had turned down a motion against the use of capital punishment on the Arabs who took part in the 1929 riots. This is not merely a moral question, Buber insisted, but an eminently political one, since execution of the Arabs would contribute to poisoning the situation and would strengthen the opposition of those who were wavering. "It would not be a sign of weakness but of power and consciousness of power if I save the life of my enemy," Buber wrote. In 1930 Scholem wrote Buber that the face of the Zionist cause, seen from the standpoint of the members of Brit Shalom (Covenant of

Peace), was in danger of becoming a Medusa head. Scholem reported the total demoralization which encompassed them, and warned Buber that he would find it unbearable if later he had to say to himself that his cause had shipwrecked while he was not there. This was a reproach to Buber, who (in contrast to Bergmann, Scholem, and Simon) postponed his ascent to the Land until the university could agree on a position for him.

In 1929, in a letter to Chaim Weizmann, Buber recommended Hans Kohn as *the* person to occupy the chair "for international peace" that was being established at the Hebrew University. Kohn was not only an expert on modern history, particularly nationalism, he was also a leading pacifist and someone thoroughly acquainted with the specific situation of the Near East. Nothing came of this effort on Buber's part, partly, as Magnes wrote Buber, because of Kohn's political stance. In the same year Kohn wrote to Buber that the events in Palestine were very bad and that "we are all guilty, for we should never have allowed it to get this far. . . . Had we, as Hugo [Bergmann] and I wanted, taken up in the early summer of 1928 an attitude agreeing in principle with the Arab demand for representation of their people, much might have been avoided. Now (through our cowardice and inactivity) the Revisionists have succeeded in delivering their blow, which is aimed only half against the Arabs, half against the executive . . . and its weak 'position.' " The results of this, Kohn prophesied, would be years of hatred, military suppression, and the moral defeat of Zionism. "*We* must *do* something to fight further misfortune, hatred, fear." "Zionism will either be peaceful or it will do without me," Kohn later informed Buber, and added that he was returning to Palestine with an unimaginably heavy heart; "for face to face with *this* Zionism I wholly despair." After growing disillusionment with a Zionism that seemed ever farther from the hopes of the Brit Shalom, Hans Kohn emigrated to America, where he became a noted professor and a member of the National Council of Judaism, an organization noted for its anti-Zionist stand.

Buber himself had a more optimistic assessment of the situation than Kohn. He told Paula at this same time that the much-despised Brit Shalom had come into the foreground of discussion, that people awaited from them concrete proposals for action, that he had proposed to lay down a clear and precise program of action for a gathering with Magnes. In this connection he spoke of Robert Weltsch as having made out famously in the crisis. "One sees at such times that one has disciples," Buber wrote; "not many but reliable ones. Hans Kohn is more doctrinaire than he, more intent on declarations than on real pathfinding through the brambles of the factual, but also good."

Common to all Buber's speeches, to most of his Zionist articles, and to the memoranda, warnings, propositions, letters, protocols, conversations, and consultations that are still hidden in archives was the Arab question. This was not merely a matter of the Arab question alone, as Robert Weltsch and Buber stressed in their speeches to Zionist organizations and sympathizers, but of *Jewish* nationalism and of the final goal of Zionism. In 1929 Buber published "Three Stations," a remarkable one-page summary of the development of the goal of Zionism. First, our key word was *culture,* Buber wrote, and we worked for a rebirth of Jewish spirit and form. But then we recognized that one cannot *will* culture, that it never appears in history as intention and goal but always as an epiphenomenon, the by-product of a life process. Then we turned to the very foundation of life which we called *religious renewal.* Then we realized that religion too is something that one *may* not will. "Religion striven for for the sake of human life, for the life of the people instead of the hallowing of God in human life, in the life of the people, is worse than irreligion because it is fictitious, unreal while playing at being the reality of realities." The third station that we arrived at, said Buber (echoing Rosenzweig), was *reality,* the whole of reality with God, world, and man—"the human fight for God in the world, meeting of persons with God in the world, redemption of God's world by men, and, as the place of the fight, meeting, and redemption, *the lived everyday.*"

In another one-page statement of 1929 Buber formulated the goal of Zionism historically. There are ages of faith in which people do their work gladly with the "in spite of all!" of the human heart. In other ages there is a lack of faith in life and people bear work as a compulsion that cannot be overcome. In the former, people discover the blessing hidden in the curse "by the sweat of your brow." In the latter, they forget it. It is easy to recognize ours as an unbelieving age, but here and there a breach has been formed, as in the second Aliyah, in which Ahron David Gordon's faith in the cosmic meaning and value of work wed "Adam" to "Adama," man to the soil.

In a third short piece "Why Must the Upbuilding of Palestine Be A Socialist One?" Buber set over against the Moscow dictatorship, based on an ideological socialism devoid of reality, and the Rome dictatorship, based on an anti-ideological greed for power devoid of spirit, the image of the nascent Jerusalem as the true marriage of spirit and reality. This did not mean that Buber nursed an unrealistically ideal picture of "Jerusalem." In a 1928 talk to a group of labor Zionists in Berlin, Buber named as postulates of a true Zionist socialism: common ownership of the land, doing their own manual labor, and the free determination by the settlers of the norms of their communal life. "As a Jewish socialist who proceeds from reality and not from ideology, I must say that these postulates cannot be attained at present," since the work of building up Palestine at that time consisted of both the initiative of the people and that of private capital. The test of the Jewish will to colonize is the specific responsibility that is different from either the hunger for profits or the renunciation of profits. There is no way to carry through the great socialist demands politically if one does not at the same time strive to realize them factually. Nor can freedom from the grind of work by reduction of the hours of work be the answer. What each person means in his or her heart when he or she says "socialism" is real community between people, direct life-relationship between I and Thou. This means a genuine communal autonomy that goes as far as conditions allow. Here too not the either-or of centralized or decentralized socialism is meaningful but the narrow ridge between them; setting the demarcation line at each hour of how much communal autonomy is possible in that situation. Nor is it just the deterioration of the relationship between worker and employer from which modern mankind suffers but also the deterioration of human relationships in general. In a reply, Arnold Zweig spoke of Buber as a seer who sees tomorrow and the day after tomorrow. This Buber denied, saying that his concern was with the present moment and the meeting in it of idea and life.

In 1929 two leading German Zionists, Georg Landauer and Gershom Chanoch, informed Buber that he had been chosen by the Hitachduth, the Labor Zionists in America, as well as by the German Labor Zionists, as their representative to the Sixteenth Zionist Congress to be held in August in Basel, Switzerland. They held Buber's participation in the Congress to be especially important and necessary for the spiritual preparation of the new generation and for the education of youth that now seemed to them the central questions for Zionism. The Zionist leader Joseph Sprinzak also held Buber's appearance at the Congress to be absolutely imperative both for the broadening of the Jewish Agency to include the support by non-Zionists and for the floor debate where Buber's words and presence would in themselves constitute a fight against Jabotinsky's Revisionists. Buber yielded to these urgent pleas and went to Basel for the last Zionist Congress, in which he actively took part.

In his speech to the Sixteenth Congress, Buber rejected the ordinary contrast between the anti-Zionist who sees Israel as less than a nation and the Zionist who sees Israel as a nation. He favored a third category: those who see Israel as more than a nation—meaning everything by which a nation is defined but rejecting the "sacred egoism" that makes the nation an end in itself. Nor can the goal of Zion—the beginning of the kingship of God for all human people—be postponed until the life of the nation is secure. "If we do not will more than life, we shall also not win life." "The end does not hallow the means, but the means profanes and distorts the end." He who does evil for the sake of good perverts his own soul so that it is no longer capable of doing good. To Buber that applied to the group quite as much as to the individual.

In this connection Buber recalled a conversation about Zionism that he had with the great German sociologist Max Weber. If Zionism erects a small state like all the other small states, Weber prophesied, it will remain with them on the periphery of history and, like them, will disappear. But if instead it builds up a spiritual power, then it will remain in the center of history and will endure. Making this concrete and specific in relation to the Arab question, Buber called not for declarations, such as emerged from the Twelfth Zionist Congress at Karlsbad in 1921, but for practical action by a standing commission that would concern itself with every issue touching on the Arab question. Such an organization could not be guided by a formula but by a direction. In the same way, speaking Hebrew is not itself enough without a direction-giving content. Therefore, Buber wished as decisive for Palestine "a Hebrew humanism in the most real sense." Among the young people whom he had come to know in Palestine a dreadful amount of sacred egoism prevailed. A Hebrew humanism would lead them from the path of nationalist assimilation to that of national pioneers.

THE ARAB QUESTION

Speaking in Berlin in October 1929, Buber emphasized again the inseparability of land, people, and task and pointed to the small experiment of the kibbutz as more important than the enormous Russian state centralism: only in the kibbutz was there really *topos*, place—

concreteness of a social transformation not in institutions and organizations but in the interhuman immediacy itself. Applying this to the Arab question, Buber told how Max Nordau, when he discovered there were Arabs in Palestine, ran to Theodor Herzl and said, "Then we are doing wrong." To those who say one must do wrong to live as a people, Buber replied, Yes, as long as one does only so much in every hour that one may be truly responsible for it. He defined true responsibility as that genuine actual imagining, or inclusion, that would enable the Jews in Palestine to imagine what it would be like if *they* were the people already living in Palestine and the Arabs were the newcomers who came there to colonize it. Only when we know how we would react to that can we learn to do no more injustice than we must in order to live.

Such responsibility was a *political* matter, not simply an ethical one. The British "protection" of the Jewish national home not only made it an extension of British imperialism but also subjected the Jews in Palestine, equally with the Arabs, to the British policy of divide and conquer. A genuine national pride, in contrast, Buber wrote, would bring the Jews nearer to the Arabs so together they might build up the land. The only truly Palestinian forms are those of the Arabs. "We have not lived *with* the Arabs in Palestine but *next* to them," Buber said, and added that if this continued to be the case, the situation in Palestine would inevitably deteriorate to the place where the Jews would find themselves living *against* the Arabs. It is characteristic of Zion that it *cannot* be built with every possible means but only *bemishpat* (Isaiah 1:27), only "with justice," Buber said in Antwerp in 1932. "For Judaism is the teaching that there is really only One Power which, while at times it may permit the sham powers of the world to accomplish something in opposition to it, never permits such accomplishment to stand." If the goal is to be reached, the way must be like it. Lies cannot lead to truth, nor violence to justice. "I sometimes hear it said that a generation must . . . 'take the sin upon itself' so that coming generations may be free to live righteously." This is self-delusion and folly; for the children of such a generation "will usually turn out to be hypocrites or tormented." Affirming once again the secret power in the depths of history that confirms our faith, Buber concluded that we can be true peacemakers, God's co-workers, only in the active life of our own community and its relationship to other communities.

In 1929 Buber's chair for the study of religion fell through, partly because of the opposition of the Orthodox who rejected unconditionally Buber's teaching religion. Magnes then proposed to create a position for Buber as life-rector of the Hebrew University. This offer greatly excited and pleased Buber. "The bomb is planted," he wrote to Rosenzweig. "Magnes has invited me to come to Jerusalem as the 'academic overseer' (lifelong rector) of the University. He himself will remain the Chancellor. What to do? . . . decline (But how does one decline something like this?) or accept, postponing the step as long as possible." Magnes had agreed to allow Buber to come more than a year later, in October 1930, and in the first two years to spend the months of May to October in Europe. Writing to Paula, Buber said, "His offer surprised me; it means a partial abdication in my favor. The whole way in which he made it pleased me very much and did me good. . . . Yesterday I asked him your question on the telephone, whether it is a sinecure or a 'real' position; for I could only accept the latter. . . . there can be no doubt that the position is a real one, with serious work and responsibility, but also with far-reaching influence—and naturally also with the conflicts that are inherent in it. . . . Objections will certainly be made from certain Zionist circles, but Magnes seemed sure he could overcome them—chiefly, perhaps, because he has the Americans on his side. (Incidentally I have been invited to make a lecture trip to America. Would you make fun of that? I have an instinctive disinclination, but I don't know whether there are real grounds for it.)"

For Paula, who had given up her religion, her family, and her city to marry Buber, this meant a still greater sacrifice. Philo-Zionist though she was, she knew no Hebrew and could not but miss her beloved mountains and forests, the source of many of the stories which she had written and published. "I understand well, dear heart, how difficult a decision that means for you," Buber wrote her, "and I know that I may only propose it to you if I, in so far as it depends on me, see to it that you can live in a manner suitable to you and worthy of you. But for me too it means a not unimportant displacement. It is an offer to which it is very difficult to say yes—and yet it would be still more difficult to say no. For here I am offered for the first time in my life an office that at once demands greatness and makes greatness possible." Buber concluded, as in Adam's speech to Eve at the end of Milton's *Paradise Lost*, "You must know that I would rather be a vagabond with you than the academic overseer of this planet without you."

Paula answered that things must work out as they must and that, to her surprise, she even felt her present life was actually too hollow, too impoverished and savorless. "I could not truly consciously have desired what has popped up here: still it is as though all the doors have sprung open." In a later letter to Paula, Buber reported that in the discussion of Magnes's proposal the scientists, who formed the majority of the faculty, demanded that the faculty itself select the academic overseer. The whole matter of such a change in the structure of the university was then turned over to a commission "of which a majority are for me," Buber added. Whatever happens, Buber concluded, "I propose to make possible a broader and more active way of life for us. You must feel yourself freer to do your work and to move about more in the world. You must be able to give up a part of the housework, and that means we must make the necessary changes in the house."

Magnes's dream of Buber's being the life-rector of the Hebrew University did not materialize.

CHAPTER 2

Education

BUBER'S ATTITUDE toward education was quite close to his attitude toward psychotherapy. Both he saw as quite concrete illustrations of his statement that "All real living is meeting," but in both this meeting is founded on mutual contact and mutual trust without the full mutuality of reciprocal "inclusion," or "experiencing the other side of the relationship" (a concept Buber first put forward in 1913 in the "Dialogue after the Theater" chapter of his book *Daniel**). This "normative limitation of mutuality" in no way implies that either authentic psychotherapy or authentic education, in Buber's view, is anything other than genuine dialogue. The mediating figure between them is the *zaddik* and his relationship to his Hasidim. One of the tales that is found in Buber's later rendition of *The Tales of the Hasidim* is called "The Strength of Community." In this tale the Baal-Shem, who felt, as often, that a destiny greater than could be described in words hung on his

---

*See Volume One, pp. 159–164.

prayer, was unable to make a traditional blessing of the risen moon because of the dark clouds that obscured it. Every time he sent someone out to look, the sky was darker still until at last the Baal-Shem sat on his chair in helpless dejection. At that very time, his disciples became so enthusiastic over the service that their Master was doing for them that they danced through the streets and into his room and, without even noticing his mien, pulled him up into the dancing circle. At that moment, the person watching outside called out that the night had suddenly grown light: "In greater radiance than ever before, the moon curved on a flawless sky." Here is unmistakable mutuality without identity of function or role.

One of Buber's lasting associations during his years in Germany was that with the progressive children's school Odenwaldschule, located in a forest not far from his home. Personally close to its leaders, Buber also came there as visitor and, occasionally, speaker. "In the Odenwaldschule it was beautiful," Buber wrote his friend Franz Rosenzweig about one such visit. "One could see in the eyes of the fifteen- to eighteen-year-olds how they took in what I had to say about names and still more what I read—in a fresh way, almost as in the Lehrhaus," the free Jewish school for adults that Rosenzweig had founded in Frankfurt.*

Buber had an equal, though not so untroubled, impact on progressive educators. He was invited to give the keynote address at the Third International Pedagogical Conference of the International Work Circle for the Renewal of Education, which was held in Heidelberg from the second to the fifth of August 1925. The overall theme of the conference was "The Unfolding of Creative Forces in the Child," and it was in response to this theme that Buber produced his important essay on "Education" written three years before "Dialogue." Buber saw his task as in large part a critical one—critical both in relationship to the theme of the conference and in the program—and he warned the leaders of this in advance. Part of the reason for Buber's stance was the tendency to arrogate "creation" to human beings: "Man, the creature that can form and shape what has been created, cannot himself create. But every person can open the creative to his or her self and to others. He can summon the Creator to save and perfect his image." Only times which knew a human image of general validity, such as the Christian, the gentleman, the citizen, could answer the question, "To

*See Volume One, Chapter 13.

what must we educate?" Today only the imageless image of God remains to dominate and shape the present human material. With every child that is born creation begins anew. But that creation can only be given direction by the educating person who brings the educative forces of the world into his responsibility to God. The educator is set in the midst of the need which he experiences in inclusion, and he brings this need into the imitation of the God who is hidden but not unknown:

> When all "directions" fail there arises in the darkness over the abyss the one true direction of man, towards the creative Spirit of God brooding on the face of the waters, towards Him of whom we know not whence He comes and whither He goes.
>
> That is man's true autonomy which no longer betrays, but responds.

This conclusion so baffled Sir Herbert Read that when he set Buber's essay on "Education" at the center of his book *Education through Art* he changed the imitation of the imageless God into the responsibility of the teacher to represent his society. It takes on greater meaning, however, in the essay "Imitatio Dei" ("The Imitation of God") which Buber wrote in 1926, the year after "Education." Unlike the Christian who can imitate the life of Jesus, the Jew is set the paradoxical task of imitating the imageless God by perfecting that part of the divine image entrusted to him by God. To imitate God means to walk in his ways—the *human* ways made visible in God's commandments *and* those inimitable secret ways of God that we only understand through suffering. When God breaks in our tent, like Job's, we experience, beyond all mercy, grace, and righteousness "the terror of the other, the incomprehensible, ununderstandable works." In this sense the "creation" entrusted to the person wins a legitimate connection with the task of educative dialogue.

The second reason for Buber's stance provides us with a classic illustration of his life as an "encounter on the narrow ridge." In place of the easy opposites of conservative versus progressive, or discipline versus freedom, Buber offered a third, more concrete and realistic alternative of education as dialogue: The teacher makes himself the living selection of the world, which comes in his person to meet, draw out, and form the pupil. In this meeting the teacher puts aside the will to dominate and the will to enjoy the pupil that threaten "to stifle the growth of his blessings." "Either he takes on himself the tragedy of the person, and offers an unblemished daily sacrifice, or the fire enters his work and consumes it." The greatness of the educator lies in the fact that his or her situation is completely *unerotic*— that is, not chosen on the basis of what the teacher likes or dislikes. "He sees them crouching at the desks, indiscriminately flung together, the misshapen and the well-proportioned, animal faces, empty faces, and noble faces, in indiscriminate confusion, like the presence of the created universe; the glance of the educator accepts and receives them all."

The teacher is able to educate the pupils whom he finds before him only if he is able to build real mutuality between himself and them. This mutuality can come into existence only if the child trusts the teacher and knows that he is really there for him. The teacher does not have to be continually concerned with the child, but he must have gathered him into his life in such a way "that the steady potential presence of the one to the other is established and endures." "Trust, trust in the world, because *this* human being exists—that is the most inward achievement of the relation in education." But this means that the teacher must be really there facing the child, not merely there in spirit. "In order to be and to remain truly present to the child, he must have gathered the child's presence into his own existence as one of the bearers of his communion with the world, one of the focuses of his responsibilities for the world."

If the act of inclusion is quite real and concrete, it removes the danger that the teacher's will to educate may degenerate into arbitrariness, or willfulness. This "inclusiveness" is of the essence of the dialogical relation; for the teacher sees the position of the other in that person's concrete actuality yet does not lose sight of his or her own. Unlike friendship, however, this inclusion must be largely one-sided: the pupil cannot be expected to be concerned about the teacher's becoming educated through their interchange without the teaching relationship being destroyed thereby. Inclusion must return again and again in the teaching situation. Through discovering the "otherness" of the pupil the teacher discovers his or her own real limits; also through this discovery the teacher recognizes the forces of the world which the child needs to grow and he draws those forces into himself. Thus through his concern with the child, the teacher educates himself.

The two attitudes of the "old" and the "new" educators that Buber cited in his address on "Education" are still dominant in educational theory and practice today. On the one hand, there are those who emphasize the importance of the so-called objective education to be obtained through the teaching of Great Books, the classical tradition, or technical knowledge; on the other, there are those who emphasize the subjective side of education and view it as the development of creative powers or as the assimilation of the environment in accordance with subjective needs or interests. The old educators picture education as the passive reception of tradition poured in from above, in Buber's image "the funnel"; the new educators picture education as drawing forth the powers of the self that are already present, in Buber's image "the pump." In education as dialogue the pupil grows through his or her encounter with the person of the teacher and the Thou of the writer, composer, or artist. The reality that each presents becomes alive for the student: it is transformed from the potential, abstract, and unrelated to the actual, concrete, and present immediacy of a personal and even, in a sense, reciprocal relationship. This means that no real learning takes place unless the student participates, but it also means that the student must encounter something really "other" before he or she can learn.

Thus Buber offers a third alternative to the famous controversy between the "Great Books" approach which stresses a uniform classical education to correspond to a universal and timeless human nature and the developmentalist approach which stresses an education for immediate needs. "The great productions of the human mind are the common heritage of all mankind," writes Robert Maynard Hutchins. "They supply the framework through which we understand one another." John Dewey, in contrast, advances the idea of education as a continuous reconstruction of experience in which principles are only learned effectually in connection with their use in social and natural contexts—the present environment. Buber, in contrast to both positions, proposes an education that will produce persons able to respond to the demands of their particular historical situation. Classics should be studied in order that students may become whole persons able to influence others and not for the knowledge itself. Not universal principles but our present situation furnishes the criterion for selection of educative material, for this alone gives the growing generation what it needs in order to withstand this hour. We begin, certainly, with what Buber calls a "real text," but the meaning is not already in the text but comes into being in the moment in which a voice speaks to us from the text and we respond—in the present. The interpreter does not *possess* the meaning of a work. She discovers it anew in genuine meeting, and it is through just such discovery that the teacher is able to communicate the meaning of a text to her students.

It is not freedom and the release of instinct that are decisive for education, Buber declared in direct opposition to the trend of "progressive education" shared by most of those participating in the Heidelberg conference, but the educative forces that meet the released instinct. Proponents of the old, authoritarian theory of education do not understand the need for freedom and spontaneity. But proponents of the new, freedom-centered educational theory misunderstand the meaning of freedom, which is indispensable but not in itself sufficient for true education. The opposite of compulsion is not freedom but communion, Buber asserted, and this communion comes about through the child's first being free to venture on his own and then encountering the real values of the teacher. The teacher presents these values in the form of a lifted finger or subtle hint rather than as an imposition of what is "right," and the pupil learns from this encounter because he or she has first experimented.

Buber's assertion that freedom is the springboard to communion but not in itself the goal is entirely consonant with his definition of true freedom in *I and Thou* as the freedom to enter into relationship, the freedom to practice decision "before the Face" as long as one lives. Yet we also can detect an unmistakable autobiographical note in this statement growing out of his profound personal identification with Gustav Landauer during the Munich Revolution *and* his simultaneous feeling that Landauer's entering the government of the first Räterepublik was a serious error on his part:

> Freedom—I love its flashing face: it flashes from the darkness and dies away, but it has made the heart invulnerable. I am devoted to it, I am always ready to join in the fight for it, for the appearance of the flash, which lasts no longer than the eye is able to endure it, for the vibrating of the needle that was held down too long and was stiff. I give my left hand to the rebel and my right to the heretic: forward! But I do not trust them. They know how to die, but that is not enough. I love freedom, but I do not believe in it. How could one believe in it after looking in its face? It is the flash of a significance comprising all meanings, of a possibility comprising all potentiality. For it we fight, again and again, from of old, victorious and in vain.

We can also sense, in the paragraph that follows, Buber's contrast between those like Landauer who really involved and sacrificed themselves and those who use "freedom" and "rebellion" as political slogans and catchwords:

> It is easy to understand that in a time when the deterioration of all traditional bonds has made their legitimacy questionable, the tendency to freedom is exalted and the springboard is treated as the goal and a functional good as substantial good. Moreover, it is idle sentimentality to lament at great length that freedom is made the subject of experiments. Perhaps it is fitting for this time which has no compass that people should throw out their lives like a plummet to discover our bearings and the course we should set. But truly *their* lives! Such an experiment when it is carried out, is a neck-breaking venture which cannot be disputed. But when it is talked about and talked around, in intellectual discussions and confessions and in the mutual pros and cons of their life's "problems," it is an abomination of disintegration. Those who stake themselves as individuals or as a community, may leap and crash out into the swaying void where senses and sense fail, or through it and beyond into some kind of existence. But they must not make freedom into a theorem or a programme. To become free of a bond is destiny; one carries that like a cross, not like a cockade. Let us realize the true meaning of being free of a bond: it means that a quite personal responsibility takes the place of one shared with many generations. Life lived in freedom is personal responsibility or it is pathetic farce.

Buber may also have been thinking of that week in 1919 when he had imaginatively to experience in his own body the blows with which Landauer was brutally kicked to death, when he gave as his first illustration of inclusion in his Heidelberg lecture a man who kicks another and then unexpectedly feels his kicks from the other side:

> A man belabours another, who remains quite still. Then let us assume that the striker suddenly receives in his soul the blow which he strikes: the same blow; that he receives it as the other who remains still. For the space of a moment he experiences the situation from the other side. Reality imposes itself on him. What will he do? Either he will overwhelm the voice of the soul, or his impulse will be reversed.

The English novelist D. H. Lawrence describes exactly this situation in his classic novel *Sons and Lovers* when the husband of the woman Paul Morel has been having an affair with waylays him, knocks him down, and kicks him in the side:

> Still dazed, he felt the blows of the other's feet, and lost consciousness. Dawes, grunting with pain like a beast, was kicking the prostrate body

of his rival. . . . He made off across the field into Nottingham, and dimly in his consciousness as he went, he felt on his foot the place where his boot had knocked against one of the lad's bones. The knock seemed to re-echo inside him; he hurried to get away from it.

Another concrete example of inclusion that Buber gave is even more certainly autobiographical; for no one who has not had the experience he describes could possibly have imagined it. Since this experience is sexual, it makes us think of the monograph on sex that Buber himself had planned to write for his series Die Gemeinschaft, but later abandoned in favor of Lou Salomé's essay "The Erotic." It also brings to mind how basic Buber's relationship to his wife Paula was not only for his life but also for the very development of his philosophy of dialogue:

> A man caresses a woman, who lets herself be caressed. Then let us assume that he feels the contact from two sides—with the palm of his hand still, and also with the woman's skin. The two-fold nature of the gesture, as one that takes place between two persons, thrills through the depth of enjoyment in his heart and stirs it. If he does not deafen his heart he will have—not to renounce the enjoyment but—to love.
>
> I do not in the least mean that the man who has had such an experience would from then on have this two-sided sensation in every such meeting—that would perhaps destroy his instinct. But the one extreme experience makes the other person present to him for all time. A transfusion has taken place after which a mere elaboration of subjectivity is never again possible or tolerable to him.

It was surely Buber's own experience of "inclusion," or what he was later to call "personal making present" and "imagining the real," that caused him to emphasize in this speech on education the all-important but, even today, almost universally ignored distinction between "inclusion" and "empathy," which latter Buber describes as a "familiar but not very significant term." Empathy, as Buber here used it, is almost an aesthetic category—gliding with one's own feeling into the dynamic structure of an object, a pillar, a crystal, the branch of a tree, or even of an animal or man, understanding and tracing it from within with the perception of one's own muscles through "transposing" oneself. Such transposing means the exclusion of one's own concreteness and the extinguishing of the actual life situation. Inclusion is the opposite of this: it means extending one's own concreteness and fulfilling one's actual life situation in such a way that one experiences the complete presence of the reality in which one participates, living through the common event from the standpoint of the other without forfeiting anything of the felt reality of his or her own activity. (Some humanistic psychologists, such as Carl Rogers, use the term "empathy" to cover both of these meanings. But just in so doing they fail to make the distinction between an "identification" which may be pure aestheticism or even projection and the genuinely two-sided dialogical reality that is central to healing, teaching, friendship, and love.)

Buber's address "Education" aroused a storm of controversy among the assembled educators and involved him in constant exchanges both in the plenary session and in the smaller workshops that made up the two-week international conference. Elisabeth Rotten, in reporting on the conference, described it as passionate wrestling and contending. What was most important to Buber, however, was that his speech brought the battle into the open, in the true space of decisions and in the inwardness of the person, thus foreshadowing a future dispute within the camps of the educators themselves. This wrestling and contending in no way meant for Buber an alienation from the leading German educators who had invited him to give the keynote speech of the conference. In the short Foreword to the printed edition of the address, Buber wrote: "Foremost among those into whose hands I should like to lay this little book, stand those friends who have helped me in my efforts to serve the truth of education—from the beginning in the (unpublished) conference 'for the renewal of essence of education' in Heppenheim an der Bergstrasse in 1919 to my present efforts to teach in Germany, Switzerland, and Holland, and my plans for Palestine."

A different level of education was the annual "decades" organized by the French philosopher and philologist Paul Desjardins in France, who from 1910 on brought together at the Abbaye de Pontigny in France philosophers and artists from many countries in the search for an antimaterialistic renewal of life. Writing to Paula from Pontigny in September 1929, Buber described less the encounters themselves than his impression of the architecture and art of Paris, which he visited for the first time, and of Pontigny itself. These descriptions give us an insight into how important art continued to be for Buber throughout his life, even though he no longer focused as much on it as he had during his student years. "In Paris," Buber wrote, "Notre Dame naturally made the greatest impression on me. From such a structure one learns that there is a classic and a Roman Gothic and that the classical belongs organically together with the Roman. In the Louvre only

Leonardo's painting of Anne, Mary, and the infant Jesus did not at all disappoint me; I could reach no real relation with the colors of the 'Virgin of the Rock.' Rembrandt's Hendrikje is wonderful. A not insignificant painter whom I got to know only here is Courbet. Delacroix is represented by many paintings, yet not favorably. There is something of the late Tintoretto about him at which one would wonder if one did not know him from elsewhere." It is clear, Buber concluded, that one needs a minimum of three weeks to visit Paris. Of Pontigny itself Buber wrote that it was very beautiful. Of the abbey there still stood a somewhat built-up part with a splendid arched hall in the first floor and an almost equally delightful, smaller dining room below. The hall led to a very well-equipped library. Next to this preserved part of the abbey the old church still stood intact. Around it were large, beautiful gardens, meadows, and little forests. Desjardins told Buber that he had acquired the whole property in 1910 after the death of his children and had developed it to keep it alive. Buber confessed that he had to accustom himself here to a somewhat more exact and objective form of discussion, as in the exchange on the astronomical revolution of the sixteenth and seventeenth centuries. In addition to several famous French scholars, there were a number of young Englishmen, a few Germans and Italians, and one person from India. "All the arrangements are at once stimulating and restful," Buber wrote. "Real tradition is hidden therein, ancient life-wisdom; but also something genuinely personal, which comes from the person of Desjardins, toward whom I find myself most sympathetic—an older man, very gentle and silent, but of a great spiritual and intellectual liveliness." A quarter of a century later in the Preface to his little book *Images of Good and Evil* Buber spoke of these *"Entretiens de Pontigny,* founded and directed by my unforgettable friend Paul Desjardins."

A week later Buber wrote to Paula from Pontigny that it had oppressed him "directly and bodily" to learn how much she was suffering from the heat. Then in quite another form of "inclusion" he wrote her that the church in Vézelay would have said still more to her than it did to him. "Its vestibule has an intensity that is hardly less than that of San Zeno. It is a church to which people make pilgrimage. Its medieval epic workmanship coincides with the splendid statement of its founder: The works have begun, the wars are finished. In Vézelay St. Bernard preached the way of the cross; on the mountain that bears the church was the camp of the Pope and around it the accoutrements of Barbarossa, Richard the Lionhearted, and the French."

Meanwhile Buber was also continuing his work on specifically Jewish education, particularly the adult education at Rosenzweig's Frankfurt Lehrhaus. In 1922–1923 Buber lectured on "Original Forms of Religious Life" (Magic, Sacrifice, Mystery, Prayer) and gave a seminar in which he analyzed Ancient Near Eastern, Greek, Jewish, and Christian writings. The lecture series included the material that Buber intended to publish as the second of his five projected volumes, under the title "The Basic Forms of Religious Life." One Frankfurt father told Buber, with some disapproval, that his eleven-year-old daughter had said to him that she wanted to visit Buber's lecture because in her school "propaganda" was made for it. Buber confessed himself not too happy with this report: "How can I say something real about the mystery cults to an eleven-year-old . . . ?" he asked Rosenzweig. His second lecture course that year was on "Prayer" with a seminar in the interpretation of Psalms. During the same year, Erich Fromm, then a sociologist and student of Jewish lore, lectured on Karaite Judaism, and Gershom Scholem, just before leaving to work at the Hebrew University Library in Jerusalem, gave a course and led study groups in the Book of Daniel and the Zohar Hadash, an important Kabbalistic text.

In the meantime Rosenzweig continued to put pressure upon Rudolf Hallo not only to study daily Gemara (Talmudic commentary on the Hebrew Bible), which he did, but to go further in accepting the forms of traditional Jewish life than he was able to do. Unable to accept Rosenzweig's call for "an open-minded but rooted conservatism," Hallo resigned as administrator of the Lehrhaus. Hallo sent Buber a touching letter in which he said that he did not want to look back on this action as something that caused a break in his new relationship with Buber, which had been so valuable to him and done him so much good. "My step was solely in regard to myself and Franz Rosenzweig," he wrote, and in the end, with much pain, these two had parted with mutual understanding. "Do not take this letter as an attack and self-justification," he pleaded, "but as a loud cry finally uttered by one to whom the total silence of the other has begun to be uncanny." Buber, however, in an undated letter to Franz Rosenzweig, said that Eugen Rosenstock-Huessy had told him of Hallo's action, "of which all understanding is beyond me—outside of the so-called psychological, of which I unwillingly make use."

In the same letter Buber suggested to Rosenzweig that if he could not find a replacement such as Scholem, who was unavailable, Rosenzweig might set up an honorary committee to direct the Lehrhaus, as part of which Rosenzweig could count on Buber's aid. "I am of the opinion that the Lehrhaus can and shall be preserved." On July 17, 1923, Rosenzweig wrote a joint letter to Eduard Strauss, Buber, Richard Koch, and Ernst Simon asking them whether they could take over the leadership of the Lehrhaus without him. Simon responded in the negative, as a result of which the leadership from then on was shared among Rosenzweig, Buber, Strauss, and Koch. Buber at that time took Simon severely to task for his unwillingness to help out in this situation. "Your answer to Rosenzweig's letter has affected me painfully," Buber charged. "It is entirely lacking in human response. Have you then, you fine and proud young people with your preoccupation with literature and history, with directions and institutions so lost the natural human glance of love that you can no longer recognize the gestures of your brother who is in pain? And are you too 'matter of fact' to pour a drop of restoring wine in your vinegar?" They were like Job's friends, Buber suggested, but if God put them into Job's situation, as he had Rosenzweig, they would no longer think themselves in the right! "I hope you understood fully why I say this to you," Buber concluded.

Three months later Simon wrote a long and impassioned letter to Buber protesting against his way of conducting his seminar on Hasidism and, by implication, explaining his decision not to cooperate in the leadership of the Lehrhaus. "You have demanded of the people assembled there that they really 'express' themselves," Simon wrote, with the result that there developed "an at times hysterical, at times shameless, kind of questioning, typically carried out almost exclusively by women, which deeply repelled not only myself but also a great number of the younger and older people and hurt them at the very core of their beings. Although you stood your ground heroically and said a great many things worth hearing, you did not take my hand which offered to rescue you from the assault of the hysterical and the less than honest." After long pondering on why Buber himself seemed to be unaware of this situation, Simon came to the conclusion that it was connected with Buber's lack of any sense of his public and the spurious use that it made of his truth. This, moreover, Simon saw as closely connected with Buber's metaphysical position, which was expressed in *I and Thou* and which Simon protested against, namely the lack of any sense of the *tragic*. "Our human existence is *constituted* by the fact that we have eaten of the tree of the knowledge of good and evil. . . . We know shame and with it the tragedy of *sex*." To know men we must see them neither as animals nor as angels, but as creatures expelled from paradise and condemned to the tragedy of *work,* beings who represent a mixture of the dust of the earth and the divine soul and who, if they wish to bind themselves to God, must take on themselves the *tragedy of the law.* Buber's error of paying too little attention to the "law" carried with it, Simon declared, the corresponding error of paying too much attention to the relationship to his fellowmen. In contrast to Hermann Cohen, who was an Idealist, Buber would not be one at any price. Yet he fell into it ever again when he took "standing before the Face" for the *only* side of "reality" and acted accordingly. "The reality of our human life has a tragic double face. . . . You believed yourself to be standing 'naked before God' and, in fact, stood naked before Fräulein H.—a fearful sight! Everyone who loves you must inwardly grieve at this, and you do not notice it." The "I-Thou" relation cannot be naïvely presupposed in the unmessianic world but must be tested in each individual case. In a totally accidental fellowship, such as that of the Lehrhaus, in which, next to much that is genuine, there are, also, hysteria and the lust for religious sensation ("the worst of all!"); consequently, there can only be *indirect* communication. This does not apply to you alone, Simon added. In shameless questions and still more shameful answers lie the central danger of the Lehrhaus, "the reason why I cannot take part in its direction."

Buber did not respond immediately to this letter, at least not in written form. But he wrote Rosenzweig about it, commenting, "He is right, but only on the far side of love." Rosenzweig replied that Simon had shown this letter to him in advance and added, "Naturally he is 'right.' As right as one can be who does not believe that a minyan can turn a group of tradesmen into praying men. The translation of sensationalism into genuine need is not, of course, demonstrable. Yet one must believe in it, and even E. Simon will one day believe in it. . . . when he comprehends the healing forces of freedom, which now he can only hold to be a poison flower (which it certainly *also* is)." This letter of Simon's stands in striking contrast to his letter to Buber of two months earlier when, in connection with his editorship of *Der Jude,* he informed Buber that he considered it a great good fortune to have experienced Buber's real faithfulness to the smallest detail, his responsibility to the word. "I have learned a great deal for myself from this." Grete Schaeder feels that Buber replied to Simon a half year later in his speech "Education," in which he made it clear that the relationship between teacher and student cannot be a fully mutual one, and she implies that this speech may reveal the impact of Simon's letter. Buber's greatness showed itself not only in his intellectual reply to Simon's criticism, Schaeder adds, but also in his human greatheartedness: he simply accepted the "disciple" Simon as friend.

In 1923–1924, as part of an increasing stress on the study of Jewish sources in the Lehrhaus program, Buber lectured on the Baal-Shem, discussed the various Hasidic interpretations of the first sentence of Genesis, and lectured on Jewish eschatology accompanied by a reading of the Fourth Book of Ezra. Also lecturing at the Lehrhaus that year was the man who first influenced Buber toward Zionism (even before Theodor Herzl), Dr. Nathan Birnbaum. Birnbaum had developed from atheistic Zionism through Yiddish to strict observance of the Jewish Law and affiliation with the most Orthodox branch of Judaism. The fact that he spoke in an institution at which Buber, the *apikoros* [heretic], taught caused the Orthodox weekly to protest against the "academic freedom which is unknown to Halakhah [the Jewish religious law]" and which "the concept of religious purity of traditional Judaism cannot tolerate."

Thus the Lehrhaus made manifest the spirit of dialogue that Buber himself increasingly stood for within the branches of Judaism as well as between Judaism and Christianity—the understanding of issues which did not gloss over differences. In 1923–1924, Buber presented a course on Hasidic teachings and conducted a seminar on the Hebrew originals. After giving lectures in 1924–1925 on the "Suffering Servant" in Isaiah, and in 1924–1925 on "The Sayings of the Fathers" from the Talmud, it was only natural that in 1925–1926 Buber engaged in a critical discussion on Christianity with the Protestant minister Hermann Schafft of Cassel. "Buber," writes Glatzer, "who more than any other contemporary Jew attempted to interpret Judaism to the non-Jewish world, made (and still makes) the point very distinct where the Jew must say 'No' to Christianity and thus to the spiritual structure of the Western world."

One of the most important differences between Judaism and at least one major strain of Christianity—that going from St. Paul and St. Augustine to Luther and the Neo-Orthodox—is in the attitude toward sin, particularly original sin, and evil. This is no simple contrast of opposites, however, and for a deeply thinking Jew like Buber the human as well as the theological reality of evil was a problem with which he had to wrestle ever anew. More than a quarter of a century later, this struggle was to bear fruit in Buber's anthropological understanding of evil in the book *Good and Evil* and in his Hasidic chronicle-novel *For the Sake of Heaven*. The latter, titled *Gog and Magog* in the German and Hebrew originals, was already occupying Buber's thought during and after the First World War, though his two attempts to write the novel then and later proved unsuccessful. The only two people who knew of this concern were Buber's wife Paula and Franz Rosenzweig. Gog, from the land of Magog, a mythical figure spoken of in Ezekiel, was one day to become so powerful a force of evil that he would challenge God to combat. At that point, in this apocalyptic account, God will be forced to send down the Messiah and redemption will be at hand. "The 'Gog' oppresses me very much," Buber wrote Rosenzweig, "but not just as a subject for a novel. Rather I fight with full clarity of mind, entirely different from all fantasy, to track down how 'evil' belongs to the coming of the kingdom." In this connection, he added, a saying of Napoleon's which he formerly did not understand suddenly became lightning clear to him. "At Elba he once said that his name will remain as long as *le nom de l'Éternel.*" In another letter to Rosenzweig, "As far as Gog is concerned, it is good that today I am forty-five years old. Otherwise the fellow would gobble me up. Try to imagine, yesterday I suddenly awoke from an apparently dreamless sleep and saw bodily before me the Phoenician devil with pinched lips staring at me with a superior air like that of the Roman Imperator of the old Rembrandt in the Carstanjousel self-portrait ('Oh, Rembrandt was not a fantasist,' said the curator to me, when I tried to draw his attention to the fact that the 'bust' when well lit becomes a *face*)." At the end of 1923, Buber notified Rosenzweig that he had not dared to work on the Gog for a long while. "He has caused me too much pain."

The course in Hasidic teachings that Buber gave at the Frankfurt Lehrhaus he later published under the title *Das Verborgene Licht* (The Hidden Light)—the identical title that he was later to give to his new and enlarged collection of Hasidic tales in the Hebrew edition (*Or Hagganuz*). When he had read the booklet of Hasidic sources that, at Scholem's urging, Buber published along with his preceding Hasidic book—*Der Grosse Maggid*—Rosenzweig wrote Buber in 1923: "You must certainly draw what you have seen out of the material in which it is hidden; that is more important than any statistical correctness. But should there not also exist books in which what you have seen is more of an accompaniment? Historical books?" This question, which was to be hurled at Buber many years later by Gershom Scholem as an accusation of "unscientific" interpretation, was answered by Buber in the following year through the plan of a many-volume complete edition of

Hasidic sources, *including the formal books of Hasidic teachings,* that he and Agnon were undertaking together. On Buber's forty-fifth birthday he wrote Rosenzweig: "The work on the *Corpus Hasidicum* is already in process." Seven volumes were envisaged to begin with: 1. The Baal-Shem; 2. The Second Generation; 3. The Third Generation; 4. Nachman; 5. The Epigone; 6. Chabad; 7. Interpretations of the Bible (*Toroth* in Hebrew), sayings and parables, systematically ordered, were probably to fall into two half-volumes. Every year at least one volume was to appear. The next month he told Rosenzweig that he was thinking of entrusting the *Corpus Hasidicum* to be written in Hebrew, to a younger person to whom he would supply all the material. "The series of Hasidic books in German I must, of course, complete," he added.

Buber did not give up his plan for the series of systematic volumes on Hasidism, but it was nonetheless aborted by a misfortune which Agnon could not surmount. A fire in Agnon's house destroyed four thousand books, all his possessions, and a great deal of his unpublished writing, including a half-completed novel, many parts of which he had read to Buber. Among the other manuscripts the almost completed volume of the *Corpus Hasidicum* was destroyed, which led Agnon to give up the plan "for years." Buber knew that probably meant forever. In any event the possibility of close cooperation was removed by Agnon's emigrating to Palestine in the fall of 1924. Rosenzweig, citing the fact that Carlyle rewrote his history of the French Revolution after the whole manuscript was accidentally burned, wrote Buber that he could not conceive of the *Corpus*'s not coming into being. "Only death eradicates, not fire." Nevertheless, the project was not taken up again, despite considerable correspondence between Agnon in Palestine and Buber in Germany concerning new Hasidic material that Agnon had turned up. When Buber came to Palestine many years later and proposed to Agnon a similar cooperation, Agnon declined. Nahum Glatzer testified that the *Corpus Hasidicum* was to include the formal teachings of the Hasidic *rebbes.* "I did the legwork for them," Glatzer said to me.

In 1924, in an effort to make the best possible adjustment to his growing paralysis, Franz Rosenzweig himself prescribed in detail methods for nursing, for his communicating with those around him, and for his study and writing. Several nurses broke down under the strain of serving him, which included lifting, bathing, feeding, and helping him to walk a few yards, two and a half hours in just getting him out of bed and dressed (because the stretching of the legs brought on cramps, slipping, pain, and the repeated necessity of bending his legs for him), an hour for breakfast and even longer for other meals. Yet Rosenzweig wrote: from about eleven o'clock in the morning until about one in the afternoon; from half past four until eight; and after dinner until midnight or longer. When he could no longer turn pages of his books, the nurses were summoned by a turning of the head as he read difficult talmudic passages. When oral dictation became impossible as the paralysis of his organs of speech intensified, a specially constructed typewriter enabled him to indicate one letter at a time, though soon only his wife Edith was able to guess which letters he meant, as Nahum Glatzer relates:

> Through years of close association Mrs. Rosenzweig had acquired an instinctive understanding which seemed miraculous to outsiders. Mrs. Rosenzweig also managed every conversation with visitors, by guessing often recurring words after the first or second letter. The patient's extraordinary memory enabled him to dictate and have typed in this fashion, during three or four hours work, the final draft of what he had worked out, down to the smallest detail, during a sleepless night. This method was followed up to the time of his death.

In 1925 after he had been invited to write the article on Buber for the *Jüdisches Lexicon,* Rosenzweig confessed to Buber:

> To parody, and exclaim: Here you may view the holy beast of the Jews, and *no* mystic! is something I can and will do. It is a cry that must be raised for the sake of the good cause, and in such cases I don't take cover behind my soul. But to portray you, to write "about" you, is something I can't do. My illness has removed me to such an extent from my older friends that I could, today, write about them, just because I can no longer, or only to a lesser degree, write to them. But you, who entered on the "seventh day of the feast" are still much too "new (and ever again new) a face" for me to be able to portray you before the public. I must leave it at the fleeting image on my retina, and I hope it will not change while I live.

On Rosenzweig's fortieth birthday on December 25, 1926, Buber presented him with a map containing handwritten contributions by Rosenzweig's friends. In his letter of thanks Rosenzweig particularly noted the presence of a letter from Buber's wife, which he had not expected—"Her letter was the great surprise of the day"—and added by way of comment that when a man is in his thirties he is still always something of a baby: one is allowed occasional stupidities. But when he enters his forties, then he is finally and irrevocably grown up.

During the 1920s and continuing into the 1930s the underlying thought and program of the Frankfurt Lehrhaus served as a model for the establishment of similar institutions in Stuttgart, Cologne, Mannheim, Wiesbaden, Karlsruhe, Munich, Breslau, and Berlin. In many of them Buber was just as active as he was to be in the reopening of the Frankfurt Lehrhaus in Nazi Germany. Meanwhile Rosenzweig drew Buber further into teaching by persuading him to accept the lectureship in "Jewish Religious Philosophy and Ethics" at the University of Frankfurt.* In urging Buber to take over this position that had originally been intended for himself, Rosenzweig pointed to the elasticity of the university framework, the danger that it might become just one more institution for the training of rabbis, and the effect that Buber's presence and his "guaranteed *apikoros* personality" would have on the character and direction of the Jewish faculty that might later be appointed. "This can be done only by someone who is wholly free of any undue deference for the existing university, and who, at the same time, brings to the job the kind of personal reputation which will forbid the university's interfering with him."

It was not at all easy for Buber to make up his mind to accept the academic chair created for Rosenzweig but vacated by his illness. "If I begin work at a university," he confided to Rosenzweig, "even in this happily loose connection, I cannot restrict myself in the first semester to exercises but must declare myself and my cause as you would have had to do. Thus I must explain how *Religionswissenschaft* (the scholarly study of religion) and how 'Ethics' are possible and, in addition to that, how that is truly 'Jewish.' Would I be so independent, so responsible only to the legitimate court [God], that I could do this without holding back?" Later he informed Rosenzweig that he had to tell him something that had been pressing on him vaguely for some time but that, along with other things, had become clear to him in the deep clarity of a sleepless night: "I need for my own work more time than I had thought." This meant, he concluded, that he could no longer honestly comply with the decision he had given Rosenzweig about accepting the academic position. "My heart is deeply pained that I have once again, as so many times before, lived like a twenty-year-old. I must now really collect myself, simplify my life. Take this to heart. Forget that you are

---

*See Note in Sources for Chapter 2.

'younger'—what does that mean? I have just read how Paul said that he had an undamaged conscience in all ways, both toward God and men. I would like to know how one does that!"

Although Buber finally accepted the position, a comment he made to his friend Hugo Bergmann, in a letter of 1936, when the Nazis forced Buber to leave the position, casts light on the spirit in which he did it: "That I—after giving up a university lectureship as a young man and rejecting a prestigious academic position [at the University of Giessen] as a forty-year-old—accepted the call to the Frankfurt chair, is bound up with my relationship to Franz Rosenzweig in a manner that I must perceive as tragic. It had the character of a sacrifice." How little those who knew Buber suspected that this was the case! Shmuel Agnon, the Hebrew writer and later Nobel Prize laureate, was sitting on a balcony with the Hebrew poet Bialik and Ahad Ha'am when the news reached them that Buber was ready to take on the university lectureship. "Whatever Buber undertakes, he will do thoroughly and well," commented Ahad Ha'am.

In 1930 Buber was promoted to a professorship at the University of Frankfurt, not in Jewish religion and ethics (his original appointment), but in the general history and study of religion, a change which did not seem to displease Buber, since he referred to it as a "springboard." Thus, in the midst of so many other educational activities, Buber continued to occupy a full-time academic position with all the duties that it entailed. The amount of work in various fields that Buber accomplished during the period of the Weimar Republic, if we try to get an overview of it, is staggering and suggests not only great energy and genius but also remarkable self-discipline and order.

CHAPTER 3

·—————————————————·

Rosenzweig and the Law

·—————————————————·

THE GREATEST and best-known divergence between Martin Buber and
Franz Rosenzweig was in their attitude toward the Jewish Law—disagreement all the more striking given their closely similar attitude
toward revelation as neither objective reality nor subjective feeling but
the Word which arises and takes its meaning from the dialogue between God and man. Revelation for both men takes place within the
I-Thou relationship, and it is a command addressed not to "one" but
to "thou." Yet Rosenzweig saw a necessary relation between revelation
and law which Buber could not admit. Rosenzweig came closer and
closer to a full observance of Halakhah during his life while Buber
remained open to the teaching as a whole, yet committed to the Torah
as command only insofar as it became revelation for him.

In the volume in celebration of Rabbi Nehemiah Nobel's fiftieth
birthday, Ernst Simon tells the story of how Buber went to visit Rabbi
Nobel and his wife. When it came time to have a bite to eat, Rabbi
Nobel asked Buber delicately whether he would perhaps like to wear

a very small yarmulke (skullcap) for the occasion. Observing the look on Buber's face, he added, "Or would even the smallest one be too large for you?" "In a traditional Jewish home," Buber replied, "I would not be averse to wearing one. But with you, Rabbi Nobel, I will not grab hold of the small end of the Halachot [the Jewish laws] in this way." Then Rabbi Nobel recited the benediction silently, as if there were only two present, for only when at least three are present may it be said aloud.

It was in 1923 when the collected *Speeches on Judaism* appeared that Rosenzweig was able to get that overview of Buber's developing thought on revelation and law in Judaism that prompted Rosenzweig's writing of his famous letter "The Builders." In the last of Buber's "Speeches on Judaism"—"Herut" (On Freedom)—Buber contrasted the false desire for security of the dogmatists of the Law with the "holy insecurity" of the truly religious man who does not divorce his action from his intention. Religious truth is obstructed, contended Buber, by those who demand obedience to all the commandments of the Jewish Law without actually believing that law to be directly revealed by God. To obey the Mitzvot [the commands of God] without this basic feeling means to abandon both them and oneself to an autonomous ethic. The relation to the Absolute is a relation of the whole man, undivided in mind and soul. To cut off the actions that express this relation from the affirmation of the whole human mind means to profane them. The image of man toward which we strive, asserted Buber, is one in which conviction and will, personality and its deed, are one and indivisible.

The dogmatists of the Law will reply, he said, that spirit remains a shadow and command an empty shell if one does not lend them life and consciousness from the fountain of Jewish tradition. "Otherwise your direction will be self-will and arbitrariness rather than what is needful. How can you decide between that part of God's word which appears to you fresh and applicable and that which appears to you old and worn out?" Buber answered this challenge by praising the willingness to risk oneself continually without hoping to find a secure truth once and for all.

> O you secure and safe ones who hide yourselves behind the defence-works of the law so that you will not have to look into God's abyss! Yes, you have secure ground under your feet while we hang suspended, looking out over the endless deeps. But we would not exchange our dizzy insecurity and our poverty for your security and abundance. For

to you God is one who created once and not again; but to us God is he who "renews the work of creation every day." To you God is one who revealed himself once and no more; but to us he speaks out of the burning thorn-bush of the present . . . in the revelations of our innermost hearts—greater than words.

We know of his will only the eternal; the temporal we must command for ourselves, ourselves imprint his wordless bidding ever anew on the stuff of reality. . . . In genuine life between men the new word will reveal itself to us. First we must act, then we shall receive: from out of our own deed.

Writing in 1920, the Orthodox leader Jakob Rosenheim interpreted Buber's position on the Law in "Herut" as a dangerous glorification of subjective feeling at the expense of the objective content of actions. Rosenzweig's response in "The Builders" was much more sophisticated because it arose out of a dialogical point of view much closer to Buber's own. The word that in Isaiah 54:13 is read "thy children" is read in the Talmud "thy builders," Rosenzweig pointed out, implying that on the children rests the responsibility of being the builders of the tradition of Judaism. "You have been," Rosenzweig told Buber, "the leader of my generation and the one that came after it in freeing the teaching from the fetters which the nineteenth century put upon it. But you have not made the same step in your understanding of the Law. Here you still distinguish between what part of the Law is 'essential' and what is not." Referring to himself as one whose statements concerning the Law are not based on the experience of having reached the goal but on that of seeking and being on the way, Rosenzweig pointed to the contradiction he felt in Buber's failure to develop his understanding of the Law parallel to his understanding of the teaching. "You have liberated . . . us from the imminent danger of making our spiritual Judaism depend on whether or not it was possible for us to be followers of Kant," said Rosenzweig in what was an indirect acknowledgment that Buber had finally won the upper hand in his soul over his Neo-Kantian teacher and friend Hermann Cohen.

You point to a new principle of selection, through which the vast subject matter of learning (*Lernstoff*) you unfurl can again become a *teaching* (*Lehre*), a principle more trustworthy than anyone has attempted to set up. You introduce the concept of inner power. For inner power is what you demand when you ask him who learns to stake his whole being for the learning, to make himself a link in the chain of tradition and thus become a chooser, not through his will but through his ability.

We accept as teaching what enters us from out of the accumulated knowledge of the centuries in its apparent and, above all, in its real contradictions. We do not know in advance what is and is not Jewish teaching. . . .

Buber's alleged failure to overcome the distinction between "essential" and "inessential" in connection with the Law led Rosenzweig to ask him whether the Law he was speaking of was not really the Law of nineteenth-century Orthodoxy. Was not Jewish Law really

the law of millennia, studied and lived, analyzed and rhapsodized, the law of everyday and of the day of death, petty and yet sublime, sober and yet woven in legend; a law which knows both the fire of the Sabbath candle and that of the martyr's stake? the law Akiba planted and fenced in, and Aher trampled under, the cradle Spinoza hailed from, the ladder on which the Baal Shem ascended, the law that always rises beyond itself, that can never be reached—and yet has always the possibility of becoming Jewish life, of being expressed in Jewish faces?

Rosenzweig's own support of the Law was based upon the covenant that God has made, not with our fathers, "but with us, these here today, the living." "The souls of all generations to come stood on Sinai along with those six hundred thousand, and heard what they heard." The difference between the forbidden and the permissible must cease to exist, wrote Rosenzweig. "Not one sphere of life ought to be surrendered." The essential sphere is not that of Jewish deeds as opposed to extra-Jewish deeds but that of naturally grown freedom in which all possible activity, that which can be done, has become one. As with the teachings, the content of the Law must be transformed into the inner power of our actions: general law must become personal command.

Law *(Gesetz)* must again become commandment *(Gebot)* which seeks to be transformed into deed at the very moment it is heard. It must regain that living reality *(Heutigkeit)* in which all great Jewish periods have sensed the guarantee for its eternity. Like *teaching*, it must consciously start where its content stops being content and becomes inner power, our own inner power. Inner power which in turn is added to the substance of the law.

The selection of that part of the Law which the individual shall perform is an entirely personal one, claimed Rosenzweig, since it depends not upon our will but upon what we are able to do. Hence in contrast to the Paulinian all-or-nothing, Rosenzweig envisaged a gradual growth of the Law in consonance with the personal existence of the doer. This means that no one can or should even wish to anticipate the boundary of the Law or what belongs to its sphere. "We do not know how far the pegs of the tent of the Torah may be extended, nor which one of our deeds is destined to accomplish such widening."

In a statement reminiscent of the unconditional and almost passive obedience of Kierkegaard's knight of faith, Rosenzweig declared, "A decision based on ability cannot err, since it is not choosing, but listening and therefore only accepting." Reminiscent too of Kierkegaard is the strictly personal nature of the command: "No one can take another person to task . . . because only *I* know what *I* can do; only my own ear can hear the voice of my own being which I have to reckon with." Despite this statement, with Buber, as with Rudolf Hallo, Rosenzweig felt it necessary not only to teach but also, however respectfully, to take to task: "I could not believe that you, who have shown us again the one path to the Torah, should be unable to see what moves us as well today along the other path." Indicating that he spoke not only for himself but for others, Rosenzweig concluded: "My words open up a dialogue which I hope will be carried on with deeds and with the conduct of life rather than with words."

"Your 'Builders' has moved my inmost soul," Buber responded, "and appears to have broken through a secret door. If I answer you (which hopefully will be granted me after my return from Karlsbad), I must now really express what has long been withheld. In terms of ideas, yes, but at the same time autobiographically—much more intimately so than in the Foreword [to the collected edition of his *Speeches on Judaism*]; for what I really have to say to you can only be taken from the secret archives of the person."

To this Rosenzweig replied that he had sought to write "The Builders" in such a way that no reply would be necessary, at least not "today and here." He would be happy if Buber wanted to reply, but he had preserved in his heart the real answer that Buber had sent him over a year before. The only additional response that Buber made in writing occurred in two letters the following year. "What you say about the fact of *teshuvah* [the turning] is, of course, said to me from the heart. But you do not thereby answer the question which is central: How can I as a person repent (not merely regret) what I have not done as a person? How can I turn back with my soul where I have not turned away with my soul?" To this he added in a letter about prayer that he had believed himself lost and had found unhoped-for help. Before this happened, he had found the real word on which all depended. "I did not find it in myself, but I found it. In the prayer 'prescribed by law'? No . . . but in what had once been taught me—and whose resonance still remained with me in my fortieth year—in a crisis of the soul at the Lemberg synagogue. Now there came before me the rustle of the mystery I had known as a child and it made my heart flutter."

Buber urged Rosenzweig to publish "The Builders," and when he learned from Ernst Simon that Rosenzweig had agreed but then reconsidered, he urged him to have it printed without waiting for a reply. Actually the only reply that Buber ever made was in the form of letters, and it was not until seven years after Rosenzweig's death that Buber consented to have his correspondence with Rosenzweig on the Law published in the *Schocken Almanach*. In his introduction to "Revelation and Law," as this correspondence was entitled in the almanac, Buber wrote that he had not written a formal answer to Rosenzweig "out of a hesitation that did not have himself as its subject but the life of the Jewish community in this world-hour."

In the first of the letters in which he responded personally to Rosenzweig, Buber said that if he did write it would contain nothing in disagreement with the details of "The Builders"; for he agreed with everything that followed from the letter's premises but not with the premises themselves. In a rare personal confession of belief, Buber said that it was his faith that prevented him from accepting Rosenzweig's premises. It was an integral part of Buber's personal being that he could not identify the Law and the word of God, nor could he imagine that this position would ever change for him. He experienced this fact so keenly during the week preceding his letter, he said, that it even penetrated his dreams. Thus Buber made a distinction between revelation and the giving of the Law that Rosenzweig had failed to make:

> I do not believe that *revelation* is ever lawgiving. It is only through man in his self-contradiction that revelation becomes legislation. This is the fact of man. *I cannot will to obey the law transformed by man if I am to hold myself ready for the unmediated word of God directed to a specific hour of life.* [Italics added.]

It was thus the immediacy of the dialogue with God that made it impossible for Buber to follow Rosenzweig in affirming the whole of the Law to be divine prior to one's personal appropriation of it. It was not, as Nahum Glatzer has suggested, the fact that Buber was the "spokesman of a new, universal, religious and philosophical orientation" in contrast to "Rosenzweig, who found his peace in the practice of Halakhah where the . . . longing for salvation is resolved in the sober conformation to the Mitzvoth."

Rosenzweig in his reply questioned whether Buber and he really differed in faith; for even for him who observes the Law, revelation is not law-giving. "We do not consciously accept the fact that every commandment can become law, but that the law can always be changed back into a commandment." Buber, however, could not accept this "always": for we do not know in advance that any particular part of the Law can always be changed back into a commandment in any particular situation. Rosenzweig failed to consider "that it is the fact of man that brings about transformation from revelation to what you call commandment *(Gebot)*." Rosenzweig accepted the command as from God and left open only the question of whether the individual could fulfill it, whereas Buber remained closer to the immediacy of dialogue and made the real question whether it actually is a command of God to oneself.

> I cannot accept the laws and the statutes blindly, but I must ask myself again and again: Is this particular law addressed to me and rightly so? So that at one time I may include myself in this Israel which is addressed, but at times, many times, I cannot. And if there is anything that I can call without reservation a *Mitzvah* within my own sphere, it is just this that I act as I do.

As the correspondence continued, Buber found it necessary to make clear to Rosenzweig that while man was for him a law-receiver, God was not a law-giver. This led Buber to the decisive statement of his difference from Rosenzweig and from most observant Jews, including many of his own followers like Ernst Simon: "Therefore the Law has no universal validity for me, but only a personal one." This did not mean either individualism or anarchism, but dialogue: "I accept only what I think is spoken to me." As an illustration, Buber cited what was for him a developing relationship to the Sabbath: "The older I become, and the more I realize the restlessness of my soul, the more I accept for myself the Day of Rest."

"I am responsible for what I do or leave undone in a different way than for what I learn or leave unlearned," Buber asserted to Rosenzweig. But Rosenzweig insisted that for Buber too the separation of revelation and teaching was also a thorn and a trial. He asked Buber to think not of petty Midrashim, but of the Christian dogma. "For me, too, God is not a Law-giver," declared Rosenzweig. "But He commands." It is man who by his inertia changes commandments into law, "a legal system with paragraphs, without the realization that 'I am the Lord,' without 'fear and trembling,' without the awareness that the man stands under God's commandment." A still more remarkable statement, one that was omitted from the English translation in *Jewish Teaching and Learning,* acknowledged Buber's response to the question of the command to be as legitimate as Rosenzweig's own:

> For the Law as for the teaching I assert universality only for the hearing, not for the doing. . . . Only when you experience it as unnecessary for your Jewish being to say Yes or No—in this one case— only then do you divide yourself here from me. Whether you say Yes or No is unimportant. I said recently to Goldner, . . . the point is that Buber's No is perhaps more important for the "Building" than Ernst Simon's and my and your Yes.

An interesting side commentary on Rosenzweig's position is offered in a letter of Rosenzweig's to Ernst Markowicz in which he points to "The Builders" as an answer to his desire to take over the Law lock, stock, and barrel. "You have wanted to devour it too quickly, hide and hair, without wanting to wait for those hours of grace that make the new and strange into the natural and familiar. And then, you have not learned Halakhah in the right way; without doing that, the mere deed easily becomes worthless." To the Orthodox leader Jakob Rosenheim, Rosenzweig wrote in December 1924 reproaching him for having compared Buber with Aher, and himself with R. Meir. "Aher" was the famous Talmudic heretic R. Elisha ben Abuya, dubbed "the Other," whose disciple R. Meir remained personally loyal to him despite his apostasy. Rosenzweig denied that he was Meir and still more that Buber was Aher. "Since I have come to know Buber more closely, hence in the last three years," Rosenzweig wrote, "I have not stood in a teacher-pupil relationship to him except for the difference in age. I relate to him as a moral personality as I do to very few men. No, he is not Aher." One of Buber's early poems, from his "Jewish Renaissance" period, was an imaginative re-creation of the situation of Aher and his loyal disciple R. Meir!

Nahum Glatzer once remarked that in "The Builders" Rosenzweig was more Buber than he actually was himself—that he was leaning over backwards to find a common ground of discourse in order to communicate his own position on the Law and persuade Buber to come closer to it. This does not gainsay the real sympathy and understanding that Rosenzweig showed for Buber's position. But a letter of November 1924 written in response to the report of a discussion in the Frankfurt Lehrhaus shows how right Glatzer was in stressing Rosenzweig's own growing orthopraxy. Reacting to Glatzer's statement that only the election of the people of Israel has divine origin, but all the details of the Law come from man alone, Rosenzweig questioned "so rigid a boundary between what is divine and what is human." If the Law as a whole is the condition of being chosen and the people's chosenness depends upon their doing the deed and only in doing it knowing the command, then the only question is to what degree "this Law originating in Israel's election coincides with the traditional Jewish law. But here our doubt must be genuine doubt which willingly listens to reason and is as willing to be swung to a 'Yes' as to a 'No.' " No outsider could accept a single commandment as a "religious" demand, for it is religious only "when we cause it to come alive by fulfilling individual commandments, and transpose it from the objectivity of a theological truth to the 'Thou' of the benediction." The contrast Buber made in *I and Thou* between expressing and addressing God, Rosenzweig applied to the individual commandment: "Only in the commandments can the voice of him who commands be heard." Because this is so, no general principle, theological or otherwise, can relegate some part of the commandments once and for all to the "human" as opposed to the "divine": "I should not venture to dub 'human' any commandment whatsoever, just because it has not yet been vouchsafed me to say over it: 'Blessed art *Thou.*' "

It is in this same vein that Rosenzweig responded to the last letter that we possess from Buber to him on the Law. The question concerning the Law, like that concerning God, should not be treated in the "third person." "I, too, do not know whether the Law 'is' God's law. I know that as little, and even less than I know that God 'is.' " From this it follows that Rosenzweig would never dare state in a general sentence the limits of legitimate interpretation. "Here commences the right of experience to give testimony, positive and negative." In a curious analogy, given his earlier recourse to Christian dogma as teaching Buber would not accept, Rosenzweig declared, "As I concede to a Christian a historic and personal right to prove an exception, so

I believe in the right of the Law to prove its character as an exception against all other types of law. This is the point where the question put forward in *The Builders* claims to be an answer to your question." If Buber's life *today* does not admit of this answer, still "The Builders" opens up for him "a view of tomorrow." Yet in every case it was not Rosenzweig but Buber who restricted himself to personal testimony and refused to make any statements of a general nature either for or against the Law, much less any attempt to persuade Rosenzweig that he should or would come in the future closer to Buber's own witness. This was eminently the case with Buber's final letter of June 1925, to which Rosenzweig replied in the way we have seen:

> Whether the "law" is God's law is and remains for me the only question that is really sounded in my soul from abyss to abyss. The other abyss really does not answer this question with silence. But if it should answer it with Yes, I would not ponder whether the law is a force making for the wholeness of life—that would then be irrelevant. On the other hand, no ever so certain affirmation of this or any similar question could take the place for me of that missing—not quietly but thunderously missing—Yes.
>
> Revelation is not lawgiving. For this statement I would hopefully be ready to die in a Jewish world-church with Inquisitorial powers.

"Lawgiving has remained foreign to my heart," Buber wrote Rosenzweig the following year. "I must acknowledge its existence, but I belong only to it, not it to me."

CHAPTER 4

The Buber-Rosenzweig Bible

DESPITE THEIR BASIC divergence on the relation of revelation to law, Buber and Rosenzweig were able to work together on what became for each of them his most profound and serious life task: the translation of the Old Testament from Hebrew into German. The impetus for the translation did not come from Buber, but from the young Christian publisher Dr. Lambert Schneider. Before founding the publishing firm Verlag Lambert Schneider in 1924 at the age of twenty-five, Schneider had been and done many things. During the war he had been a soldier against his will, and when the war ended and the government of the Kaiser fell, he became a revolutionary and Spartacist—the communist branch of the so-called German Revolution which took over in Munich, when Gustav Landauer and his friends were unable to form a stable government during the first Räterepublik, the revolutionary government in Munich. He was thrown in prison and beaten for having been a Spartacist, but he was released in time to study and even, at a very young age, acquire a doctorate of philosophy. It was at that time that he met his first wife, Gertrude Schimmelburg. She came from a well-situated, highly respected Jewish family of Munich. She painted, sculpted, and sought to compensate for her "Jewish complex," in Schneider's words, by pursuing all kinds of dangerous sports. Schneider had met her on a ski hike and mountain climb. In 1933 she was fatally injured on a similar training climb.

It was as a university student that Lambert Schneider first discovered the Bible for himself, in particular the Old Testament, "and this splendid and fascinating book, often understandable only with difficulty, often vexatious, never again loosed its hold on me." "I sensed," he confessed years later, "how unsatisfactory translations are, in particular those in which the translator, without willing to do so, reads tendencies into the text that do not belong there." Some of these tendencies were Christian, some of a modern philosophical nature. Both were equally unsatisfactory to Schneider, who, not feeling up to the task of learning Hebrew and Aramaic, wanted a new translation by a Jew, by a man who was familiar with the original text and for whom at the same time the German language was a powerful instrument of expression. This led him to think of Martin Buber, who was already at that time the one German Jew recognized by German intellectuals as both an important contributor to German culture and a representative of Judaism.

Schneider wrote a letter to Buber in which he stated his proposal for a new translation, and Buber invited him to visit him at his home in Heppenheim an der Bergstrasse. A few days later Schneider sat facing Buber in his study. While he explained his wish to Buber, the latter's brown, kind eyes rested on him, "and he listened to me attentively, so attentively and openly as no one had listened to me for a very long time."

> Then he took from a shelf Luther's translation of the Bible, opened it to a passage, read it aloud to me and translated the same passage freely from the Hebrew text to show me that my view had its justification. But at the same time he made clear to me what inconceivable work, what responsibility lay in such an undertaking—all this without grandiloquence—and let me know that he did not believe he could accept such a task which would claim his time for years. All this was put forward so simply and plainly that I made no attempt at all to press him further and stood up to take my leave.
>
> Outside the sun played in the first green leaves of the trees. It was very silent in the street and in the house as Buber, standing by his desk, began

once again to speak. He did not want to refuse me definitely but wished to talk the matter over with his friend Franz Rosenzweig. Because such a request from a young man who was a Christian, seemed to him a sign that he could not dismiss without further ado. He would give me a response soon, he said, and then gave me his hand in parting.

On the way to the train station in Heppenheim, I regarded my plan as having fallen through; for his last words seemed to me to be only a little consolatory speech for my return journey to Berlin. Yet eight days later the publisher's contract for the translation was already drawn up. It was no little speech for my way back; it was an answer of Martin Buber's in the deepest sincerity.

What it is to listen and to answer I know since that first meeting with Martin Buber.

The translation that Schneider initiated and that Buber and Rosenzweig carried out not only gave Schneider the direction for his publishing work but also inculcated in him, according to his own later testimony, the freedom from prejudice that enabled him to withstand all the political confusions of Nazi Germany. Buber received from Schneider a monthly honorarium for the work of translating the Bible independently of the publication of the individual volumes. He was dependent upon this monthly payment, and when it was not forthcoming, he had to take up other literary tasks. But Lambert Schneider did not want this, since it meant postponing the translation. Leo Baeck, to whom he went for advice, said to him that he should turn to Salman Schocken, who he was convinced would help him. Schneider went to see Schocken and became so engrossed in talking to this man (who later founded his own publishing company, which took over the Buber-Rosenzweig translation) that it was only on leaving after several hours that he remembered why he had come. "But tell me, Mr. Schocken, what will become of my contract with Buber and the Bible translation?" he asked. "The contract will remain in force and the translation will proceed," Schocken replied, "and we shall talk about that next weekend."

Buber's remarkable assent to Schneider's proposition can be understood on many levels. Everything that had gone into Buber's understanding of the World as Word had prepared him for this decision— his concern for translation of many languages into German; his concern for myths, sagas, and legends; his only recently matured philosophy of dialogue with its emphasis upon lived speech and the back and forth of address and response; even his concern for drama and for poetry. Without all this he would not have been ready to turn to such a task.

The idea of the task itself was not a new one to Buber. Already before the First World War, Buber had made plans for a translation of the Hebrew Bible into modern German. At that time he held that only a community could undertake this, a community, what is more, that was also personally bound to one another, and that in this way they could help one another in their work at a deeper level than is ordinarily possible. Before the war, according to Buber's testimony, such a community was about to come into being and an agreement had been reached between it and a great publishing firm ("not a Jewish one!" comments Ernst Simon) which was to publish the translation gradually in individual volumes (not in the order of the canon). Among the contributors Moritz Heimann, Efraim Frisch, and Buber, all of the "Thursday Group," had already agreed among themselves what each of them should work on first.

Fortunately, the war brought these plans to naught; for only in the following decade did the project come to maturity in Buber and attain a fundamental and methodical clarity. "I now learned for the first time," Buber later recounted, "to understand directly what kind of a book it is—in meaning, in language, in structure—why, despite all, it had to be installed into the contemporary human world, namely, re-stored to its original power; why—and how." The stepping stone to the translation itself was the translation of the medieval Jewish philoso-pher Yehuda Halevi's poems, which occupied Rosenzweig in 1923. Rosenzweig had frequently turned to Buber for advice, and he dedi-cated the book to him. Along with the particular examples they soon reached the point where they discussed with each other the prob-lematic of translation in general and the task of the translator. Without being aware of it they found themselves impelled to ask: Is the Bible translatable? Has it already been really translated? What remains still to be done? How is it to be translated in this age?

Buber visited Rosenzweig and read him Schneider's letter propos-ing the translation of the Bible, to which he added that he was inclined to accept the proposal but only if Rosenzweig would join him in the task. Buber noted that this statement at once gladdened and disturbed Rosenzweig. Later Buber understood: Rosenzweig no longer, to be sure, expected to die in the next weeks or months, as he had in the early period of his illness, but he had given up believing he had much time at his disposal. By offering Rosenzweig a share in this task, Buber implied that he was capable of years of the most intensive work. It meant entering into another reckoning of the future. From this stemmed the expression used on the title page "zu verdeutschen *unternommen* von Rosenzweig" (literally, "undertaken to translate by Rosenzweig").

Rosenzweig's basic view at that time (which he also expressed in his postscript to his translation of the poems of Yehuda Halevi) was that Luther's great work must still be the foundation for every attempt in the German language, thus that no new translation but rather only a Luther-revision could be undertaken—to be sure, an incomparably more inclusive and penetrating one than anything which had been so designated up until then.

Buber, in contrast to Rosenzweig, did not believe that they should start with any restriction, not even the relatively flexible one set by undertaking a radical revision of Luther's translation. Only an experiment, demanding and using the whole person, hence a bold plunging ahead that knew and made use of all earlier translators but bound itself to none of them, could yield an acceptable answer to their question of whether the Bible could and should be translated anew. This is the path they finally took, but they arrived there only indirectly. Rosenzweig said (that is, he indicated on his laborious apparatus one, two, three letters of each word, which his wife Edith then guessed and spoke): "We will make a try at it." It was clear that what he meant was: We shall decide this controversy practically by testing both methods on a chapter of the Bible and thus ascertain whether one of these methods, and if so which one, was a possible road for them. "Which chapter?" asked Buber. "The first," Rosenzweig replied.

They began, naturally, with the attempt to revise Luther. They took one verse after the other and changed what, according to their knowledge and consciousness of language, seemed to need changing. After a day's work a heap of ruins stood before them. It had turned out that one could get nowhere by this method. It had turned out that Luther's Old Testament remained a majestic piece of work, but it was no longer a relevant translation of the Bible. Only four months before Rosenzweig had written to Buber, "Precisely as a German Jew I hold a new official translation of the Bible not only as impossible but even as forbidden and only a Jewish revised . . . Luther Bible as possible and allowed." Now, after the experiment, he wrote his friend Eugen Mayer, "Believe it or not, this translation began as a revision of the Luther

Bible. Step by step and at the beginning only unwillingly (me) and with heavy heart (Buber) we broke away from the Luther text. It simply did not work. . . . What will now become of it, I do not know.''

Actually Buber did not turn away from Luther with as heavy a heart as Rosenzweig suggested; for he described his next step as attempting to translate the first chapter of Genesis into German according to his own idea of how it should be done. When Rosenzweig had read the manuscript several times, he wrote Buber: "The patina is off, therefore it is as good as new, and that also counts.'' This sentence introduced excellent comments, which had already been preceded by a series of others—altogether a masterpiece of helpful criticism. Thus the common work began. Rosenzweig saw his role in this common work as that of the founding muse (Diotima and Xantippe in one person), as Buber's was in Rosenzweig's translation of Yehuda Halevi. But that, added Rosenzweig, is no small thing, even though he felt he knew much less Hebrew than Buber.

The form of the cooperation between Buber and Rosenzweig remained the same until the latter's death. Buber from time to time translated and sent to Rosenzweig pages of his first translation of the text, mostly by chapters. Rosenzweig answered with his comments: rejections, hints, proposals for changes. Buber made use of these at once in the form of changes insofar as they made immediate sense to him; and about the rest they corresponded. What they could not agree about, they discussed during Buber's Wednesday visits (Buber lectured every Wednesday at Frankfurt University and spent the rest of the day at the Rosenzweigs'). The same process was repeated with the second version of the translation through three sets of proofs. With the pages of the first version, Buber gave Rosenzweig the reasons why he had translated it thus and not otherwise, in order to make an overview easier for him. In order to spare him looking through books, Buber described for him the controversial opinions concerning each of the difficult passages, from the earliest exegetes to the most recent essays in scientific journals. Nonetheless, the correspondence often had to go on for weeks concerning a single word. Thus in the framework of an exchange of letters the Bible became illuminated in the most living commentary possible. Rosenzweig wrote to a rabbi that he had, during the Bible translation, learned a great deal that he did not know when he had written the postscript to his translation of Yehuda Halevi—not only because each new task demanded a new method but because Buber had opened to him new insights into method.

Buber proposed that Rosenzweig should receive 15 percent of the author's honorarium, but Rosenzweig at first declared that quite impossible. "You are the poet. I am the muse. Even the strongest of muses does not enter into publisher's contracts. That is our muse's *Point-d'honneur.*" The most he would accept was to have his name on the title page. Later Rosenzweig conceded to the extent of reckoning up that he found his traces on a fifth of the verses and therefore might accept a fifth of the honorarium. In 1929 when Buber told Rosenzweig that he might be going to Palestine if Judah Magnes finally arranged the chair for him at the Hebrew University, Rosenzweig lamented that Buber would not find time for the translation in Palestine—"because Palestine eats men up"—or in his return visits to Germany—because he could not shake off the European claims on his time. And even if Buber were to read and work in German in Palestine, he would lack the really driving impetus for such a specifically Golus (exile) work. "I believe in the holiness of the compulsion of the 'Conditions' (*Umstände*)," Rosenzweig wrote to Buber. "And even though in the firm B-R, your share in the work amounts to eighty percent and mine twenty, the goal and effect of the work is determined by my goal and work, that of the Golus Jew." It is cruelly ironic that these words of Rosenzweig, written just a few months before his death, were tragically contradicted by history, which dispatched most of the German Jewish readers for whom Buber and Rosenzweig labored. On the other hand, Buber finished the translation in Israel, where it became, for many Hebrew-speaking Jews, a commentary, an aid, and an inspiration to go more deeply into the original.

In a celebration at Buber's house in Jerusalem in 1961 marking Buber's completion of the translation of the Bible more than thirty years after Rosenzweig's death, Rosenzweig's friend Eugen Mayer spoke of how Buber had devoted most of his time to the indescribably difficult and time-consuming task of working together with Rosenzweig and thus filled the latter's final years with satisfaction and meaning. "For him who does a gracious deed for a great one of Israel," Mayer cited from the Midrash, "it is as if he had done it for all Israel." Rosenzweig himself fully appreciated what working with Buber on the Bible meant to him. When Buber sent him the last piece of the book "In the Beginning" (Genesis), Rosenzweig responded with a poem thanking him for making it possible for him to live through this work:

That every beginning may be an ending,
I have learned.
"Into life," I wrote, free of the burden of writing—
After barely two years
The hand ready for action became lame
The tongue ready for speech stood still,
So there remained to me only the Scriptures.

Yet the beginning became for me this end:
What I wrote
Has remained—I owe it to you, dear one,
No written thing. Nothing merely written.
We wrote the Word of the beginning,
Primal deed that vouches for the meaning of the end.
And thus began the Scriptures.

The phrase "Into life" Rosenzweig took from the concluding words of his lifework, *The Star of Redemption*. For it was his intention then to put aside writing for activity, such as the Frankfurt Lehrhaus, and it was this as much as anything that led Rosenzweig to reject the lectureship in history offered him by his great teacher Friedrich Meinecke.

Buber responded to Rosenzweig's poem by asking Rosenzweig to address him by the German *Du*, or "thou," the symbol of intimate friendship. "With Florens Christian Rang," Buber confessed, "it was not easy for me in the beginning," and with Paul Natorp the difference in age prevented it and the formal usage remained. "But between us, thank God, the difference in age is not so great." Rosenzweig replied that it was not at all difficult for him to address Buber as "thou," for he had done so all too often in silence. The difference in age did not so much account for the distance between them, "Although a nearly ten-year span of human world-experience increased it—for you were already a public figure at twenty while I still danced to the Rumpelstilt-skin riddle at thirty—but a feeling of respect that till now I could express by my usual signature to my letters. I almost regret giving up that [signature]; but it will remain as my silent undertone, as formerly my silent thou."

In 1927, Rosenzweig confided to a professor friend that he was happy that Buber had made possible for him this work, "this continuous living in the two languages that I love." In the same year Rosenzweig expressed his thanks through a privately printed change in the dedication to Buber of the second enlarged edition of his hymns and poems of Yehuda Halevi. In the public edition, it read simply, "Dedicated to Martin Buber," but in Buber's copy was printed, "For the new vision of the seventh day" [of creation]. Buber, for his part, wrote Rosenzweig after his first attempts at translating Genesis that this work had a stirring effect on him like a gift of grace, "and to a large part thanks to working together with you." A half-year later when Buber wrote Rosenzweig that for the second time in his life he found it necessary to sharply restrict his activities, he added that this, of course, in no way meant any curtailment of their common work, translating the Bible.

One of the most charming chapters in the Buber-Rosenzweig Bible translation were the reactions of Rosenzweig's young son Rafael, whom Buber's wife declared looked *so* much like his father and, like him, was so definite a personality. As Buber and Rosenzweig worked at the translation, Edith Rosenzweig read passages of it to their little son Rafael, and they delighted in his response. "I have considered," Rosenzweig wrote Buber in 1926, "that when the Torah is finished, we carvers should make a selection for the schools; naturally not for the lower classes. That would show whether it could be a popular book." But, Rosenzweig added, "Rafael needs no selection; he treasures it all. And he has besides a nose for what can be criticized in our Genesis. Recently he declared: 'I like Adam and I like Eve and Abraham and Sara and Lot and (before) the serpent, but the dear God is wicked and water is wicked.' " "My responsibility in translating the Bible is much greater, to be sure, than that in translating Yehuda Halevi," Rosenzweig wrote in 1927 to Buber's future son-in-law the poet Ludwig Strauss, "as I see almost daily with Rafael who is learning to speak from the Bible although in his head the content of the Bible and of Grimms' fairy tales are completely mixed up." But the speech of the Bible is the stronger, Rosenzweig added. "Aside from that I believe too that his inner Rosenzweig often lacks the necessary antiphonal voice of his inner Buber." When little Rafael was five, he still insisted, despite all assurances to the contrary, that his papa and Uncle Buber were the authors of the Bible! When Rafael was seven, Buber told the Rosenzweigs of the biography of him that Hans Kohn was writing and said that along with the astonishing amount of material, much of it unknown to Buber himself, that Kohn had dug up, there was also, God be thanked, much more that still remained unknown. Rosenzweig said: "Rumpelstiltskin." At that, Rafael, who had been painting at the table, shouted out jubilantly, "Ah, how good that no one knows" and continued ingenuously with "that I have translated the Bible!" instead of with the words of the fairy tale that Rosenzweig had been sure he would say. Buber, never put out of countenance, responded, "Now just not that; one knows that I am translating the Bible." Whereupon Rafael, without reflecting, said, "that I have made so many beautiful things."

When the great Enlightenment Jew Moses Mendelssohn translated the Hebrew Bible into German in the eighteenth century, his goal was to teach the German Jews German, and for that purpose, even though, as in Yiddish, he used Hebrew letters, he made his translation as German as possible. The goal of Buber and Rosenzweig was the exact reverse, as Rosenzweig himself recognized: to make the Bible, even in German, as Hebrew as possible and thereby bring the German Jews back to the original text. For this reason, even today, the Buber-Rosenzweig Bible serves many Israelis as a commentary on the Hebrew original. This does not mean that they made the task of the reader any easier than the original. On the contrary, as Gershom Scholem pointed out in the 1961 celebration marking the completion of the task, Buber's and Rosenzweig's chief intention was to exhort the reader to go and learn Hebrew and to do this, they left the clear clear, the difficult difficult, and the incomprehensible incomprehensible. Rather than smoothing out and making pleasant, they left the text purposely rough and crude, never providing a transition or a completion where the Hebrew does not do so.

If the Bible translation thus aimed at bringing back to Jewish learning the German Jews to whom it was primarily addressed, it also consciously intended to reach and teach the German Christians. Eight years before Hitler's rise to power, Rosenzweig saw with prophetic clarity the importance of their common work in combating German Christian anti-Semitism. One basis of this Christian anti-Semitism that both Buber and Rosenzweig clearly recognized was the new strain of Marcionism propounded by the liberal theologian Adolf von Harnack. In his book *The Essence of Christianity,* Harnack suggested that Christianity should divest itself of the Old Testament and the "wrathful" God of biblical Judaism, even as the Gnostic heretic Marcion had suggested in the third century. "Today," Rosenzweig wrote Buber, "the situation for which the new Marcionites have theoretically striven is already present in actuality. When the Christian today speaks of the Bible, he means only the New Testament, perhaps together with the Psalms, which then he mostly believes already belong to the New Testament." "Thus in our new translation of the Hebrew Bible," Rosenzweig concluded, "we are becoming missionaries." To his friend Eugen Mayer, Rosenzweig wrote: "I often fear that the Germans will not tolerate this all-too un-Christian Bible, and it will become the occasion for the new Marcionites of today striving to drive the Bible out of German culture. But after seventy years of such a Golus Babel [confu ion of exile], new inclusion can follow—and in any case—the end is not our business, but the beginning and the beginnings."

Rosenzweig's prediction proved all too true with the Nazis. Already in 1928, Wilhelm Stapel in an essay, "Antisemitism and Antigermanism," described the language of the Buber-Rosenzweig Bible translation as "half jargon" through which one could "most easily recognize the difference between the German and the Jewish attitudes of relationship to speech." Buber's disciple and friend Hermann Gerson, leader of the German Jewish socialist youth group known as Die Werkleute, asked Buber why they had translated the passages cited by Stapel in the way they did. In his reply Buber remarked that Stapel's whole tirade about the "Jewish Moses" showed itself to have arisen out of his lack of knowledge of the German language. "In contrast to the Luther and all other former translations," Buber wrote Gerson, "we are ready, in order to save a treasure such as this, to go the limits of the German language—without overstepping them."

The German Christian Bible scholar Karl Thieme had an understanding of the intention and accomplishment of the Buber-Rosenzweig Bible very different from that of Stapel. "As surely as this work is inconceivable without the Jewishness of its creators," he wrote, "so surely is it removed from any confessional stamp: It is a titanic attempt to go back behind all the different versions, each according to its own understanding of biblical religion, and behind two millennia of Christianity, to recapture the pre-Christian genuine origins of the Holy Book." To Scholem's judgment that "there was a utopian element in their undertaking," Thieme replied, "Certainly. But only thus could such a work arise—a work which we serious Bible scholars could today so little imagine ourselves without as without the Septuagint and the Vulgate."

To understand the impact of the Buber-Rosenzweig translation, we must comprehend both the general spirit that informed it and the specific characteristics of the translation that served as guidelines in the work of the two friends. Simon singles out three interconnected characteristics that distinguish this Bible translation from all others: the oral element, the sensual element, and the maximum preservation of the Hebrew form of speech in a foreign idiom through which, in Buber's own words, the Bible was liberated from the "plague of familiarity." "Do we mean a book?" wrote Buber. "We mean the voice. Do we mean that one shall learn to read? We mean that one shall learn to hear. There is no other way back to the Bible than that of the turning, which turns us around on our axis, until we are directed not to an earlier stretch of our way but to the way where the voice is to be heard. We wish to break through to the spokenness of the Word, to its having been spoken. The Bible is to be read *in living Presence.*" This is the claim that the Buber-Rosenzweig Bible makes on "the man of today." "We proceed from the insight," wrote Buber, "that the Bible stems from living recitation and is destined to living recitation, that speech is its true existence, writing only the form of its preservation." In 1926 Buber and Rosenzweig together responded to critics by asserting the ever-renewed presentness of the spoken word in the Bible to all ages:

> We believe that the word that has become writing in the Bible faces every age, our own as much as any past age, alien, distant, and hostile, but that this work preserves the strength in every age to seize those who hear it. . . . It wants to speak to every age, in every age, despite every age. We do not know whether it will take our translation work into its service and into what kind of service. We have only one thing to be concerned with: to be *faithful* to it.

Buber and Rosenzweig expressed the importance of the oral as opposed to the written, of sound as opposed to sight, by dividing their translation of the Hebrew original into "cola," or breathing units. Though these may appear at first glance like the format of poetry, they are actually the length of phrase or clause that can be said comfortably in a single breath so that the punctuation is not paragraphs or sentences or rhyming units but the length of a breath if the text were, in fact, read aloud. Ernst Simon describes these cola "as a special rhythm, the origin of which is not aesthetic but respiratory, that is, fitted to the division of the scripture into segments divided according to the tempo of reading aloud, like the cadence of the traditional melodies by which the translation was influenced without being submissive to it." Simon even cites the testimony of an experienced Baal Koreh, a man who reads the Bible aloud in the synagogue, that the Buber-Rosenzweig translation could be chanted! "Our translation is the first *colometric* one," wrote Buber in 1927 in response to the criticism of Emanuel bin

Gorion, "i.e., the first that gives to the text its natural articulation, regulated by the laws of human breath and of human speech, each one of which represents a rhythmic unit."*

The uniqueness of the Bible, wrote Rosenzweig in an article in honor of Buber's fiftieth birthday, can be indicated only through the book that is read aloud, not the book that is written. The Bible is not the most beautiful book in the world, the deepest, the truest, or the wisest, continued Rosenzweig, but it is the most important, and this importance is bound up with its oral character. This oral character is, in turn, bound up with the deeply dialogical quality of the Bible. The writtenness of the Bible lies on it like a light garment. In the moment when the psalms are prayed, the laws obeyed, the prophecies believed, they at once lose their monological muteness, find voice, and call the eternal Partner to dialogue. But the human partner, too, is constantly summoned to dialogue. Continually, the psalms awaken men to prayer, the laws awaken men to obey, the prophecies awaken men to belief. Even the epic is secret dialogue which, under the husks of its epic past, is carried over into full anecdotal presentness and what is awakened to deed, hope, love, becomes knowledge, teaching, revelation.

One of the most moving tributes to the spoken quality of the Buber-Rosenzweig translation was made by the great Protestant theologian Paul Tillich when he spoke at Sarah Lawrence College in 1952. At dinner a professor whose own mother language was German asked Tillich what he thought of the Buber-Rosenzweig translation in a way that left no doubt that he expected Tillich to go along with him in depreciating this "grotesque endeavor." But Tillich responded with a great appreciation of the translation—based, he testified, on belonging to a circle in Germany that regularly read it aloud together.

One of the most important presuppositions for restoring the spoken and heard quality of the Bible was the rediscovery of the original power of metaphor through finding, and in some cases even creating, comparable German words. It was this aspect of the Buber-Rosenzweig Bible that made it seem strange and contrived to many, especially on a first reading, but it was precisely this which gave it its great power. For it deliberately set out to shock the reader out of the familiar and hackneyed into the original address and response of the spoken word, and it succeeded in doing this as no Bible translation before or since has

---

*See Note 1 to Chapter 4.

done. So far from meaning that Buber and Rosenzweig took liberties with the original Hebrew text, it meant a greater faithfulness—the faithfulness which dares to stand in direct dialogue with the original rather than allowing the influence of Luther's or any other translation to guide their hand. So their faithfulness was not to the traditional interpretations but to the traditional version of the Hebrew text from which, according to Ernst Simon and others, the translators deviated only in the very rare and exceptional cases where it seemed to them absolutely necessary. It is this faithfulness which resulted in the deliberate strangeness of the language, which by its alien, unusual sounds served, as Rosenzweig said, to trouble the complacency of those who imagine they already possess "the Book." For this is "the only book among all the books of humanity which is forbidden to find the end of its course in the storehouse of the cultural possession of humanity."

From the Septuagint on, all translators had endeavored to transport the Hebrew Bible into their *own* spiritual world. Even Jewish translators and exegetes could not escape these tendencies to modify the Bible to fit Western theological and cultural ways of thinking and speaking. The fundamental direction of the Buber-Rosenzweig Bible was the opposite.

Buber and Rosenzweig rejected the calcified theological terminology of "spirit" in favor of the still-living metaphor of *Braus Gottes,* which Everett Fox translates close to the Hebrew original of *ruach* and the German *Braus,* as "rush of spirit" or "rushing wind," recalling the famous verse from John, "The wind of the spirit bloweth where it listeth."* That primordial rushing that goes forth from God, commented Buber, is neither nature nor spirit but the two in one, prior to any split, so that it takes on its natural form in "wind," its psychological, or soul-form, in "spirit." In the Bible *ruach* everywhere means a happening. "To render this, our translation speaks of *'Geistbraus'* (rush of spirit) not of *'Geist.'* "

Perhaps the most significant of these changes from written to spoken and from static to dynamic is the Buber-Rosenzweig translation of the Hebrew *kadosh* not as "holy" but as "hallowing." *Kadosh* does not mean a state of being but a process: that of hallowing and of becoming hallowed. Moses stands before the thornbush not on holy ground but on the ground of hallowing. When Aaron is consecrated as a priest, he is clothed in the garments of hallowing and anointed with the oil of

---

*See Note 2 to Chapter 4.

hallowing. The Sabbath is a festival of hallowing, and the sons of Israel are called by God to become people of hallowing (not a holy people).

This rendition at one stroke changes the whole meaning of the relationship of God to the world and of the sacred to the profane and lays the groundwork for Buber's later characterization of Hasidism as regarding the profane not as an antagonist of the holy but as the not-yet-hallowed, the not-yet-sanctified. No separate spheres of sacred and profane insulated from one another by taboo can endure before the onrushing *Geistbraus* of the God of spirit *and* nature. If we apply this change to the translation of a familiar Hasidic tale, the power of this understanding of hallowing the everyday or sanctifying the profane becomes unmistakable:

> The rabbi of Kobryn taught: God says to man, as he said to Moses: "Put off thy shoes from thy feet"—put off the habitual which encloses your foot, and you will know that the place on which you are now standing is ground of hallowing. For there is no rung of human life on which we cannot find the hallowing of God everywhere and at all times.

Holiness is not a simple state accessible to the enlightened who can see through the illusion of existence. It is a *task* in which man's hallowing and God's hallowing meet. When Rabbi Mendel of Kotzk's question as to where God dwells was answered by citing the verse, "The whole earth is full of His glory," he retorted, "No, God dwells where man lets Him in!"

To carry through their sense of God's name as presence rather than essence, as word of address rather than an object to be magically conjured, Buber and Rosenzweig capitalized personal pronouns in their translation of the Hebrew Bible. Buber spoke of the necessity of finding in the Western language a correspondence that will engender in the reader a feeling of sureness streaming out of the name, not expressing the God-with-me, God-with-you, God-with-us conceptually, but in embodied presence. What had been previously translated as the Lord was now rendered as I, THOU, HE—that is, extrapolates Everett Fox, as "I who am-there with you, You who are-there with me, He who is-there with me." This means, as Rosenzweig explained, recognizing all Platonizing tendencies and guarding against their indirect philosophical consequences. God does not name Himself at the thornbush as Being but as Existing, as being-there, as being present, being with, coming to, and helping those whom He addresses. Thus the absoluteness and eternality of God is really the capacity of this present moment and any future moment to be one in which I find myself addressed in my present existence. The eternality of God's presence is here, as in *I and Thou*, not the *"eternal"* Thou but the *eternally* Thou, the ever-renewed concreteness and uniqueness of the meeting with the Thou. Starting from Moses' relationship to God, Buber comments: "Man cannot 'see' God's face (in our terminology: he cannot make God into an object), but he can let himself be addressed by him in his inmost self and stand in dialogue with him (in our terminology: he can become a partner to God)." When Ernst Simon first read the Buber-Rosenzweig translation of *ehyeh asher ehyeh*, he complained to Buber about his taking it on himself to alter the great formula of the identity of God with himself (I am that I am). "Buber answered me with a short sentence that I shall never forget," recounts Simon: " 'God makes no philosophical pronouncements about himself and speaks in no formulae." God says to His creature what he needs to know—that He is there with him, is present to him, but in always new, never-to-be-anticipated forms, in the forms of this, His creature's, own life situations, and that what matters thus is nothing else than recognizing Him again and again in them.*

The Hebrew Bible wants to be read as one book, wrote Buber, so that none of its parts remain shut within themselves; rather each remains open to the other. It wants to be present to its reader in such intensity as one book that in reading or reciting a certain passage it brings to mind those passages connected with it, especially those identical, close, or related to it in speech, and that they all illuminate one another in such manner that they come together into a theologoumenon—a conception that is not expressly taught but immanent in the words, emerging from their relations and correspondences. The repetition of the same or similar-sounding words, or words and phrases the same or similar in root within a passage, within a book, within a group of books, shows the linguistic relationship between the prophets and the Pentateuch, between the Psalms and the Pentateuch, between the Psalms and the Prophets.**

One striking example of this linking of words through sounds or roots is from the story of Jacob and Esau. Jacob, who has obtained by trickery his father's blessing of the first-born, must, after he returns

---

*See Note 3 to Chapter 4.
**See Note 4 to Chapter 4.

from fourteen years of service with his Uncle Laban, face the wrath of his brother Esau and with it the possibility that Esau will kill him. The night before he is to meet Esau, he goes apart alone and encounters a strange man with whom he wrestles until dawn and whom he will not let go until he has received his blessing. After this trial, Jacob is now ready to go to Esau to seek forgiveness, to repair the injured order of existence, and, if necessary, to give his life in the process. Thus what was won by deviousness could be retained only by open-hearted directness and great personal and spiritual courage.

These meanings are not read into the text. They are already present as hidden connections that need be brought to light only by paying attention to the significant repetition of leading-words or motifs.

The integral connection between the story of Jacob wrestling with the "angel," which is so often dealt with out of context, and his flight from the wrath of Esau and his returning to face it, is given in the text through the repetition of the motifs of covering the face and seeing one's face, the parallel between seeing the face of God and seeing the face of Esau, and the parallel between the blessing, or gift, which God gives to Jacob and that which Jacob gives to Esau.

Esau links Jacob's name "heel-sneak" with the way in which he has twice sneaked what was his: first his birthright, then his father's blessing (Genesis 27:35–36). This mean way of fighting is atoned through the good, the name that has become shameful replaced by one that is hallowed. Soon God himself expressed the renewal of the man Jacob-Israel, and completes the blessing, but only after he is reconciled with his brother Esau. The blessing between man and man is followed by that between God and man.*

In the Introduction to his translation of a selection of Nietzsche's writings, the American philosopher Walter Kaufmann suggests that Buber and Rosenzweig took their cue for the leading-word style of the Hebrew Bible from Wagner's leitmotifs (though, as Grete Schaeder points out, there is no statement of Buber's that would testify to his having a special relationship to Wagner's music). In both cases "an unobtrusive cross reference" is established, writes Kaufmann, "an association which, even if only dimly felt, adds dimension to the meaning." What is more, Kaufmann claims that no major writer is as biblical in this respect as Wagner's one-time admirer and later opponent Nietzsche, who "knew the Bible so much better than many people

*See Note 5 to Chapter 4.

today." And Kaufmann himself, in this context, acknowledges the influence of the Buber-Rosenzweig *Leitworte* principle on his own translation of Nietzsche.

From Nietzsche's sister Elizabeth Förster-Nietzsche to Hitler, Nietzsche's thought was scandalously distorted into the scripture of an anti-Semitism which he himself regarded as a barbarous stupidity. If Hitler had had his picture taken next to the bust of Wagner, instead of Nietzsche, it would have been far more appropriate, since Wagner's "Nordic" music really was accompanied by a strong strain of anti-Semitism. Whether Wagner's leitmotif was influence, stimulus, or merely a convenient borrowing of a name for an independently discovered principle, its connection with the Buber-Rosenzweig Bible makes for all sorts of ironic overtones—from the Nazi denigration of the Hebrew Bible as the "Jewish book" to the great comfort that the Buber-Rosenzweig translation gave to the German Jews during the first years of the Nazi regime. It also dovetails with one response that Buber received in a letter from his old friend the poet Alfred Mombert. "Our old eternally-new Bible, which has sent forth so many powerful streams into the German language, has the highest claim to receive a new life from the German language. And today is also again capable and ripe to do so as it has not been for a very long time. For close behind our German language stands today a still greater: German music."

In the same letter Mombert prefaced this statement by a more personal one: "Nothing could so delight me," he wrote, "as that you have now laid your hand on precisely what remained for you to do: the translation into German of the 'oldest primordial proclamation' (*Urkunde*) of the human race (Herder). Here, if anywhere, is the eternal Palestine, visible to all ages and peoples." Later, when he had received a new volume of the Buber-Rosenzweig translation, Mombert confessed that splendid as it is, for a long time he could not bring himself to read the Luther translation because of its "thick layer of Christian-churchly varnish" and "European culture." "That I can again read the Pentateuch directly next to the Gilgamesh-Epoch of the Babylonians and the Avesta of the Persians and next to the Pyramid-Texts—without having to curse the believers and the parsons—is a great joy to me!" And Mombert, whose first contact with Buber in 1907 was in connection with the latter's efforts to get material on Oriental ecstatic confessions for his *Ekstatische Konfessionen* (anthology of mysticism), added in a still later letter: "Your translation is to be classified in the libraries under 'Orientalia' and not under 'Theology.' " In 1930 Mombert wrote Buber of his joy at possessing the new translation of Isaiah. Realizing that the traditional text is *not* the last word, that new possibilities of innovations and heightenings have been demonstrated in the same language "is for me a rejuvenating experience."

The Buber-Rosenzweig Bible translation "has been universally acclaimed as a miracle of fidelity and beauty," wrote the Germanicist Solomon Liptzin in a book on refugees from Nazi Germany. This statement might be somewhat in accord with the later recognition that the translation has received, much more indeed in the thirty years since Liptzin wrote that statement. But the original reactions were of a very mixed nature. The noted Hebrew writer Emanuel Bin Gorion (Emanuel Berdyczwesky) composed a long, highly critical essay on the Buber-Rosenzweig translation shortly after the first volumes appeared. After he received the book *Im Anfang* (In the Beginning, or Genesis) Gershom Scholem wrote Buber a long letter in which he praised the "splendid factual clarity" of the translation but protested against its exalted tone, which reminded him of a Hasidic *niggun*, or wordless melody. Buber in his answer replied that in Scholem's letter he had found the only serious criticism that he had encountered until that time. In his letter about Genesis, Scholem explained, "I do not dare to think in what tone you will translate the prophets" if Genesis is already so exalted in tone. In 1930 when he received the translation of Isaiah he wrote Buber that he found this beloved text a stranger to him and again centered in on the problem of pathos (a problem which Buber's younger friend Abraham Joshua Heschel affirmed as the very heart of biblical prophecy). Buber again singled out Scholem's criticism as the most serious and relevant he had received, but he declared that to him the whole of the Bible was an expression of pathos and that in the prophets it was only heightened. "Of course, when the prophet really cries out, the form of the *cola* is split asunder."

"The strongest, most stiff-necked and demanding of the critics of your work," Scholem later said to Buber, "was yourself, the artist, the master of speech, the *homo religiosus* who tirelessly wrestled for the exactness and fullness of expression which alone could correspond to your intentions." And many years later Scholem added his own testimony to that of the many others who have found in the Buber-Rosenzweig translation an invaluable commentary on the text itself. "Many of us have again and again, when we read difficult passages of the Bible, asked ourselves, what would 'the Buber' say—not otherwise than we ask, what does Rashi [the great medieval Jewish commentator on the Bible] have to say?"

The great German-Swiss novelist and poet Hermann Hesse wrote in three separate places, "I must also name the Bible translation of Martin Buber, with the sincerity and strictness of its struggling for the word, one of the noblest strivings of the German spirit in our time." When Hesse nominated Buber for the Nobel Prize in Literature in 1949 and again in 1958, he gave as the basis for his proposal, along with other things, the translation of the Bible. Buber's son Rafael who, as a communist, was by no means close to his father at this time, wrote in 1926: "Genesis is very beautiful in your translation. I gladly read in it and often in so doing have the feeling that I am reading Hebrew. . . . It is not only the faithful rendering in the rhythm of the Bible but also the primordial text in the beautiful German language. At any rate I read it in German and understand it in Hebrew." The Hebrew writer Shmuel Agnon was also one of the translation's most sympathetic supporters. "That you have accepted our translation with such enthusiastic agreement, with so deep and warm an understanding of its nature, has been a real source of happiness for me and for Rosenzweig," Buber wrote Agnon. "Here in Germany the book has become a veritable object of battle." In addition to those who rejected it because it claims to say something new beyond Luther, there were those who were unable to read a word of the original who nonetheless uttered the most definite judgments. "But the truth can only be held back for a time. . . . We receive ever more expressions of acknowledgement, indeed of enthusiasm, both public and private, and do not doubt its ultimate victory." Although Rudolf Hallo wrote Buber that he needed to be convinced of the rightness of the translation, he said that he awaited the fifth volume as one would await a revelation and added, in his next letter, "Before your disclosure in your letter that you feel *called* to your work, I stand silent and disarmed."

Among those who responded were a number of eminent scholars and translators of the Hebrew Bible. One of these, Benno Jacob, wrote: "It is an epoch making accomplishment which, considering the changed times, may stand of equal rank beside Luther's translation of the Bible. Of course, that can only be judged by those who know both languages. Above all you have attained what, if I understand you rightly, you really wanted: to *restore* the *original* language. . . . In a word,

I know no translation which so very much replaces the original and yet so very much presses one to learn the original itself." The great Bible scholar Alfred Jeremias wrote Buber that he saw the translation as a "pneumatic" rendering out of the depth of Jewish spiritual life, the mysticism of the everyday, the hallowing of the profane, hence out of Jewish, as opposed to Christian, messianism. They had done for the believing Jew what Luther had done for the believing Christian by his translation of the New Testament.

In replying to the sharp but respectful criticism of the litterateur Rudolf Borchardt of the Stefan George school of poets, Buber used of himself the same phrase that Elisha uses in Buber's mystery play *Elijah* —"taken into service." This task he did not see as touched by Borchardt's criticism, which stemmed from the assumptions of the school of biblical critics of Julius Wellhausen, a comparative method that involves a complex theory for the sources of the five books of Moses, leaning particularly on parallels with Babylonian religious practices. Rudolf Pannwitz, who later was to write a pointed attack on Buber's approach to Christianity and Gnosis, wrote perceptively of the Bible translation that it did not aim to recast the Bible in the German language but rather to stretch out the German language to the point where it could receive the Hebrew spirit and tone of the Hebrew Bible.*

For many members of the Jewish and Zionist youth movements, Ernst Simon recounts, the translation served first as a sort of substitute for the original. Finally, however, it became to them a bridge to the original because of its strange Hebraisms which transcended the bounds of the usual framework of the German language. To those who know Hebrew the translation has proved of great value as one of the most important exegeses of the Bible. The Buber-Rosenzweig Bible came as both the supreme cultural achievement and the termination of what Buber himself called the German-Jewish symbiosis. Ernest M. Wolf, like Scholem and Simon, testified to its great importance for Jewish youth both as a substitute for the original and as a favorite commentary, or *targum,* on it. It gave a solid foundation to the renaissance of Jewish learning that had been stirring from the early years of the century, even before the impact of Hitler's anti-Semitism, and "regular and systematic courses in Bible study became one of the major forms of educational endeavor in the Jewish community."

---

*See Note 6 to Chapter 4.

There was hardly a meeting, a seminar, a conference, or a camp of Jewish youth organizations where Bible study was not part of the program, and usually a major and central part of it. . . . Had the generation of young Jews that went through the Buber-Rosenzweig school of Bible reading and Bible interpreting been permitted to grow up and to remain together, they would probably have become the most Bible-conscious Jews since the days before the ghetto-walls had fallen in Europe.

Rosenzweig himself, far from expecting and desiring "universal acclaim," positively rejected it as either a realistic or a desirable goal. "We may only and exclusively write for the one percent," he wrote to Buber, "with a side glance to the ten percent. The eighty-nine percent do not concern us. If we had to write for them, we should never have begun." The one percent would understand immediately what *Braus* means or who HE is, the ten percent only after hard work, the eighty-nine percent never. In a later letter Rosenzweig wrote Buber that "whoever expects a work of art, simply cannot understand us. Although it *is* one." It is not visible as such any more than the elegance of a mathematical proof is visible to anyone except a mathematician.

The Bible translation, which was to occupy Buber until he entered his final coma two days before his death, was as central to his life and thought as it was to Rosenzweig's. The progress from the easy to the hard word and the understanding of the world of words as event and happening, which laid the groundwork for *I and Thou*, came to still fuller flowering and maturity in the work of the translation. It was no accident that the translation itself should be carried on as a continual dialogue between the two friends, for the life and thought of whom the "World of the Word" had become central. Only in such dialogue could the "World of the Word" take on its full reality. The question that had oppressed Buber as a boy helping his grandfather with Rashi remained a continual source of wonder to the two friends who took the bold plunge into the hitherto unexplored territory of recapturing the original, spoken ancient Hebrew in the modern, written German: "What does it mean and how does it come about that one 'explained' something that was written in one language through something which was said in another?"

Writing to a friend after the completion of the Book of Samuel, Rosenzweig said of the translation: "It was a heavy task, Buber says the heaviest of his life." What this heavy task meant to Buber personally as a progress from the "easy word" to the hard one is vividly portrayed by the poem "Confession of the Author" which Buber wrote in 1945 and dedicated to Ernst Simon:

Once with a light keel
I shipped out to the land of legends
Through the storm of deeds and play,
With my gaze fixed on the goal
And in my blood the beguiling poison—
Then one descended to me
Who seized me by the hair
And spoke: Now render the Scriptures!

From that hour on the galley
Keeps my brain and hands on course,
The rudder writes characters,
My life disdains it honor
And the soul forgets that it sang.
All storms must stand and bow
When cruelly compelling in the silence
The speech of the spirit resounds.

Hammer your deeds in the rock, world!
The Word is wrought in the flood.

Who or what was it that descended to Buber, seized him by the hair, and commanded him to "render the Scriptures"? Not a voice from heaven but the address heard in the situation itself. Buber's Bible translation too is a "Word to the Times"—a faithful listening and response to the demand of the hour, which in this case meant bringing the biblical word to an age probably more alienated from and hostile to it than any earlier one within the history of Judaism and Christianity. Nowhere is this prophetic voice in an alien world expressed with more force and clarity than in Buber's essay "The Man of Today and the Jewish Bible," one of the first fruits of the biblical translation and the beginning of three decades of serious concern with the interpretation of the Bible. Beginning with the simple statement that "the theme of the Bible is the encounter between a group of People and the Lord of the world in the course of history," Buber immediately sets this theme in tension with the "intellectual" man of our time for whom "the spirit imposes no obligations," since "everything except everyday life belongs to the realm of the spirit." "Nowadays 'religion' itself is part of the detached spirit," one of its subdivisions which only serves to reinforce the dualism between "spirit" and "life." That is why Buber later sardonically described religion as "the great enemy of mankind." The so-called Old Testament, in contrast, is the greatest document of a reality in which the spirit is made incarnate and everyday life hallowed, in which the Torah is designed to cover the natural course of man's life and the covenant is a demand not for religiosity but for real community. The man of today, who "has no access to a sure and solid faith," can, nonetheless, "open up this book and let its rays strike him where they will, without prejudgement or precommitment."

Buber describes this possibility of opening oneself to the Bible in terms of the three categories that Rosenzweig had placed at the center of *The Star of Redemption*—creation, revelation, and redemption. Creation is the origin, redemption the goal, revelation the midpoint between the two—but not a fixed midpoint, such as the revelation at Sinai, but our present perceiving of that revelation. Not only is such perception possible at any time, but a psalm or a prophecy is no less "Torah," i.e., instruction in the dialogue with God, than the story of the exodus from Egypt. If the history of this people points to the history of all mankind, "the secret dialogue expressed in the psalms and prophecies points to my own secret." Revelation, then, takes place ever anew in the present *if I am there*, something which the man of today resists in his innermost being. He sees history as chance or fatality rather than as the "awful and splendid moment of decision—your moment and mine no less than Alexander's and Caesar's." But precisely because it is your moment it does not belong to you but to the meeting itself, and this implies living in genuine responsibility, which is just what the man of today does not want. "Man of today resists the Scriptures because he cannot endure revelation. To endure revelation is to endure this moment full of possible decisions, to respond to and to be responsible for every moment." If this is a logical extension of *I and Thou*, it is one to which the concreteness of the history of the Bible and of the present has lent new force and seriousness. Here, indeed, is the link between *I and Thou* and Buber's 1928 essay "Dialogue," in which every event is seen as a "sign of address."

The man of today also resists the knowledge of creation in favor of process and determinism. Here "process" is used, as in *I and Thou*, as the unfree link between cause and effect rather than the creative novelty of Bergson and Whitehead. Yet the reality of creation is still open to him "because every man knows that he is an individual and unique." "Another first man enters the world whenever a child is born," and this new beginning is an opportunity not for the abolition of the world or its improvement but its genuine transformation. What is most difficult of all, however, is to grasp redemption existentially, from our own experience. The lived moment leads directly to the knowledge of revelation, thinking about birth indirectly to the knowledge of creation. "But in his personal life probably not one of us will taste the essence of redemption before his last hour." Yet here too there is a way, if we have, not what Paul Tillich called the "courage to be," but what I have called the "courage to address and to respond," a way that can be understood, said Buber, by recalling our own "hours in the lowest depths when our soul hovers over the frail trap door which, at the very next instant, may send us down into destruction, madness, and 'suicide' by our own verdict." In those hours we feel the touch of a hand which reaches down to us and wishes to be grasped—if we can only have the incredible courage to take the hand and let it draw us up out of the darkness! Thus redemption, like revelation, is not a one-sided act of God but a dialogue, a partnership between God and man. We can know, like Job, that our Redeemer lives, that He wishes to redeem us, only if we are ready from our side to accept His redemption with the turning of our whole being, *teshuvah.*

The modern *Lebensphilosophie,* with which Buber himself was once identified, that philosophy of life which exchanges the life-drunk spirit for the detached intellect and thus degrades it, which inverts the relation between creating spirit and receiving life and thus inverts the primordial conditions, exalting life to the madness of its sovereignty and driving it into absurdity, has deepened the need of modern man, blocked his self-awareness, and made any attempt at rescue far more difficult. The Bible, which teaches the holy marriage of spirit and life and rejects the subjugation of spirit to life just as it rejects every enslavement of life by spirit, still has the power to help the man of today in his innermost need. It can do this through those ties between the history of creation and revelation that point to how the Bible is to be read: *in living presence.* It teaches man what it means to be God's partner in creation: that there is no split between the "religious" and the "social," that God and the "oppressed and needy" belong together. For God dwells in the "high and holy" places *"and* with those who are broken, and bowed down in spirit" (Isaiah 57:15). The biblical world of faith is not a higher religion into which one can withdraw oneself from the evil of the lived everyday. It means that heaven shall be built on earth and nowhere else. One may not turn to God if one has turned away from the responsibility to one's own everyday. The biblical repetition and varying uses of *ruach* show the power of the

Bible to lead the man of today to the insight that the dualism between the realm of spirit and that of natural law is false from the beginning; that man must himself help to build the dwelling of the holy or it will not be built.

What truly matters is not a "return to the Bible," Buber concludes, but rather, taking up again the genuinely biblical unity of life with our whole time-entangled life and multiplicity of soul, withstanding our present historical situation in dialogical responsibility and Bible-true openness to faith. In the light of this essay, the words with which it concludes now take on new meaning: "Do we mean a book? We mean the voice. Do we mean that one should learn to read? We mean that one should learn to hear." The spoken quality of the Bible is inseparable from the demand upon our existence for *teshuvah,* for the turning of our whole being so that we find ourselves, not back on some earlier stretch of our way, but there where the voice is to be heard!

CHAPTER 5

·———————————————————————————·

Tragedy, the "Suffering Servant,"
and Rosenzweig

·———————————————————————————·

IN 1925 BUBER wrote and published in *Masken,* the journal of the Düsseldorf Playhouse, a short essay titled "Drama and Theater. A Fragment." Thirty-five years later this piece, written because of Buber's work with the theater, came full circle when the directors of New York City's avant-garde Living Theater expressed their sincere enthusiasm for it by regularly reproducing the whole of "Drama and Theater" in the Living Theater program for William Carlos Williams's play *Many Loves.*

Buber sharpened and intensified the question of the relation between drama and theater before attempting to answer it. Drama as poetry, he declared, "is something entirely different from the drama of theater." Drama as poetry he defined as the rising to artistic independence of dialogue, an element that was tolerated only with reluctance by the epic, and even in the narrative is given only as much space as is needed to move the action forward. The statement that in drama dialogue carries all action does not mean "dialogue" merely in the conventional sense in which it is used in the theater. It means dialogue in the full sense of Buber's now mature philosophy of dialogue: address and response and the reality of meeting and of the "between." Regarded as a species of poetry, drama is "the formation of the *word* as something that moves *between* beings, the mystery of word and answer." This mystery is not one of union, harmony, or even complementarity, but of *tension;* for two persons never mean the same thing by the words that they use and no answer is ever fully satisfactory. The result is that at each point of the dialogue, understanding and misunderstanding are interwoven. From this tension of understanding and misunderstanding comes the interplay of openness and closedness, expression and reserve, that mark every genuine dialogue between person and person. Thus the mere fact of the *difference* between persons already implies a basic dramatic situation as an inherent component of human existence as such which drama only reproduces in clearer and heightened form.

It is this recognition of *difference* which explains the polarity, the vis-à-vis, *and* the tragic conflict arising because "each is as he is." But this is also at the heart of the distinction between dialogue and Socratic dialectic. *Dialogue* recognizes differences and never seeks for simple agreement or unanimity. *Dialectic,* in contrast, begins with the categories of "the same" and "the other," but excludes the reality of "the between" and with it the recognition of real otherness as that which can be affirmed even in opposing it. Thus both the original assumption and the goal of dialectic is a unified point of view. The dialectician's faith in logic as the arbitrator and common denominator not only of his inner reflections but of the dialogue between person and person is essentially single-voiced, monological, and pseudo-universal.

If the play as poetry is communication in tension across all barriers of individuation, the play as a theater production, according to "Drama and Theater," originates in the elemental impulse to leap through *transformation* over the abyss between I and Thou that is bridged through speech. Buber illustrated this process of transformation of the actor into the hero by the experience of primitive man, who if he assumes the aspect and gestures of another being—an animal, a hero, a demon—can *become* this other being; for example, the Australian and the kangaroo, the Thracian who danced the satyr in the train of Dionysus. The "identity" they achieve with the being they represent is not "acted," yet it is a play; for it disappears as soon as masks and attitudes are stripped off. In the fourth dialogue of *Daniel,* Buber had already described, less clearly but a great deal more fully, this primeval origin of dramatic transformation.

The most striking illustration that Daniel gives of transformation is the ancient Dionysus play which represented the procession dancing and singing in honor of Bacchus and the nuptials, passion, and resurrection of the God. The young man who had been selected and had prepared to sacrifice his body for the body of the savior stood light and detached before the dark intoxication of his companions:

> His foot struck the earth like the foot of a young steer; the streams of pallor and of blood mixed themselves on his skin like fire and water, and when his cheeks became red, they had the color of new wine. In his eyes, however—which were not seeing, only existing eyes—dwelt the transformation "to winds and waters and stars and the birth of plants and animals," and his free limbs completed it. . . . more ingenious than Gunnar Helming and more believing than the Gauri-maiden—what was it that happened to him? What was it that happened in him? Did not the secret of magic rest on him to which all virginal peoples are devoted: he who transforms himself into the God lives the life, does the deed, works the work of the God? Did he not *realize* the God in and with his soul as in and with his body?

This dramatic transformation is not yet fully a play; for the latter comes into being only in the long development and involvement which produces actors and spectators vis-à-vis each other and which in its modern and degenerate form replaces rather than complements the transformation: "The spectator to whom the action that he beholds is no longer a reality penetrating his life and helping to determine his fate and the actor who is no longer overcome by the transformation but is familiar with it and knows how to make use of it mutually correspond." The actor knows himself looked at, looked at without awe and shame, and he himself plays without awe and shame, as in a show. In the theater of Aeschylus, in contrast, what took place on the stage was neither an illusory imitation of a past happening nor a delusive production of the imaginary, but rather a sacred reality that *concerned* the life of each of the watching and listening audience, concerned it with primal power so that awe and shame were still present both to the beholders and to the beheld.

In Greek tragedy, drama as poetry and drama as theater are joined into one. The spiritual principle of dialogue and the natural one of mimic transformation-play combine to produce true drama, a Janus-faced reality looking simultaneously back to the written drama and forward to the "living theater." These two principles relate to each other, Buber claimed, as love to sex; for love needs sex in order to become embodied and sex needs love in order to attain spirit. This analogy at first glance seems odd but at second glance, not at all so. "Drama and theater" and "love and sex" are not analogous: they are two aspects of the same reality—the dialogue between I and Thou. Sex, like the transformation of the actor into the hero, is a natural and elemental union, while love, to Buber, like the *word* that arises between person and person in drama, is the affirmation of *otherness*. And for both, spirit, the relation *between* I and Thou, is primal, and the structure of theatrical production or the interaction of natural impulses is the "It" which the relationship employs and transforms.

For this reason the theater needs drama more than drama needs the theater. "The theater that is not obedient to drama bears the curse of soullessness that, for all its luxuriant variegation, it can hardly stifle for the hour's duration of its magic show." An age of unperformed drama is a heroic and lonely Eiron.* But "an age in which the self-glorious theater treats all drama as material and occasion for its phantasmagoria" is a pitiful boaster, one which says what it does not know and speaks its word without faithfulness to the mystery of address and response.

It is clear that Buber considered the theater of the age in which he lived to be a pitiful boaster. For the faithless public and the faithless theater to be redeemed from fear to awe, a great work of teaching is necessary, a work in which the theater itself can take part only when it recognizes the supremacy of drama and submits itself to the command of the *word*. But to do this does not mean to retreat from the spoken word to the written. Rather it means to preserve in all faithfulness the tension of agreement and disagreement, the mutual affirmation of otherness that lies at the heart of "I and Thou."

> The word that convulses through the whole body of the speaker, the word that serves all gestures in order that all the plasticity of the stage construct and reconstruct itself as a frame, the stern over-againstness of I and Thou, overarched by the wonder of speech, that governs all the play of transformation, weaving the mystery of the spirit into every element—it alone can determine the legitimate relation between drama and theater.

---

*Greek: a dissembler, one who says less than he thinks, as in Socratic irony.

The problem of the relation between drama and the theater found dramatic expression in the 1926–1928 correspondence between Buber and Hugo von Hofmannsthal concerning the latter's play *The Tower*.

The influence of Hofmannsthal on the young Buber we have already seen,* and this influence was in many respects lasting. Albrecht Goes repeatedly characterizes Buber's mature style as possessing the "severe grace" of Hofmannsthal. When Hofmannsthal sent Buber greetings on his fiftieth birthday, Buber replied by telling Hofmannsthal that his personal and literary existence had been of great importance to Buber from his youth on for his own connection with German culture—right up to the present. A speech of Hofmannsthal's on literature ("Das Schrifttum als geistiger Raum der Nation") that Buber had just read was for Buber a new, especially clear and beautiful sign of this continuing bond between the two men, for it expressed an insight common to them. "The world only becomes a unity for those who are whole in themselves," wrote Hofmannsthal in this speech, and he designated as the highest value "that spirit become life."

Hugo von Hofmannsthal was born in Vienna on February 1, 1874, of mixed Austrian, south German-Jewish, and Lombard antecedents. When he entered the University of Vienna in 1892, four years before Buber, he was already famous as a poet. Nearly all of his lyrical poetry was written during the nineties. In 1899, Hofmannsthal had begun to write for the stage, and from about 1908 until his death, he collaborated with both the composer Richard Strauss and the famous producer Max Reinhardt. After the First World War, he dedicated much of his effort to the idea of the European community and was the guiding spirit behind the Salzburg Festival, an annual festival of music and drama known throughout Europe. Hofmannsthal not only shared Buber's enthusiasm for the great actress Eleanora Duse, on whom he wrote three articles before the appearance of the one by Buber, but came into close personal association with her by dint of her having played the title role in his play *Electra* and Jocasta in his *Ödipus und die Sphinx*. He found in her not only individuality but universality and saw her as "the embodiment of an unnamable tragic force."

This concern for the tragic might seem strange to the many who know Hofmannsthal mainly as the author of the thoroughly charming but seemingly light "comedy for music" *The Cavalier of the Rose*, which

---

*See Volume One, Chapters 1 and 15.

served as the libretto for Richard Strauss's opera *Der Rosenkavalier*. Yet tragedy remained a central concern of this profound poet, dramatist, and thinker from his youth on and found its culmination in the last drama that he wrote before his death, *The Tower*, which the Hofmannsthal scholar Michael Hamburger characterizes as "his own most personally committed play." *The Tower* was more to Hofmannsthal than a play: "it was his reckoning with the post-war world, a last attempt to embody the substance of his own life in a myth, and a kind of moral and spiritual testament." Hamburger sees *The Tower* as "the one completed work of Hofmannsthal that fully engaged all his disparate faculties and energies—the mysticai and the worldly, the visionary and the analytical, the adventurous and the conservative—and coordinated his many-sided experience within a single imaginative structure."

There are two distinct versions of *The Tower*. The earlier version was first published in two issues of Hofmannsthal's periodical *Neue Deutsche Beiträge* (February 1923 and January 1924). The later version, undertaken mainly with the stage in mind and incorporating changes suggested by Max Reinhardt, was first published as a separate volume in 1927. The earlier version was also revised somewhat and published posthumously in 1934 in the first edition of Hofmannsthal's collected works. But the really important differences lie between the earlier version, even in the revised form it later took on, and the 1927 version. Michael Hamburger suggests that "the two versions should be regarded as two distinct works, the first more dreamlike, mythical, and utopian, the second more outward-looking, more clear-cut, and more starkly tragic in its conclusion." "That Hofmannsthal should have written these two very different versions of the play," writes Hamburger, "sheds some light on the struggles and uncertainties of his last years, his premonitions of upheavals even greater than those of the First World War, and his doubts as to the outcome."

Both the earlier version and the 1927 version are almost identical, with a few exceptions, until the end of the third act. Both begin with Sigismund, heir apparent to the throne of a seventeenth-century Poland, imprisoned for most of his twenty-two years in a dark cave in the Tower because of dire prophecies that he would rebel against his father—prophecies which seemed to have been partially confirmed when his mother died in childbirth. In both versions King Basilius finally sends for Count Julian, the courtier who has kept Sigismund prisoner all these years. Julian pleads with Basilius for a test to show that his charge, whom he has taught and befriended as well as kept in irons and fed worse than an animal, is really a gentle creature and not a demonic rebel. The meeting between the King and the Prince becomes a "mismeeting" when the King curtly rejects Sigismund's plea that Basilius, his mother and father in one, kiss him, for he had never been kissed by a human being. Basilius demands that Sigismund be only the noble prince and not the son, but Sigismund, used to killing rats and vermin in his cave, attacks his father and insists that from now on he is himself the king. In both versions the king recovers, Sigismund is overpowered and with him Julian, who had given him the royal standard while Basilius lay apparently dead.

It is here that the two versions diverge significantly. In the earlier one the King spares the lives of Sigismund and Julian but has Sigismund shut up again in the cave in the Tower and Julian constrained to remain there permanently as his jailer. After a year a rebellion that Julian has been plotting is on the verge of success. He comes down to Sigismund's cell and demands that he come out to be the symbolic leader of the people who have risen up against Basilius. But Sigismund refuses to have any part in Julian's schemes.

Before Sigismund dies he receives a visit from the Children's King, who tells him that he, Sigismund, was only an "interim King." It is the Children's King, close to nature and pure, who seems to be destined to enter the "Promised Land" to which Sigismund, his blood-brother, could only point. Sigismund, to vary the figure, is the "suffering servant" of Deutero-Isaiah; the Children's King is the Messiah come. "We have built cottages, and we keep fires alight in the forge, and turn swords into ploughshares," the Children's King says to Sigismund. "We have proclaimed new laws, for it is always from the young that laws should come." Sigismund, in contrast, has no true place in history. He knows that there is no place for him in time, and the Children's King says the same of him after his death. The people cry out to him: "Do not leave us! Endure with us!" But the two boys who have accompanied the Children's King are too satisfied with Sigismund's function as a stepping-stone to their master to see his death as tragic: "Let him die!—rejoicing!"

This revised first version, the one published in the *Collected Works* in 1934, was the manuscript text that Hugo von Hofmannsthal sent to Martin Buber in 1926. It was Buber's criticism of this moderately revised version that impelled Hofmannsthal to consider the changes that he finally made in the fourth and fifth acts, changes so radical that the first and second versions are considered two distinct plays and are printed as such in the fourth drama volume of the definitive edition of Hofmannsthal's collected works. If the correspondence between Buber and Hofmannsthal on *The Tower* thus throws great light on Hofmannsthal's 1927 version, it is equally revealing as to Buber's approach to drama and the theater and their inextricable connection with tragedy and the "suffering servant."

Writing to Hofmannsthal from his home in Heppenheim an der Bergstrasse on April 2, 1926, Buber told the dramatist how great an impression *The Tower* had made upon him and how grateful he was to Hofmannsthal for sending it to him. "Now one may again believe in the existence of tragedy in our time," Buber added—a statement the importance of which is all the greater in the light of his earlier criticism of Gerhart Hauptmann and Frank Wedekind for eliminating precisely those elements from modern drama that might make tragedy possible. But in the second paragraph of this short letter, Buber referred tersely and without explanation to "my objections to some things in the last act" and suggested that these might be discussed orally, since he was thinking of visiting Austria again after a long break the following summer. "But much more important than any objection," Buber concluded, "is the fact that this work exists and that one must acknowledge it and you."

On May 8, Hofmannsthal replied to Buber from his home in Rodaun, outside of Vienna with an urgent request that he elucidate his objections:

> You must clearly have sensed that I had not sent this tragedy to this or that person whose name happened to pop into my head but that in sending you this play I wanted to thank him whose presence, so long as we are living at the same time, has comforted and encouraged me in many moments.
>
> What you write me is infinitely friendly and does me great good. But you have an objection. I beg you from the heart to spell it out. Do not leave its expression to a meeting which chance may prevent. I by no means consider this work to be so fully finished. . . . Your objection can only have a productive function for me.
>
> Even if I thereby inconvenience you, I dare ask of you: express it in a few sentences. It will not need to be in detail. I will understand what is decisive from this intimation; it will urge me on, and the secret thought that we contemporaries stand in a relation of creative alliance will be confirmed to my great joy.

Buber's immediate response to this appeal was a letter of May 14 which was not a mere intimation but a full and direct statement of what he could and could not confirm in Hofmannsthal's tragedy:

> My objection, as I probably already wrote you, concerns only the last act. Everything before that works on me completely convincingly, but this does not. The reason for this, I feel, is that, unprepared, unmediated, two new spheres are included in the action that do not appear to me atmospherically credible. The one is the world of spirits, which, to be sure, has a clearer effect in the new version than in that of the *Beiträge* (because the gypsy girl is simplified), but is still only magic-mirror-like and problematic. More critical, however, to me is the other, that of the "new generation." This Children's King does not have, like Fortinbras, the dramatically legitimate function of leading from the tragedy back into history. He signifies what is both outside of tragedy and outside of history—the Messianic. But for that, as beautiful as he is, he is not true enough. Now Sigismund himself is a messianically intended figure tragically come to grief. In the very place where this most painful event should have become most inexorably visible stands one who "relieves" him of his mission. Nor is he an antagonist already known to us (even if perhaps silent for a long time) but someone who has just now appeared; what is more, only lyrically, so to speak, not dramatically. Therefore, our participation flags here nor can it be animated by any lively interest in the spectacle. Something of the sort could probably only become real in the epiphanies of Greek tragedies. There the fact of the distance between gods and men within the same corporeal world allowed, made possible the resolving change of perspective: the divine could overcome the humanly factual in the outcome of the play. With us the perspective of one generation is merely replaced by that of another, but this is not real in *The Tower* as is that on which the drama is built: the sight of genuine tragedy which you have succeeded in creating is suppressed by that of a charming but not truly comforting fiction.
>
> You must certainly have understood that the objection that I have here hastily expressed according to your wish, I feel so strongly precisely because I feel your work so strongly. If it were made against a lesser work than this, it would have no legitimacy.

At the end of this letter Buber asked Hofmannsthal whether he had received the first volume of the Buber-Rosenzweig Bible translation that he had asked the publisher to send him some months before. "I should like very much to discuss some time with you some of the questions about our language-situation that are connected with it." The connection between this postscript and the main body of the letter is no casual one. Without understanding Buber's developing attitude toward the world of words in general and toward drama and the theater in particular, one cannot understand Buber's translation of the Bible nor can one understand Buber's essentially dramatic interpretation of biblical Judaism in which speech itself is event and event is speech. More specifically, the whole concern for the origin of the messianic that underlay Buber's series of interpretations of the "Old" and New Testaments made it impossible for him to accept the pseudo-messianic character of the Children's King and the softening of the real tragedy of Sigismund in favor of this utopian fancy. Where T. S. Eliot saw "Christian hope," Buber rightly saw the evasion of tragedy that is the product of the very despair that it covers over. Yet he also saw the basic lines of genuine tragedy in the play which Hofmannsthal could bring into relief by removing the phantasmagoria of the gypsy and the charming lyricism of the Children's King.

Buber had no Aristotelian view of tragedy as providing a spiritual catharsis—a view which depended, for its meaning, on a reconciliation with the Greek order (*moira*) impossible to modern man. He knew that the tragedy of contradiction between persons because "each is as he is" is in its deepest meaning an integral part of life. But he also understood the genuine meaning and comfort to be found in the realistic acceptance of tragedy when, as in the conflict between Theodor Herzl and his friend Davis Trietsch, he set foot on the soil of tragedy and gave up the perspective of "right and wrong." It was only many years later, Buber wrote in recounting this incident, that he learned "how out of the grave of being in the right the right is resurrected." This "right" is no longer a matter of a "point of view" but of the spirit working in the depths of history, the arrow of the "suffering servant" that is not drawn from its quiver and yet is not without real messianic effect. Here Buber's interpretation of drama and tragedy and his interpretation of the messianic development within biblical Judaism are one.

Hofmannsthal's first response to Buber's statement about the fifth act of *The Tower* was a short letter of June 8 in which he thanked him many times "for your good and to me very important letter."

> I am not at all sure to what extent this version is to be regarded as the definitive one, and I shall fully include in my reflection what you have expressed.

Shall one really see you once again in this country so neglected by the most important Germans? I would rejoice in it with my whole heart. In old sympathy—participation—and may I not say: friendship,

Yours,

H. H.

The meeting between the two men did take place: a long letter from Hofmannsthal to Buber of December 19, 1926, refers to it. In this letter, Hofmannsthal also says: "I shall send you the new version of *The Tower* in January: it does not contain what disturbed you—and in which you were right. (Also there are still deeper changes.)" In a reply written on Christmas day, 1926, Buber revealed the great importance to him of *The Tower* and of the changes that Hofmannsthal, at his prompting, was making in it: "I look forward to the new version of *The Tower* with good expectation—I have the distinct feeling that here will be the testimony for the continuance of drama in our time, something for which I had already ceased to hope."

If, as Hamburger says, in the process of tidying up, "some of the more mysterious motifs" get lost, such as the gypsy's role as the "vengeance of the material, maternal, time-bound" (Hofmannsthal's own interpretation), the second version is unquestionably the more effective both as drama and as theater, and for the very reasons that Buber expressed and to which Hofmannsthal agreed. At the end of the third act of the 1927 version, the King sentences both Sigismund and his teacher Julian to be beheaded in public. An uprising saves Sigismund from death only hours before he is to be executed. Sigismund, ready to be led away by the people who have come to acclaim him, goes to the window to reply to their calls and is shot by the sharpshooters of his enemies. As he dies, he lays on his friend the doctor an unmistakably messianic charge: "Bear witness that I was there even if no one recognized me." These are the last words of Sigismund and the final words of the play. By removing the sinister phantasmagoria and the charming fantasy to which Buber objected, Hofmannsthal laid bare the tragedy at the heart of the play, the clear sense of which had led Buber to write in his first letter about *The Tower*, "Now one may again believe in the existence of tragedy in our time."*

In 1929 Buber wrote an essay on the Hebrew theater that had successfully established itself first in Europe and later in Tel Aviv. In this

---

*See Note to Chapter 5.

essay, "Reach for the World, Ha-Bimah!" Buber brought this understanding of the relationships among drama, theater, and tragedy to a new depth that prepared him for the writing of his own mature biblical play *Elijah*. Jewish drama has the potential for what Greek and Christian drama lacks: the understanding of the "right" of the biblical covenant which places upon us the task of bringing forth redemption out of the very contradictions of earthly existence. This "right" only "dwells" in us, "in the midst of our uncleanness" (Leviticus 16:16); we do not possess it. We must *from there* experience the world as it is, in its dramatic reality—in its deep substantial antithesis and contradictions, which are not to be overcome by the categories of being right and being wrong.

Here the contrast between T. S. Eliot's "Christian hope" and Buber's response to the first version of *The Tower* and its merely symbolic redemption takes on a deeper religious significance. In the Christian drama, according to Buber, revelation and redemption coincide. Redemption has taken place and henceforth there exists two worlds—the redeemed, in which no antithesis and contradiction, hence no dramatic reality, any longer persists, and the unredeemed, the world behind God's back, which consists of nothing other than antithesis and contradiction. If a genuine Jewish drama comes into being, it will make present to the whole reality of life the word of the God who "dwells in the midst of our uncleanness." Here we can see the final merging of Buber's understanding of drama and the theater with his deepest understanding of the biblical covenant:

> What saved Judaism is not, as the Marcionites imagine, the fact that it failed to experience "the tragedy," the contradiction in the world's process, deeply enough; but rather that it experienced that "tragedy" in the dialogical situation, . . . it experienced *the contradiction as theophany*. This very world, this very contradiction, unabridged, unmitigated, unsmoothed, unsimplified, unreduced, this world shall be—not overcome —but consummated. . . . It is a redemption not from the evil, but of the evil, as the power which God created for his service and for the performance of his work.

In "Biblical Leadership," a lecture Buber delivered in Munich in 1928, his understanding of biblical dialogue deepened to include the paradox of historical success and failure and with it an understanding of redemption and messianism as inseparable from the suffering of the "servant" depicted in the famous passages about the suffering servant in Deutero-Isaiah, familiar to most English-speaking people through Handel's great oratorio *The Messiah* if not from the Bible itself. The purpose of God is fulfilled not by might nor by power but "by my spirit," says the biblical text. If this is so, then the Bible knows nothing of the intrinsic value of success. Even the life of Moses consists of one failure after another. It is the prototype of the secret leadership which works not through success but through failure.

> What we are accustomed to call history is from the biblical standpoint only the façade of reality. It is the great failure, the refusal to enter into the dialogue, not the failure in the dialogue, as exemplified by biblical man. . . . The way, the real way, from the Creation to the Kingdom is trod not on the surface of success, but in the deep of failure. The real work, from the biblical point of view, is the late-recorded, the un-recorded, the anonymous work. The real work is done in the shadow, in the quiver.

How thoroughly this understanding of the connection between genuine dialogue and historical failure permeated Buber's consciousness at this time is shown by two other "Words to the Time" which he wrote at this juncture, both of which are far removed from the context of the Bible. In the fall of 1928 Buber gave an address on "China and Us" for a conference of the China Institute at Frankfurt-am-Main which he concluded with the assertion that what we can receive from China as a viable way comes not from Confucianism but from Taoism. But the Taoism that Buber here expounded was not concerned with "living unity," as was his "Teaching of the Tao." It was concerned with historical success and failure. Our age has begun to learn "in the bitterest manner, indeed, in a downright foolish manner," that historical success is of no consequence. We have begun to doubt the typical modern Western man "who sets an end for himself, carries this end into effect, accumulates the necessary means of power and succeeds with these means of power." The Taoist teaching (*wu-wei*), that genuine effecting is not interfering, not giving vent to power, but remaining within oneself, points us to that powerful existence that at first appears insignificant or even invisible yet endures across the generations to become perceptible in another form. "There where we stand or there where we shall soon stand," Buber prophetically concluded, less than five years before Hitler came to power, "we shall directly touch upon the reality for which Lao-tzu spoke."

In 1929 Buber took up this theme of the hidden leadership in still a different context—that of Zionism, modern politics, and Max Weber's famous sociopolitical concept of charisma. It was at this time that Buber recounted, as a contribution to a number of recollections of Theodor Herzl by his contemporaries, that conflict between Herzl and Davis Trietsch which we have already discussed in connection with Buber's early Zionist politics.* At the end of this story of how he first set foot on the soil of tragedy, Buber inserted a reflection which came directly from his fiftieth year and not his twenty-fifth. If Trietsch's fiancée with the flashing eyes who impelled Herzl to answer as he did showed a dreadful lack of objectivity on Herzl's part, the fact that his opponent had one human being who would take his part that way may have raised in Herzl's mind the question as to whether there might not be another reality, different from obvious world history—"a reality hidden and powerless because it has not come into power."

> . . . whether there might not be, therefore, men with a mission who have not yet been called to power and yet are, in essence, men who have been summoned; whether success is the only criterion; whether the unsuccessful man is not destined at times to gain a belated, perhaps posthumous, perhaps even anonymous victory which even history refuses to record: whether, indeed, when even this does not happen, a blessing is not spoken, nonetheless, to these abandoned ones, a word that confirms them; whether there does not exist a "dark" charisma.

Buber did not suggest that the man who acts in history could allow himself to be overwhelmed by such questions; for if he did so, he might have to despair and withdraw. "But the moments in which they touch him are the truly religious moments of his life." Here religion is not just the meeting with the "eternal Thou," or even "dialogue," but the suffering of the servant in the depths.

Whether or not in writing about the "dark charisma" of Davis Trietsch Buber was also thinking of his own life-experience of one political disappointment after another—an experience which he was to go through again and again in the remaining thirty-six years of his life —it is certain that he associated his friend Franz Rosenzweig with the "suffering servant," an association which became clear and unmistakable in the last years of Rosenzweig's life.

"I am happy that seeing Hans Trüb has pleased you," Buber wrote Rosenzweig after his Jungian analyst friend had visited the sick man.

*See Volume One, Chapter 4.

He added no comment about Trüb as a thinker but spoke instead of Trüb's hobby as a singer. "When he comes again, he will bring with him his mandolin and will give you a concert of folk songs. He is, in fact, what is called in the North a bellman-singer." In the same letter Buber commented to Rosenzweig concerning his friends Hugo von Hofmannsthal and Jakob Wassermann, "Have you noticed the growing isolation of all these men? 'The wilderness grows.' " When Trüb wrote Buber about this same visit, he also did not speak of Rosenzweig as a thinker but about the enormous personal impact the visit had on him, tied up with which was his clear discernment of Rosenzweig as a suffering servant—in the Christian *image* of crucifixion, as Buber himself wrote of his friend Landauer after his murder. "In his room something in me was touched that I cannot name," Trüb wrote. "Is it the human person that moves in its wholeness and at the same time remains still?" Just because this visit was the most significant moment for him of that year (1926), Trüb felt that he ought not interpret it. "That day is ever again present for me. I see Rosenzweig physically before me, walled in in his crippled body." Despite the enormous obstacles to his turning to the world, Rosenzweig does not turn away from it, he added. "Day after day he places himself in his suffering and gives us report of the imperishable life of the human person." His presence, as it spoke to Trüb, bore witness as to what life is in this world, where perhaps in this moment Rosenzweig was for the first time really created again by God. "I dwell with this dying man wholly from my heart. I recognize the unshakable fact of the progressive course of his illness and am deeply sad because of it. But in my whole depths I am shaken by the fact that with all of this the person himself remains undiminished, present in full value. Will he from the moment when he closes his eyes, when he can no longer give any sign, be any less present than earlier when he could still walk and speak, or than now, when only a thin thread of possible communication joins him to us? I love Rosenzweig for the sake of his cross. He will continually work good in my life."

On Friday evening, December 6, 1929, Rosenzweig was attacked by a feverish illness that developed into a severe bronchial pneumonia. After forty-eight hours of sleeplessness and gasping for breath, in which those around him tried in vain to find a comfortable position for his paralyzed limbs and to make out what he wished to say, on Monday, December 9, he fell into a refreshing sleep. On Monday afternoon, the doctor, who had given up the idea of using an oxygen tent in order that

Rosenzweig might communicate with his family, consented to his request that he be brought to his chair in the study. It took two hours to transfer him from his bed to his chair, where he slept from 1:00 P.M. to 4:00 P.M. When he awoke he took some food, the first in several days, and asked that his hand be brought into position for a dictation, to be transliterated into the copybook used for his correspondence with Buber. Pointing to the letter plate of his typewriter, letter by letter, he spelled out slowly and laboriously ". . . and now it comes, the point of all points, which the Lord has truly revealed to me in my sleep: the point of all points for which there. . . ." He was referring, as Buber himself has said, to one of the passages on the suffering servant from Deutero-Isaiah. The writing was interrupted by the entrance of the doctor, whom Rosenzweig, with infinite trouble, managed to ask (through their spelling out the alphabet and his nodding) whether the B'nai B'rith Lodge, of which the great German Jewish thinker and spiritual leader Rabbi Leo Baeck was president, had acceded to Baeck's extraordinary request, actually a decree, that the Lodge buy seven thousand copies of the Buber-Rosenzweig translation of the Pentateuch. The doctor, an influential member of the Lodge, was not at all sure what the outcome would be, but realizing this might be his last chance to talk with Rosenzweig, he said the Lodge would accept, an answer which seemed to please Rosenzweig, who decided not to finish the interrupted sentence, the last he ever wrote. Sometime after one o'clock in the morning of December 10 he died.

The burial took place on December 12 at the Frankfurt cemetery. In accordance with Rosenzweig's wish, there was no funeral oration. Martin Buber read Psalm 73, which contains the inscription Franz Rosenzweig chose for his headstone. This psalm, from which the inscription for Buber's own headstone was taken thirty-six years later, is one of those which Buber interprets in his book *Prophetic Faith* in connection with the "God of the sufferers," the "suffering servant," and the mystery of God suffering with the *zaddik,* the "proven" man who suffers for God's sake. "As the coffin was lowered into the grave," Nahum Glatzer recounts, "the sun broke through the clouded skies; a majestic rainbow appeared."

In 1954, I gave a lecture on Rosenzweig and Buber at the Habonim Synagogue in New York City on the occasion of the twenty-fifth anniversary of Rosenzweig's death. This synagogue, under the leadership of Rabbi Hugo Hahn, had as its members many of Rosenzweig's closest friends from Germany, such as Eduard Strauss; and Nahum N.

Glatzer, Rosenzweig's chief interpreter, came down from Brandeis University for the occasion. In preparing for this lecture, which was about the personal friendship of Rosenzweig and Buber as much as about the "New Thinking" which they shared, I found myself deeply moved by the final years and death of Franz Rosenzweig. In a letter which I wrote to Martin Buber, I shared these feelings and asked Buber whether Rosenzweig might not be regarded as a saint. "The word 'saint' is too Christian for Rosenzweig," Buber responded, "but he was, I believe, a suffering servant of the Lord." In 1933 the first of one hundred Schocken Bücherei (little books), published by Salman Schocken's newly founded publishing house, was the Buber-Rosenzweig translation of the chapters on the suffering servant (Isaiah 40–55), appropriately titled (both for the content of the book and the time of the rise of Hitler) *Die Tröstung Israels* (The Comforting of Israel).

A week or so after Rosenzweig's death, Buber wrote an essay about him which he titled "Für die Sache der Treue" (For the Cause of Being True). Pointing out that in the "New Thinking" Rosenzweig had written that "Truth has ceased to be what 'is' true and has become what must be confirmed as true," Buber spoke of how Rosenzweig set aside the writing of books after the completion of *The Star* in favor of a life in which he wished to confirm the truth as husband, father, teacher, learning from the Torah and working in Israel. But then it was made clear to him that this was still "too little to become My servant." "An unspeakable load, unspeakable, was to be laid on and borne by him" —his illness. Instead of dying within a year, as he had expected, he had to suffer for eight years. "In those eight years Rosenzweig confirmed in the Face of God the truth that he had seen. Lamed in his whole body, he fought for the truth through being true." Imprisoned in the chains of sickness, he did not slacken in his service to the spirit, but the spirit was wholly incorporated in the hallowing of the everyday. "More than by his words, he taught directly and indirectly by his very existence." His doctors said of him that he was a "phenomenon of the spirit," but Buber insisted that he was a phenomenon of the spirit that willed to become wholly manifest in concrete existence.

Faith alone would not account for such great endurance and determination, Buber asserted. It needed the companionship of humor. Faith means taking a vow, but humor is necessary to fulfilling this vow in the midst of all the vexatiousness and contrariness of existence. He who believes accepts life as a whole; but to accept life in its individual events, moment by moment, a life of the utmost pain, requires a deep-seated humor. "In all these years of suffering I have admired nothing in Rosenzweig so much as his smile. . . . it arose out of the basic genuineness of the creature. It was not superior and not resigned, it was full of faith and presence. The jokes that stood on almost every page of his comments on my translation manuscript were entirely natural jokes and yet like prayers of thankfulness."

In a 1956 essay in which he contrasted Rosenzweig with Heidegger and other existentialist thinkers as one who really let his truth transform his life and really lived it in his life, Buber again reverted to this theme of faith and humor. Rosenzweig's paralysis was so monstrously difficult for a thinker such as Rosenzweig because it crippled not his thoughts but his expression of them. Yet I can testify, wrote Buber, out of our unique contact through six years of working together, how Rosenzweig, sinking ever deeper into the abyss of sickness, remained uninterruptedly faithful to his service. "The great lesson that I at that time received from my younger friend was the merging of faith and humor in such a test." If faith is a trust which withstands each situation, humor is a smiling acceptance of existence as it is—as Rosenzweig did repeatedly through the imperturbable smile of the lips that he moved with such difficulty and through his jokes, made despite the utmost physical obstacles to any kind of communication. Humor is here both servant and blood-brother of faith. "It is thus that an existence that confirms the truth appears."

At the end of his "Gleanings," the collection of short fragments, poems, and essays that Buber selected to be preserved in book form just before his death, Buber placed the short answer to the question of what happens after death that he wrote for a French journal in 1927 and that was printed in German in 1928 on his fiftieth birthday. That Buber took the trouble to write this statement out for Rosenzweig in the French in which it was originally printed suggests that he may have been thinking of Rosenzweig and his imminent death when he wrote it.

> We know nothing of death, nothing other than the one fact that we shall die—but what is that, dying? We do not know. So it behooves us to accept that it is the end of everything conceivable by us. To wish to extend our conception beyond death, to wish to anticipate in the soul what death alone can reveal to us in existence, seems to me to be a lack of faith clothed as faith. The genuine faith speaks: I know nothing of death, but I know that God is eternity, and I know this, too, that he is my God. Whether what we call time remains to us beyond our death

becomes quite unimportant to us next to this knowing, that we are God's —who is not immortal, but eternal. Instead of imagining ourselves living instead of dead, we shall prepare ourselves for a real death which is perhaps the final limit of time but which, if that is the case, is surely the threshold of eternity.

Buber sent to his poet friend Alfred Mombert a copy of his memorial essay "For the Sake of Being True." In his letter of thanks Mombert wrote: "I have also heard your voice in the old Kuno-Fischer Auditorium, which spoke mysteriously of the servant of God. In your further work may the spiritual promptings of your friend not be wanting to you!" Hans Kohn, who had just finished his intellectual historical biography of Buber, wrote Buber from Jerusalem that the totally unexpected news of Rosenzweig's death had struck him most painfully. "I saw him only once . . . a living monument of the strength of the spirit which conquers all." "I understand," he added, "how hard this must have struck you. The Bible, the 'New Thinking,' your whole last ten years were so inwardly bound up with Rosenzweig, in your work and in your life. I hope that his death will lead you to new activity in the completion of the translation of the Bible—the spiritual task common to you and him."

CHAPTER 6

Religious Socialism and Die Kreatur

FLORENS CHRISTIAN RANG

BY 1922, two years before it ceased publication, Buber had already turned over the actual editorship of *Der Jude* to Ernest Simon. He felt the need of getting on with his own work, such as *Ich und Du,* but he also felt the intra-Jewish dialogue too confining for the needs of the time. As a result, from 1922 to 1932, Buber gave ever more time and energy, both in speaking and writing, to Jewish-Christian dialogue, particularly within the post–World War I movement of religious social-ism and, from 1926 to 1930, in coediting the journal *Die Kreatur.*

The impetus to found *Die Kreatur* (The Creature) had come to Buber through his close friendship with Florens Christian Rang, the former pastor turned lawyer with whom he had had the argument about Jew-ish representatives in Easter of 1914 at the first and only meeting of the Forte Kreise. The kiss of peace which the two men exchanged at the time proved to be more enduring than the superpatriotic and nationalist stance that Rang adopted during the war and which he himself deeply regretted and sought to atone for after the war. Buber opened *Die Kreatur* with an editorial acknowledging and adopting Rang's belief that every religion is in an exile that only God can liberate it from but that there is need for genuine dialogue between each of these houses of exile without presuming to abolish the separateness of the religions in favor of any universal "essence" of religion. In 1932 Buber dedicated *The Kingship of God,* his first scholarly work on the origin of messianism in the Bible, to his Jewish friend Rosenzweig and his Christian friend Rang.

Rang's first name was Christian. He himself added the "Florens" before it in the middle of his life to suggest the flowering of Christianity: "Bloom, frozen Christ!" By his ruthless honesty and powerful emotions he won the friendship and respect of Buber's friend Hugo von Hofmannsthal, who saw Rang as typical of the German essence which burned all bridges behind it and expressed itself obscurely because of its tendency to run ahead of what was communicable. Rang also came into close association with the educational and religious circle that arose after the Heppenheim conference of 1919, including such men as the progressive educator Theodor Spira, Paul Natorp (the old philosopher of whom Buber spoke in the second of his "Report on Two Talks"), Hermann Herrigel, Ernst Michel (a devout Catholic), and Alfons Paquet, a man immersed in the European cultural movements of the time. Rang, like Buber, was deeply concerned with messianism, and, again like him, saw the advent of Jesus as a messianic rift, since Jesus' words that the kingdom of heaven would come were not fulfilled.

Rang's active attempt at penance for his earlier position was expressed in his 1924 book *Deutsche Bauhütte,* in which he called on Germans to use their economic resources for the rehabilitation of France and Belgium. To this volume Buber himself contributed an essay. Rang was also connected with Eberhard Arnold's Bruderhof, a communal outgrowth of the youth movement and the war which later identified itself with the Anabaptists [a radically pacifist Protestant Reformation movement of three centuries before] and emigrated to South America and then the United States.

As Buber's friendship with Rang had begun in a fruitful tension, so it continued even after Rang's radical rejection of his former German patriotism. For Rang had more faith in economics and the state than Buber had. Rang published *Deutsche Bauhütte* in Eberhard Arnold's press. Buber's letter-essay in it praises Rang for liberating those who stood close to him from critical passivity. But at the same time Buber declared that it is necessary to draw each day anew the demarcation lines between the redemption and the unredeemedness of the world, the spirit of love and violent nature, realization and resistance. This implied to Buber a rejection of dependence upon the state in favor of personal and communal social action. This does not mean, said Buber, that we belong to the passive standers-by who share in the guilt of the state by declining all responsibility for it. Rather, we break the ban that divides the lived responsibility of the individual person from the seemingly soulless collectivity by transforming the institutions of the state from their neutrality and estrangement into the directly personal. This means not only that the Germans should give as individual persons to help the Belgians and French but also that this help should go directly to those in need in those countries and not to their governments. You know, Buber concluded, what I see in the state: the "status quo," the visible embodiment of the present stage of the nonrealization of the kingdom of God. "In Liebe Dein," signed Buber, who, despite his philosophy of "Ich und Du," addressed only his very closest friends as *Du,* or Thou.

In 1924 Rang developed a serious illness. In June, Buber wrote Rosenzweig that he had just visited Rang in the clinic at Giessen, where he was laid up with neuritis, and that Rang had sent Rosenzweig his special regards. Characteristically, Rang liked very much Rosenzweig's translation of the poems of Yehuda Halevi but could not bear the tone of the afterword. On October 4, Rang died. Buber wrote to Rang's widow Emma from Rome, where the news had reached him, "Now I know why I felt again and again that I must immediately return to Germany and to Christian—and as often as it came I dismissed this premonition as a foolish impulse! It is hard for me to take in that I can no longer see him again with mortal eyes, no longer hear his voice with mortal ears." "I am not fearful for him," Buber added. "He who, as hardly any other, was a confirmation for me of the eternal existence of the spirit, is now confirmed in eternity. But how forsaken it leaves us, his friends! He was to us an emissary of the Judge and an emissary of the Redeemer; he put us to the test and helped us at the same time. That he was present did not make life easier, not at all, but happily difficult, blessedly difficult. How shall we do without him whose love witnessed to us of the love of God? I am certain that his presence—not in our thoughts alone but in all reality—will remain in our midst and strengthen us and that we, no matter how forsaken, are not torn from community with him."

In the first issue of *Die Kreatur* in the spring of 1926 Buber dedicated the journal to Rang. Jurist, philosopher, and theologian in one, Rang served his circle of friends, the political, social, and economic needs of the time, and the demands of real community. He stood in genuine dialogue with the Catholic Church (with which he broke because of the dogma of the infallibility of the Pope) and with Judaism. He knew from within himself the cleavages and contradictions of the age. Rang found the narrow ridge between the Catholic conception of the sacraments as founded upon an objective consummation and the subjective piety of Protestantism. He sought the way of faith in the actualizing of the whole of existence.

RELIGIOUS SOCIALISM

Rang was a Christian Socialist, and it was with Christian socialism and religious socialism in general that Buber found common cause in the years of the Weimar Republic. Education of the people, politics out of faith, socialism derived from the Gospels or from the prophets, formed for Buber and his circle a social concern that stayed clear of the state and of party politics. Of the two German-speaking movements of Protestant religious socialism, Buber stood nearer the Swiss group that formed around Leonhard Ragaz, and its journal *Neue Wege*, than to the Berlin circle that formed around Karl Mennicke, Eduard Heimann, and Paul Tillich. Ragaz was one of Buber's closest friends in Christian circles. His friendship with him reached back to the second decade of the twentieth century and continued in a warm and vital relationship throughout the Second World War. Buber found in Ragaz the greatest understanding of the true meaning of Israel, and the decade-long dialogue between them led to a meeting of minds that took place between Christian and Jew on a large scale only after the Second World War. For both these men, as Grete Schaeder has pointed out, the prophets of Israel and the teaching of Jesus stood on common ground in the admonition to turn one's personal and social existence back to God and to the message of the kingdom of God which such turning must precede. Both felt that this message had become fossilized in the legalism of Orthodox Judaism and in the dogmas of the Church and that it must be awakened to new life. Both distinguished sharply between traditional religion and the genuine message of Israel and of early Christianity.

Although Buber's major sympathies lay with Ragaz's religious socialism, he also met with religious socialists of all types during the 1920s, including a conference held at his home village of Heppenheim in 1928 in which he was a central figure. It was at one such meeting that Buber first met Paul Tillich, a younger man than Buber, well known in certain circles but not yet the world-famous Protestant theologian that he later became. At that time Tillich held that the *kairos,* the historical situation of that moment, demanded the building of religious socialism. After he emigrated to the United States he felt that the *kairos* had changed and turned his attention to other matters, although always living "on the border," as he wrote in the autobiographical sketch at the beginning of his early book *The Interpretation of History.* In this respect he was close to Buber with his own encounter on the "narrow ridge." The first meeting between the two men illustrated very concretely Buber's narrow ridge and Tillich's life on the border. As a member of a committee of socialists, some religious and some not, Tillich reported to the larger conference the conclusion that a word should be found to replace "God" in order to unite in the common cause of socialism those who could use this name and those who could not. After he had given this report, Tillich himself has recounted, a short man with a black beard and fiery black eyes stood up in the back and said: "Aber Gott ist ein Urwort!" You cannot do away with a primordial word like God, said Buber, even for the sake of attaining unity. "And he was right!" Tillich exclaimed.

In 1922 Ragaz wrote, "But before all else I remind you of men like Gustav Landauer and Martin Buber who proclaim a state-free and non-violent socialism in the sense of a genuine community of men built upon love." In a letter to Ragaz early the following year, Buber said that what concerned him most was to experience in all seriousness how far community can go and whether there where it ceases, only the personally fateful historical differences rule or the question of truth itself. Buber informed Ragaz that together with the great Protestant theologians Karl Barth, Friedrich Gogarten, and some others, he was arranging a gathering devoted to this question for the days around Easter and that he hoped very much that Ragaz could join them.

When Ragaz invited Buber in March of the same year to speak to his circle about Zionism and the meaning of Judaism, Buber responded with characteristic directness: "I have said all I have to say about the

meaning of Judaism and therefore cannot now publicly speak about it.
. . . I do not speak often in public, only when something in particular
needs expressing; every speech is a serious and difficult matter for me,
and it is not given me to 'describe' anew what I have already said." "To
distinguish between the subjective life-experience *(Erlebnis)* and the
subjective-objective event *(Ereignis),*" Buber added, in a comment on
his Introduction to the collected *Speeches on Judaism,* "is something that
a life-experience-event *(Erlebnis-Ereignis)* of a catastrophic nature
taught me in a way that struck me to the quick a few years ago: three
days and nights of uninterrupted presence." This is an unmistakable
reference to Buber's total, body-mind "imagining the real" event of
Landauer's being kicked to death by the soldiers in 1919.

In a letter to Rosenzweig in 1923 Buber informed him that he was
going to take part in a conference on "religious socialists" in Rosenzweig's home city of Cassel under the leadership of Rosenzweig's old
friend Eugen Rosenstock-Huessy. His being invited was of more than
personal interest, he added, because the movement was thereby stepping beyond the limits of Christianity. In 1931, however, Buber wrote
his young disciple Hermann Gerson, an influential leader of the Jewish
youth movement, that the many invitations to conferences of "religious socialists," without any limitations on the word "religious," yet
carried out in the sign of Christ, had led him to the decision to revive
an old plan of founding a "union of Jewish religious socialists" in
Germany and Palestine. Buber asked Gerson to take over the leadership of the German groups, a task which Gerson declined on the
grounds that "religious socialism" in general had for him a questionable, intellectual, and unreal flavor that the proletariat rightly and
responsibly rejected. Gerson excepted from this judgment the activities of men like Paul Tillich and Eduard Hermann who were highly
active in the socialist, political movement. Buber responded by pointing to the religious socialism of Ragaz as the more living in his opinion.
Buber did not intend by this union of Jewish religious socialists an
exclusive group but precisely the contrary—groups whose representatives could be sent to the more general religious socialist conferences
so that they would in fact be general and not merely Christian, with
Buber as the sole exception. As late as November 1932, Buber was still
writing to Ragaz about his intention to assemble Jewish socialists and
stated that he had recently received a new impetus from Holland to
carry out this intention. Both Buber's intention and the fact that it
never became a reality illuminate the limits of genuine Jewish-Chris-

tian dialogue during the Weimar Republic while presaging its decline into caricature under the Nazi regime that came into power a few months later.

A wholly different level of Jewish-Christian "dialogue" was the contribution that Buber chose to make to a special 1925 issue of *Der Jude* on anti-Semitism and German peoplehood. Even though he was no longer editing *Der Jude,* the editor let Buber see the other essays in the issue before it went to press. Buber found the word "Pharisee" so often misused and misunderstood by the other contributors, including some Christians who stood very close to him, that he chose to write an essay on "Pharisaism." In this essay he uncovered, without ever having to underline it directly, the connection between anti-Semitism and the anti-Judaism built into Christianity from the Gospels on—a connection which many educated Christians only became aware of, if at all, after the Second Vatican Council forty years later. It was the Sadducees not the Pharisees who were the literalists who tore asunder the Torah—the pointing of the way contained in the sacred history and sacred book—and the lived moment, the way of man. By doing so they put themselves in opposition to the might of the living spirit that again and again proclaims itself by way of human speech. The Pharisees, in contrast, by honoring the oral tradition as well as the written, lifted the Torah into the arena of world history. "Just because their interpretation of the scripture was in the end truer to human existence, which is rich in changes, than to the unchanging text; just because they expounded upon the fixed text only in order to subdue the streaming reality in the name of God, did they serve him who does not will his manifestation to be encapsulated but, rather, like the work of his creation so also that of his revelation, 'renewed every day.' "

The reason why the Pharisees are generally misunderstood, of course, is that they are caricatured in the New Testament as strict legalists and narrow followers of rules, which was true of the Sadducees and, to a much lesser extent, of the school of Shammai but certainly not of Hillel, who lived seventy years before Jesus and whose school without question had great influence upon Jesus' own emphasis upon God's mercy, love, and compassion. And the reason why the Pharisees are thus caricatured is the polarization—less visible in the earlier Gospel of Mark, but very evident in the other two synoptic Gospels—between Jesus and his opponents, who were all portrayed as self-righteous legalists and hypocrites. Therefore, Buber had to take up in this essay the relation of Jesus to the Torah, a subject which he only dealt with at the length that it demanded in his 1950 book *Two Types of Faith.*

The same problem that Buber encountered in the meetings on religious socialism he encountered in the German movement for education of the people (Volkhochschul) at the center of which stood the Hohenrodter Bund, which brought together leading educators yearly from 1923 to 1933. There was no Jewish representation in it as such, but individual Jewish men, later active in Jewish adult education in Nazi Germany, were invited, above all Buber himself. At the sixth annual week of meetings, in 1928, Buber was the principal figure. To the central theme of "World View and Adult Education" Buber contributed his address "Philosophical and Religious *Weltanschauung,*" in which he set forth his philosophy of dialogue, or the I-Thou relationship, and in so doing named as holy ground the place where an insecure man steps forward, for "only as insecure persons can we fulfill the hour." One could speak here of a certain amount of Jewish-Christian dialogue but only in a marginal sense, since what Buber was representing was neither an organization of Jewish educators nor Judaism as such but only his own personal philosophy, which he applied to the problems of education in general and of Jewish education in particular. The same was true when in 1931 there was a joint meeting of the German section of the World Union for the Renewal of Education with the Hohenrodter Bund. Buber found the meeting of these two groups still more of an "encounter on the narrow ridge." It laid on his comrades and himself the task of distinguishing between what from the opposing side was something new and positive that could be accepted and made their own and what had to be held in check when the countergroup's claim to intellectual superiority grew almost to hubris.

Writing to Ragaz in 1928, Buber reaffirmed his conviction of the possibility of a meeting of a few men "in all seriousness and stillness" to take counsel with one another on the realities of socialism at that point in history. It was in that same year that Buber wrote his "Three Theses of a Religious Socialism," a highly condensed and forceful statement of the essence of what he had come to understand this phrase to mean. This statement began significantly with a quotation from Leonhard Ragaz: "Any socialism whose limits are narrower than God and man is too narrow for us," and it expanded on that quotation in a way that Ragaz could wholeheartedly second. Each—religion *and* socialism—needs the covenant with the other for the fulfillment of its own essence. *"Religion,* that is the human person's binding of himself to God, can only attain its full reality in the will for a community of the human race, out of which alone God can prepare His kingdom," and the fellowship of man, equally, can develop only out of a common relation to the divine center "even if this be again and still nameless." The two need each other as do body and spirit, call and response. Either alone is meaningless and fictitious, and that, Buber pronounced, was precisely the case with all the prevailing religious forms and socialist programs. The point where the two can meet in truth is concrete personal life—standing and withstanding in the abyss of the real reciprocal relation of the mystery of God and the mystery of man. To do this, man must live both what he believes and what he seeks to accomplish in such a way that the means that he uses are like the goal he pursues.

JEWISH-CHRISTIAN DIALOGUE AND ENCOUNTER BEFORE *DIE KREATUR*

To some extent most of Buber's activities during the 1920s, even his translation of the Hebrew Bible, can be seen as part of a Jewish-Christian dialogue, as well as being in many cases a dialogue with his fellow Jews, as at the Frankfurt Lehrhaus or in connection with Zionism and the proposed Hebrew University in Jerusalem. In many cases, as with Rang and Ragaz, this dialogue was a genuinely reciprocal one. A signal example of such reciprocity was Buber's dialogue with Albert Schweitzer, who became famous throughout the world not just through his writings about Jesus, and his reverence for life, but also through his lifetime of service in Lamberéné, Africa, during which he became the living embodiment of what he wrote. Buber's own relation to Christianity was decisively influenced by the writings of Schweitzer. Following Schweitzer, Buber understood the figure of Jesus in terms of his message of the coming of God's kingdom and the mystery of suffering of the servant of God in Deutero-Isaiah. He did not, as Grete Schaeder has pointed out, follow Schweitzer in extending the eschatological expectation of a speedy coming of the kingdom to Paul but regarded Paul, in his later works as in his earlier ones, as a representative of an inauthentic, Hellenized Judaism.

"Being open to the world and withstanding concrete reality were always a measure," writes Schaeder, "of whether a Christian thinker could come close to Buber." Among these thinkers were such Neo-Orthodox, or dialectical, theologians as Karl Barth, Emil Brunner, Eduard Thurneysen, and Friedrich Gogarten. Their conversion into Christology of Buber's I-Thou relationship between God and man, Buber could not, of course, follow (as is demonstrated at length in the chapter on "Christianity" in my book *Martin Buber: The Life of Dialogue*). Unlike his friend Rosenzweig, Buber could not acknowledge the equal validity of Judaism and Christianity, one as being already in the eternity of God, the other as being the historical way to God. "We cannot simultaneously stand within and look with the objective eye that gives equal validity to two opposing *claims*. We know the Christian claim only from the outside and we cannot accept it." If each fights for the sake of Heaven, that does not mean that either side possesses some Hegelian overview of the progress of spirit in history toward a perfection in which all differences will be abolished or suspended.

From July 20 to July 25, 1925, Buber gave a series of lectures on "The Belief in Rebirth" at an academy at Amersfoort, Holland. The response of the Jungian psychiatrist Hans Trüb to this event is a far better example than any public debate could be of genuine Jewish-Christian dialogue. "My thoughts return to Amersfoort day after day," Trüb wrote Buber in August. "This one short week illuminated our whole past and future lives," he added. "We all seek for the same One that you revealed to us through your heartfelt speech. It *could* not be misunderstood. The absolute integrity with which you shared with us *what your eyes see* [italics added] is a present which we can only accept with the deepest gratitude. I know indeed that ever again in the present the 'great' happens, that there where persons really meet the infinity of creation reveals itself to us. But that a man without holding back takes it upon himself to live this faith makes me happy." To this Buber responded: "Your words have gladdened my heart. I too think warmly about Amersfoort, as about a young tree that one may trust."

In what Trüb wrote about Amersfoort he best expressed that aspect of Buber's personality which I myself found central in my personal encounters with Buber more than a quarter of a century later. Although the great emphasis of Buber's philosophy, as of his interpretation of biblical and Hasidic Judaism, is on the word—on hearing and responding—first of all Buber was a person who *beheld*—not with the analytical eye of the thinker or the aesthetic eye of the artist or the subjective eye of a person trying to select from his encounters with the world what would confirm the opinions and mind sets he already had, but with the calm, open, genuinely interested but not personally biased eye of one who chooses reality just because it *is* reality. Only then did the next two stages which Trüb spoke about come into play—living without reservation what he knew and speaking about it to others from the heart.

As far as Jewish-Christian dialogue is concerned, one might say that Buber was meeting such an open-minded Protestant as Trüb at least halfway in speaking on spiritual rebirth, even if he did so from the standpoint of the call for *teshuvah,* the turning of one's whole existence to God. The way was already there for him in his work with individual patients, Trüb wrote Buber a month later, but he did not know how to transmit the experience of his meeting with the Thou in life to the public for whom he wrote. Buber, by what he said and was, illuminated for him the stretches of the way that lay before him as brother, as teacher, as fellowman. Trüb did not express gratitude to Buber for showing him the way to God but to God for showing and opening for him the way to Buber. While going his own way gladly, he wanted Buber to know how closely tied he felt to him and at the same time not to feel this tie as a burden.

In October 1925 Buber received on the same day three requests for permission to translate his Hasidic books—one from an Englishman, one from Ludwig Lewisohn, himself an important writer in America, and one from a Frenchman who belonged to Claudel's circle which, under the title Le Roseau d'Or, brought out ten books a year. Only the third of these letters did Buber find noteworthy because it said (in French), "There are above all Catholics among us and Catholic extremists (Claudel, Maritain, Chesterton, etc.). But it is precisely as Catholics that we desire to become acquainted with the mystical philosophy of Hasidism. For a long time their teaching has been dear to my heart. . . . It is necessary that Christians know that there exists among their elder brothers an elevation of the spirit. . . . We see in you an indispensable element."

DIE KREATUR

In 1924, Buber allowed the highly successful periodical *Der Jude* to cease publication, except for occasional special issues, not only because he wanted to concentrate on his own philosophical and scholarly work but also because he was moving in the direction of Jewish-Christian dialogues. This direction took on its fullest concrete and symbolic expression in his founding the first high-level periodical coedited by a Protestant, a Catholic, and a Jew. This journal, *Die Kreatur* (The Creature), was also highly successful and prestigious, and during the four years that it lasted (1926–1929) Buber gave to it almost as great devotion as to *Der Jude*. Rang had suggested calling the journal *Greetings out of the Exiles*, but Buber preferred the more positive title *The Creature*, indicating the basis on which the three different religions could come into fruitful dialogue. "The journal wants to speak of the world—of all beings, of all things, of all events of this present world —in such a way that its creatureliness, its having been created, becomes recognizable. Always bearing the creation in mind, each creature to which we turn becomes noteworthy." "Trust also the growing generation, the era ascending out of the hiddenness." As Eugen Rosenstock-Huessy later put it, *Die Kreatur* spoke once again from the heart as though the already threatening madness of the Hitler time were long past.

This co-working of three faiths had already been foreshadowed, Rosenstock pointed out, by the Patmos Circle that emerged at the end of the First World War. In it such Protestants, Catholics, and Jews as Franz Rosenzweig, Karl Barth, Hans and Rudolf Ehrenberg, and Rosenstock-Huessy himself founded Patmos Press, which published from 1919 to 1920 "The Books of the Crossroad." But the three editors of *Die Kreatur* belonged to no common circle. Rather, Buber with great care and thought chose a Protestant and a Catholic thinker each of whom made "meeting" real in his own sphere. The process of choosing itself was indicative of the goal of the journal. At first among the German Catholics only Ernst Michel was acceptable to Buber, such common work not being possible with Romano Guardini and Friedrich Gogarten. Michel was indeed someone who was very close to Buber for many years to come. In the end, though, it was not Ernst Michel but Joseph Wittig whom Buber chose as the Catholic coeditor, and Wittig, a Catholic priest and professor, did not belong to any of Buber's close circles. Among German Protestants, outside of the disciples of Barth (whom Buber seems to have excluded in advance), Buber could think of only two—both religious socialists with whom he had worked in common. The first of these was Leonhard Ragaz, who had his own journal; the second, Paul Tillich, whom Buber saw as very gifted but still immature and above all still unclear, though open and ready to change. The person on whom Buber's choice as the Protestant coeditor finally fell was Viktor von Weizsäcker. Unlike Wittig, von Weizsäcker was not even primarily involved in religion or theology but was a practicing psychiatrist who made an important contribution to psychosomatic medicine as well as being a pioneer in applying the I-Thou relationship to psychology, psychiatry, and the medical profession in general.

In his memoirs, von Weizsäcker relates that he first met Buber one evening at the home of the famous author Emil Ludwig, who lived in a villa in the forest behind a castle—ironically enough the very house once lived in by the poet Stefan George, who hated Ludwig and whom Ludwig hated. A group of remarkable men came to Ludwig's home from time to time—writers, philosophers, editors, and thinkers, among whom was Martin Buber as well as Hans Ehrenberg of Rosenstock-Huessy's Patmos Circle. After a number of such meetings in the course of the years, Buber approached von Weizsäcker with the proposal that he coedit a journal with him. Von Weizsäcker had to overcome serious misgivings before he could agree, because of the difference in their age (Buber was ten years older), Buber's fame as an author, plus an unsureness as to Buber's direction with regard to this journal. He recognized at the same time that Buber had without question broken through from the literarily and aesthetically cultivated author that he had been to an earnest man who had taken on himself the responsibility of religious and philosophical seriousness—something that von Weizsäcker himself had begun to undertake.

In July 1925 von Weizsäcker wrote to Buber that he was not ready for so serious an undertaking unless it grew organically out of his own way and direction, as was true of Buber. In the end von Weizsäcker let himself be persuaded to become the coeditor of *Die Kreatur*. After his own piece, "The Doctor and the Patient: Pieces of a Medical Anthropology," had been published in 1926, he wrote to Buber that a part of his person that had long remained hidden was being revealed, as a result of which he found himself ever more willing to express himself in writing. Writing Hugo von Hofmannsthal in 1926, Buber particularly referred him to von Weizsäcker's essay "The Pains" in the third issue of *Die Kreatur* as one that helped point to the basic stance of creaturely existence, first attained by rejecting Idealism and then by divorcing it from psychologism. In these early essays von Weizsäcker did indeed lay the foundation for a whole new approach to the doctor-patient relationship, one based upon question and answer and on the partnership of physician and client rather than on the expertise of a

scientist about an object. As opposed to objective or subjective knowing, he called this "transjective." The real concern of *Die Kreatur* was
not cosmology, as Buber had earlier suggested, but anthropology—
philosophical anthropology which opened itself to the problematic of
the human creature, including the relationship of the human to all
created beings and things.

As strange as Buber's choice of a psychiatrist as the Protestant editor
of *Die Kreatur* might seem, the choice of Joseph Wittig as the Catholic
editor was even stranger. At first glance, Wittig would seem, of the
three of them, the most representative of his religion, being both a
priest and a professor of Catholic theology. But von Weizsäcker's later
observation that "The Catholic was no proper Catholic, the Protestant
no proper Protestant, and the Jew no proper Jew" was true for Wittig
in even more startling degree than of his two coeditors. Through his
book *Jesus in Palestine, Silesia, and Elsewhere,* Wittig had become the
best-known and most effective of Catholic popular writers; so he did
not suffer from that "invisibility" of which Buber spoke to Rosenzweig
when considering von Weizsäcker. Wittig made visible the religious
form and being in all the things and events of the world, according to
von Weizsäcker. He saw the divine as appearing constantly in human
and natural existence. He was the son of a carpenter, a professor of
church history at Breslau since 1911, a simple pastor with naïve and
childlike faith, yet a man of distinctive and uncommonly stubborn
character. He emphasized the co-working of God in the activity of
creation more strongly than the Church allowed, which brought his
teaching near to Luther's concept of justification. In 1927 he coau-
thored a book with his Protestant friend Eugen Rosenstock on *The Altar
of the Church.* It was Rosenstock who brought Wittig into contact with
Buber. But the coauthorship of a three-volume book with Rosenstock
did not make Wittig more Protestant. Rosenstock, in fact, looked upon
himself as in many ways more Catholic than Wittig.

Wittig's principal conflict was not with the Church but with the First
Bishop of Breslau, Adolf Cardinal Bertram. Wittig opposed the petrifi-
cation, neglect, and perniciousness of preaching and confession. It is
not the fulfillment of prayers and other things prescribed by the
Church that leads to redemption, he held, but an inner renewal which
only divine grace can help. These can be seen as Protestant heresies,
von Weizsäcker contended, only when one no longer breathes the
fresh air of a spiritually alive person concerned about the salvation of
the human being and not about satisfying his own vanity. Cardinal

Bertram, more a regent of the Church than a shepherd of souls, never spoke with or even saw Wittig. Bertram demanded a revocation, and Wittig responded that first he had to be shown his errors. The cardinal then demanded that Wittig take once again the apostolic vows. Wittig replied that one cannot repeat a vow, for that would make all vows valueless.

It was in the midst of this feud between Cardinal Bertram and Father Wittig that Buber invited Wittig to be the Catholic editor of *Die Kreatur.* On July 28, 1925, Wittig wrote Buber that he had told Rosenstock that he would serve in this capacity, which for him meant entering the company of those whom he wanted to be near. Rosenstock's personal knowledge of him was the one credential he brought. But, first, Wittig thought, he ought to ask his bishop or at least tell him of his intention in order to preclude his having to leave his new colleagues by some eventual official prohibition. A recent communication from the bishop to the faculty of his seminary had reminded the priest-professors that they needed the Church's assent for every collaborative enterprise in books and periodicals, and not just for the theological ones. Wittig then raised the question with Buber as to whether he would want him as coeditor under such circumstances. "Cut off from the Church, I think I would be of no use to you," he said, and then added with typical humility that while he was indeed the person Rosenstock said he was, he did not have Rosenstock's scholarship. "For the trust and love that speaks out of your lines," he concluded, "I am thankful to you as one is thankful for good fortune. That will remain even if it turns out to be impossible for us to work together."

Buber's reply to Wittig made it quite clear that Wittig represented Catholicism by what he was and did, wrote and said, as a person, and not by his official position in the Church. To Wittig's first question as to whether Buber would agree to his complying with the canonic law, Buber asserted categorically, "I have turned to you in truth as the unique person that you are. That means that I had lived through in my consciousness, as much as I was able to, your personal situation including, naturally, your office and your order and have accepted it insofar as I can from the standpoint of my task." This statement in turn touched on the second question of whether, cut loose from the Church, Wittig would be of no value to Buber. To this Buber's response was equally categorical: "Because I have turned to you in truth as the person that you are, therefore—may I be allowed to say this in all respect and humility as one praying man to another—nothing on this earth could ever take away from you your representative character as a Catholic in my eyes."

A half year later, in February 1926, Wittig formally accepted the coeditorship of *Die Kreatur* in a touching letter that said that if all living beings are born in anxiety which is then succeeded by joy, his own editorship of *Die Kreatur* must be something very living. Although his excommunication from the Church had not come by Christmas, as he anticipated, Wittig, after a night-long talk with Rosenstock, suddenly decided to accept Buber's invitation, unaccompanied by any doubting or vacillation.

In April 1926 von Weizsäcker wrote Buber confessing his delight over Wittig's personality. "Wittig is a disarming man," he wrote, but he also expressed his fear that Wittig's views might leave him sitting forever in a village instead of working up from peasant to pope. Toward the end of May, Cardinal Bertram made a final demand that Wittig recant his views. Wittig's refusal automatically placed him in excommunication, which even the Pope, who had read one of his books and found it "beautiful," was powerless to do anything about. It was not until 1946, when Wittig was sixty-seven years old, that the excommunication was lifted. To von Weizsäcker, Wittig's excommunication seemed a catastrophe for *Die Kreatur;* for his own strongly expressed desire that there be a Catholic editor meant for him a Catholic in good standing. He even proposed that they suspend *Die Kreatur* if necessary and find other ways to influence people. Buber responded that he had already written Wittig saying that at the slightest sign from him they would make it officially known that he was no longer an editor of *Die Kreatur.* But Buber did not agree to find some other way to influence people, and he categorically stated that if Wittig *wanted* to remain as editor, as far as *he* was concerned he would hold fast to him. "We already anticipated this possibility." Even if it were a major excommunication from the community of the Church and not just from its sacraments and offices, Wittig could never cease to be a Catholic. Some time later, in expressing his delight over a particular statement of Wittig's, Buber wrote Rosenzweig, "Such expressions one hears only from Catholics." "Wittig also has a good ear," Buber wrote. "The editors for *Die Kreatur* are set." The most poignant expression of Buber's personal response to Wittig was his statement to Rosenzweig, "Wittig's letter awakens Rang's voice in my ear."

While by no means restricted to a particular circle as in the case of Rosenstock's Patmos publications, the contents of the three volumes of *Die Kreatur* show clearly how it became a center for a group of kindred spirits concerned with education, psychotherapy, religious socialism, international understanding, religion, and poetry. Many of Florens Christian Rang's essays were published in it posthumously, as well as essays by such seminal thinkers and writers as Lev Shestov, the Russian Jewish existentialist; the Catholics Wilhelm and Ernst Michel; Franz Rosenzweig, Ernst Simon, Hermann Herrigel, Nicolas Berdyaev, Hugo Bergmann, Hans and Rudolf Ehrenberg, Eugen Rosenstock-Huessy, Alfons Paquet, the poet Ludwig Strauss, Hans Trüb, Marie Louise Enckendorf (the widow of the famous sociologist Georg Simmel), the Protestant theologian Eberhard Grisebach, Margarete Susman, Eduard Strauss, and Walter Benjamin. Most of these names appear not once but several times in the three years of publication. It was here that the classic exchange of letters between the two Russian thinkers M. Gershenson and W. Ivanov was first published in translation. For the two dialogical psychotherapists, Hans Trüb and Viktor von Weizsäcker it served as the pump primer that started them on distinguished writing careers. Joseph Wittig wrote several beautiful and essentially dialogical pieces for *Die Kreatur,* and Buber himself first published in it such important writings as "Education," "Dialogue," and "Gandhi, Politics, and Us." Rosenstock-Huessy wrote Buber that the third issue of *Die Kreatur* possessed an "unheard-of beauty"—an "awesome symphony" that answered his own earlier criticism of a lack of specific direction.

Wittig meanwhile married a former student of his who had served him as housekeeper (in order not to compromise her, suggested von Weizsäcker), moved to near Heppenheim, and had several children and a happy family life. Von Weizsäcker found himself more and more impressed by Wittig's writings and asked Buber whether Rang and Wittig had known each other, echoing unknowingly Buber's own sense of an affinity between the two men. The one thing that troubled von Weizsäcker was Buber's silence as editor. In contrast to *Der Jude,* Buber never wrote any editorials for *Die Kreatur.* This was a deliberate, self-imposed limitation to avoid his possibly dominating this exchange of free and profound spirits. While honoring this silence, von Weizsäcker asked Buber whether it was not up to him, the most summoned man of the hour, to set an example that would avoid the danger of the will to produce which would be the death knell of *Die Kreatur.* According to von Weizsäcker's own later testimony, however, *Die Kreatur* did not end because of any decline of quality but simply went out of existence when it had served its function as a forum for the chorus of rich and creative voices that it had brought into polyphonic and, often, antiphonal harmony.

The last issue of *Die Kreatur* announced the death of Franz Rosenzweig and printed some fragments from his unpublished writings. Here appeared the only other editorial note aside from the one that opened the first issue: "This journal, which we began in the memory of Florens Christian Rang, we wish to conclude in the memory of Franz Rosenzweig. It derived its editorial foundation stone from Rang, its name from Rosenzweig. What it has been able to say and effect will remain for all time bound up with the remembrance of these two great exponents of the one reality." The lasting value of *Die Kreatur* is attested by those persons who have kept its volumes as cherished possessions throughout the years and by its recent reprinting as a whole by a German publishing firm.

What Wittig's association with Buber meant to him is expressed in a touching letter which he wrote Buber after the appearance of the last issue. "I must let speak the word from the heart that came from many years: 'What will become of us now?' I do not mean you and me but us. . . . This question is the only thanks that I can express to you for our being together in the last four years. Therefore, I ask you to let me continue to share in your works and in your life. . . . I know that there will be a life for us after the completion of *Die Kreatur.* But it will always be for me an Easter day whenever we meet each other again, whether in work, a letter, or a visit."

One such "Easter day" for Wittig came in 1932 when he received Buber's little gem *Zwiesprache* (Dialogue), now published separately as a book. Although Wittig must have at least glanced at it when it appeared four years before in *Die Kreatur,* now he read it from the first page to the last. Thinking then of all that his parents and pastors had said to him in his youth about "praying without ceasing," he recognized it again in the content of Buber's *Dialogue.* "Now in the evening," Wittig concluded in the letter he wrote Buber that same day, "I am deeply moved by the friend whom I love teaching people to pray."

With the exception of Buber's claim that there is room in "dialogue" for religion in all its forms, there is nothing either directly or indirectly about prayer in the book. Yet Wittig was not wrong; for this important sequel to *I and Thou* (and for many people a better introduction to Buber's philosophy of dialogue than that more poetic book) is linked unmistakably both to Buber's work on the Bible and to the central motif of *Die Kreatur:* that the Creator speaks to his creatures through the "word" of creation—that everything is a "sign of address"* if we open ourselves to it and respond. Here "the world as word" has come into the maturity of the "life of dialogue" in which not only religion, education, drama, art, and knowledge have their place but all of human existence in its possibilities of going forth to meeting and of the new "word" that is the product of that meeting. Only here the central terms are not "I-Thou" and "I-It" but "dialogue," which allows the other to exist in his, her, or its own right and not just as a product of one's experience; "monologue," which waits for the other to finish speaking so one can make one's "point" or drive one's argument home; and "reflexion," which bends back on oneself and prevents one from awareness and response. Buber speaks here of the worker in his factory who can have a dialogue with his machines; of the employer who can be there for the individual worker when he steps up to him; of Jesus —who loved only the "loose, lovable sinners" and not the self-right-eous, but who *stood in genuine dialogue* with the latter as with the former. He contrasts "social workers" who never have to do directly with any of the many persons with whom they work and the man who has only enemies but who relates to those enemies so personally and directly that it is their fault if the enmity does not flower into friendship.

In a letter to Ernst Simon, Buber spoke of *Dialogue* as "the little book of my heart," and it is indeed a book that emerges from the heart, uttering words that with their simplicity and power have gradually found their way into the minds and hearts of countless people the world over. "I believe in general that I have given no 'answer,' " Buber wrote, "not merely no total answer, but also no piece of one, rather a pointing in the literal sense." The great Russian-Jewish existentialist Lev Shestov (1866–1938) wrote an essay responding and contending with *Dialogue*—which he published in German and in French. On the other hand, the great Eastern Orthodox existentialist Nicolas Berdyaev wrote an article on *I and Thou* and *Dialogue* (in the Russian émigré journal *'Put*) in which he made the incredible statement that Buber was concerned only with the dialogue between God and man and not that between man and man. When I asked Buber how such a total misunderstanding was possible, he replied that Berdyaev, whom he knew at the "decades" at Pontigny, was a person who was better at speaking than listening!

*See Note to Chapter 6.

Perhaps the most fascinating and opaque part of *Dialogue* is the "Original Remembrance" with which it begins. In this subsection Buber recounted a dream which recurred to him with all sorts of changes, sometimes after an interval of several years. This "dream of the double cry" always took place in a "primitive" world, meagerly equipped—a vast cave, a mud building, or the fringe of a gigantic forest. It always began with an extraordinary event unrolling at a furious pace, such as a lion cub tearing the flesh from Buber's arm, to be followed suddenly by a slower pace in which Buber stood there and cried out—joyfully and fearfully, with pain and/or triumph depending upon what preceded it—an inarticulate, rhythmic cry, rising and falling, swelling slowly to a long and slow fullness that is almost a song. Then from far away came the "same" cry but uttered or sung by another voice, not an echo but a true rejoinder, corresponding to the dreamer's original cry in such a way that he experienced in his dream the certitude that *now it has happened.* The last time the dream recurred, two years before Buber wrote *Dialogue,* no answering call came. But this time, the answer came not from the distance, but from the air around him. It came noiselessly as if it had always been there and only awaited his opening himself so that it could be given him, as a real rejoinder, more perfect than the others precisely because it was already there. By "original remembrance," Buber wrote Simon, he meant the dream as a recollection of a primordial world *(Urwelt)*.

"Dialogue" here does not necessarily mean speech; for there is also silence which is communication, as when two men sit next to each other in a railway carriage, one whose being seems to say that what counts is being really *there,* the other of whom is a man who holds himself in reserve, keeps himself aloof—not as an attitude but as the impenetrable barrier of being unable to communicate himself. In this hour of silent dialogue the seven iron bands around this man's heart burst asunder, in response to his partner, and he releases in himself a reserve over which only he has the power. Communication streams from him to his neighbor, who receives it unreservedly as he receives all genuine destiny that meets him. This is no experience or knowledge that can be borne away with him but nonetheless a true event: "For where unreserve has ruled, even wordlessly, between persons, the word of dialogue has happened sacramentally."

The life of dialogue does not mean having much to do with others but really being present to those with whom we have to do. That is why "dialogue" cannot be identified with "love." Real love is the highest form of dialogue but by no means the only one, whereas that love which does not reach out to another is monologue masking as dialogue, the proper name of which is Lucifer. The life of dialogue is the real contrary of the cry, heard in twilight ages (such as the Germany of the Weimar Republic and the America of the 1960s and early 1970s), for universal unreserve. "He who can be reserved with each passer-by has no substance to lose." It is in this connection too that Buber gave the essential response to those who say one must first become a whole person, achieve "individuation" or integration, before one can transcend the self and go out to dialogue with the other. Although dialogue between mere *individuals* is a sketch which can be filled in only by a dialogue between *persons,* by what can we really become persons, Buber asked, better than through "the strict and sweet experiences of dialogue" which teach us the boundless contents of the boundary?

In *Dialogue,* Buber came as close to irony as in any of his voluminous writings. Real dialogue does not have to be with someone one already knows. It can be found in the tone of a railway guard's voice, in the glance of any old newspaper vendor, in the smile of a chimney sweep. But monologue disguised as dialogue is the great dissembler that masquerades as the interhuman. Buber's irony became even stronger when he turned to the "kingdom of the lame-winged Eros," which, already in the Weimar Republic, had taken on the manifestations that Rollo May so accurately depicts in *Love and Will* as a repression of the true eros by sex. The varieties of "erotic man" that Buber described are again that most cruel hoax of monologue that passes for dialogue.

There a lover stamps around and is in love only with his passion. There one is wearing his differentiated feelings like medal-ribbons. There one is enjoying the adventures of his own fascinating effect. There one is gazing enraptured at the spectacle of his own supposed surrender. There one is collecting excitement. There one is displaying his "power." There one is preening himself with borrowed vitality. There one is delighting to exist simultaneously as himself and as an idol very unlike himself. There one is warming himself at the blaze of what has fallen to his lot. There one is experimenting . . .—all the manifold monologists with their mirrors, in the apartment of the most intimate dialogue!

In opposition to true community stands not only individual monologue, but the collectivity, the totalitarian states of left and right in which, bundled together without *Thou* and without *I,* hostile and separated hosts march into the common abyss. True community emerges only out of the breakthrough from the repressed and the pedestrian to the reality of the between; "No factory and no office is so abandoned by creation that a creative glance could not fly up from one working-place to another, . . . an unsentimental and unreserved exchange of glances between two men in an alien place." It is this that guarantees the reality of creation.

JEWISH-CHRISTIAN DIALOGUE DURING AND AFTER *DIE KREATUR*

Buber's dialogue with committed Christians (Protestant, Catholic, and Eastern Orthodox) by no means ended with *Die Kreatur.* It continued, indeed, as long as he lived. There is abundant evidence as well that the turning toward the other that impelled Buber to found *Die Kreatur* continued unabated in the three years between its demise and the Nazis' ascent to power. In *Dialogue,* Buber had written:

> A time of genuine religious conversations is beginning—not those so-called but fictitious conversations where none regarded and ad-dressed his partner in reality, but genuine dialogues, speech from cer-tainty to certainty, but also from one open-hearted person to another open-hearted person. Only then will genuine common life appear, not that of an identical content of faith which is alleged to be found in all religions, but that of the situation, of anguish and of expectation.

These dialogues of open-hearted persons meant responsibility in the face of the "claim" of reality, answering a real address unmediated by any conceptual world view. "The first person whom I thought of in this connection was you," Buber wrote Albert Schweitzer in connection with inviting him to a conference in Karlsruhe. "You have for a long time been exemplary for me of the direction that I mean."

Although Buber was widely accepted by the Christian world as apos-tle and spokesman for Judaism, he made no claim to be representative either of rabbinical Judaism or of any synagogue or official group. Similarly he was not himself interested in dialogues with official Chris-tians but with committed persons. Not seldom the two were at vari-ance. The Rhine-Main *Volkszeitung* had received a severe warning from the bishopric because of its printing of the report of the address

"Philosophical and Religious World-View" which Buber had given in the 1928 conference of the Hohenrodter Bund, the educational movement with which he had long been connected. Buber's speech was seen as replete with modernisms that were dangerous for its readers. Josef Nielen, a student chaplain and later a professor of Catholic theology, defended the speech as free of anything offensive to Church dogma, but the bishopric's stricture against it included a list of "errors."

Theodor Bäuerle, founder and director of the Folk School in Stuttgart and an active leader of the Hohenrodter Bund (into which circle he introduced Buber), wrote Buber in January 1929, confessing that the theme "Religion and Revolution," which had been proposed for a dialogue between Buber and him at the Jüdisches Lehrhaus in Stuttgart, was too difficult and touched him too personally for him to be able to carry through a public dialogue before a large audience. Buber agreed to this, and their dialogue took place the following month on "Religion and Politics." But the real dialogue was in the letters between them. Buber found Bäuerle's letter very important to him personally, but he did not feel that the dualism that Bäuerle feared was inevitable if one recognized that this world is neither God's nor the devil's but rather its own and man's. Only when we think of God's demand as perfection do we fall into dualism. We cannot live without force, but in each situation, in each surrounding we can make real a tiny amount of nonviolence. The lecture hall itself is an image of the world in which we must persist. "Does not the vinegar of misunderstanding and *with* it the drops of genuine spiritual wine—of being understood—belong to the meaning and shape of our lives? Is not the pillory our true home, ours, the humans, who do not *have* the spirit but wish to bear witness to it?

There is a significant parallel between the correspondence of Buber with the young theologian and Semiticist Hans Kosmala, who wrote Buber in 1932 in deep distress over the invitation of the distinguished Bible scholar Alfred Jeremias to be the director of a mission to the Jews, and "Two Foci of the Jewish Soul"—the speech that Buber gave in 1930 to one of the four German Christian missions to the Jews. To Kosmala, who confessed himself at home in Buber's sphere of thought, Buber wrote that it depended upon his own inner strength and the conditions that he set whether he could take on a missionary position such as this and remain spiritually alive. To the German mission Buber declared that he was opposed to their cause as a Jew who waits for the

Kingdom of God and regards missions such as theirs as springing from a misunderstanding that hinders the coming of the kingdom. The first focus of the Jewish soul Buber saw as faith—not in the sense of the belief that God exists but in the sense of *emunah,* the trust that though God is wholly raised above man and beyond his grasp, he is present in immediate relationship with human beings and faces them. The biblical "fear of God" is the creaturely awareness of the darkness out of which God reveals himself, the dark gate through which man must pass if he is to enter into the love of God. If one tries instead to construct a theological image of God as simply love, one runs the risk of having to despair of God in view of the actualities of history and life or of falling into self-deception and hypocrisy. The fear of God is merely a gate, however, not a dwelling in which one settles down, as some of the Barthian and Neo-Orthodox theologians who emphasized the "wholly otherness" of God seemed to feel. This also means that no primordial "Fall," or original sin, can abridge man's power to turn to God and imitate him. Because this is so, we cannot do God's will by beginning with grace but by beginning with ourselves, our will which, poor as it is, leads us to grace.

The second focus of the Jewish soul is the corollary of the first: the recognition "that God's redeeming power is at work everywhere and at all times, but that a state of redemption exists nowhere and never." While the Jew experiences the touch of God's nearness that comes to him from above, he also experiences, more intensely than any other, the world's lack of redemption and feels the burden of the un-redeemed world on him. Redemption means to the Jew not the individual soul but the soul *and* the world inseparably bound together. As a corollary to this attitude toward redemption, Buber articulated here for the first time the distinction between the "prophetic" and the "apocalyptic" that became the cornerstone for all his later understanding both of biblical Judaism and of early Christianity. Prophetic faith preserves the oneness of God and the world, whereas the apocalyptic belief falls into an essentially Manichean dualism:

> The prophetic promises a consummation of creation, the apocalyptic its abrogation and supersession by another world, completely different in nature: the prophetic allows "the evil" to find the direction that leads toward God, and to enter into the good; the apocalyptic sees good and evil severed forever at the end of days, the good redeemed, the evil unredeemable for all eternity.

The prophetic is the call to man to turn back to God in the present; for "those who turn cooperate in the redemption of the world." "Man cannot bring down grace by magic or any definite act; yet grace answers deed in unpredictable ways."

The Jewish belief in the *non-*incarnation of God and the unbroken continuity of human history means that premessianically the destinies of Judaism and Christianity are divided. "To the Christian the Jew is the incomprehensibly obdurate man, who declines to see what has happened; and to the Jew the Christian is the incomprehensibly daring man, who affirms in an unredeemed world that its redemption has been accomplished." But when both Christian and Jew care more for God than for our images of God, "there are moments when we may prepare the way together."

Between Buber and Albert Schweitzer there was, as we have seen, a mutual influencing and a mutual confirmation. "Your books are very dear to me," wrote Schweitzer to Buber in December 1932. "Alas, fatigue and frightful work hinder me from writing to you as I might. But you should know that I have not forgotten you and that I follow all your work with interest and would be so happy to speak with you once. . . . How often I envy you and your peaceful and quiet creating! My lot is unrest and a multiplicity of tasks in the midst of which I must struggle to collect myself for my work. Often I can almost do no more." *The Hidden Light* (Buber's first collection of Hasidic tales published after *The Great Maggid and His Followers*) "is splendid," Schweitzer exclaimed. "How much life there is in the rabbis! I feel so much of this sort—Jeremiah and Isaiah and Ezekiel are splendidly translated. But especially valuable to me is *Dialogue,* where you give of your inmost self and where I find so much that we have in common. . . . For this so wonderfully simple and deep self-sharing, I thank you especially." It is no accident that Schweitzer mentioned in the next paragraph his own book that he was completing on "The Mysticism of the Reverence for Life"; for it is undoubtedly this central theme of his life and thought that made him feel so close to Buber's understanding of dialogue as a way of life that not only applied to the relationships between persons but to art, knowledge, and our relationship to (*all*) the beings and things among which we find ourselves.

CHAPTER 7

Martin Buber at Fifty

THE YEAR BEFORE Buber's fiftieth birthday he wrote in his Foreword to his collection of Hasidic tales and teachings of his early premonition that, no matter how he resisted it, he was inescapably destined to love the world. He also confessed that he could not imagine his own existence without the existence of God:

> It is not merely in appearance that God has entered into exile in His indwelling in the world; it is not merely in appearance that in His indwelling He suffers with the fate of His world. And it is not merely in appearance that He waits for the initial movement toward redemption to come from the world. . . . How it happens that this is not appearance but reality . . . that is a mystery of God the Creator and Redeemer, not more mysterious to me than that He is; and that He is is to me almost less mysterious than that I am, I who write this with trembling fingers on a rock bench above a lake.

When Buber was fifty, he heard of a lecture by Edmund Husserl, the German philosopher who founded the school of phenomenology that influenced thinkers such as Maurice Merleau-Ponty, Martin Heidegger, and Jean-Paul Sartre. Anxious to hear Husserl, Buber went to the lecture hall, where someone from the Philosophical Society recognized him and asked him to sit at the head table. When Husserl appeared, he gave those at the head table a quick greeting before stepping up to the lectern. "My name is Buber," Buber said. Husserl was taken aback for a moment and asked, "The real Buber?" Buber hesitated to give any further explanation, whereupon Husserl exclaimed: "But there is no such person! Buber—why he's a legend!"

The first book on Buber was published two years before his fiftieth birthday by the German Protestant Wilhelm Michel: the slender, beautifully written *Martin Buber's Path into Reality*. The second was written for Buber's fiftieth birthday by his old friend from the Bar Kochba circle, Hans Kohn, but was not published until two years afterward— the voluminous *Martin Buber: His Work and His Time,* a cultural history of central European Jewry. Michel saw Buber as paradigmatic of the time because Buber had taken the scattered fragments into himself and made them whole, confronting the illusions of the age with an image of reality. Michel ranked Buber among the influential German speakers of his time, someone whose words led to decision and reality. With what in retrospect seems tragic irony, Michel asserted that Buber "belongs to us": "There lives in him the *German* world-hour, no matter how exclusively he may seem to concern himself with the particular question of Judaism. . . . One does not speak the German language as he does without deeply and seriously entering into the destiny of the people from whom this language stems." Commenting on this statement, Ernst Simon wrote, "No German intellectual had ever before expressed such recognition of a representative of Judaism," and added, Buber "is the first Jewish author to enter German cultural history on an absolutely equal footing of give and take both with regard to his general as well as his specifically Jewish contribution."

Hans Kohn's *Martin Buber* was the first thoroughly scholarly study of the development of Buber's thought in the context of his time. As such, it laid the foundation for all the many subsequent studies that have been made of Buber and his thought during the nearly half century since it was first published. Insofar as it went (up to the end of the 1920s), it was exhaustive, and it also included the first full bibliography of works by and about Buber up to that time. In addition to Kohn's labor of love there were at least four separate Festschriften celebrating Buber's fiftieth birthday: one was a special Buber issue of the Zurich periodical *Der Lesezirkel* (The Circle of Readers); a second, a special Buber issue of *Das werdende Zeitalter,* the journal of that circle of progressive educators to which Buber had been close for more than a decade; a third, a special issue of *Der Jude,* revived by Buber's friends for this occasion; and a fourth, a book with contributions from a great many key figures, solicited and edited by Karl Joël and entitled by him *Aus unbekannten Schriften* (From Unknown Writings).

Karl Joël introduced *From Unknown Writings* with a highly significant distinction between that unknown which can never be revealed and the hidden unknown which is the very source of revelation. It is to the hidden unknown that Buber consistently pointed, as in the title of his Hasidic tales, *The Hidden Light,* and his interpretation of the hidden depths of history in the "suffering servant," and the "dark charisma" that confirms the anonymous man. Leonhard Ragaz talked of the deep sharing between Jew and Christian in Buber's and his common belief in the building of the kingdom of God in all reality in earthly existence and exclaimed, "Is it not splendid that we may carry on such a dialogue with each other?"

The most moving anecdote about Buber was that which his educator friend Elisabeth Rotten related in the introduction to her selection from the revelations of Sister Mechtild von Magdeburg. Speaking directly to Buber, she reminded him of how, six years before, a small circle of his close friends were gathered at his house in lively conversation around his table and how this conversation elicited from Buber a statement that she often found illuminating her way in the years since. " 'One must also love the evil,' you said to us, 'yes—but in the way that the evil wants to be loved.' Your glance said to us still more than your words alone could have said. We had been speaking of the Quakers' belief in the good in all men and of our strong attraction to it but also of the danger of losing sight of the reality of evil. . . . Your simple words, your embracing glance solved this dark and tormenting riddle of life that had oppressed us."

A significant counterpart to Buber's statement on evil narrated by Elisabeth Rotten is found in his comment on Max Brod's contribution to the special Buber issue of *Der Jude.* Speaking to Brod of three of his novels, Buber protested: "One may not voluntarily accept evil into one's life. Evil enters our lives entirely willy nilly. To defend ourselves against it, we should always will only to penetrate the impure with the pure. The result will probably be an interpenetration of both elements; still one ought not anticipate that result by saying 'Yes' to the evil in advance." Hermann Hesse testified to the enormous impact on his life

of Buber's Hasidic tales; the Christian theologian Friedrich Thieberger wrote of the new biblical belief that he and Buber shared, and
many prominent Zionists, such as Leo Hermann, Adolf Böhm, Markus
Reiner, Robert Weltsch, Ernst Simon, Viktor Kellner, Felix Weltsch,
and Siegfried Lehmann, founder of the Jewish National Home, wrote
of Buber's contributions to Zionism and Judaism. Hugo Bergmann
contributed a philosophical study of "Concept and Reality" in the
thought of Buber and the German Idealist philosopher J. G. Fichte.
Several letters from the early correspondence between Buber and
Chaim Weizmann were also published in this issue. One contributor
even told of how Buber at fifty outran his companions when they left
his house for a spontaneous run in the night! "The life of people in
this age sucks dry with mighty drafts, strikes out with mighty thrusts,"
reflected the distinguished writer Arnold Zweig. "But it would have no
depth were there not here and there on the earth persons who sit like
this man Buber in Heppenheim and give it that tiny injection of iodine
without which its fire, spirit, and central creativity would be a mere
mechanical process."

Writing to Buber from Jerusalem, Hugo Bergmann recalled in a
most intimate way all that Buber had meant to him and his friends over
the years from the first time when as a high school student he read
"with glowing cheeks" Buber's first article in *Die Welt*, through his talks
in Prague and the *Speeches on Judaism* which were published on the basis
of them, through the circle of men that he gathered around *Der Jude*
and the Prague Conference, where A. D. Gordon's Hapoël Hatzaïr and
Buber's own followers joined in a socialistic Zionism. In his early years
in Palestine, Bergmann confessed, it seemed to him that he was drawing away from Buber until their personal meeting showed him how
close they were and how much they felt *carried* in his presence. On
Buber's fiftieth birthday, Bergmann, as spokesman for himself and his
friends, confessed his group felt more keenly than ever how little their
generation had attained, how unclear their relation was to Palestine,
to Zionism, to tradition, and how weak was their impact on their
contemporaries. "We have on your birthday only one prayer," Bergmann concluded: "May the small group of men who have banded
themselves around you with your help find their way in the years to
come and be given the external conditions that will enable them to act
as a group and you . . . be given the health and strength to accomplish
what we, in love and in care, await from you."

In thanking his younger friend, Buber told him how he too had taken the other directly to his heart. "With a feeling of responsibility, to be sure, and the anxiety stemming from that, but also with joy." "Since the beginning of our acquaintanceship, I have never ceased to think of you with love. Your manner, at once serious and gay, patient and impatient has always done me good."

"The numerous contributors to your *Festgabe* are only the leading voices of a great band who feel themselves bound to you and listen to your voice," wrote Buber's publisher Lambert Schneider. Proud as he was of being the publisher of Buber's works, Schneider added, Buber as a person meant almost more to him than his works. As a "birthday present," he informed Buber that he had decided to let *Die Kreatur* continue publication for a third year: "I cannot bring myself to let it go." Ernst Simon wrote Buber that even in his beloved Rabbi Nobel he had not found such devotion to his fellowman as in Buber and added that if he himself should become a teacher and learn to exercise this chief of virtues—to practice love without the intoxication of power —it would be because Buber had been his teacher. "Your letter has touched my heart," Buber replied, "confirming, then admonishing, then the admonishing passing into the calmness of being there for each other. It is beautiful, comforting, yes full of promise that there exists this human knowing about the humanity between different generations."

Many who were not as close to Buber personally also wrote to him of what he had given and continued to give them. Ernst Joël touchingly shared with Buber the fact that it was Buber's enormous encouragement that enabled him to go through the streets and into the dreary dwellings of the proletarian quarter in which he chiefly worked and to spend long monotonous hours visiting the children who were entrusted to him, work which otherwise might easily have been unnerving. Buber called Ernst Joël "the noblest person in the German Youth Movement." In 1914 Joël's "radiance streamed forth to all," said Buber, but after his return from an English prison camp Joël became only a silent server in East Berlin, throwing off all intellectuality. He was "a great helper." He was much beloved by both Martin and Paula, and his sudden death in 1929 came to them as a great sorrow. Moshe Ben-Gavriêl wrote Buber from Jerusalem that if he had been able to glimpse the contours of a living Judaism in the midst of shoreless enthusiasm and boundless disappointment, he owed it in great part to Buber's books. Shmuel Agnon wrote a tribute in Hebrew from Palestine in which he compared Buber to the "precious Jews who open inns somewhere far from Jewish settlements on the off-chance that a Jew will pass by seeking kosher food."

> Buber writes in a foreign language, and would satisfy thirsty souls with pure ideas. His "new" Hasidism is not a new creation, but one that is beloved anew by him from day to day. He often comprehends the mystery of an idea far better than he who first expressed it, and sometimes elevates small matters to lofty heights, as he raised Hasidic tales to the level of universal legend.

In significant contrast to all these is the long letter from Nelly Braude-Buber, Buber's sister from his father's second marriage. Addressing him as her "beloved, old Cina" (an abbreviation for Marcina, the Polish equivalent of Martin), she wrote from Lodz, Poland, how difficult it was to stand at a distance and dare to reach out a hand of greeting to him when she knew so little about him and most of that secondhand from their father. But this shyness was overcome by the greater fear that Buber might think she had not thought of him on this special day. Actually, not only his fiftieth birthday but every birthday and not only his birthday but every day from childhood on was special because her loyalty to him was so deep that "it fills my own home and illuminates my every day." Even though she could not understand all the books that he sent her, she believed that she had understood *him* well and constructed her life in *his* sense when day after day she fulfilled her service to the small children of their elementary school and did her work with patience and love. "Thus I try to transpose your words, which I do not always understand, into everyday work." "God bless Paula, who is your life's support and treasure," Nelly added, but she also told her brother of how much their father loved him and how gladly he received every word by and about Martin. But when he complained that he heard so little from Martin, then his face would suddenly take on a sad look and she would realize suddenly that, despite his lively walk, his clear eyes, and his clear understanding, he was an old man. "You will not become a stranger to me," her letter went on, "even when I do not see you for a long while and do not write you. But our children know nothing of this bond. Does not that pain you too?"

What Nelly said about Buber's relationship to his wife Paula was, if possible, an understatement. Buber expressed the special meaning that his fiftieth birthday held for him by writing for Paula the poem

"On Looking Backward," in which he acknowledged, as we have seen, how she helped him overcome the madness and delusion that tempted him and, through her refusal to offer him false confirmation, helped bring him to the place where he could make real decision and find true direction. Buber's seminal essay "Dialogue," published when he was fifty, was dedicated to "P."—Paula:

> The abyss and the light of the worlds,
> Time's need and eternity's desire,
> Vision, event and poem:
> Were and are dialogue with you. *

BUBER'S FAMILY AND FRIENDS

Nelly Braude-Buber went to see her parents twice a year in Lemberg, formerly Galicia but after the war part of Poland. That Buber, who lived much farther away, was as totally out of touch with his father as her letter might seem to imply is gainsaid by a letter which he wrote to Rosenzweig sometime in the twenties in which he said, "My father became sick in Vienna and had to be taken to a sanatorium." Presumably he was taken there by Buber himself, who was probably meeting him there at the time and who used this occurrence to explain why he had no time to write Rosenzweig at that point or to delve further into a common concern. In 1924, after his winter semester of teaching at the University of Frankfurt, Buber visited his father in Poland in connection with "an important family matter." In 1925 Buber wrote to his father wishing him best wishes for his birthday and, as usual, sent him the latest books he had published, in this case his Bible translations. Carl Buber wrote of his surprise that his son had taken on a project of such magnitude and his joy at receiving the books. He also predicted that Martin would have great success in the world as a result of it, the rays of which will warm "all of us." In 1930 Buber journeyed again to visit his father in Lemberg, and in 1931 his whole family went there for the funeral of his stepmother. On that occasion Buber spoke of his eighty-three-year-old father as "a man of astounding strength and

---

*See Note A in Sources for Chapter 7.

uprightness," proving that the admiration which he felt for his father as a boy had in no way diminished.

Martin Buber's son Rafael, or, as his family nicknamed him, Raffi, remained in friendly communication with his parents during these years. But in his political views and acts he moved very far from them. He became a communist for a time and married a woman who was also one—Margarete Thüring, who later became known for her book *Under Two Dictators,* describing her experiences in the Nazi extermination and the Soviet slave-labor camps. In a letter of 1923 Buber wrote of how painful their relationship with Raffi was—for he had given them all kinds of worries. "Now," Buber wrote, "he is visiting us with his wife and a most darling child, named Barbara, who resembles my wife." But the following week Raffi was going to Worpswede to join the settlement of Heinrich Vogeler, a painter and German communist who migrated in 1925 to the Soviet Union and spent the rest of his life there. Although Buber, as a federalistic, communitarian socialist was certainly pained by his son's becoming a communist, there were far more practical concerns which upset Martin and Paula, in particular the schooling and upbringing of Barbara and later of her younger sister Judith. In 1928 these concerns came to a head in the difference between Martin and Paula, on the one hand, and Margarete Buber-Neumann, on the other, in regard to Barbara's education.

Margarete came to visit in order that they might together try to come to an agreement. This proved to be in vain, and Paula Buber took the unusual step of going to the courts and getting custody of both Barbara and Judith, presumably on the grounds that their parents' way of life prevented their raising the children as they should. Thus, ironically, family history repeated itself, even though for very different reasons, and Buber's grandchildren came to live with him as he had with his grandparents. This irony came full circle when Barbara lived with Buber in Jerusalem in his old age and helped to take care of him.

The second and younger child of Martin and Paula was Eva. When Eva was a little girl, she saw on Paula an old necklace. "How old is it?" Eva asked. "Three hundred years," Paula replied. "Mommy," exclaimed Eva, "I had no idea that you were already *so* old as that!" Writing to a family friend living in Jerusalem in 1923, Buber said that Eva was exactly as always he knew her: "She does not change but remains always the child and the world creature that bears its certainty in itself. My wife finds it hard to take. . . . the demonry of everyday life at present." Eva, of more delicate build and of more sensitive and aesthetic nature than her older brother Rafael, two years later became engaged to and then married Buber's friend the poet Ludwig Strauss.

The almost physical pain which remained with Buber all his life as a consequence of the brutal murder of his friend Gustav Landauer was intensified in 1927 by the death of Landauer's oldest daughter Lotte after an operation. Since Landauer's second wife, Hedwig Lachmann-Landauer, had already died, it was Lotte who tried to keep Buber and her father's other friends informed of his situation during the trying days of the first and second Räterepublik in Munich. It was she who telegraphed Buber, "Father is out of danger," words which all too quickly proved untrue, and it was she who informed Buber in 1922 that Landauer's ashes were kept in an unworthy place in a basement, thus moving Buber to arrange with Fritz Mauthner and Landauer's other friends in 1925 to erect the monument in Munich. Of the three daughters, she was the most responsible and mature—and the only one at the time of her death who was married. Martin and Paula traveled together to Karlsruhe in Breslau on August 16, 1927, to be present at the funeral. Buber himself delivered the memorial address, which Lotte's husband Max Kronstein wrote down and presented to Buber in December in a bound handwritten booklet of fifteen pages. This address was for Buber a heavy duty, but a duty of the heart. "Gustav Landauer's daughter—that means," said Buber, "the connection with a great life of fire and spirit, . . . of love and devotion to humanity." But it also means, he added, the connection with "a death in which the monstrous, sheerly apocalyptic horror, the cruelty of our age was delineated." In a genuine marriage such as Charlotte Kronstein lived, there is something reconciling that can even now in some measure overcome the cruelty of our age. Where one person stands so near another as Charlotte did with her husband and her child [a daughter, Marianne, who has lived for many years now in Scarsdale, New York], then presentness extends beyond death—in the underivable uniqueness of the person that is made manifest in the great bond of husband and wife. "We do not send into the darkness of Nothing our farewell greeting to Charlotte Kronstein but into the eternally living mystery." "My body and my heart disappear," Buber quoted from his own translation of Psalm 73, but "the rock of my heart is God in eternity."

Another warm friendship that Buber had—one that was not so close as that with either Landauer or Rosenzweig but that lasted a great many years longer—was that with the German-Swiss poet and novelist

Hermann Hesse. In 1927 Buber felt compelled to express to Hesse how very attached he was to his novel *Steppenwolf.* It was to Buber as though it were a through-and-through living being, a genuine person and not a "personality," and a friend—"in no way an always friendly friend, but a friend." In order to experience that, Buber added, one must have really read the book in contrast to the critics who mention it without having opened themselves to it.

As a present to Buber in Christmas of 1927 Hesse sent him "a few poems." Buber was unable to write him his thanks for them until a few days before his fiftieth birthday because of an operation that Paula had to undergo. But he assured Hesse that his present was received from the depths of his heart. In 1932 Buber wrote Hesse thanking him for his little novel *The Journey to the East,* which had been published that year in Berlin. It was, said Buber, "an astonishing and delightful book, pure and right. It does one good that such a book is still possible." Buber promised to send Hesse that year and the next some publications, scientific and otherwise (undoubtedly *The Kingship of God,* among others), that represented for him "a great piece of life." Hesse wrote Buber that it made him glad to receive such an enthusiastic response to *The Journey to the East,* which was so little understood. "With the years," Hesse added, "it is as if I suffer my writings rather than create them. I cannot protect myself against what makes them understandable only with difficulty. One of them, *Steppenwolf,* has been wholly and totally misunderstood, and just because of this misunderstanding has become a popular success!"

At the end of 1926, Max Brod wrote Buber that he would receive shortly Franz Kafka's greatest novel, *The Castle,* which had just been published by the Verlag Kurt Wolff, and that this work would bring to Kafka's writings the broader public they merited. But it was *The Trial,* a hand copy of which Brod had earlier sent Buber, which interested Buber most. "I have read this book in all its parts as one that deeply concerned me," Buber wrote, "and even where it oppressed or disturbed me, I have remained in an undiminished relationship of trust to it. If Kafka's pure human face had remained here for us," Buber added, "I would have said to it: We have to do with the meaningless until the last moment. But while we suffer all the entanglements of the absurd, are we not ever again aware of the meaning that shows itself to be not at all of our kind and yet turned toward us, thrusting through all the fumes to the chambers of our heart, which attains and receives it? So this goes into your ear, dear Max Brod, as if it were his," Buber concluded, and said that he would gladly write about Kafka: as soon as he *could*—"I find it very difficult," he confessed, and it was not until the 1950s, in fact, that Buber could write on Kafka.*

"Kafka's *Castle* was for me a subject not of reading but of real happening," Buber wrote Brod a month later. "It is a corporal embodiment of the mystery within it that concerns the survivors in their innermost life." "What you write me about Kafka is so true!" Brod replied. "The general echo is still weak, but such a word from you already by itself justifies for me the editing of this manuscript that was so anxiously protected by Kafka himself. Do you know that in the last year of his life he got his friend Dora Dymant to throw twenty thick notebooks into the oven while he lay in bed and watched them burn?" Five years later Max Brod, in his tireless and selfless devotion to the writings of his friend Franz, proposed to Buber a plan to publish a "pointing" to Kafka by six famous German authors—Martin Buber, Gerhart Hauptmann, Hermann Hesse, Heinrich Mann, Thomas Mann, and Franz Werfel—and, if he could find their addresses, the French novelist André Gide and the poet Paul Valéry, in order to interest the public in the three novels published out of the manuscripts still extant after Kafka's death (manuscripts which Kafka himself directed Brod to burn, but which Brod instead had the courage and greatness to edit and publish).

Buber's inclusion of psychotherapy in the life of dialogue (as opposed to any attempt to make the life of dialogue a subject of psychological investigation) was already obvious in his 1923 address "The Psychologizing of the World" to the Jungian Club of Zurich, of which Hans Trüb was a leading member. Some months after a meeting with Buber in October 1925, Trüb wrote Buber on how important it had been to him when Buber had asked, in response to an account of a case that Trüb gave him, whether his female patient was afraid of responsibility. "If one makes present to himself the whole depth of its meaning," wrote Trüb, "one comes of necessity to the question with which you ended your lectures in Holland: 'Are you ready, with your whole, collected person. . . . to be responsible for your existence with nothing other than your 'I am there'?" Trüb had found himself instinctively moving in this direction for the past six years, to the place where he had himself in his practice replaced the emphasis on "analysis" with an emphasis on the event of meeting which cannot be reduced to the

---

*See Note B in Sources for Chapter 7.

psychological but lies *between* persons. This led him to share his own responses with the patient, a method which he himself called "analysis of relationship" in a lecture to the Zurich Analytical Club four years before. "The object of our consideration must not be the 'other' but the reality of our relationship." To this, Trüb was helped not just by Buber's writings but by his glance. "I know your work as a true, honest report of what has again and again been seen by your good, true eyes, in which you have placed your trust at every moment—even the most shattering ones. Your glance is to me unforgettable. It is penetrating and yet in no way injuring; severe, unrelenting, and yet of unmistakable kindness!"

Buber wrote to Hans Trüb in 1928, strongly encouraging him to write down in a series of images his experience of the limits of psychology, to tell from within what he and his "patients" went through in common. "To such writing," Buber said, "grace will not be denied." And that is how it turned out for Trüb in the years to come. Trüb, even in his turning toward dialogical anthropology and away from analytical psychology, still remained in essential *Auseinandersetzung*—dialogue and contending—with his master and teacher Carl Jung. The same can be said of Ludwig Binswanger, the founder of "existential analysis," who remained a lifelong friend and friendly opponent of Sigmund Freud even though he too was influenced very strongly by Buber (and Heidegger)—in this case by the writings of Buber more than the person. In 1932 Buber had his publisher send a copy of his book *Dialogue* to Binswanger, who responded that, knowing *I and Thou* well, he did not experience any difficulty in reading this sequel. What made the greatest impression on Binswanger was the second part of the book and in particular the sections on Thinking, Eros, and Community as well as the "Conversation with the Opponent" in the third part of the book. "Since I was already early summoned to giving direction to a 'great-impulse,' " Binswanger testified, "but am at the same time a doctor who would gladly become ever more a human being, the way that is indicated here is the way of my total existence—hence not only that of thinking and striving, but also what is experienced daily 'in my own body.' "

In 1930 Buber wrote his old friend and Zionist co-worker Robert Weltsch that the news of the death of his wife Martha had shattered his soul. "It had become so much a matter of course for me that you had this quiet, good woman, to know you in the shelter and home of this union, that it is now painfully, bewilderingly difficult to take in the fact that in this cruelest of ways, such as happens to us only through the destruction of the central relationship of our lives, you have become alone. Your friends, among whom I feel myself more strongly than ever, can seek to give you, in the presence of being with each other, what friendship has to offer. But only the hand that struck the blow can work healing. When the destroyed union with the beloved being is immersed in the mystery itself, it becomes for us, no less incomprehensibly, a consolation. Thus I have experienced it, thus I wish it for you with all the strength of my wishing."

The undiminished strength of Buber's own central life-relationship was demonstrated once again in 1926 when he left it to his wife Paula, who was with her daughter in Düsseldorf, to communicate with their son-in-law Ludwig Strauss how he felt about the question of the circumcision of their first child, Martin Emanuel. "I have learned in the course of my life," Martin wrote Paula, "that we in exile may not forgo the original authentication of our belonging, no matter how we may feel personally. It is the only one given to us. Through it we personally carry forward the 'covenant,' which in exile does not have the community as its bearer." Inconsistent as this might seem to some with Buber's position toward the Jewish law, this attitude should dispel the common notion that Buber was simply an *"apikoros,"* as Rosenzweig jokingly called him, who was as a matter of principle and practice totally nonobservant. The biblical covenant between God and Israel became more and more the center of Buber's understanding of Judaism, in marked contrast to that Reform and liberal Judaism that, until recently, found its touchstone of reality in the universalism of the Enlightenment and replaced the biblical covenant by the "messianism" of Judaism's "prophetic" mission to bring universal ethics to mankind.

JUDAISM, BIBLICAL AND MODERN

In 1928, the year in which he wrote his essay on "Dialogue," Buber gave classic expression to his understanding of "The Faith of Judaism" in a lecture presented to an institute of economics. In this lecture Buber claimed to be formulating the theological pillars of a popular religion, but he no longer claimed, as in his earlier *Speeches on Judaism,* that this popular religion was exclusively an underground phenomenon in opposition to the dominant rabbinical Judaism. Now he saw

Hasidism as making visible in the structure of the community a movement which holds sway over the inaccessible structure of personal life
and is to be found everywhere in Judaism in less concentrated form.
One of the most basic movements of Judaism in general and Jewish
mysticism in particular is that of Yihud, or unification. Yihud does not
merely proclaim an abstract ethical monotheism but takes on itself the
task of making real the oneness of God "in the face of the monstrous
contradictions of life." This unification takes place not in spite of these
contradictions but in a spirit of love and reconciliation which includes
them. "The unity of the contraries"—the paradoxical reality that transcends the logic that mutually excludes A and non-A—"is the mystery
at the innermost core of the dialogue." From this standpoint the "religious life" means grasping the whole concreteness of life *without reduction* and bringing it into the dialogue with God.

An important event for the future of the Buber-Rosenzweig Bible
translation and of all of Buber's own works was the decision of Salman
Schocken in 1929 to establish a Jewish publishing house. It was the
Schocken Verlag, not Lambert Schneider Verlag, that carried forward
the publication of the separate volumes of the Bible translation as they
appeared in the 1930s, and published a new edition of *Ich und Du* and
the shorter works of Rosenzweig. One of Buber's books that Schocken
Verlag published was *The Kingship of God,* a book that had gestated for
many years in Buber's mind. What was particularly significant about
this book was that it was the first fully scholarly interpretation of the
Bible that Buber had written and as such was the foundation for all the
later scholarly interpretations that followed, such as *Moses, Prophetic
Faith,* and *Two Types of Faith.* More specifically, it was published as the
first of three volumes on the origin of the concept of messianism in the
Hebrew Bible, even though the later volumes were never published as
such but only in a fragment on the anointing of Saul by the prophet
Samuel.

Buber believed that this book would establish him in the scholarly
world in a way that none of his other books had, and perhaps for this
reason he ignored his younger friend Abraham Joshua Heschel's advice not to include all the many scholarly footnotes, and all the attempts to respond to the Wellhausen and other schools of biblical
interpretation. As early as 1930 Buber wrote Schocken that *The Kingship of God* would so strengthen his scholarly position that it would be
the springboard for the establishment of a "Schocken Institute of
Jewish Studies" of which he would be the director or at the very least

would merit a Schocken Chair for Jewish history of religion at the University of Berlin. The fact that he had been named honorary professor of general science of religion at the University of Frankfurt seemed to him another impetus in this direction.

After *The Kingship of God* was published in 1932 Buber did not see it as a "projection" of his own views but a reality that simply needed the assembling of the material to reveal itself. This reality was the direct kingship of God over every sphere of Israel's life as individuals, families, communities, and as a people in relationship to other peoples. This Buber saw as the meaning of the command in Exodus, "Ye shall become a kingdom of priests and a holy nation," and he supported it with a history of biblical Judaism from Moses and Joshua through Gideon, the judge who refused the offer of the crown with the words, "I shall not rule over you and my son shall not rule over you but the Lord God of Hosts," through the kings who were anointed as the viceroy of the true King and whose task, therefore, was to realize the demand of the covenant for true community. By the same token the disappointment of the prophets in the kings who separated the service of God from the practical affairs of their rule over the peo;ле gave rise to the image of a future king and then eventually of a fu' лre *nabi* (prophet) and a remnant of Israel who would answer God's demand. Hence the mixture of demand and comfort in the messages of the prophets who "spoke truth to power."

Buber's approach to history in *The Kingship of God* does not mean a dismissal of the comparative aspects of the history of religions, but it guards against the blurring of the historical figure which is caused by the now widespread shifting into the primitive. What Buber means here is not the history of religion but the history of faith, grasping quite concretely the relation of God to Israel, the living presence of the invisible God who "speaks out of the thornbush of the present," and accompanying and facilitating all this intuition as an organ of knowing.

The heart of *The Kingship of God* lies in its repeated theme that the human being must enter into the dialogue with God with his whole being: it must be "an exclusive relationship which shapes all other relations and therefore the whole order of life." This exclusiveness demands a "religious realism," a will to realization of one's faith in the whole of one's existence, that cannot be present in a polytheism which sees a different God in each phenomenon of life. The Sinai Covenant is not to be understood as a limitation on the essence of God, as if he were somehow less absolute for having entered into it. Like his revelation to Moses, it says only that he, the hiding and revealing God, will be present with the people in the future, that he will be there as he will be there. It does not mean that Israel is in some way dearer to God than other peoples. Israel is chosen only to fulfill a charge, to become a "holy people." Until this charge is fulfilled, the choice exists only negatively.

The unity of spirit and law in the judge is succeeded by the king, who had security of power without spirit, and the prophet, who had spirit without power. The kings were commissioned by God and responsible to him, but they tended to sublimate their responsibility into a divine right granted without obligation and to regard their anointing as demanding of them a merely cultic acknowledgment of YHVH's kingship. It is the failure of the kings in the dialogue with YHVH which resulted in the mission of the prophets. The "theopolitical" realism of the prophets led them to reject any merely symbolic fulfillment of the divine commission, to fight the division of community life into a "religious" realm of myth and cult and a "political" realm of civic and economic laws. The God of Isaiah whom one knows to be Lord of all is not more spiritual or real than the God of the Covenant of whom one knows only that "He is King in Jeshurun," for already he makes the unconditional demand of the genuine kingship.

Buber's approach to the kingship of God as a direct theocracy or a "theopolitical state," is itself a striking example of walking the narrow ridge. The highest binding, which by its very nature knows no compulsion, is not, of course, realized in any actual state, since every state rests, more or less, upon compulsion. Therefore, every fight for the realization of the rule of God in political life contains the lasting danger of erring on the side of compulsion or of freedom. On the one side of the narrow ridge, the power of the dominant element becomes self-serving, and then there arise the "apes" of theocracy—hierocracy or rule by priests. On the other side, freedom becomes its own goal and anarchy threatens as "empty license." The narrow ridge between these two abysses is the drawing of the demarcation line in each hour in such a way as to approach as nearly as possible to making real the kingship of God in human community.

Joseph Wittig wrote Buber in June of 1932 that he had sat for five days long at the foot of Buber's teaching chair and had heard his voice while reading *Königtum Gottes.* It awakened in him the memory of the God whom he acknowledged thirteen years ago, the God who goes with the people in their wanderings and exile. But only now had the power of that vision come over him through Buber's book. He described his reading of *The Kingship of God* as a spiritual exercise heightened by the recognition of Buber's intensive scholarly research. Around 1919 he came to see God as the one who gave him his task, and that remained a meaningful blessing to him as long as he had tasks. Now, however, he felt as if God had let him fall out of his hand. Although he wrote well into the night he felt himself lost with no sure captain to guide him. The recent political changes seemed to have turned the Lord of Hosts into a mere field chaplain. "Rarely have I been so shocked at how Godless the world has become."

"I have read your book on the kingship of God with burning interest," the Swiss theologian Emil Brunner wrote in June 1932. "At last! —finally we have a book about the Old Testament that is written out of understanding and not out of misunderstanding."

> Not only do I expect much from its effect on our Old Testament theology; it has also helped me to understand anew and better. For years I have repeatedly stated that we have no need so pressing as a real understanding of the Old Testament. . . . Your book seems to me to be the first to have really broken through, through the comfortless schematism of objectivizing history with its evolutionary waltz which flattens everything to the same level. . . . We cannot be thankful enough to you for this.

Buber asked Brunner if he would be willing to publish his opinion of *The Kingship of God,* to which Brunner replied that he could not publish a criticism or review in a field in which he was not himself a scholar. That his high opinion of *The Kingship of God* was in no way a fleeting one is shown by the statement made years later in his book *Man in Revolt* that Buber's *Kingship of God* contained more real philosophy of history than any book on the philosophy of history.

The great Jewish historian and man of the spirit Leo Baeck wrote Buber that the analysis of the historical tendencies of the text was indispensable here, and that one could almost say that here text and commentary were one. Baeck's hope was that in this respect Buber's book would provide a new direction; for without an understanding of the historical paradox no access to the Bible is possible. Hugo Hahn, one of the leading German rabbis (he later was the rabbi of a New York Jewish congregation that carried on the spirit of Franz Rosenzweig), wrote Buber that his book would call forth a whole new Bible generation. Every young theologian would need to study it and read it again and again. The book is ostensibly *about* religion, yet, with all its scholarship, is itself a religious book, a witness to the religion of Israel, a *significant* new understanding of the Bible.

Gershom Scholem, in the course of a long letter with penetrating critical questions, said that the principles to which Buber had given a concrete application in *The Kingship of God* opened up a wholly new line of Bible scholarship the significance of which for every level of Jewish reality was incalculable. Professor Joseph Klausner, the eminent scholar of Judaism and early Christianity, of the Hebrew University in Jerusalem, declared that *The Kingship of God* advanced new ideas and judgments of great significance for the history of religion in general and for that of Israel in particular.

The importance of the people is not as a goal in itself but as the beginning of the kingdom, Buber said in a radio talk of 1930. The "chosenness" of Israel is not for power and majesty but for this long way of pain and overcoming, leading to the hallowing of the interhuman realm, the founding of the community that will serve as a beginning. "We Jews are a community based on memory," declared Buber in a 1932 essay, an expanding memory which sustains and quickens Jewish existence. For the core of history does not consist of a series of objective events but of a sequence of essential attitudes toward such events, themselves a product of collective memory handed down from parent to child. To Buber nothing was so ominous as the disappearance in the past century and a half of this collective memory and the passion for handing it down. The magnetism of Palestine, the possibility of establishing a new continuity in the Palestine community, and the very existence of the Jewish communities of the Diaspora—all depend upon making real again the words of the Passover Haggadah: "We, all of us, have gone forth out of Egypt."

Buber characteristically named his 1932 collection of essays and speeches about Judaism *Fight for Israel* (Kampf um Israel). In the same letter in which he informed his young friend and disciple Hermann Gerson of his choice of this title in place of his earlier idea of "Service to Israel" he responded to Gerson's torment caused by the illness of the latter's fiancée and the incurable ailment of a close friend: "To doubt God (and still not despair) seems to me to belong to true faith, and it is one of the greatest teachings of the Bible that God rejects Job's friends but confirms Job (42:7)." Buber too was a fighter with and for God, like Job.

JEWISH MYSTICISM AND HASIDISM

In our search for understanding the development of Buber's thought in response to the events and meetings of his life we are not helped much by the dates of the publication of his books. For Buber, even more than for most authors, events in a distant past germinated in his mind, took on tentative form and shape, were tested, thought through, postponed for a time when he could free himself enough from other commitments to give them the concentration they deserved. This is certainly true of *The Kingship of God,* but it is also true of many other of his lifelong concerns, such as Judaism, Hasidism, socialism, education, art, and the theater. What is more, what appears to be a simple continuity of interest, as with the Bible and Hasidism, was for Buber, again and again, a rediscovery and fresh beginning in response to the events of that particular period of his life. For example, in 1924 Buber wrote a reply to an article about Hasidism by the eminent Protestant theologian Karl Ludwig Schmidt in Schmidt's theological journal. Although he agreed that Hasidism preserved the Jewish law, Buber denied that it did so in a doctrinaire way. Rather it was an expression of a spirit in which the highest potentialities of the human being, the redeeming power of intention, took part. Such a statement by Buber gives us an insight into how he reconciled his total devotion to Hasidism with his own very different attitude toward the observance of the Jewish law.

Again, the fact that Gershom Scholem had moved to Palestine and was doing active research on Hasidic materials there that Buber did not have access to occasioned a good deal of correspondence between them. In 1924 Scholem wrote of his desire to found a section on Jewish mysticism in the National Library in Jerusalem and proposed that he, Buber, and two other scholars of Hasidism—Simon Dubnow and Samuel Horodetsky—contribute their private collections as a foundation for it. In his reply Buber congratulated Scholem on his marriage: "We cannot picture you as a husband without a certain stretching of our imaginations," Buber wrote, "but our good wishes are with you; and undoubtedly the married state is the right one for all persons, with the exception perhaps of the pure philosopher." In 1930, Scholem wrote Buber of his regret that he could not visit him in Europe and discuss with him his studies in Jewish mysticism and particularly in the Lurian

Kabbala, which laid the foundation for the teachings of Hasidism. In 1932, Buber wrote Scholem that when his pressing work on the translation of the Bible allowed it, he hoped to write "a Hasidic theology," which meant for Buber a presentation of Hasidic teaching understood from within but *not* that Buber himself was or ever wanted to be a theologian. The presupposition for such a theology, Buber added, was, of course, a presentation of the Kabbala by Scholem upon the foundations of which Buber could build.

An entirely different sort of exchange took place between Buber and his old friend the poet Alfred Mombert in 1924 when Mombert received from Buber the collection of Hasidic tales titled *The Hidden Light* (Das verborgene Licht). "When a new work of yours appears," wrote Mombert, "I lay everything else aside; for it deals with something absolutely essential and ultimate. With each new book I experience ever more strongly that such books are produced only on the path of a long love." What Buber said in his Preface about the marriage of the "hidden light" with the "manifest light" Mombert singled out as the eternal contending of the poet. "How dreadful, impossible is the burden laid on the poet!" he concluded. Agnon too hailed Buber in connection with *The Hidden Light:* "Often your speech attains such simplicity that it is as if you were one of the disciples of the school of the blessed Baal Shem. You have the merit of having sublimated the provincial anecdote into a cosmic legend." This is precisely the "merit" that Buber later successfully overcame in his transmission of Hasidic tales as "legendary anecdotes"! In a 1926 letter to Agnon, Buber speaks of their common work plan, still a possibility in both their minds, and says he has already finished an almost complete transcription of all the stories about the Baal-Shem. In the same letter Buber complains that Agnon mentioned nothing personal in his letter. "You must know how heartfelt an interest I have in your life."

In 1927, Agnon sent Buber the collected materials that he possessed on Hasidic stories. Agnon complained of the slowness of the copier, of an earthquake that had shattered the walls of his house and left a crack in the roof, and of the haste with which he had to work in order to meet the deadline of the authorities to be out of the house in twenty-four hours in case of a new quake. "Haste is the devil's work," wrote Agnon, "and I had to experience it with my own body. All my household implements, books, and manuscripts were scattered wildly about." Returning to their common work on the *Corpus Hasidicum,* Agnon promised to have transcribed for Buber some wonderful stories that he had heard in Jerusalem from old Hasidim. In 1928 Buber told Agnon that his work translating the biblical Book of Samuel with its many textual difficulties had forced him to postpone for a while "our Hasidica," but he hoped in the immediate future to send him an organized manuscript. Four years later Buber again explained that his other work (most probably *The Kingship of God*) had prevented him from sending Agnon the organized material for the first volume of the *Corpus Hasidicum,* but he hoped to do so in May, including not only the stories but also the transcription of the formal teachings which he would systematically arrange at the same time.

In 1927 Buber published a little book of fragments from the books of disciples which he entitled *The Baal-Shem-Tov's Instruction in Intercourse with God.* Although the text itself was completed many years before, the Introduction, which was new, contrasts significantly with the emphasis upon *hitlathavut,* or mystic ecstasy, in "The Life of the Hasidim" section of *The Legend of the Baal-Shem.* Buber did not now deny that Hasidism is a mysticism, but he defined this "realistic and active mysticism" in such a way that it is not essentially distinct from "the life of dialogue":

> The Baal-Shem will probably be extolled as the founder of a realistic and active mysticism, i.e., a mysticism for which the world is not an illusion, from which man must turn away in order to reach true being, but rather, the reality between God and him in which reciprocity manifests itself, the subject of the message of creation to him, the subject of his answering service of creation, destined to be redeemed through the meeting of divine and human need; a mysticism, hence, without the intermixture of principles and without the weakening of the lived multiplicity of all for the sake of a unity of all that is to be experienced (*Yihud, unio,* means not the unification of the soul with God, but unification of God with His glory that dwells in the world). A "mysticism" that may be called such because it preserves the immediacy of the relation, guards the concreteness of the absolute and demands the involvement of the whole being; one can, to be sure, also call it religion for just the same reason. Its true . . . name is perhaps: presentness.

The indwelling glory of God is pictured by the Kabbala and Hasidism as the Shekinah, and the Shekinah is pictured as a woman, exiled from her husband, walking with torn and bleeding feet the dusty roads of the world. This imagery becomes sexual when the Baal Shem, in a boldness peculiar to Jewish mysticism, compares prayer to the coupling of man and woman. First, he suggests that at the beginning of prayer man should move up and down and later cleave motionlessly, since "Prayer is a coupling with the Glory of God." Then he states that as in bodily coupling only he can beget who uses a living limb with longing and joy, so in spiritual coupling only he begets who performs teaching and prayer joyfully. Then he compares prayer to "the bride who at first is adorned with many garments, but then, when her friend embraces her, all clothing is taken from her."

CHAPTER 8

Hermann Gerson and the "Work Folk"

THE JEWISH YOUTH MOVEMENT AND BEN SHEMEN

THE YEARS OF DISILLUSIONMENT after the First World War were particularly so for the Jewish members of the German youth movement, who had hoped in vain that the Kaiser's promise of equal status for the Jews would become a reality. Many of these joined the *Blau-Weiss*, the specifically Jewish youth movement in Austria and Germany, on which Buber had a profound influence. A large proportion of the Jewish Youth Movement was sympathetic to Zionism as expressed in Buber's early "Speeches on Judaism" with their emphasis on people and the tie of blood and believed that the "Jewish question" could be solved by the complete separation of the two peoples. For some of its members, the Jewish Youth Movement was a continuation of the Bar Kochba movement in Prague, and during the 1920s Buber was the great name for the Vienna *Blau-Weiss* leaders, as he had been in the previous decade for the Bar Kochbans. The *Blau-Weiss* was dedicated to the creation of a Jewish nation. Yet the Jewish Youth Movement was like the German youth movement in general in its emphasis on close identity with the landscape, traditions, and beliefs of the Volk, and it was the *German* landscape and language in which these Jewish youth had grown up. Their dreams "ripened under pine trees not under palms," observed Moses Calvary, himself a thoroughgoing Zionist who left Germany for Palestine in the early 1920s.

Buber's concerns with education, socialism, the Youth Movement, the Bible, Judaism, and Zionism had a more lasting influence on Siegfried Lehmann's Jewish Folk Home, which moved from Lithuania to Berlin during the First World War and after the war transplanted to Palestine where, instead of serving the Jewish refugees from Eastern Europe, it served the immigrants to the Land. Continuing the tradition of the German youth movement, the youths of Ben Shemen wandered all over Palestine visiting the various settlements, especially those where like-minded youth groups dwelled.

The idea that underlay the education at Ben Shemen, as at most of the kibbutzim, was that of a Jewish people living together in a *righteous* way and working on their own land in Eretz Israel. Here the Youth Movement was not an expression of a protest against the adult world, nor was it a longing to build alongside the dreary reality a second idyllic life of wandering. It was the clear expression of a desire to become part of that world the older generations, despite hunger and fever, had created out of the malaria-infested marshlands, a new world of agricultural communes living together in brotherhood. Later, after Buber came to live in Palestine, he reestablished connections with Ben Shemen, and his influence permeated it even more deeply through Arieh Simon, the successor to Siegfried Lehmann.

HERMANN GERSON AND THE WERKLEUTE

Through his close bond with Hermann Gerson, the leader of the "Work Folk," Buber had an even more dramatic impact on one segment of the Jewish Youth Movement in Germany and its transformation into an actual kibbutz in Palestine. "Folk Education as Our Task," an address that Buber gave at the twenty-first meeting of delegates of the German Zionists in 1926, the very year in which he met Gerson, affords us an insight into the deep significance of Buber's master-disciple relationship with Gerson for Buber's own understanding of his place in the Zionist movement. Here Buber portrayed his understanding of the Jewish settlement in Palestine as a colonization continued over many generations, "allowing the participation in the generation-work of the community to be included in the atmosphere of a new normality." This colonization was to be carried out by an élite of Jewish youth who already had a firm foundation in the folk education of their former homeland. But here Buber asserted that two basic human types were needed for this task—the Halutz, or pioneer, and the helper. Here there becomes visible, as Grete Schaeder has pointed out, not only Buber's conception of the way in which Palestine should develop but also the role that he intended for himself while he ever again postponed his own immigration: that of the helper. Corresponding to the folk schools in Palestine there must exist institutions in the Diaspora that will teach what Buber called the "Seinstradition"—the handing down of values, the *institutional* linking of the generations through teaching, as opposed to anything occasional, provisional, and temporary.

The Jewish Youth Movement cannot fulfill this task, Buber said, because its leaders are not persons who hand down existence and teaching. The succession of its generations are not included in the great connection of the generations. "That is also the reason why we see the often gloriously living generations of the Youth Movement—the Jewish as much as the German—disappear one after the other, as though they had never lived in an inspired present."

It is clear from this that Buber felt that the task was laid on him in some measure of turning to the youth and helping them become the pioneers who would enregister themselves in an organic succession of generations. With the emergence of Hermann Gerson as one of his staunchest disciples the way seemed to open for Buber to do just that, since Gerson was already one of the acknowledged leaders of the Jewish Youth Movement in Germany. Through Gerson Buber might hope to help found a genuine "Youth School."

In late November 1926, Hermann Gerson wrote Buber a long letter from Berlin which initiated a relationship between them that, with serious breaks, was to last until Buber's death forty years later. After thanking Buber for what his books had meant to him, Gerson introduced himself as a member of the German Youth Movement for many years, as a "comrade" in the German-Jewish Wanderbund, and as a disciple of Gustav Wyneken (1875–1964), the leading pedagogue of the Youth Movement, who from 1906 to 1920 was the director of the Free School Community of Wickersdorf, which he founded together with Paul Geheeb. Two years earlier, Gerson had read Buber's Introduction to his Hasidic collection *The Great Maggid and His Followers* and his *Three Speeches on Judaism*. Through them, Buber restored to Gerson, who came from a fully un-Jewish home, his Jewishness—and an essential content to his life which went far beyond the opportunity to be active in a party. Buber had opened a whole new world to him, Gerson testified—a narrow ridge between the prosaic reality of the everyday and the exalted world of thought. He had thereby given him a touchstone for distinguishing among all sorts of subtle philosophies and the spirit that presses for realization. Gerson even testified that through this awakening he had attained to a religious life, one which refused to regard God as a *mere* idea or projection of the human spirit. Thus Buber had become for him the true leader. After this introduction, Gerson asked Buber, in effect, if he would accept him as a disciple, would teach him what was essential for his life. He closed by assuring Buber that this was not a case of adulation for a "great man."

Buber replied within a week that he was ready to meet with him personally if he would come to Heppenheim some morning (only in the morning could he spare time from his work) and give him a week's notice beforehand. At the end of January 1927, Gerson asked Buber's permission to assemble a group of young people who might read the Bible together with Buber. He also asked Buber his opinion of the issue between an ethics based on the truth and an ethics based on inner authenticity, such as the creed adopted by the united German youth bands in 1913 which united in the "Free German Confession" to shape their lives according to their own decision, on their own responsibility, with inner truthfulness. Buber replied that our concern is unconditionally with truth even though we can never "have" the truth. We can attain authenticity, or genuineness, only if we aim at the truth and allow the former to emerge as a by-product. There is no reliable yardstick for ethical decisions, Buber added, but there is the *one* direction to the living truth.

The questions Gerson addressed to Buber were by no means simply theoretical. As the leader of the Kreis (Circle), the most important group of the German-Jewish Wanderbund Comrades, he was faced with very real ethical problems. It was his desire to transmit Buber's teaching to his comrades, few of whom would know Buber's thought in the same depth as he and still fewer of whom had personal access to Buber. Gerson wanted, like Buber, to combine the German and the Jewish, personal authenticity and genuine community, socialism and a care for the quality of the life between persons. To begin with, however, his circle was not distinctively Zionist.

Moritz Spitzer, who founded the Jungzionistiche Blätter in 1928, wrote Buber that he did so to fill a great need. "I don't know if you are aware," he wrote, "how extraordinarily problematic the relation of the youth, even those that are in some way organized as Zionist, has become toward Zionism. The Jung-Jüdische-Wanderbund, the left socialist branch of the Jewish Youth Movement, the liveliest and most clearly defined of the Bunds, is still imprisoned in a narrow and often absurd interpretation of the Halutzim (pioneers), which in every case is more valued politically than personally." Buber replied to Spitzer that never, not even during the war, had he been so concerned about the youth, never was his desire to help them so great as now. The only hope that Buber saw in this difficult situation was to turn from general solutions and slogans to immersion in the concrete, the present, and the personal, even the most personal. This growing consciousness of the task facing him led Buber to the lasting resolution never to evade a call which came to him from the youth. Buber wrote Gerson in August 1928 that he was planning to lead a course for the representatives of the youth groups.

Although both his work and his lecture commitments, including many to the Jewish Youth Bunds, limited the time that Buber could give to Gerson, he was truly present to him as a teacher in the deepest sense of the term. In response to a letter from Gerson, Buber wrote him in 1929: "I would very gladly see you again—I do not feel the connection with you as so 'little' as you think—on the contrary, I regard every genuine disciple (the other kind is painful) as a direct gift of God." Gerson complained to Buber of how little community was realized in the Jewish Youth Movement. Even the so-called turning toward Jewishness was often only superficial. In two journals of different Bunds, Gerson was attacked with the old reproach of utopianism and being unrealistic. He gave up being leader of the German-Jewish Wanderbund "Comrades," the liberal-religious direction. But he still felt responsible for the realization in the life of the Bunds of those of Buber's truths that he had made his own. Yet even though he was constantly aware of the central place that Buber's existence had in his life, he was still troubled by those critiques of the life of dialogue that questioned its importance. Gerson too had to walk the narrow ridge of the concrete between two types of absolutist abstractions: those who rejected the whole personal sphere in the name of the suprapersonal idea of building up Palestine and those who rejected it as a bourgeois, sentimental luxury which distracted from the one true task—the proletariat's fight for liberation. Gerson found himself particularly troubled by the question of whether the life of dialogue was important to everyone or only to the religious.

In Gerson's activity with his Bund these questions were particularly vital, especially in relation to the close circle that he built up within his Bund of those who wanted to break through to real life in community. "I am very important to this circle," he said to Buber. In 1930 he shared with Buber the doubts his circle experienced when confronted by the arguments of the communists and the Halutziuth (pioneer movement). He succeeded in reassuring himself by applying Buber's stress on the importance of the "now and here" to the "harder" task of remaining in Germany and in Europe rather than going to Palestine, and he even cited Buber's Munich speech "How Can Community Come into Being?" as support. He saw as their common central goal the creation of a Jewish milieu in Germany—via a spiritual union with Judaism accomplished through learning. In this connection his group opened in Berlin in 1929 a "School of Jewish Youth" closely similar in goals and methods to the Lehrhaus in Frankfurt. Because of its emphasis on communities of workers, Gerson saw this school both as the concrete starting point for their task and as the beginning of community living.

In the face of such a barrage of important problems, Buber begged Gerson not to be so importunate in asking him questions, the responsible answers to which could be arrived at only after intensive reflection. Gerson confused willingness to answer with the capacity to answer. Buber had not failed to respond to real questions, as he had in general recognized Gerson's to be, but his ability to answer was *presently*—because of physical exhaustion—diminished. Gerson did not imagine with sufficient concreteness the condition of a really overstrained person. "I feel very bitter that for so long I could not speak to and question you," Gerson wrote Buber. "Once for all," responded Buber, "do not ever believe that when I am silent or express myself in brief form that I 'have something against you.' That is never my attitude toward a person to whom I stand in relationship. Should I ever have anything against you in my heart, then I would not allow it to lie there but would say to you directly what was wrong. Please picture to yourself for once in a basic and lasting way that, in spite of a temperament given to moods and caprices, I am a hard worker—with a work day from which I can wrest some 'free time' only through extraordinary efforts and with all kinds of interruptions."

Gerson envisaged for his branch of the Jewish Youth Movement the double task of building a Jewish milieu in Germany and taking on the responsibility of the German socialists for meeting social needs. The first task evoked in his mind the plan of attempting to re-create a center like that of Siegfried Lehmann's Volksheim, only with stronger emphasis on Jewish learning. Buber wrote Gerson (in a letter in which he said he could not address him as *Du*) that he liked very much Gerson's idea of re-creating the Volksheim and thought that it might accomplish at one and the same time both of Gerson's tasks.

Gerson prepared himself for these tasks not only through his immersion in Buber's thought and his active intercourse with the members of his circle but also by studying at both Leo Baeck's Hochschule für die Wissenschaft des Judentum (Advanced School for the Knowledge of Judaism) and the University of Berlin, where he earned his degree in 1931 through a dissertation on the development of the ethical views of Buber's own teacher, the famous sociologist Georg Simmel. The synthesis of non-Zionist Jewish nationalism, non-Orthodox enthusiasm for Judaism, and noncommunist revolutionary socialism, which Gerson combined with Buber's religious socialism, his existentialist religion, and his Hebrew humanism, was "so complex," Grete Schaeder opines, "that it could only find a resonance among the bourgeois intellectuals in Germany." She also holds that in the shelter of his bourgeois existence Buber underestimated both the severity of the economic and political problems following the economic crisis of 1929 and the growing anti-Semitism that brought about the rapid economic decline of the Jewish petite bourgeoisie. In light of the politicization and polarization that followed both in Nazi Germany and in Palestine (in totally dissimilar ways) these explanations of the later history of Gerson's "Circle" can only be seen as tragic half-truths.

Like the Bar Kochbans who had been influenced by Buber's "Speeches on Judaism" a generation before, the Young Jewish "Comrades" asked the existential questions of what it meant to them personally to be Jewish. Although they began as almost assimilated Jews from nonreligious families, their turning toward Judaism was less a "conversion" than a gradual taking on of what could be meaningful to them —learning Hebrew, celebrating the Sabbath, reading the Buber-

Rosenzweig translation of the Bible, learning Jewish history, and identifying themselves with that continuity of the generations that Buber
called destiny. This existential approach by no means implied the
liberal idea of free individualism. They were simultaneously concerned
with the Jewish people and with creating a true Jewish community
based on the spiritual, ethical, and social values of Judaism. Thus they
did not make the nation an end in itself; nor did they accept the 613
mitzvot, or commands of the Jewish law, in any "leap of faith," but, like
Buber himself, faced every religious commandment separately. Like
Buber too, they started from the "national universalism" of the biblical
prophets, the modern parallels to which they found in the same cultural clusters as Buber did—the anarchosocialist ideas of Gustav Landauer and later the religious socialism of Paul Tillich, Leonhard Ragaz,
and Buber himself. They were active in Jewish learning and in social
and political work. Even the average members studied the Bible, Jewish history and sociology, talmudic commentary and legend. "All the
members participated in the Bible courses which were held weekly
within the framework of the Schule der Jüdischen Jugend," reports
Eliyahu Maoz (Ernst Mosbacher), "and also in summer and winter
camps (sometimes under the personal guidance of Buber)." Following
the Buber-Rosenzweig approach, they did not focus on how the text
originated but on what it said.

Like the Zionists in speaking of their German homeland as the Galut
(exile), they nonetheless worked in Jewish social welfare, educational
groups for young Jewish workers, or in the Home for Young Jewish
Unemployed as steps in re-creating a social, national, and spiritual
center of Judaism. Without denying that the fight for social revolution
would claim victims, they rejected, as Buber himself repeatedly did, the
communist doctrine that the end justified the means. They aimed at
a synthesis between Marx and Buber which accepted the Marxian
method as a way of explaining historical, political, and economic facts,
but rejected Marxism as a total ideology or *Weltanschauung.* In all this
they were more concrete and realistic than the other two sections of
Kameraden—those who continued to adhere to the old liberal German-
Jewish ideology, such as that of Hermann Cohen, and those who accepted socialism but rejected Jewishness as anything more than an
accident of origin.

The "Rechenschaft," or accounting, which Gerson wrote for the
periodical of the Kreis in 1930 gives us a still deeper insight into the
unique synthesis between Buber's teachings and the ever new prob-

lems that the Kreis had to contend with. Gerson began by quoting Buber's statement, "The German Youth Movement errs because it imagines that youth is a goal in itself and does not recognize that it should be the instrument of a fulfillment." He continued by spelling out in detail his complaint that the unity and the wholeness of the person had been destroyed in favor of separate spheres, such as the intellectual, the emotional, the physical. The "private" life of the modern person Gerson saw as wholly egocentric, monological, ruining all relationships between persons. One uses the other as a means to one's personal end with the result that there is neither immediacy of human relationships nor any communal life. Gerson called for a new image of the human—a turning to one's fellowman, a rejection of general formulas in favor of taking seriously each unique situation and each unique person. For the same reason he rejected the abstractions of "all or nothing" in favor of the "as much as is possible," the meliorism of Buber's *quantum satis,* which establishes the line of demarcation constantly, according to the specific address and resources to respond to each new situation. The courage to make decisions, the courage radically to realize their highest calling, meant for Gerson the recognition that "the true community is the Sinai of the future," as Buber wrote in *Der heilige Weg.* The Bund that concerned Gerson was a community in which the different generations are united, and not just the youth. The living together of people of various ages can be fruitful beyond our imagination, he declared.

Gerson's total acceptance of Buber's language and thought was accomplished by a determined effort to look, speak, and act like Buber down to the beard, the diction, the pronunciation. At the same time, as Gerson admitted in 1966, he was so concerned with his role as charismatic leader of his circle that he was chary of bringing Buber together with his followers too often lest his own position be in some way threatened. "To be prepared means to prepare," Gerson quoted from one of Buber's first "Three Speeches on Judaism." In the light of the development and radical change of the Werkleute we cannot help wonder whether the thoughts, speech, and mannerisms that Gerson had "made his own" and the *way* in which he had appropriated them had really prepared him for the unforeseeable new situations that he and his circle had to confront.

Under Gerson's leadership, Palestine was explicitly rejected by the Werkleute as the goal of their communal life in favor of transforming "modern civilization" in Germany. "For us who are concerned about a new, nontheological, reality-true form of religion," said Gerson, "what matters is to authenticate it in that difficult modern situation which is the destiny of modern man and will probably remain so."

Buber rejected the comparison that Gerson made between the Werkleute and Hasidism. For "only a total life-structure can be compared with Hasidism, one therefore which embraces all spheres of life insofar as it can be codetermined by the person and the whole of life until its end. A youth movement of your kind is barred from doing that by its very nature; it can only do it first in some 'beyond'—which until now none has done. You feel yourself, in fact, that what is essential is not those few golden hours that we snatch from the rest of life but our work in the world outside. You say it in your letter to your comrades —but, I feel not yet sharply and decisively enough."

The Werkleute movement made very great demands on its members, including trying to influence their choice of professions. They advocated the "social" professions, such as teaching, social work, and medicine, and downgraded business and merchandising. By doing so they created an atmosphere of intellectual and spiritual activity that made the members feel that they were taking part in very important work. But they were not adhering to Buber's understanding of the life of dialogue, as he put it forth in "Dialogue," where he spoke of the possibility of a dialogue between the factory worker and his machine and between the employer and the worker who came before him as a person with a problem. When Gerson wrote Buber that a traveling salesman cannot progress in personal renewal, Buber replied: "The question of vocation is a hard nut to crack—but I cannot accept the idea that any vocation is so God-forsaken that it cannot be made meaningful, no matter how difficult that is in certain border cases."

Aside from the Halutziuth, whose older members went to Palestine as pioneers, the Werkleute was the only group which succeeded not only in maintaining the activity of its older members but even in increasing it. In the winter months of 1930–1931 Gerson sought to attack the problem of the continuation of the Werkleute through the formation within the mediating leaders of a "Core" that was closely and personally bound to him. Since this inner group represented no structure that had grown organically from the mediating leaders themselves, the "Core" could last only a short time. In November 1931, Gerson complained to Buber, "openly as your disciple," that he had noticed "with a feeling of extraordinary bitterness that the young people known to me, especially the Bund youths (naturally outside of our Circle) know so little of you." He added that he hoped this did not sound like a demand that people follow Buber, which, of course, it did. Gerson, like Buber, was much concerned about how strongly the young people had been politicized so that they substituted political Jewish ideas for an enduring "Hebrew Humanism," in Buber's phrase. "It is not pleasant to live in Berlin now," Gerson wrote in the first indication of the oppressive fate that so soon came upon them. "One feels the Nazi revolt so near—and can have so little hope for a socialist revolution."

At Pentecost the ideological development of Gerson's Kreis, which had brought it into ever greater conflict with the two other sections of *Kameraden,* led to a formal split into the communist scout movement Schwarzes Fähnlein, the German nationalist "front troops," and the majority of *Kameraden* in the center—members of the Kreis and some others who together formed the Werkleute under Gerson's leadership. The three elements that characterized the Werkleute were: a religiously based social concern, commitment to the Jewish people in exile, and revolutionary socialism. Noting that community is more than mere comradeship and that the social and the Jewish questions are allied, Gerson nonetheless stressed that what was most important was not what they had in common or any world view but the life of dialogue in which individuals and groups persevered. From this he reached the remarkable conclusion that their fight could be fought only there, in Europe, and not in Palestine. "This is our life-ground: to seek with our lives whether there is not room here for all that gives life meaning."

Buber, in his response to Gerson's letter, said he did not see why the Palestine question had to be solved in terms of general principles. The solution would be easier if it were approached practically. Those who were suitable for Palestine and for whom Palestine was suited should be guided in that direction. In such a case making a new connection was more important than the tearing apart of old ones. "I am in general against principles," wrote Buber, "which only too easily violate the personal posing of the problem. . . . We do not need 'community'—that is nothing—but a community *out of persons,* and this can very well arise out of a decision to renounce but not out of renouncing decision. Genuine decisions like a ploughshare turn up the soil of individuality so that it becomes fruitful."

In a letter of September 1932, Buber wrote Gerson that in his opinion Gerson was too preoccupied with the conscious task of "being-in-the-world" and serving God, instead of just being in the world spontaneously and serving God as he happened to at any given time. "You are still too much of a 'billiard player' and too little a 'tennis player.' I know exactly how that is; for at your age (aside from the fact that I was more light-hearted than you), it was just the same with me." In the same letter Buber spoke of Gerson's forthcoming marriage: "Naturally one does not know when one 'marries' whether one 'will remain ready to involve his existence where necessary.' But what is important is precisely that one does *not* know; that one remains uncertain, that when one moves to meet someone one has to withstand the test in its *whole* burden, unmitigated by any simplified life-style. To remain truly insecure is to remain insecure in the face of this test." In a remarkable anticipation of the blessing that Elijah was to give to Elisha in Buber's "mystery play" of a quarter of a century later, Buber wished that Gerson and his fiancée "experience the true blessing of life, that which comes out of contradiction."

Looking back on his relationship with Buber during those early years, Gerson wrote much later:

> He was a master of conversation—and each conversation with him reached its high point when his partner in conversation shared with him the central problems which beset him in the intellectual, political, or personal sphere. When I got to know him in 1927, he had already made it a rule to answer personally every letter that he received; and when he accepted a young person as his personal disciple, then he shared in all that person's joys and sorrows. This great capacity to listen, to conduct a dialogue with individuals and with historical happenings—this rare capacity is that which determined Buber's person and made every conversation with him into a life-experience in which clarification, deepening, and encouragement wonderfully united.

It was at Gerson's request that Buber in 1932 wrote his essay "Why Study Jewish Sources?" for the syllabus of the School of Jewish Youth that Gerson directed in Berlin along with Moritz Spitzer. It was in the spirit of this essay that Gerson wrote a circular letter to his Circle on April 15, 1933, recognizing that the place of realization may change —more specifically that the task of the Werkleute now lay in Palestine and not Germany—but that the work on the Bible and Jewish history should not be forsaken in favor of swelling the ranks of the already numerous party Jews who had no historical vision. "One of our tasks in each place—also and especially in Palestine—is for us to concern ourselves with a Jewish existence that forms part of the chain of spiritual tradition. We can hope for a real Jewish productivity only out of this link with former generations." The Werkleute's identification with German culture, Eliyahu Maoz has pointed out, was based upon a selection of those aspects which represented the German contribution to European culture in general. With the rise to power of the Nazis in 1933 and the anti-Jewish boycott and restrictions that went into effect in April 1933, the foundation for their identification with German culture was swept away and with it all their vacillations about their relationship to the Halutzim. In April 1933 the decision to establish a Werkleute-Kibbutz in Palestine was unanimous. Although in his circular letter of April 1933 Gerson wrote at length of the innumerable tasks and difficulties and the social, pedagogical, cultural, and political problems that lay ahead of them, the radical changes that in fact awaited them far outstripped his imagination and that of the other members of the Werkleute. Gerson became a Moses who entered the Promised Land but no longer as Moses. His charismatic leadership ended in a tragic way that he could not have anticipated.

PART II

Nazi Germany

(1933-1938)

CHAPTER 9

The Hour and Its Judgment

"OF ALL THE JEWS IN EUROPE," writes Nora Levin, "the dazed and bewildered Jews of Germany were most unprepared for the fate that was to engulf them." When the state abruptly prohibited them from describing themselves as "members of the German Folk," the shock "deprived them of the moral and cultural essence of their life." Shortly after the Nazis took power, they declared a Boycott Day on April 1, 1933, against the buying of goods from any Jewish store. At Buber's house too there appeared an S.A. man (a member of the Storm Troops that helped bring Hitler to power) who lifted his hand in a Nazi salute and announced to Buber that a boycott march would take place in front of his house. Buber observed mildly that he probably could not change anything, but the S.A. man turned to him with a question: "Herr Professor, we have different signs: 'Jewish Business,' 'Jewish Law Office,' 'Jewish Doctor,' but none of these fit you. What sort of sign shall we put in your window?" At this Buber observed laconically that the choice must be left to the S.A. officer; for he himself had no label.

The S.A. man looked about critically at Buber's study and observed the impressive library that lined the walls. Finally, an illumination came to him. "I have it," he announced happily, and drew from his briefcase a sign, "Jewish Bookdealer." "We shall put that in the window," he decided, and that is what happened.

The German Jews still hoped that this was only a transitory phase that would soon pass. The Jewish community of Berlin cabled the Chief Rabbi of Britain urging that all "acts of propaganda and boycott" be stopped, for fear that such "false news" would create difficulties and "tarnish the reputation" of what they still insisted on considering their "fatherland." The very violence and extremism of Nazi anti-Jewish propaganda confirmed some in their illusions because such barbarism strained their credulity.

When Martin was thirty-eight years old and Paula thirty-nine, they had moved from Berlin to Heppenheim, a charming, flower-mantled village in the Bergstrasse wine-growing region south of Darmstadt. There they lived for twenty years in a three-story gray house at Werlestrasse 2, a quiet corner in a residential neighborhood. During those years Buber appeared to his neighbors as an unusually shy man who spoke seldom, someone out of whose way even children stayed, as though they were afraid of him. He always wore a long black beard and a black hat that sat on his head "like a duckpond." Buber could be seen nightly through a big window of his house, sitting up very late, his head framed by both hands, deeply engrossed in his books. Paula Buber described him in those days as someone who was so absorbed in his work that people mistakenly thought him unaware of what was going on around him. But those who really knew him, as she did, knew that he was always fully aware of and very much concerned with the events of the household, the city, the country, and the world. What appeared to strangers as absent-mindedness was really an extraordinary capacity for the most intense concentration.

Paula Buber described what the Nazi takeover in Heppenheim was like in her novel *Storm of Gnats: A Year in the Life of a Small City,* written after their emigration to Palestine and published only in 1951. The ironic though compassionate point of view with which the myriad peccadilloes and absurdities of Heppenheim are described in this novel is not too different from Buber's own attitude. Buber never discussed politics but once admitted to the parents of a schoolmate of his son Rafael that he did not hate the Nazis, but merely scorned them.

Hedwig Straub, the Buber maid from 1930 to 1936, recalls that in 1933 Albert Einstein was a regular visitor at the Buber house, as was the mayor of Jerusalem, and that they were always discussing the possibilities of emigration, which, when it happened, took Einstein to America and Buber to Palestine. Only in 1952, three years before Einstein's death, did the two friends meet again.

During the Second Reich many German professors had blindly supported the expansionist aims of the government and had made their lecture halls breeding grounds of virulent nationalism and anti-Semitism. The very insistence of the Weimar Republic on complete academic freedom had been used by these professors to undermine the democratic regime. A great many professors were fanatical nationalists who wished the return of monarchical Germany, and by 1932 the majority of university students appeared to be Hitler enthusiasts. After 1933 the vast majority of university faculties knuckled under to the Nazification of higher learning. Although one-fourth of them had been dismissed by the Nazis for being Jews, liberals, or communists, the number of those who lost their posts through defying National Socialism was exceedingly small. In the autumn of 1933, the very time when Buber was ousted from his position at the University of Frankfurt, such luminaries as Professor Ernst Ferdinand Sauerbruch, the surgeon; Martin Heidegger, the existentialist philosopher; and Wilhelm Pinder, the art historian, took a public vow to support Hitler and the National Socialist regime. When Heidegger came to lecture at Heidelberg, the faculty, assembled on the stage, had agreed in advance to get up and leave as soon as he got up to speak. When Heidegger arose, one young professor, Arnold Bergstraesser, stood up, but no one else did. Then he in turn sat down while Heidegger subjected the professors who had not yet turned Nazi to a tongue-lashing such as had never before taken place in a German university!

In October 1933, Buber resigned his professorship and did not wait for the official dismissal. He received many expressions of sympathy from German professors. Buber remained in Heppenheim in connection with the intellectual world that had fallen into consternation and confusion. His house became a kind of shrine for Jews and Christians seeking advice and help. Scholars and spiritual personalities of Germany, who had formerly stood in academic or even friendly relations with Buber, sought to justify themselves to him when they joined this or that form of the National Socialist movement. In the first years many

"Aryans" showed their defiance by visiting Buber and expressed in person or in letters, sometimes intentionally on open postcards, their misgivings about what was happening in Germany.

The Nazi search of the Buber home in Heppenheim in March 1933 was actually quite uneventful. As Buber himself said, the respect for books and authority of the ordinary German prevented their resorting to any violence—in the face of a library of 20,000 books. What happened was simply that two young boys in brown uniform appeared unannounced before him to conduct a search of the house without knowing what to look for. Buber was suspect as a famous Jew. They dimly sensed that his spiritual resistance represented a danger for their "new order" without knowing what form that danger might take. When they came on Buber, he was sitting at his desk working at the translation of the Bible. The one in charge demanded, "What are you doing here?" "I am translating the Bible," Buber answered. The brown-clad man looked mistrustfully at the long sheets of paper covered with Buber's clear, beautiful handwriting and observed skeptically that that was much too long for the Bible. It was the Talmud. Buber denied this and pointed to the already printed volumes of his translation. This in no way convinced the literal-minded S.A. man. "The Bible," he said, "is only just *one* book that one receives at confirmation." Finally Buber proposed that the Protestant pastor be fetched as an "expert" on the matter. The latter testified that this really was the Old Testament. Since he appeared credible in the eyes of the S.A. officer, the house search ended there.

The ravages and brutality of the *Kristallnacht* in November 1938 left such an impression on the mind of the Heppenheimers that even a close friend of Rafael's reported years later that while he stood outside in the Buber garden a gang of Nazi rowdies, led by Wilhelm Koch, the local party chief, hurled stones at the house and finally broke into it. "Tossing books left and right, Koch finally came across the picture of the naked Venus de Milo. 'So, Pig,' snarled Koch, 'that's the kind of bastard you are!' struck Buber over the head with the book and stormed out"—evidence so detailed that we could not help believing it if we did not know that Buber had left Germany six months before November 1938, when *Kristallnacht* occurred. It may, indeed, have been an unconscious telescoping of the earlier search about which Leonhard Rettig knew, and the later events that marked the real heightening of the Nazi terror. What actually happened was that the Nazis destroyed all the furniture in the house in Heppenheim, which still belonged to Buber, and the three thousand volumes that still remained in his library, and then sent him a bill demanding that he pay them 27,000 marks! By this time the respect for books was no longer in evidence.

One of the most ironic touches of the Nazi accession to power, equaled only by Rosenberg's quoting Buber's *Speeches on Judaism* at the Nuremberg trials because of Buber's emphasis on the importance of "blood" for the people, was the fact recorded by Agnon that Goebbels, Hitler's propaganda minister and, along with Goering, number two man, praised Hitler as a *Künder,* or Proclaimer, the special German translation of the Hebrew *nabi,* or prophet, that Buber and Rosenzweig used in their Bible translation. A colleague of Buber's at the University of Frankfurt was Ernst Krieck. Buber himself described Krieck, after he turned Nazi, as having too much sense of responsibility for the Nazis to appoint him as the Minister of Culture of Prussia, even though he was the only man whom they might seriously have considered. In a periodical edited by him, Krieck published an anti-Semitic essay on "the Jewish God." Buber offered him through a third party a statement clarifying only those things which were factually incorrect. Krieck replied to this third party that he had great respect for Buber, but that the latter was still too naïve. He did not understand at all that this was a *political* journal!

In a letter of February 1933 to Ernst Simon, who now lived in Jerusalem, Buber showed himself to be not at all a prophet in the popular sense of that term. He wrote Simon that he did not anticipate a change of power in favor of the Nazis and that only if that were to be the case was a real persecution of the Jews and the passage of anti-Jewish laws to be anticipated. Nor was he any more realistic than his fellow German Jews when in a letter of March 28, 1933, he wrote Simon that the Nazis' search of his house had been carried out in a thoroughly correct and uneventful fashion, "as was not otherwise possible," and lamented the distortions in the foreign press, especially the American. On April 2, the day after the beginning of the boycott, Nikolaus Ehlen, an influential Catholic layman and founder of the Catholic "Greater German Youth," communicated to Buber how much they were thinking of him "in these days." "As living Christians and especially as Catholics and also as born but also baptized Germans, we can do no less! No, we must do it if we do not want to betray Jesus." On April 10, Emil Brunner wrote to Buber from Switzerland that he had thought of him every day during those weeks. He would have written earlier, he added, had he not feared to embarrass him by so doing. "God has richly blessed your work until now. In these bitter times too he will not desert you. Your people have always had to find God 'in the depths.' " Though Brunner had a Christian interpretation of the songs of the suffering servant in Deutero-Isaiah, he confirmed Buber's Jewish interpretation as well. "The time of wandering in the desert that has now begun for you can also be a time of great revelation. God grant it," concluded Brunner and signed, "Deeply bound with you in faithfulness and love."

It was Nahum Glatzer who in a letter to Buber from London of April 27, 1933, spoke the truly prophetic and pathetic words of the situation of the Jew in Germany. Dismissed by the Nazis from his position at the University of Frankfurt, as Buber had not yet been, Glatzer foresaw, since he thought ghettos no longer possible, not the confinement of the Jews but their destruction. "They want to exclude us entirely, but we cannot exclude them? Can we bear this cleavage? Can we live in the midst of so much enmity? Must not each, in any way he can, escape?" He would have remained with the community as long as there was one, were it not for his pregnant wife. But he wisely saw that if he were to leave it would have to be now. "Do you believe that I shall ever again find a foothold?" he wrote Buber. "It torments me that I do not know whether I am right."

"If your wife is expecting a baby, no one can responsibly advise you to return," Buber responded. "But the question of how much can be borne can only be tested practically," he added. "For my part I shall now seek whether I can bring something about for the community." Buber was not dismissed, but he had a letter from the rector of the university warning him against giving his lectures and seminars in the summer semester of 1933, which also meant that there would be no publicity surrounding it, unlike the dismissal of Glatzer and others that was reported in the *London Times.* "I do not believe that I shall still lecture in Frankfurt," Buber concluded.

Max Picard, a historian and philosopher of art and culture, wrote Buber from Sorengo in May 1933 of a conversation that he had had with Karl Wolfskehl, the distinguished poet and writer from the circle of Stefan George. "It is a shame," Picard said to Wolfskehl, "that George, who preaches the heroic, does not find a word to say against what is happening today." "George has always concerned himself about the eternal things," answered Wolfskehl. Picard responded by asking whether it was not a matter of eternity when one attacked the

Jews, the people of God, and whether this moment is not the moment of eternity. "I am ashamed," Picard wrote Buber, "that I sit here and am not attacked with them."

In April 1933, Buber wrote the first of his great responses to the "judgment" of the hour, "The Jewish Person of Today." "The Jewish man of today is the inwardly most exposed person in our world," Buber declared. "The tensions of the ages have selected this point in order to measure their strength on it. They want to know whether man can still withstand them and they test themselves on the Jews. . . . They want to learn through his destiny what man is." Split into two, a fallen part and an unconquerable one, the Jew knows that the unconquerable covers, shields, and endures for the fallen.

But the most famous of Buber's responses to the situation, the essay "The Children" published in May in Robert Weltsch's *Jüdische Rundschau,* did not take a heroic stance but rather portrayed the full pathos of the situation.

> The children experience what happens and keep silent, but in the night they groan in their dreams, awaken, and stare into the darkness. The world has become unreliable. A child had a friend; the friend was as taken for granted as the sunlight. Now the friend suddenly looks at him strangely, the corners of his mouth mock him: Surely you didn't imagine that I really cared about you?
>
> A child had a teacher, a certain one among all the others. He knew that this person existed, so everything was all right. Now the teacher no longer has a voice when he speaks to him. In the courtyard the space that leads to him is no longer open.

The world's familiar smile has turned into a grimace, and there is no one to whom the child can tell his anxiety, no one he can ask why everything is the way it is. The child's rage can find no outlet but smolders inside and turns into *ressentiment.* "This is how a child becomes bad." The judgment of the hour is not only that against the Nazis but also that against Israel.

> . . . "Israel" means to practice community for the sake of a common covenant in which our existence is founded; to practice in actual living the community between being and being, person and person, toward which end creation was created. And today this means to preserve directness in a world which is becoming more and more indirect, in the face of the self-righteousness of collectivities to preserve the mystery of relationship, without which a people must perish in an icy death.

But have we not started out ourselves on the road toward becoming a self-righteous collectivity?

The contrast that I make in *Touchstones of Reality* between the "community of affinity," or like-mindedness, and the "community of otherness" is clearly at the heart of Buber's distinction between Israel as a "self-righteous collectivity" and Israel as a people open to the covenantal task of building community with other peoples. Even though externally it had "been impeded or thwarted in a thousand ways," Buber still demanded of Israel that it practice community and directness, "standing by the members of the German nation in unbroken personal integrity, without reservation and free of animosity, wherever we encounter them, in such a way that we are able to see each other and recognize one another." Cruelly difficult though it is, "human openness is a dire need."

In May 1933, Buber's old friend Gustav Lindemann wrote him on the occasion of the dismissal of Ludwig Strauss, the husband of Buber's daughter Eva, from his university post. "The National Movement has no room for my work on 'grounds of race,'" Lindemann reported to Buber, "although with Louise I worked on the foundation of the German theater for almost thirty years." Hans Johst, the president of the Reich's Chamber of Writing, appropriated for the Nazis the playhouse that Lindemann and the actress Louise Dumont had led by calling it *"Germany's* work in Düsseldorf." By the same token, only a non-Jewish supporter who was ready to see the theater conform to the "spirit of the times" would be allowed to reopen it. "I can no longer sing my song; my throat is stopped up," lamented Lindemann. "Today I can say that God was gracious to Louise in taking her to himself a year ago."

What was to happen to great numbers in the 1950s and early 1960s took place—although, unfortunately, to a much lesser degree—even at the time of the Nazis: Buber's person was a call to the Christian conscience, even of those whom he did not know. At the end of May 1933, the German pastor and superintendent Joachim Ungnad wrote Buber thanking him for all that he had read of his, particularly his translation of the Psalms and the Prophets, and expressing to him how much he too suffered "from all the frightful injustices that you and your people and fellowbelievers have experienced in this time of persecution. In God's hand everything becomes a blessing! My wish is that God lets you experience all this as such in this difficult time."

However naïve Buber may have been about the Nazis in February he more than made up for in June. "Things do not look so good in Germany," he wrote Hans Trüb. He doubted whether he could complete his work there: "The atmosphere has a constricting destructive effect on one's soul." Yet Buber's need to work was greater than ever: "I have begun to bring in the harvest of a great piece of my life." Despite all that was taking place, Buber did not falter in his own work during the five years that he still remained in Germany. This is all the more remarkable because in the course of the year that followed he took up an enormously demanding task of Jewish education that occupied him until his departure from Germany.

Neither did Buber falter in his prophetic task of speaking to the German Jewish community in its time of crisis. In the summer of 1933, he wrote a "theological note" titled "In the Midst of History" in which he unmistakably referred to Hitler as the man who arrived at power because he had no inhibitions about doing away with fellow-creatures. Resuming his preoccupation with the Servant and the hidden history, Buber declared that "whether a person is powerful or powerless makes no difference in the role he plays in the dialogue of history." Viewed from its secret depths, history is a dialogue between the Deity and mankind in which often the person who does not succeed is the one who has been faithful to the dialogue, and, as Buber said of Davis Trietsch after his public shaming by Herzl, secretly confirmed. The arrows God leaves in his quiver are in no way inferior to those he shoots; for the Divine Presence wanders throughout history in exile and bears the suffering of all the suffering servants. God is not only all-powerful but also all-suffering. He is "nigh unto those who are of a broken heart." From this standpoint, history can be understood only when we are the ones addressed and to the degree that we make ourselves receptive. We are flatly denied the possibility of making an objective judgment concerning history's meaning, but we are permitted to know history's challenge to and claim on us. This is not a "subjective" meaning but one that can be caught only with one's personal life.

"How could I venture," Buber quoted the great Hasidic *rebbe* Levi Yitzhak of Berditchev, "to ask you why everything happens as it does, why we are driven from one exile to another, why our enemies are allowed to torture us!" Like Buber in his rejection of *gnosis*, Levi Yitzhak said he did not want to know the secrets of God's ways—he could not endure them. "But I beg you to show me what this, which is happening at this moment, means to me, what it demands of me, what you, Lord of the world, are telling me by way of it." Here we can understand clearly Buber's approach to "The Hour and Its Judgment." At no time did he see the Nazi persecution of the Jews as a just punishment brought upon Israel for its sins. Yet he did not fail to ask what meaning even these absurd and horrible events might have for *all* Jews in the world today. He did not "justify" history as the will of God, but he brought it into the dialogue with God. So that he too could cry out with Levi Yitzhak, "Ah, I do not long to know why I suffer, but only that I suffer for thy sake!"

It is in the same spirit that Buber approached the Jewish New Year's Day in September 1933, the first since the Emancipation which German Jewry experienced under great duress. Of all the festivals of all the peoples, only this holiday represents the exalted and awesome truth that all the forms of the world again and again approach renewal, but in the shape of judgment. The renewal of the soul standing in judgment is its turning, its *teshuvah.* The decision whether the world will endure depends upon the turning. The "judgment" that Buber perceived for German Jewry in that hour of crisis was that everyone perceived his own need *and* that of those close to him. "But who of us suffers the need of the Jewish people as a whole whose very existence is being put to the test through the destruction of that symbiosis with the German people which has been, up till now, confirmed through life and work? Which of us takes on himself the burden of the problematic situation that suddenly towers monstrously above us? Who recognizes his own guilt in all this and turns from it . . . in such a way that through him the turning of the whole people takes place? . . . Who preserves German Jewry in its hour of judgment, who stakes himself so that it will be renewed?"

Buber's old friend, the educator Elisabeth Rotten, wrote Buber on the last day of 1933 of how much she wished that she could economically afford to ask him whether she, a lifelong passionate philo-Semitic German Quaker, might not give free courses at the Frankfurt Lehrhaus which Buber was then reopening. "In the past," she confessed, "I proceeded from the problems, needs, and realities of the present and drew attention to the 'imperishability' of the past in order to show how slowly ideas take root and bear fruit, and nonetheless the significant persons of all ages and peoples reach out their hands to one another. Now I have withdrawn wholly into history." Her greatest comfort, she concluded, was that all of her disciples knew exactly where she stood.

In a January 1934 address to the Frankfurt Lehrhaus on "The Jew in the World," Buber characterized the Jew as the insecure person pure and simple. Such partial security as other peoples have enjoyed he has been deprived of. Living on ground that may at any moment give way beneath its feet, the Jewish people has experienced every symbiotic relationship as treacherous, every alliance or union as temporary. This is why the Jewish Diaspora is characterized by Jews as the *galut*, or exile. This wandering, forsaken community has had for the peoples in whose midst it has lived something ghostlike about it, something uncanny *(unheimlich)*, homeless *(heimlos)*, that cannot be assimilated into the majority culture. The Jews were always the first victims of fanatical mass movements, such as the Crusades of the eleventh century, and were blamed for mass misfortunes, such as the "Black Death." Even when they tried to adjust to their environment, like the Marranos who converted to Christianity in Spain and remained secretly Jewish, that adjustment failed, and the Inquisition followed upon Marranism. Only in being faithful to the prophetic call to realize community can the Jewish people attain its own unique security, asserted Buber.

Buber was not only concerned with the Nazi threat to the Jewish people but also with its threat to Christianity. In 1934, when Buber attended the Eranos Conference at Ascona, Switzerland, centering on the analytical psychologist C. G. Jung, he found himself compelled to respond publicly to the vicious attacks on Christianity by a number of Nazis who were present. "It is not usually my role to defend Christianity," said Buber as he rose to his feet, "but in this case I must do so." The Nazi ideologist Professor Erich Karl Hermann Hauer, who also attended the Ascona Conference, felt a strong affinity with Buber and wanted to establish a connection with Mussolini, in whom he expected to find resonance and understanding for Buber's thought. Buber was, in fact, invited to give some lectures in Italy in 1936, but he did not want to enter that Fascist country even though it had not yet fallen under the Nazi hegemony and become anti-Semitic.

In January 1934, Buber received a remarkable letter from a Protestant woman who, largely under Buber's influence and just because of the Nazis, wanted to convert to Judaism. This woman, Elisabeth M., although not Jewish, felt herself closer to Judaism than "unfortunately most present-day Jews." Another remarkable letter from a non-Jew was that which Margret Boveri sent to Buber in March of 1934. She could not agree with Buber in his assumption that the non-Jews could not understand the position of the Jews. "For it seems to me there is more community in human beings than can be destroyed by the one-sided 'thousand-year politics' of the Nazis and their deep-rooted inheritance of prejudice." Thanking Buber for his book *Kampf um Israel* (Fight for Israel—1932), she concluded her long letter to Buber, who was to her *the* representative of the Jews, by describing to him what she had been suffering and contemplating all this time "in order to fill in a little the deep chasm" that the Nazis had attempted to carve out between her and him.

The well-known German novelist, writer, and pastor Albrecht Goes later described this period in Nazi Germany as one when any person in responsibility was assailed by the dilemma of speaking untruthfully or keeping silent untruthfully, at a time when much of life that had seemed dependable proved unreliable and many advisers had no advice to give. At that time Buber's books—*Dialogue, I and Thou*— "were as important to us as bread." "At that time we encountered a word such as that from the Hasidic wisdom, 'There is nothing more whole than a broken heart,' as confidence against all illusion, hope where there was nothing to hope, a way among the brambles." At that time, too, witnessed Goes, "it counted for not little that the man who wrote these words was still among us, that his lamp burned at night in Heppenheim on the Bergstrasse."

In August 1934, after a long and passionate discussion about unlimited responsibility, Goes lay awake at night and suddenly saw Buber tied to this conversation. He heard again the words that Buber wrote on responsibility at the end of "My Way to Hasidism," "words that are as close to me as Genesis or 1st Corinthians 13 or Goethe's 'Urwort Orphisch' "—Buber's description of the true *zaddik* as the person who does not turn away from but withstands the enormously threatening, thousandfold questioning glance of individual lives, "the person who hourly measures the depths of responsibility with the sounding-lead of his words." Goes found it a great comfort to hear those words anew in his solitude, to sense, alongside the quiet breath of his sleeping wife, another breath in the room—"the breath of the responsible world, your world." "Our life is a stone thrown into the water, out of which circles of activity and responsibility arise." But these circles come up against walls and banks that want nothing of their influence, that reject this responsibility with brutal determination. What can be our attitude in the face of this passivity or activity? "I ask you, as a very young man who cannot truly find himself in this age of alienation," whether I should wish to be "a doctor to the incurable." "Do I have as a man and a pastor a mission to the brutal teacher, to the slippery but 'correct' steward of an estate whom no word can reach, to the mysterious prisoner who will not admit an iota of guilt, to the honest master craftsman who commits arson, to the unshakably secure adulterer? And these are only the concrete cases of this week." "I do not complain, I only ask," Goes concluded. Buber replied with a postcard suggesting the need of personal talk between them (a meeting which did not, in fact, take place until nineteen years later) and then quoted from the conclusion to his 1919 essay, "What Is to Be Done?": "You shall not withhold yourself" (Deuteronomy 22:3).

When we find ourselves unexpectedly in a situation in which the foundations of our existence are called in question, we must ask ourselves what forces are at our command, said Buber in the spring of 1935. This wholly unapologetic self-examination is meant for our ears alone, even though it be overheard by a world that is no longer open to our address. "But does it become us to practice self-criticism on the open-market where we are ringed round by a loud criticism that contests our right to existence and denies our worth and our values? Yes, it becomes us." Not self-justifications but the calm, untroubled knowing about faithfulness and unfaithfulness in our own life sets itself against the accusation.

In March 1935, Ernst Michel wrote Buber expressing his regret that Buber had to give up his lectures at the Lehrhaus because of a Nazi prohibition issued on February 21. "I was saddened but not surprised," Michel added, and expressed hope that Buber would use the leftovers from these lectures for his work among them. Michel told Buber that he had written down, edited, and was having typed his notes on Buber's lectures on "Judaism and Christianity." (Buber told me that Michel's notes greatly facilitated his writing of *Two Types of Faith* sixteen years later.) Michel also informed Buber that he had mailed him a copy of a paper, "Genuine Overcoming of Liberalism," "that no one here dares to print." "The sphere of activity in Catholic circles is ever narrower," Michel added, describing himself as one who made no secret of moving ever further from Christology and sacramentalism. "I feel myself more and more a sectarian without wanting to give up my native ground."

In July 1935, Buber informed Hans Trüb that he had to abandon his plan to give a second lecture for the Eranos Conference at Ascona. "I am more exposed than before, and I have been advised, at any rate until the prohibition against lecturing is lifted (a new attempt has been made by the Zionist organization which is not entirely hopeless), not to come forward even abroad, even in so neutral a setting." "I have a great longing to talk with you," Buber added. "The last months have been very difficult for me and I must 'include a new element.'" Just over a week later, Buber wrote Trüb that he could resume his teaching activity (in the Lehrhaus, of course, and not in the university) but not lecturing and giving papers, even abroad.

In 1936 Schocken Verlag published in its "Library of Little Books" a selection of twenty-three psalms in the original Hebrew with Buber's translation. In his Foreword to this selection, which he titled "Out of the Depths I Call unto Thee," Buber seemingly dealt with the psalms but actually, existentially, spoke to the great need of his time. There is no sharp line to be drawn, he asserted, between the psalms of personal need and those expressing the hope for rescue of the community. The words of the personal complaint are themselves an offering to God. The Psalmist awaits the renewed speech of the God who seems to have forsaken him. Again and again the Psalmist cries out, "How long, O Lord, how long?" Yet the Psalmist does not cease to hope for the "return" of liberation and in the middle of despair sees in a waking dream a "newly created people" arising on a newly built Zion. It is indeed difficult to live as a stranger among the "haters of peace"; yet the work of suffering appears as a planting: "He who sows in tears shall reap in joy." The psalms are the *vox humana*. At every age in which there is no longer "faithfulness amongst the children of Adam," they speak to us anew of our human weakness and of our human strength. In conversation with Schalom Ben-Chorin in 1956, Buber said: "The time of Hitler was the most terrible that I have lived through, but even in that time there was a holy meaning in history, there was God . . . only I cannot say how and where."

In early October 1936, Buber reported to Trüb the unexpected cancellation of his passport, and by the end of October this vexation continued, despite his hope for a speedy restitution. In December 1936, Buber turned to Hermann Hesse for advice as to a Swiss publisher who might publish a new novel by his wife Paula. She had been excluded from the Reich's Chamber of Writers because of her "Jewish marriage." At this time Buber was obliged to take a two-week trip to Lvov, in Poland, because his late father's estate was threatened with forced parceling.

In the midst of these increasingly vexatious problems, Buber did not cease to speak to the Jewish community concerning the self-knowledge that the crisis might bring to it. In 1937 in Prague he addressed himself in particular to "The Prejudices of Youth." The crisis in the community can be overcome only through personal responsibility, he stated. Yet young, as well as old, evade this demand for steadfastness, escaping into membership in a "collective" for which one needs decide only once and which, from that moment on, relieves one of all further worry and responsibility. *True* membership in a group, in contrast, can be the most serious and constant test of responsibility. While belonging to the group with passionately active and fierce love, the individual must refuse to let any group slogan interfere with standing up for what is right and rejecting unworthy and inadequate means to the group's goals. One must pledge the whole of one's responsible personality in a courageous demand for true realization and fight against false interpretations and applications of the just demand of one's group. That these words, so like what Buber published in 1936 in "The Question to the Single One," are not directed to the Nazi totalitarian state alone is shown by the fact that he spoke them in Prague to Jewish youth. The rise of one collective always carries with it the threat of a counter collective, as Buber recognized five years before the Nazis in his essay on "Dialogue":

> Bundled together, men march without *Thou* and without *I*, those of the left who want to abolish memory, and those of the right who want to regulate it: hostile and separated hosts, they march into the common abyss.

An inkling of the toll which living in Nazi Germany took on Buber's spirit is given us by a letter of January 1937 to Hermann Gerson, who was now settled in a kibbutz in Israel. "I can well imagine," Buber wrote, "that now in this difficult time of your life you had expected more support from me and rightly so. The worst of it is that it has also been for me a difficult time, perhaps the most difficult (if not the most violent) of my entire previous life, a time of heavy threat to soul, spirit and survival. If not needing any earthly help (for there is no help *for that*), I have been still less able to help, less able to *be* there than at any time during the past twenty years." Someday, if he could write it down, Gerson would understand. Unfortunately, Buber never did, and we too must content ourselves "with this communication from heart to heart."

Looking back on "The End of the German-Jewish Symbiosis" in January 1939, after he had already immigrated to Israel, Buber described the co-working of the two peoples as an existential synthesis in the depths terminated through an intervention of the "host state" which in its "machinelike thoroughness" and "calculated frenzy" "appears quite strange in the history of Western man in the twentieth century of the Christian era." Buber described the symbiosis of the German and Jewish spirit, "as I experienced it in the four decades I spent in Germany," as the first and only one since the Golden Age of the Jews in Spain that had been *fruitful.* This was a fruitfulness found in every area of German existence. It was evidenced not only by individual accomplishment but also by such phenomena as the transformation of Stefan George's poetry by his Jewish disciples into a historical and cultural phenomenon. It was also evidenced by the application of the ideas of the Jewish thinker Edmund Husserl by Heidegger and others of his German disciples to the methodological foundations of various branches of knowledge. "I myself have, in intellectual association with Germans of prominence, experienced again and again how out of the depths common ground was unexpectedly ploughed up and became shared words and symbols." The end of this symbiosis means a deeper rupture in the German spirit than can be imagined today, Buber claimed. In this connection, Buber cited Paul Tillich's statement a year before the rupture that "The Jewish principle"—the prophetic principle of the intellect—"has become our own fate and a 'secessio judaica' would be separation from our own selves." If the continuity of development in German intellectual life is ever resumed, Buber said, "it will of necessity reestablish its ties with those values which supported the symbiosis, and with those works which resulted from it. But the symbiosis itself is terminated and cannot return," although the German Jews, who escaped from German soil onto Jewish ground, "bring to us something of that noble element of the German soul which is being denied and stifled by their tormentors."

This generosity to the nobility of the German soul meant no sentimentality on Buber's part about the demonry of the Nazis.

On November 26, 1938, Gandhi published a statement in his paper, the *Harijan,* in which he suggested that the Jews in Germany use *satyagraha,* or soul-force, as the most effective reply to Nazi atrocities. In a public reply which Buber wrote and published along with one by Judah Magnes, Buber took Gandhi to task for his statement that these persecutions were "an exact parallel" to those of the Indians in South

Africa in 1905 and in so doing revealed the full pathos of what he and his fellow Jews had been through in Nazi Germany. "What the rage of the enemy could not bring about, the friendly address has effected," Buber wrote. "I must answer."

Let the Nazis, the Lords of the ice-inferno, affix my name to a cunningly constructed scarecrow. . . . But you, the man of good-will, do you not know that you must see him whom you address, in his place and circumstance, in the throes of his destiny?

Jews are being persecuted, robbed, maltreated, tortured, murdered. And you, Mahatma Gandhi, say that their position in the country where they suffer all this is an exact parallel to the position of Indians in South Africa at the time when you inaugurated your famous "Strength of Truth" . . . campaign. . . . But, Mahatma, are you not aware of the burning of synagogues and scrolls of the Torah? Do you know nothing of all the sacred property of the community—in part of great antiquity, that has been destroyed in the flames? I am not aware that Boers and Englishmen in South Africa ever injured anything sacred to the Indians. . . . Now, do you know or *do you not* know, Mahatma, what a concentration camp is like and what goes on there? Do you know of the torments in the concentration camp, of its methods of slow and quick slaughter? . . . Indians were despised and despicably treated in South Africa, but they were not deprived of rights, they were not outlawed, they were not hostages to induce foreign powers to take the desired attitude towards South Africa. And do you think perhaps that a Jew in Germany could pronounce in public one single sentence of a speech such as yours without being knocked down? . . . In the five years which I myself spent under the present régime, I observed many instances of genuine *satyagraha* among the Jews, instances showing a strength of spirit wherein there was no question of bartering their rights or of being bowed down, and where neither force nor cunning was used to escape the consequences of their behavior. Such actions, however, apparently exerted not the slightest influence on their opponents. . . . A diabolic universal steam-roller cannot thus be withstood. . . . Testimony without acknowledgement, ineffective, unobserved martyrdom, a martyrdom cast to the winds—that is the fate of innumerable Jews in Germany. God alone accepts their testimony, and God "seals" it, as is said in our prayers. . . . Such martyrdom is a deed—but who would venture to demand it?

On November 19, 1938, some five months after Buber had gone to Palestine, the Nazis staged the infamous *Kristallnacht,* or night of broken glass, to divert the people temporarily from war. The pretext for the riots was found in the slaying of a German official in the Paris embassy by a Jewish youth desperately trying to avenge his parents' suffering during their deportation from Germany to Poland. Nora

Levin describes the pogrom of *Kristallnacht* as "an orgy of arson, property destruction and murder of Jews on a scale not yet experienced in Hitler Germany." These "spontaneous demonstrations" were carefully organized and guided by Reinhard Heydrich (a key Nazi figure who controlled the S.D. [Security Service], the Gestapo, and Criminal Police) and were carried out by S.S. men and Storm Troopers, not in uniform, who had been provided with hammers, axes, crowbars, and incendiary bombs. Thousands of shops, homes, and the synagogues were destroyed; many Jews were brutally murdered, and twenty thousand Jews were sent to Buchenwald and other concentration camps.

Writing on the first anniversary of *Kristallnacht,* Buber declared that the German state, in annihilating a minority which had not transgressed against it, was shaking the foundations of its own existence. The regime which destroys its minorities must collapse soon or the population will lose its desire to serve the state. Buber spoke of the state to distinguish it from the German people who concurred with or tolerated it but who did not act on their own initiative.

> What happened in Germany a year ago was not an outbreak of a nation's passion, of widespread Jew-hatred, nor was it so in any action committed against us in these seven years. It was a command from the upper level and was executed with the precision of a dependable machine. For two weeks during the preparation of the Nuremberg Laws, school children came by the windows of my house in Heppenheim every morning at six o'clock and sang the pretty song "Only when the Jew's blood squirts from the knife." . . . On the next morning we waited in vain for the procession. In Poland I saw what elementary Jew-hate is—an outbreak of instinctual drives; I have never seen it in Germany.

Buber did not exempt the German people from culpability. On the contrary, he suggested that it was an old habit of the German people to obey those in power and see them as God-sent. "It is apparently quite difficult for a German to distinguish between God and success and to imagine a God who does not go forth with strong battalions, but rather dwells 'among the bruised and downcast' (Isaiah 57:15)." Even the true intellectuals in Germany seemed "inclined to believe in everyone who takes over the business of politics and carries it by force with uninhibited harshness." Even those who helped persecuted and suffering Jews were often inwardly in basic agreement with the tendency of the persecutors although regretting their grossness.

In January 1939, Buber had stated that "the Jewish share in the

German economy . . . was constructive and educative" and that "it was not a parasitic existence; their whole humanity was put to the task and it bore fruit." In his analysis of the new anti-Semitism in November, Buber stated, in contrast, that the problematical Jewish relationship to the economics of the ruling nations is a consequence of the fact that the Jews of the Diaspora have no share, or only a very minor one, in the basic production, in the laborious gathering of raw materials, the hard work on the soil in agriculture as well as mining. This situation makes the Jews conspicuous in times of great economic hardship, and the deep bitterness of those whose lives seem hopeless needs only a political catchword to explode. Here too Buber saw the demand of the hour as a need for self-knowledge and self-judgment: "Those who threw the spark into the powder keg will not escape judgment. But we are not fulfilling our duty by mourning and complaining. We must learn from what has happened and transform what we have learned into action." Buber's greatest fear was that people in Palestine might learn the wrong lesson and imitate in the name of the Jewish cause that "golem on whose brow the name of Satan is inscribed," that "cruelty that functions like a machine" and that "seizes, desecrates, and destroys our communities one after the other."

The Nazis called Buber the "arch-Jew," a designation which he quoted with pride in his address on the occasion of his receiving the Peace Prize of the German Book Trade in 1953.

To Buber, Hitler was only the caricature of Napoleon, the "demonic Thou" toward whom everything flames but whose fire is cold, the man who was Thou for millions but for whom no one was Thou. The only remarkable thing Buber saw in Hitler was his being possessed—in the literal sense of the term—as the consequence of his impotence. Hitler's idea of the higher race was not really biological, Buber held. It stemmed from Nietzsche. Actually Hitler believed himself to belong to the lower race, but he took it on himself arbitrarily to define the higher race so that he could count himself a member of it. In conversation with Werner Kraft, Buber pointed to Lao-tzu's sentence, "What one will destroy, one must first allow to become great." *This* is the reason, Buber held, why one only fought Hitler so late.

Buber's friend the writer Max Picard after the war called Hitler, in Buber's language, the supreme monologist: "Never did any of his speeches call for an answer. His speeches were nothing but monologues, enormous accumulations of monologic cries." This is exactly how Buber himself saw Hitler. In my essay "The Bases of Buber's

Ethics" in *The Philosophy of Martin Buber* volume of The Library of Living Philosophers, I wrote, "One's antagonist may, indeed, be the devil or Hitler, but even such a one must be faithfully answered, contended with." In his "Replies to My Critics," Buber commented that he held no one to be "absolutely" unredeemable—by God. But speaking not "of God, but solely of myself and this man," he felt constrained to reject my interpretation:

> Hitler is not my antagonist in the sense of a partner "whom I can confirm in opposing him," as Friedman says, for he is incapable of really addressing one and incapable of really listening to one. That I once experienced personally when, if only through the technical medium of the radio, I heard him speak. I knew that this voice was in the position to annihilate me together with countless of my brothers; but I perceived that despite such might it was not in the position to set the spoken and heard word into the world. And already less than an hour afterward I sensed in "Satan" the "poor devil," the poor devil in power, and at the same time I understood my dialogical powerlessness. I had to answer, but not to him who had spoken. As far as a person is part of a situation, I have to respond, but not just to the person.

In 1963 Buber reaffirmed what he had written in "The First" in April 1933, thirty years before: that the decisive thing was not what had befallen the Jewish community in Germany but how they related to that happening. "What I at that time wrote down, I meant not only for that opening stage of the crisis. It also applied to the final stages, for the catastrophe that began to become manifest five and one-half years later and that remains inscribed in world history as the greatest crime that was ever initiated by a state organization as such."

In his exhortations to German Jewry collected in *The Hour and Its Judgment*, declared Ernest Wolf, Buber revealed himself a genuine "teacher of his people." The awareness of the destruction that hovered over them gave tragic pathos and prophetic urgency to his words. "Like the prophets, the speaker rebukes and consoles at the same time. But he consoles far more frequently than he rebukes. And he hurts only to heal all the more deeply and lastingly."

CHAPTER 10

Jewish-Christian "Dialogue"

AS IMPORTANT AS the prophetic demand and comfort that Martin Buber brought to German Jewry during the first five years of the Third Reich was his leadership in spiritual resistance against the Nazis. (Abraham Joshua Heschel, who was Buber's friend during the last thirty years of Buber's life, spoke often of his association with Buber during this period in the direction of the reopened Frankfurt Freie Jüdische Lehrhaus. "Buber gave me my first job," Heschel said and testified, "This was the period of Buber's true greatness.") This spiritual resistance to Nazism took two principal forms: Jewish-Christian "dialogues" and the organization of education for the Jews of Germany. The latter commenced only after the Nazi rise to power. The former began even before, when the coming upheaval could already be scented in the air.

In Aachen, Germany, in the fall of 1930 after a public debate between Friedrich Hielscher and Friedrich Muckermann about the meaning of the state (Reich), Buber and his friend Albrecht Schaeffer asked the two disputants whether they would meet with them privately for further discussion. When Hielscher later visited Buber at his home, he got to know not only Buber's wife, "a good-hearted, contentious Bavarian," but also his son-in-law Ludwig Strauss, whose poetry he learned to love. Through Paula Buber's pride in her Bavarian homeland and his in Silesia, they ended up by speaking not about faith but about the difference between a federal and a centralized state. Hielscher attacked the federal state, and Buber nodded in seeming agreement. But he wanted to know how it would have to be to satisfy Hielscher. When Hielscher outlined a state in which the central government was accorded the final decision about law, economy, foreign policy, and the army and only culture and instruction were left to the member states, Buber replied angrily. "Naturally, you think of the federal state and not of its members. You do not see it as the union of its members but as their master, and you give to it all that you hold to be important. The member states are graciously left to do the house work, called administration, to set flowers on the table, called art and science, and to raise the children which later have to serve the master." Then Hielscher became angry himself and cried, "How shall the whole be united unless the muscles and cords so important for the work are mastered?" "That is just it," replied Buber, more and more excited, "that you regard the whole as a work machine and not in truth as a union. . . . Here nothing is united, only commanded and obeyed."

Hielscher looked at Buber in astonishment. This man who, despite his little more than fifty years already affected one like a patriarch with his gray beard, his strong and fine nose, his comforting hands, his at once kindly and commanding gaze, had suddenly been transformed into a wrathful prophet.

And then Buber continued: "I will predict for you what will happen. You will experience what routine toil instead of purposeful growth, command and obedience instead of the union of free persons, means. Then you will recognize that you wanted to force together two realms that do not belong together, and then it will be too late, for you and for your Silesian homeland. . . . This so-called German state . . . will devour Bavaria as it will devour your Silesian land and people."

"In 1933 I recognized that Buber was right," confessed Hielscher. "In 1938 I understood it, and in 1945 I experienced it."

In a brief reply in early 1932 to Eugene Jolas, editor of the distinguished Hague journal *Transition*, Buber again prophesied clearly what was to come. Asked about "the evolution of individualism and metaphysics under a collectivistic regime," Buber replied that he saw individualism under collectivism as revolutionary, metaphysics as "partaking of the mood of the catacombs." What eventually became true for all individuals and all groups under the Nazi collective became true first of all for Buber's own people—the German Jews. The last and most memorable public dialogue that Buber had with a Christian on Judaism and Christianity in pre-Nazi Germany was that with the courageous anti-Nazi Protestant Karl Ludwig Schmidt, professor of Protestant theology at Bonn. An element of terror and greatness is added to this Jewish-Christian interchange in that it stood in the shadow of the inexorable approach of the Nazi persecution of the Jews. The common biblical inheritance of the two faiths stands in fateful tension with the religious roots of anti-Semitism in Christianity, which the Nazis exploited to the full. It was with this context in mind that Buber asked that the 1964 publication in English of his reply to Schmidt be prefaced by a description of "the circumstances under which that public dialogue was held." "The reader must understand that the atmosphere was that of an impending crisis."

In February of 1933, Schmidt wrote Buber that as a German and as an evangelical Christian he was ashamed for the new "national" (Nazi) government and for the official submission of the Evangelical Union to it. "The real church wills freedom of conscience." On January 1, 1933, Schmidt had invited Buber to a discussion on "Church, State, Nation and Synagogue." Buber proposed instead the title "Church, State, People, and Judaism"—first, because he did not feel himself authorized to talk on the behalf of any synagogue whatsoever and second, because he considered the word "synagogue" an imprecise designation which did not appeal to him as something to which he could respond.

The discussion, which took place on January 14, 1933, in the Jüdische Lehrhaus in Stuttgart and was published in full on the basis of stenographic notes in a theological journal in September, did take place under the title that Buber requested. This discussion was so noteworthy that the distinguished German-Jewish thinker Hans Joachim Schoeps devoted a whole section to it in his book *Jewish-Christian Religious Dialogue in Nineteen Centuries,* which was published in Berlin in 1937. Schmidt began by stating that the unbounded, confused anti-Semitism that Germany was witnessing must lead directly to the de-Christianizing and the de-Churching of the German people in whose midst the Jews lived and was trivializing the Jewish question to a purely racial one. The true Christian, in contrast, takes fully seriously the

Jews' claim to be Israel, the people of God; for the God of Judaism came to be understood as the God of all peoples and as such was proclaimed to the whole world. The God of Israel is no purified God-idea but a partner who shares a history with his creatures, who addresses and makes demands of them. *That* is Israel's gift and legacy to the whole of mankind. The tragic reverse side cannot be ignored, however; for in and with the Diaspora, Judaism has again and again surrendered and lost itself to the world in a process of assimilation that has turned obedience to the personal God into a philosophical view of God. The Church waits eagerly yet patiently for the Jews to leave their unfulfillment and enter into the fulfillment of the Church of Jesus Christ which is the true Israel, the Israel of the spirit. This patient wrestling must not be confused, however, with the fight against Judaism on the basis of national and state ideology which destroys the Israel of both the Old and the New Testaments and makes the fight against Judaism into a fight against the substance of the Church.

Buber replied to Schmidt orally and directly with the aid only of a few notes. In his reply he set forth essentially the teaching not only of "Two Foci of the Jewish Soul" but also of *The Kingship of God* (1932), his first book tracing the origin of messianism in the Hebrew Bible. Starting with the uniqueness of Israel as a people and a land bound to the covenant with God by its task of becoming a true community, Buber rejected the Church's view that Israel has been rejected by God —a postulate that the Church must hold in proclaiming *itself* now to be the true Israel. Despite a thousand sins and turnings away, Israel knows the covenant not as a contingent event in the world but as one that took place in the reality of the distance between God and Israel, and it knows that God will hold it in his hand and not let it fall into the fire. Buber stated this not in the context of historical success, which would have been even more absurd at that hour than in the mouths of the Israelites of the Bible. Rather it lay in the mystery of the hiddenness of the "suffering servant," the concrete *sensing* of the unredeemedness of the world and with it the impossibility of recognizing the Church's claim that the Messiah has already come in Jesus Christ. The redemption of the world is connected indissolubly with the fulfillment of creation and cannot be proclaimed in the redemption of the soul detached from the world, however much in our dying hours the soul may announce to us the coming of redemption. The corollary of this view of creation and redemption is that God cannot be fixed in any of his revelations. None of his revelations has the finality of perfection; none has the character of incarnation.

Neither Judaism nor Christianity can know the other from within; yet each may recognize the mystery of the other as genuine holiness. Jesus proclaimed the original certainty of the kingship of God and pointed to its fulfillment through renewing and transforming the conception of the servant. But Jesus' message was carried to the peoples of the world as a dualism which split the realm of community, state, and the *whole* life-answer of man from the kingdom of God, severed "religion" and "politics," and, strengthened by the power of the Church, declared Israel cut off from the task of making the human race into a community of God. The Western world has from of old denied the Jews the possibility of participating in the creative life of the land. Even when the Jews were "emancipated," it was only as a multitude of Jewish individuals and not as Israel. Since then the attempt has repeatedly been made to see Israel as simply one among the religions. But Israel without its peoplehood has no reality. Zion cannot be understood merely as a geographical place any more than Israel can be understood merely as a nation.

That his Christian partner in dialogue could refer to Israel in the context of the servant of God afforded Buber hope that in a blessed common contending Israel might be genuinely received by Christianity. Because of its faith that the human community can be transformed into the realm of God, Israel can nowhere and never be indifferent to the social and political order in which any human community is built. Every form of state is a problematic model of the kingdom of God which points to it, no matter how distorted the model is. What we call "state" is the balance of the free will for community and of the force which keeps order. From this standpoint of the double vision of Israel concerning the state, Buber explained to Schmidt the answer to his question of how the Jews, who are committed to conserving their tradition, could be so active among the revolutionaries.

Schmidt in his reply emphasized how much he and Buber were at one in recognizing that world history, seen from the standpoint of the Bible, depends on Israel and that without this there could be no dialogue between God and humankind. But he emphasized equally that where God spoke to the forefathers through the biblical prophets, he speaks to us now through his Son, and *this* speech is ultimately valid once and for all. If the Church were more Christian, the contest between it and Judaism would be sharper than it now can and may be. World history, which despite its splendor is full of horrors, has come to be what it is because the Jews have *not* entered into the Church and understood themselves as the people called by God in Jesus Christ; because they have not accepted Christianity as the true, spiritual Israel.

Buber, in his short reply, denied that a true Christian Church and a true Israel would be in sharper contest with each other, although the difference between them would persist unweakened. "God's gate stands open for all. The Christian does not need to come to God through Judaism nor the Jew through Christianity." To this Buber added a vividly concrete personal experience. He lived not far from the city of Worms, which he occasionally visited. Whenever he did he would go first to the cathedral and rejoice in its perfection and sublimity. But then he would go to the Jewish cemetery with its rubble of fallen stones and ashes. Looking from the formless, directionless stones up to the splendid harmony of the cathedral, Buber felt himself to be looking from Israel up to the Church. Yet he felt himself bound to these misshapen stones and ashes and through them directly to the forefathers, the memory of the Sinai happening between God and Israel that is given to all Jews. The need of Israel is a real need, and its shame a real shame. But there is a divine meaning in it which God, according to his promise to Israel, has not let fall from his hand (Isaiah 54:10).

The approaching onslaught of the Nazis against the Jews and the capitulation of the official German church to the Nazis gave a poignant overtone to the dialogue between Buber and Schmidt. Schmidt would in no way allow his Christian position to lend sanction to the Nazis' ideological attack on Jews and Judaism. Although he spoke from the traditional Protestant pietist perspective which linked the conversion of the Jews with the second coming of Christ, he by no means looked on Buber as someone he was personally trying to convert. Before their dialogue, he sent Buber a sketch of his talk so that Buber could see the standpoint from which he was forced to speak as a representative of his church. But, he added, I speak this way "to a human being and thinker like you with great reluctance and shame." After the dialogue, he wrote Buber how thankful he was to have participated with him in this exchange: "Our long discussion in your home in Heppenheim was for me a regular seminar at which I believe I learned a great deal. And in the train, then in the Stuttgart Hotel, and finally in the public exchange itself everything grew still more intense." Thus the representative Christian and the unrepresentative but deeply biblically rooted Jew carried on their exchange within a real personal dialogue, and this too gave it an overtone of meaning which made it a real event invulnerable to the storm clouds hanging over it.

One of the most striking Christian responses to Buber's dialogue with Christianity came not from a theologian but from Gertrud Bäumer, a writer, social politician, and fighter for women's rights who edited the journal *Die Hilfe* along with Theodor Heuss (the future president of the West German Republic), as well as the weekly *Die Frau*, and who was from 1920 to 1933 ministerial adviser in the German Ministry for Interior Affairs. Referring to Buber's participation in the Comburg seminar in Cassel, she stated that every response to Buber's words must begin with the recognition of the greatness and powerfulness of the religious world that he had presented. "Just as you say that the memory of Sinai is more than the making present of a historical fact, so was the presence of this world among us more than a report of a religious proclamation. . . . With very few persons of my own 'faith' have I felt the great immediacy of your sharing *(Mit-Teilung)*. . . . That under these conditions and in this circle [the Nazis also took part in this Comburg "Week of Work"] you spoke so freely and calmly from the ground of your being is an unquestionable victory that is compelling for all persons with whom you come in contact."

In 1932, Buber wrote an essay for a volume published in 1933 by the German Fellowship of Reconciliation which dealt with the question of whether the group can relieve the individual of his responsibility. Buber distinguished between the genuine person of faith who "trusts" within a relationship of faith, and the one who "believes in" a leader. People readily declare today that they believe in the Führer, Buber said, "but the idols with human bodies are still worse than those in the form of ideas because they can counterfeit reality more effectively." "With my choice and decision I answer for my hour, and this responsibility my group cannot take from me. My group concerns me enormously in my decision," but "no program, no tactical resolution, no command of a leader can say to me how I, making my decision, must do justice to my group in God's sight." "It may even be that I shall have to oppose the success of my group's program and carry into my group itself that 'inner front' which can run as a secret unity across all groups and become more important for the future of our world than all the lines drawn today between group and group."

All this has nothing to do with "individualism." "I hold the individual to be neither the starting point nor the goal of the human world. But I hold the human person to be the unalterable center of the struggle between the movement of the world away from God and its movement to God." This struggle takes place to an uncannily large extent in the realm of public life; yet the decisive battles are fought out in the depths of the person. "The dizziness of freedom of the generation that has just passed has been followed by the search for bondage of the present one, the unfaithfulness of intoxication by the unfaithfulness of hysteria." "This generation is striving to escape from the powerfully commanding 'ever-again' of being responsible through flight into a protective 'once-for-all.' " This essay was used by Buber as an integral part of his little book *The Question to the Single One*— published in 1936—a time when it had still greater relevance, if only as a voice crying in the wilderness.

The Protestant theologian Jakob Wilhelm Hauer wrote Buber in late March 1933 saying that he was proposing that Buber should be invited to make known the desires and positions of the Jews in connection with the "Jewish question," just as the proletarians should be consulted in matters concerning communism. He particularly referred to statements that Buber made at Cassel about how Jews should be accepted as "guests in the land" in the biblical sense of the term. These demands Hauer felt could be made more concrete, perhaps with a repetition of his Comburg speech. "The important thing is that for once it should be stated from your side what is really hoped for, what can and must be demanded according to your view." It is striking that Buber's statements at Comburg were *not* printed in the journal Hauer edited, *Die kommende Gemeinde* (The Coming Community).

In April 1933, Buber's Catholic friend the sociologist and psychotherapist Ernst Michel wrote Buber asking whether he would agree to the interpretation that a Christian pastor had made of some biblical passages in a newspaper article. The passages discussed—"An eye for an eye and a tooth for a tooth" (Exodus 21:24) and "You have heard it said: You shall love your neighbor and hate your enemy" (Matthew 5:43)—are both standard texts for traditional Christian anti-Semitism, and it is not surprising that a pastor pulled them out at this time to justify the Nazis in their treatment of the Jews. In his reply to Michel, Buber pointed out that in the time of Jesus the Jewish tradition did not understand the Old Testament passage as a *jus talionis,* a law of retaliation in kind, but as a recompensation by money, that New Testament research has placed in doubt whether Jesus actually said the words "and hate your enemy," and that in any case neither that statement nor anything like it can be found in the Old Testament. Rather it says in many passages that you should be helpful even to your enemy, that you should not "hate your brother in your heart." The word "neighbor" in "Love your neighbor as yourself" (Luther's translation) or more accurately, "Deal lovingly with your fellowman, who is like you" (Buber's own), does not apply only to one's own people, as has been thought; for in Exodus 11:2 it designates only those who do not belong to your people. "*Rea* means simply that person with whom at any time one has *directly* to do in the circle of social living together." This led Buber to repeat that statement about the guest living in your land that had so struck Jakob Hauer at Cassels: "When a stranger sojourns with you in your land, you shall not do him wrong. The stranger who sojourns with you shall be to you as the native among you, and you shall love him as yourself" (Leviticus 19:33 f.). The faithless are always inclined to hate those in whom they see their "enemy," Buber commented in conclusion. "But whoever lives in faith, Jew or Christian, can learn from a Talmudic master who never went to sleep without praying, 'May every person be forgiven who has done me any injury.' "

The interchange with Ernst Michel set the stage for a more extensive, significant, and public interchange with Gerhart Kittel, the New Testament scholar who, despite his evangelical piety and his emphasis on the Old Testament–Jewish roots of Christianity, affirmed National Socialism and represented a "Christian" anti-Semitism. In June 1933, Kittel wrote Buber that he was sending him a little book he had written entitled *The Jewish Question,* some passages of which must seem inimical to Buber as a Jew. Yet he honestly wished to do justice to Judaism, he claimed, and reminded Buber of the high esteem in which he held his lifework as shown by what he had written about it. Buber replied that he had read the book carefully and had found much in which agreement between them did or could exist. But when he read the whole he could not affirm that Kittel had done justice to Judaism. Buber objected to his speaking of *the* Jewish doctor, *the* Jewish lawyer, and *the* Jewish merchant, as if they could all be dealt with as a single class (the very stuff of prejudice), and he objected even more to Kittel's using the fact that the Jews were strangers in the land as a basis for discrimination. "Would you want this conclusion to apply to the German minorities in the world?" Buber asked Kittel and cited passages from the Hebrew Bible, such as those he had cited at Cassel and to Michel, about having one standard and one justice for host and guest alike.

Acknowledging the "obedience" which Kittel cited as one part and one part only of the awakening of a new covenant of faith in the Jewish people, Buber asked Kittel whether such "obedience" "means that we should regard our 'defamation' (Rudolf Bultmann) not only as God's just judgment but also as men's just deed?" Buber concluded by pointing out that Kittel wrote his message to a public to which Buber, as a Jew, had no access.

As it turned out, Buber was enabled to reply publicly to Kittel through the courage of his former partner in dialogue Karl Ludwig Schmidt, the editor of *Theologische Blätter,* and this reply and his further reply were reprinted in Buber's book *The Hour and Its Judgment* (1936). In his "Open Letter to Gerhard Kittel" (July 1933), Buber stated that he had nothing to say to what in Kittel's book was intended as "giving the fight against Judaism a Christian meaning." But when Kittel sought to enlist for this meaning "the cooperation of those Jews like myself who hope for a renewal of Jewish faith, then the obligation of a reply falls on me." In this connection, Buber repeated in expanded form with many citations from the Hebrew Bible what he had written in his personal letter to Kittel about "defamation" and about loving the guest in the land. Only if Kittel proceeded from this "Magna Charta of biblical faith," which binds all people in whose midst guests live and which was surely not suspended by the New Testament, would he have the right to speak about "the obedience of the strangers," in which case the question would also arise about the obedience of *the peoples:* "God does not demand of us an obedience such as you understand it. . . . It does not become us to bow ourselves to the will of a people *as the will of God."* To Kittel's statement that true Jewishness remains with the symbol of exiles wandering over the earth without rest or home, Buber responded that the "wandering Jew" is a figure from Christian, not Jewish, legend. True Judaism is always ready to see the promise fulfilled *in the next moment* and its wandering come to an end. It knows no "God-willed tragedy" that it must recognize; for it knows grace, the grace that calls mankind to its task. "History is no throne-speech of God, but God's dialogue with humanity." The "historical givenness" of being strangers is a question addressed to the peoples and to Israel, not a solution to a problem. Kittel's interpretation of the Jewish manifestation of genuine readiness for community and sacrifice in settling in Palestine as "communist tendencies" to infiltrate and poison the "countries of culture" Buber found uninformed and incomprehensible.

In November 1933, Buber published in the same journal a reply to Kittel's "Answer." To say that the emancipation was no true solution because it liberated only the individual and not the people does not justify the persecution of the Jews. "If God were ever to judge between Israel and the nations of the world, he would not fail to look at the guilt of the nations," Buber declared. To Kittel's strong denial that he defamed Judaism, Buber cited, as one example out of many, Kittel's claim that *the* Jewish lawyer obeyed the letter of the law but acted directly contrary to the German consciousness of law. If this statement that the Jewish lawyer perverts the law *as a Jew* is not defamation, Buber asserted, "then I do not know what in the world deserves such a name." Kittel instructed Buber that "a pious Judaism" would see the fulfillment of God's promise as *God's* work. "Only God can fulfill God's promise," Buber replied. "But pious Judaism, and I with it, believe that it pleases God to summon man as helper in his work." To publish these responses to Kittel was not without its dangers for a Jew in the Third Reich. But, as Schalom Ben-Chorin has observed, a civil courage was always characteristic of Buber, outwardly so tender a man but one who could become hard and severe where right and wrong, justice and injustice, were involved.

In writing Buber that he was ready to publish the "Open Letter to Gerhard Kittel," Schmidt remarked, "Whether and how long there will be room for my calling and my person in the University of Bonn and in the evangelical church becomes ever more problematic." By the time Buber's reply to Kittel's answer was published, Schmidt had already left Germany for Switzerland, where in 1935 he was given a professorship at the University of Basel. In August 1933, Ernst Lohmeyer, another courageous anti-Nazi, sent Buber a long letter concerning the "Open Letter" to Kittel. "Each of your words was to me as if it had been spoken out of my own heart," Lohmeyer wrote, while confessing to a feeling of shame that a theological colleague could think and write as Kittel had and that the evangelical church could be so silent and "like a captainless ship let itself be driven off its course by the political stormwind of a fleeting present." Expressing his bitterness at Kittel's use of religious catchwords to rationalize political measures, Lohmeyer declared that "the Christian faith is only Christian so long as it bears the Jewish in its heart." Lohmeyer, a professor of New Testament at Breslau from 1920 to 1935, was punished by the Nazis for his anti-Nazi position by being forced in 1935 to exchange his professorship at Breslau for one in Greifswald, and then, as rector of the University of Greifswald in 1946, was arrested and shot by the Russians for no known reason. From Jerusalem, Gershom Scholem wrote Buber that he had read Kittel's brochure with disgust and revolt and that of all the shameful works produced by a well-known professor this was certainly among the most shameful.

After the Nuremberg Laws of 1935, Julius Streicher's depraved journal *Der Stürmer* filled the minds of millions of readers with hatred and fear of Jews. In 1936 a delegation of German Protestant ministers, mostly village pastors, asked Buber for material against Streicher's falsifications, which he, of course, supplied. A still more significant spiritual resistance to Nazism through Jewish-Christian dialogue was Buber's publication of his book *The Question to the Single One* in 1936. Taking off from a critique and redefinition of Kierkegaard's central concept of the "Single One" *(Einzelte)* and, to a lesser extent of the nineteenth-century German philosopher Max Stirner's radical individualism, Buber, in fact, used this book as an occasion for a radical criticism of collectivism and, in connection with this criticism, of those persons, such as the Christian theologian Friedrich Gogarten and the University of Berlin professor of constitutional law Carl Schmitt who interpreted Christianity in such a way as to lend theoretical support to collectivism. In particular, Buber contrasted Gogarten's affirmation of the radical and unredeemable evil of man with the Jewish position which recognizes no "original sin." In a highly sympathetic reply to Buber's critique of Gogarten, Karl Ludwig Schmidt suggested to Buber that he write to the great systematic evangelical theologian Karl Barth for his views on the subject. Barth replied that the concept of "radical" evil was valid in Protestant Christianity *coram Deo* (before God) but not among human beings and that this confrontation of the *whole* person with the demand and judgment of God in no way affected the command to love God and to love one's neighbor. "Were it otherwise," Barth concluded, "then the whole confessional church might have remained peacefully at home in these days or exactly in that place —where Gogarten stands!" Buber concurred that man might stand as evil in the sight of God but not in the sight of a human community or institution.

In his 1948 Foreword to *Between Man and Man,* Buber described *The Question to the Single One* as "the elaboration of an address which I gave to the students of the three German-Swiss universities at the close of 1933." Although he spoke of the book as containing "some political inferences," Buber also stated in this Foreword that its publication in

Germany in 1936 was astonishing, "since it attacks the very foundation of totalitarianism." "The fact that it could be published with impunity is certainly to be explained from its not having been understood by the appropriate authorities."

That the political implications of *The Question to the Single One* were not entirely missed at the time by the educated German is shown by the letter Buber received from Hermann Herrigel, a writer, journalist, archivist, and adult educator who belonged to the circle that surrounded Florens Christian Rang and Martin Buber and some of whose essays Buber published in *Die Kreatur*. Buber's wish to hallow politics, to give it the task of making the crowd into real community and of transforming persons into Single Ones who are responsible to other persons, Herrigel saw not as politics but as work on the kingdom of God. This work can be carried on indefinitely, but politics cannot wait. Politics is to be fulfilled not through the development of Single Ones, which is a secondary task, but through leadership and domination. It is not surprising that Herrigel added that he could not share Buber's judgment about the present situation. He could not comprehend how Buber could see the substitution of a Führer principle for parliamentary rule and for personal responsibility and decision as the degeneration of responsibility and as the "laming of the human struggle for the truth." To Herrigel, the Führer principle demanded responsibility and was a collective search for truth. "I really wonder," Herrigel concluded, "that you publish a book today that . . . must bring you into the position of expressing yourself directly on the present political situation."

Buber claimed in his reply that Herrigel had basically misunderstood the intention of his book and pointed out that in a Foreword (which he had withheld because it was too personal) he had written, "I do not speak of political systems." He also pointed out that the kernel of *The Question to the Single One* was already contained in his 1932 essay "On the Ethics of Political Decision." Most of what he said applies equally to the party state and some of it specifically—a position which Buber had, in fact, taken since 1919 and earlier. "Nothing could be farther from my mind than assigning to politics, as you imagine, the task of making the crowd into real community. Politics and the politician cannot do it, but other persons shall do it because they in some measure can." Grete Schaeder suggests that this letter to Herrigel was an understandable attempt on Buber's part to create a political alibi. Despite his denials, there can be no doubt that Buber was fully aware of the political implications of this book when he published it and probably also of the personal danger to which it exposed him.

What was not explicit to the Nazi censors, we can today make explicit to ourselves and with it a new stage in the development of Buber's philosophical anthropology, his concern with the wholeness and uniqueness of the human. In *The Question to the Single One* Buber characterized the nineteenth-century German philosopher Max Stirner as "a pathetic nominalist and unmasker of ideas" who converted Protagoras' dictum that "Man is the measure of all things" into the still more questionable statement that the "Unique One," the concrete present individual, is the bearer of the world. Stirner's principal formulas were that the free man "acknowledges nothing but himself" and that "True is what is Mine." Ironically and in utmost contrast to what he himself intended, Stirner forecast that twentieth-century situation in which the rigid collective *We* rejected all superior authority and translated Stirner's "Unique One" into that *Group-*I which acknowledges nothing but itself. Thus on the second page of his book Buber already, unmistakably though not explicitly, attacked the very foundation of Nazi totalitarianism. Nor was Nazism absent from Buber's mind when he wrote on the next page of "the epidemic sickening of the word in our time, by which every word is at once deadened by mechanical repetition and changed into a slogan." We may well imagine too that Buber had Nazism in mind when he prophesied that Stirner's "open country," in which his "Unique Ones" who see the world as their property "bustle in futile and uncommitted life," must lead to Kierkegaard's "narrow pass." "I think, however, that in reality the way to this narrow pass is through that open country that first is called individual egoism and then collective egoism and, finally, by its true name, despair." Again, there are unmistakable overtones of Buber's response to Nazism when he writes, in his discussion of Kierkegaard: "The human person belongs, whether he wants to acknowledge it and take it seriously or not, to the community" and, "He who has realized what destiny means, even if it looks like doom, knows too that he must acknowledge it and take it seriously." But this confrontation with Nazism also meant to Buber that true membership in a community includes the experience of the *boundary* of this membership and that this boundary is experienced "in such agony as if the boundary-post had pierced his soul."

It is in this context that Buber criticized "that powerful modern point of view, according to which in the last resort only . . . collectives are real, while significance is attached to persons only as the workers or the tools of the collectives"—a precise definition of the totalitarian touchstone of reality. Such attempts give the political province an exaggerated autonomy and remove it from the responsibility of the "Single One" who takes part in it. One such attempt was that of Oswald Spengler, the philosopher of history, who, in anticipation of the Nazis, trivialized Nietzsche's historical thesis into a biological one. "Every attempt to interpret human action in biological terms . . . is a poor simplification," commented Buber, "because it means the abandoning of the proper anthropological content, of that which constitutes the category of *man.*" A second attempt at severance of the political from the personal was the contemporary one of the Roman Catholic exponent of constitutional law, Carl Schmitt. In Schmitt's view, the political has its own criterion, which cannot be derived from any other realm, that of the distinction between friend and foe. In opposition to this view, Buber pointed out that the friend-foe formula derives from those times in which common life is threatened and not those times when its stability seems self-assured. What is more, Schmitt by picturing the rebel as the "inner foe" mistakes the rebel's loyalty to the general order which he wishes to preserve just by changing certain aspects of it. This is a *dynamic of order* which expresses itself in the double movement of making real political structure by calling the order of any particular time into question from the standpoint of the whole dynamic.

The third attempt at severance was also a contemporary one—that of the well-known dialectical *and* dialogical theologian Friedrich Gogarten. In his book *Political Ethics,* Gogarten claimed that ethical problems receive their relevance only from the political dimension and, therefore, by implication, *not* from the religious dimension even if the political has a religious basis. Buber, in contrast, coupled the assertion that the Single One cannot win to a legitimate relation with God without a legitimate relation to the body politic, with the equally basic assertion that "I must always let the boundary between cooperation and noncooperation concerning my relation to my community be drawn by God," or more precisely, by my unique dialogue with God in the unique, concrete situation in which I find myself. Gogarten based his political ethics on a Hobbesian view of man as "radically and therefore irrevocably . . . in the grip of evil" and therefore dependent upon the State to ward off evil through its right over the life and property of its subjects. To this, Buber responded in the spirit of Karl

Barth's letter and his own reply, namely, that man is evil *before* God but not before any human order or institution that is supposedly empowered by God.

At this point, Buber introduced a decisive development in his own philosophical anthropology which was also clearly his own understanding of how such an evil as Nazism could come to be. Man is not radically anything, Buber claimed. He is "the crystallized potentiality of existence . . . in its factual limitation"—what Buber's friend Paul Tillich later called "finite freedom." The action of the human being is unforeseeable in its nature and extent; for man is "the centre of all surprise in the world." This means that man is not good or evil but both together. "Good" is the movement in the direction of reality, "evil" the "aimless whirl of human potentialities without which nothing can be achieved and by which, if they take no direction but remain trapped in themselves, everything goes awry." Put in another way, evil is the convulsive shirking of direction, the soul's not standing up to personal responsibility before God. This shirking takes place through passion or indolence, but in either case "the real historical demonries," of which Nazism was to Buber the preeminent example, "are the exploiting by historical powers of this shirking." The State *as such* cannot decide for its citizens what is their authentic direction in each new concrete situation, the "one direction of the hour to God." Yet this is what Gogarten wants the State to do when he puts *the* State in the place of the historical state, the government of the particular time, and then ascribes to this impersonal abstraction responsibility for ethical decisions. Only the Single One, who stands in responsibility, can answer for the direction of the concrete situation. Even a statesman can be this Single One, but only if he understands the establishment of power as a commission and power itself as a great responsibility. No philosophical or theological concept of the State can properly supersede the responsibility of the human person, be he servant or emperor, the responsibility for the body politic in the sight of God.

Buber's summation of *The Question to the Single One* is also explicit in its application to totalitarianism. Both person and truth have become questionable today, Buber asserted, and both are exploited by the modern collectivity. At this point, Buber confessed his own unintentional contribution to the collectivization of the person—"that struggle in recent decades against the idealistic concepts of the sovereign, world-embracing, world-sustaining, world-creating *I.*" This struggle was conducted in part by reference to the neglected creaturely bonds of the concrete human person, the realization that the thinker is bound to a spatial realm, a historical hour, to a people, family, society, vocational group, companionship in convictions. These new insights into the reality of bonds were exaggerated and perverted into serfdom by the quite different tendency which ascribed primacy of reality and responsibility to the collectivity and saw the person as merely derivative. When the individual who is joined to a whole is denied his personal voice, human perception ceases, human response is dumb, and "the immeasurable value which constitutes man is imperilled."

Truth has become questionable through being politicized, and this too has been facilitated by that sociology of knowledge that has recognized the historical bonds of man's existence as a social being. In opposition to this view, Buber advanced the precise formula that in 1952 he adverted to in "Hope for This Hour" as a cure for the tendency of mutual "unmasking" which results in universal existential mistrust: setting the proper limit to the validity of such insights and seeing man simultaneously in his conditioned and unconditioned being. "The man who thinks 'existentially,' that is, who stakes his life in his thinking, brings into his real relation to the truth not merely his conditioned qualities but also the unconditioned nature, transcending those qualities of his quest, of his grasp, of his indomitable will for the truth, which also carries along with it the whole personal power of standing his test." By neglecting to draw *this* boundary line again and again in each concrete situation, "the political theory of modern collectivisms was easily able to assume power over the principle which lay ready, and to proclaim . . . the life interests of a group as its legitimate and undeniable truth." This marks the beginning of the disintegration of human faith in the truth and of the paralysis of the human search for the truth. "In order that man may not be lost there is need of persons who are not collectivized, and of truth which is not politicized, . . . of the person's responsibility to truth in his historical situation," of the Single One who confronts and guarantees all being which is present to him including the body politic.

The Question to the Single One represents a new emphasis upon the importance of saying "I" necessitated by the collectivist and totalitarian trends of the time. To those who have coupled Buber with George Herbert Mead as an exponent of the "social self" or with Harry Stack Sullivan as an exponent of the "interpersonal" in general, Buber says here in unmistakable terms, "Not before a man can say *I* in perfect reality—that is, finding himself—can he in perfect reality say *Thou.*

. . . And even if he does it in a community he can only do it 'alone.' "
This is not the flight of the alone to the Alone of the mystic; for the
mystic gives up that saying of "I" which is necessary for love. Nor is
what is meant individualism, which asks of the person only that he
"realize his potentialities." Even morality and piety, where they become an autonomous aim, must be reckoned among the showpieces
of a spirit that no longer knows about Being but only about its mirror-
ings. Responsibility presupposes one who addresses me from a realm
outside myself and to whom I am answerable. Where no primary
address and claim by another can touch me, responsibility becomes a
delusion and the mutuality of persons is dissipated. Responsibility
means openness to the primal otherness of the other, which even in
the case of God is never Barth's "wholly otherness." Responsibility in
the face of reason, an idea, a nature, or an institution is merely fictitious; for these are but abstractions and not persons to whom we are
answerable.

But if our other is only God, excluding the world, that, too, is not
true responsibility, even if we relate to God as Thou, as does Kierkegaard's "knight of faith." "Everyone should be chary about having to
do with 'the others,' " Buber quoted Kierkegaard, "and should essentially speak only with God and with himself." Speaking with God is
something totally different from speaking with oneself, Buber commented, but not from speaking with another; for in speaking with
another, one is approached and addressed, whereas in speaking with
oneself, despite all the soul's adventures in double roles—"games,
intoxications, dreams, visions, surprises, overwhelmings, overpower-
ings"—one can still anticipate what is coming in the depths of one's
soul. What Kierkegaard really means, Buber ventured, is that the Single One has to do *essentially* only with God, and in that he contradicts
Jesus, whose contemporary he strove to be. For Jesus coupled the
command to love God with all one's might *and* the command to love
one's neighbor as *one like* oneself. Not "as I love myself," Buber commented; for (Erich Fromm to the contrary) "in the last reality one does
not love oneself, but one should rather learn to love oneself through
love of one's neighbor." God and man are not rivals: "Exclusive love
to God ('with all your heart') is, *because he is God,* inclusive love, ready
to accept and include all love." "In order to come to love, I had to
remove the object," says Kierkegaard of his renunciation of his fiancée
Regina Olsen. "That is sublimely to misunderstand God," Buber witnessed, speaking from the depths of his whole life and of his marriage

with Paula. "Creation is not a hurdle on the road to God, it is the road itself." Creatures are placed in my way so that I may find my way with them to God. The real God is the Creator, and all beings stand before him in relation to one another in his creation. "The real God lets no shorter line reach him than each man's longest. . . . Only when all relations, uncurtailed, are taken into the one relation, do we set the ring of our world round the sun of our being." Buber did not, as it appears, say that Kierkegaard's God is not the true God, only his conception of our relationship to God: "Who is there who confesses the God whom Kierkegaard and I confess, who could suppose in decisive insight that God wants *Thou* to be truly said only to him, and to all others only an unessential and fundamentally invalid word?"

Even here Buber does not lose his emphasis upon the singleness of the Single One. In order to bring all our finite *Thous* into our dialogue with the "eternal Thou" we must create for ourselves an innerworldly "monastery" which will prevent our bonds with the world from being dissipated. This loneliness in the midst of life, in which we take refuge as "retreats," is imperative if we do not wish to see our participation in the Present Being dying off. Kierkegaard is an image of the human condition for us; for he is, like us, isolated and exposed, and this is the fate of man as man. But he is not a human image which can give us meaningful direction for personal and social existence; for we know an organic continuance and grace of preservation from which, like a schizophrenic, he wants to win us into his private world as if it were the true one. Buber's "narrow ridge" is not on the fringe of life but precisely at its center: "We, ourselves, wandering on the narrow ridge, must not shrink from the sight of the jutting rock on which he stands over the abyss; nor may we step on it. We have much to learn from him, but not the final lesson." "I do not say that Kierkegaard on his rock, alone with the mercy of the Merciful, is forbidden. I say only that you and I are forbidden." Kierkegaard's view is acosmic; it denies the creation. But God the Creator does not hover over his creation as a chaos; he embraces it. "He is the infinite *I* that makes every *It* into his Thou," and we imitate God when in our human way we embrace the bit of world offered to us by saying *Thou* with our being to the beings who surround us, loving God's creation in His creatures.

What is most remarkable is that, living in Nazi Germany, Buber could still affirm the body politic as the human world which seeks to realize in its genuine formations our turning to one another in the context of creation. If Kierkegaard in his horror of the perverted forms social life takes turned away, Buber a century later had far more reason to do so. But Buber, who confessed himself in one of his Hasidic writings as one ineluctably destined to love the world, pronounced, "The person who has not ceased to love the human world in all its degradation is able even today to envision genuine social form." The form to which Buber pointed in particular was the very one that Kierkegaard shunned—marriage. In true marriage the confrontation with the body politic and its destiny can no longer be shirked. In this witness to marriage, Buber demonstrated once again how important his own marriage with Paula was to the development and continuance of his philosophy of dialogue. To enter into the sacrament of marriage is to take seriously the fact that the other *is,* the fact that I cannot legitimately share in the Present Being without sharing in the being of the other. If I do this, I have decisively entered into relation with otherness, "and the basic structure of otherness, in many ways uncanny but never quite unholy or incapable of being hallowed, in which I and the others who meet me in this life are interwoven, is the body politic." Our human way to the infinite is through fulfilled finitude, and of the many forms of finitude it is marriage that is the exemplary bond. In confirming my partner in marriage as the unique person he or she is, I come to "that vital acknowledgment of many-faced otherness—even in contradiction and conflict with it—from which dealings with the body politic receive their religious sanction." That the persons with whom we have to do have not merely a different way of thinking and feeling, a different conviction and attitude, but also "a different perception of the world, a different recognition and order of meaning, a different touch from the regions of existence, a different faith, a different soil: to affirm all this . . . in the midst of the hard situations of conflict, without relaxing their real seriousness, is the way by which we may . . . be permitted . . . to touch on the other's 'truth' or 'untruth,' 'justice' or 'injustice.' "

> But to this we are led by marriage, if it is real, with a power for which there is scarcely a substitute, by its steady experiencing of the life-substance of the other as other, and still more by its crises and the overcoming of them which rises out of the organic depths. . . .

Buber carried marriage over as a metaphor to the Single One who lives with the body politic, wed to it and suffering its destiny with it. Even if the Single One does not achieve much, "He has God's own time" and "receives God for his companion"; for he "loves God and his companion in one." He meets God by putting his arms around creation and faces the biographical and historical hour which approaches him in its "apparently senseless contradiction, without weakening the impact of otherness in it." He may not, indeed, have dialogue with Hitler as a person. But the situation in which Buber stood, the situation in which Hitler was, in Martin Heidegger's words, "the lord of the hour," Buber recognized as "God's question" to him, "whether it sound with angels' or with devils' tongues," although he also took care to add, "of course, without the devils thereby being turned into angels"—a mistake which the "pious" all too often make! No one must interfere with our hearing this claim and responding to it from the depths where hearing passes into being. Human truth is bound up with the responsibility of the person. It becomes existentially true only when we stand the test in hearing and responding. "True community and true commonwealth will be realized only to the extent to which the Single Ones become real out of whose responsible life the body politic is renewed."

CHAPTER 11

·———————————————·

Jewish Education as Spiritual Resistance

·———————————————·

ON MARCH 22, 1933, Robert Weltsch wrote Buber from Berlin that most of the German Jews had not yet taken in the fact that most probably the complete establishment of a Jewish system of schools and culture would be necessary. "The monstrous difficulty in this undertaking lies in the fact that an abrupt impoverishment of German Jewry is taking place." On March 24, Buber wrote to Hermann Gerson that if the core of German Jews (with the exception, of course, of the separatist movement of the extreme Orthodox) put their trust in him, he would be ready to take over the responsible leadership of Jewish education in Germany.

On April 1, the boycott was imposed upon all Jews in Germany, even those of one-quarter Jewish blood, although the wearing of the yellow badge with the Star of David on it was not made mandatory until September 19, 1941. It was this identification, as Nora Levin has pointed out, that made it possible later to begin the mammoth task of the systematic extermination of six million Jews. On April 4, Robert

Weltsch published an editorial in the *Jüdische Rundschau* which was itself a high mark of spiritual resistance to the Nazis and saved many Jews from suicide. "Wear the Yellow Badge with Pride!" it was titled, recalling the Church's forcing the Jews to wear this badge in the medieval ghettoes. "The Jews can only speak today as Jews," it read. "Anything else is totally senseless." The shattering of the old conceptions by the Nazi revolution is lamentable for many, but in this world only those can assert themselves who look the facts in the eyes, Weltsch declared. If the Jews want it enough, if they are mature and possess enough inner greatness, this can be a day of Jewish awakening and rebirth. Like Buber, Weltsch called the Jews to self-knowledge, and he also took them to task for not heeding and for even mocking Herzl's Zionism. The Jews have not betrayed Germany, Weltsch said. If they have betrayed anything, it is themselves. This badge of shame we shall wear as a sign of honor; for Jews are needed who are openly recognized *as Jews*. This is the *moral meaning* of the present happening. "The need produced a new relation of brotherhood, a feeling of communion that was fortunate to many," said Robert Weltsch in retrospect. "In this circle Buber was recognized by all as the central personality. Without him this period is unthinkable."

It was Martin Buber, more than any other single person, who taught the assimilated German Jews why they were suffering and by reawakening their Jewish consciousness gave them a counterweight against total despair. Before 1933, Menachem Gerson has pointed out, Buber's influence upon German Jewry was profound but not wide. After Hitler's rise to power, many who had not formerly concerned themselves with Buber or had dismissed him as an esoteric, incomprehensible prophet now found in him their pathfinder and comforter. Surprised and unprepared and lacking any clear sense of Jewish identity, they suddenly found in Buber's teaching what they needed to withstand the cruel demand of the hour. He awakened many to a meaningful Jewish existence and prepared them spiritually for Aliyah (emigration to Palestine). By his personal engagement in every type of course, program, and lecture, and by his direction of cultural and educational activities, Buber quickly became famous, along with the great Rabbi Leo Baeck, as the fearless spokesman for the German Jews. During the time of his people's greatest trial and suffering since the beginning of the Diaspora, Buber provided leadership of a rare quality, teaching them to face their ultimate destiny with courage and faith through a deeper affirmation of their Jewishness. "None of those who heard

Buber's lectures at the college of Jewish Education in Berlin will ever forget them," writes Dr. Bertha Badt-Strauss. "It was like an island of peace in the daily-renewed flaring-up of the Nazi persecution of the Jews." Perhaps even more important was Buber's organization of small groups of teachers and disciples who toiled and lived together in work communities. Through these activities, by counseling, comforting, and raising their dejected spirits, he saved countless numbers from spiritual despair.

Toward the end of April 1933, Buber wrote to Nahum Glatzer, who was already in London, that despite all present difficulties and those still to come, he was determined to remain in Germany as long as possible and to devote his forces to the erection of a new structure of Jewish education and culture. On May 21, Buber spoke to a large group of Jewish teachers and educators on the problem of laying the foundation for a self-sufficient Jewish culture. In this lecture at the Berlin Jewish Community, Buber proposed the establishment of an essentially Jewish school in which the teaching of Judaism would not be confined to separate religious lessons but would serve to illuminate the problems of the present. Although the connection between German Jews and the German civilization of the past was beyond dispute, the firm belief of the German Jews in being rooted in the fabric of German civilization was an illusion. In so doing, Buber was raising at a crucial moment an extremely controversial topic over which German Zionists and anti-Zionists had been at loggerheads in the past. How right he was in doing so his hearers learned only as the new educational policy of the Reichsvertretung der deutschen Juden (the Jewish body responsible to the Nazis) temporized, out of a conviction that large numbers of German Jewry could continue to live in Germany despite their radically insecure circumstances. The very existence of the Reichsvertretung depended upon this insistence that the Jews were not asked to renounce loyalty to German culture.

At the end of May, Buber invited Otto Hirsch, co-leader of the Reichsvertretung, and Max Gruenewald, rabbi and communal leader at Mannheim, to his home to discuss his ideas about Jewish education, and two days later he wrote Ernst Simon in Jerusalem asking him to consider working with him in these undertakings. He also went to Berlin to take part in meetings of the Reichsvertretung. Though he wrote Gerson at the time, "this hecticness is not for me," it became a necessary lifestyle for the five years he was to remain in Germany. Gerson himself later described this period of Buber's life as one of "tireless activity undertaken in an atmosphere of insecurity and anxiety." Meanwhile in Berlin, the liberals and the Orthodox squabbled as to whether some more neutral person could not be found to lead the reconstruction of Jewish education, while Leo Baeck testified that Buber was "uniquely qualified" to do so.

Buber had presented the leadership of the Reichsvertretung with two proposals for educational programs in which he stated that such a great communal work could be carried out only in a unified spirit and under a unified leadership. The task of this educational leader (Buber himself) would be to establish schools for the Jewish children who had been excluded from the public schools by Nazi laws, schools which would inculcate into the new generation the living substance of Judaism and create a human type capable of enduring under the most difficult conditions of the struggle for existence. In these proposals, he stressed the current implications as well as the historical significance of Jewish education for the social, economic, political, cultural, and religious life of Jewry. He was not concerned with an aggregate of subjects but a normative knowledge that would teach the students how to comprehend and master the present situation. Specifically, in addition to Hebrew, the Bible, and history, he wanted sociological studies of the German Jews and their culture.

The Reichsvertretung countered by bringing into being an "educational committee" in place of the unified leadership that Buber proposed. Individual members of the Reichsvertretung attacked Buber unjustly as belonging to the very union of progressive educators with which he had passionately taken issue in his speech "Education." What disappointed Buber even more was that he did not see any force arising from the youth to assist him; for without this force he could not imagine how it would be possible to break through the petrified resistance and to carry out a monstrously difficult task under the worst possible conditions.

In response to an encouraging letter of Leo Baeck ("Let the crows crow. This time no one paid much attention to them"), Buber wrote that he could not imagine carrying out the task of Jewish education within the framework of a committee and was unwilling to take part in such work. His conception of the methods to be used was bound indissolubly to the unified position of leadership that he had proposed. At the same time, he did not entirely close the door to membership on the committee, "since now too I am willing to do all in my power to make possible an 'answer to what is happening.'" In September, the

Jewish community of Mannheim offered Buber the place for his proposed "School for the Knowledge of Judaism" and offered to care for
its administration. This was made possible by the support of Max
Gruenewald, who recognized in the German Jews who had returned
to Judaism a tendency "to jump from a vainglorious German patriotism to a glorification of the East European Jew" and easily to fall into
a romanticism and idealization that blocked the road to real understanding. "It is interesting," writes Gruenewald, "that Martin Buber,
who taught him [the German Jew] the ways of the Chassidim and
pathways in the Bible, also introduced a new subject matter in the
Jewish school curriculum . . . *Gegenwartskunde:* The plain—and sometimes not so plain—facts about the conditions under which the Jew
lived in modern times and the lands in which he was to continue his
existence." At the end of his address "Our Educational Goal" (June
1933) Buber stated: "We educate for Palestine, for those for whom it
may be the land; for some strange country, for those for whom it must
be the land; for Germany, for those for whom it can be the land. It is
one human image, *one* goal, *one* education."

In November 1933, Buber reopened the Frankfurt Lehrhaus, which
he directed until his departure for Palestine in 1938. At his speech at
the opening of the Lehrhaus, Buber quoted Rosenzweig's statement
thirteen years before: "The need is urgent today, and today the means
of help must be found." "Only today," Buber commented, "because
of the situation in which we find ourselves have his words revealed
their full significance. Only today do we know in a fundamental way
what life need and the demand of the deed is." The method characteristic of the Lehrhaus, that of intensive interchange between teacher
and students, a community in which there is a transaction between
teachers and students, in which both groups learn and teach, is necessary, Buber asserted, in order to arm young Jews to meet the situation
and to meet it as Jews. To do this, it was not necessary to separate
themselves from that German part of their heritage which was theirs
whatever the attitude of the Nazis, but to strengthen and renew the
Jewish by becoming a *people* of God. This meant, said Buber, an education toward a community of memory, immediacy of living together
with one another, and a community of work. "In our history need has
always had an awakening power." Need and force can be transformed
into a freedom and blessing.

Non-Jews as well as Jews attended the courses at the Lehrhaus, as
before during the Rosenzweig era. Despite the fear that must have held

back many, there was an intellectual freedom here that was largely disappearing from the increasingly Nazi-dominated culture of the "Aryan superrace." In memoirs of the time, Buber's lectures at the Lehrhaus were described as "historic events." It was about this time that Buber's disciple and friend, and Rosenzweig's faithful follower, Ernst Simon returned from Palestine to help with the Lehrhaus and with the broader tasks of Jewish adult education that Buber undertook. Simon provided a rare example of a German Zionist who had "ascended to the Land" yet was able to respond to the summons of the hour by voluntarily returning to a Germany shrouded in the dread darkness that had not yet descended when he left.

In December 1933, Buber wrote to Otto Hirsch setting forth proposals for the school at Mannheim which he later carried over to his work in the Mittelstelle (Central Office for Jewish Education). Specifically he proposed five main subjects for Jewish students: language, Bible, community, history, and faith—all leading to a communal treatment of present Jewish problems, an organic connection of present and past, and a great organic spiritual unity that only the support of the German Jewry as such could make possible. Leo Baeck wrote Buber a week later in the name of the Reichsvertretung offering him the leadership of just such a school in Mannheim. But as the Jewish historian Professor Ismal Elbogen pointed out to Buber, it was not likely that many Jewish teachers from Berlin or Breslau would be able to come to Mannheim to teach, and Otto Hirsch too wrote Buber that it was essential that the school should have more than a "local significance." In January 1934, Chaim Weizmann wrote Buber from the London office of the Central Bureau for the Settlement of German Jews that there was hardly another personality that could, like him, prepare the German Jews spiritually and psychologically for immigration to Palestine. "It is, therefore, for me a special joy to be assured of your trust and your friendship, and this fact makes me especially strong and encourages me to carry on this difficult work with heightened force."

In March 1934, Buber wrote to Otto Hirsch that the "School for Judaism" could not be erected with any prospect of real success: while there were many members of the audience, there were not sufficient candidates to be trained as teachers nor was there any expectation of their coming to Mannheim. In its place, he suggested a central office for adult Jewish education organized along the lines of the folk schools that he had long been interested in. The task of the central office, which Buber proposed to locate in Frankfurt, would be to erect adult schools, houses for learning, "Schools for Youth," courses of different kinds. It was this proposal which served as the model for the "Central Office for Jewish Adult Education" that Buber directed for the Reichsvertretung. Through this position Buber exercised an enormous influence on every aspect of Jewish education and culture in Germany during the next five years.

In May 1934, in a short essay on Jewish adult education, Buber elaborated on his understanding of folk education. It cannot be intellectual; for it is obliged to grasp the totality of the human. But it also cannot be grounded on instincts, or "vitality"; for it must serve the living, life-embracing spirit with the whole bodily person. Nor can it be individualistic, since it has to place individuals in immediate contact with their fellows and allow even the smallest circle of community to sprout. Neither can it aim at a collectivity which has its existence only in the toil of its members and not in their genuine relationship to one another. Finally, it cannot be a universalistic education which depreciates the special forces of nature and tradition and seeks to erase the imprint of history. Neither can it see in ethnic multiplicity a final aim; for it unites this multiplicity under a common work and task. From statements such as this it is clear how Buber's total philosophy served an eminently practical function in this time of dire need.

One of the men to whom Buber became closest in the course of his work at the Mittelstelle was Otto Hirsch, a Swabian of deep-rooted Jewish piety. Hirsch responded to Buber's teaching and character not only by placing at his disposal the services of the Reichsvertretung but also, together with his friends Leopold Marx and the great choirmaster Karl Adler, by creating in the Stuttgart Jüdisches Lehrhaus a center from which Buber's personal influence could radiate far beyond Frankfurt. Of a number of Lehrhäuser that arose in Germany at this time, including some in Berlin and Mannheim, the Stuttgart center was the closest successor to the parent organization in Frankfurt. Hirsch's selfless activities in behalf of his fellow Jews exposed him to the wrath of the Nazis. Frequently arrested, he endured his periods of imprisonment "exceedingly well"—in his own opinion because of his "soldierly bearing and experience" but, in Ernst Simon's judgment, even more because of "the inflexible nobility of his character whose obvious qualities must have made an impression on the very torturers themselves." Simon also said of Buber's spiritual resistance to the Nazis through education at this time, "Anyone who did not see Buber then has not seen true civil courage."

Within the framework of the Mittelstelle, Buber summoned a conference on questions relating to Jewish adult education which met at the hostel of Hugo Rosenthal's "Land School Home" at Herrlingen on May 10–13, 1934. The adult educators who met here were given Franz Rosenzweig's essay "Education and No End" and Buber's 1926 address "Education." Buber set the tone for the conference with a keynote address in which he showed by the example of the Danish folk educator Nikolai Grundtvig (1783–1872) how a national crisis can give a decided impulse to adult education. "If a man wishes to bring his 'personality' through the crisis intact," Buber told his fellow educators, "then it is bound to crumble for then the crisis has what it wants —an object that is brittle enough to be cracked by it." In this statement, Buber was faithful to the Hasidic teaching that if one wants to reach a new stage, one must first become nothing, i.e., let go of the old form in order to achieve a new one. Only through a new response could the German Jews retain their community and dignity in the face of the Nazi desire to atomize and destroy them. Other educators spoke on women's questions, the study of the contemporary world, instruction in Bible, Hebrew, and Jewish history, musical instruction, and the retraining of young people for immigration to Palestine. Buber's own lecture was followed by one on "Forms and Institutions" delivered by Professor Ernst Kantorowicz, Buber's first collaborator in the conduct of the Mittelstelle and his successor after Buber's immigration to Palestine. Kantorowicz came from an entirely assimilated Prussian milieu with no knowledge of or tie to Hebrew, Jewish religious life, or Zionism. A radical member of the youth movement, following Gustav Wyneken (a noted pedagogue, who in 1906 founded with Paul Geheeb the Land Education Home Free School Community), until the Nazi rise to power he stood shoulder to shoulder with the underprivileged youth and workers in the social struggle and worked with the Social Democrats in youth work and vocational education. As a director of the pedagogic section of the Free German Higher School (Freies Deutsches Hochstift), he often crossed swords with the ideologists of National Socialist educational theory. "Without the National-Socialist 'revolution,'" comments Simon, Buber and Kantorowicz "would never have been able to work together at a Jewish task."

It was in the Mittelstelle that the authentic tradition of the German adult education movement was carried forward after its destruction by the Nazis. The main teaching staff of the Mittelstelle was nominated in Herrlingen but was extended in June by Simon's return from Palestine and was constantly enlarged by those taking part in Jewish cultural activity centrally or locally. In bringing together formerly conflicting Jewish youth groups, Buber rejected the language of "tolerance" and "neutrality" in favor of that of "making present the roots of community and its branches" and of "solidarity, living mutual support and living mutual action." In these designations, he saw the "model of the great community," the "community of communities."

In 1935, Buber brought these thoughts together in one of the bulletins of the Mittelstelle, under the title "Education and World View." "For the formation of the person and, accordingly, for the formation of the great community growing out of persons and their relations," he wrote, "everything depends upon how much one actually has to do with the world that one is interpreting." Therefore, the decisive question about a world view is whether it furthers one's vital relationship to the world or obstructs it. The world view does not need to get between him and the world. On the contrary, it can help him strive to grasp the facts faithfully if it keeps his love for this "world" so alert and strong that he does not grow tired of perceiving what is to be perceived. "In discussing a text from Jewish literature, such as the Bible, I know that no interpretation, including my own, coincides with the original meaning and that my interpretation is conditioned by my whole being."

> But if I attend as faithfully as I can to what it contains of word and texture, of sound and rhythmic structure, of open and hidden connections, my interpretation will not have been made in vain—I find something, I have found something. And if I show what I have found, I guide him who lets himself be guided to the reality of the text. To him whom I teach I make visible the working forces of the text that I have experienced.

Here we see not just Buber's method of interpreting the Bible, but that faithfulness of the "lived concrete" that informed all his teaching and his living. He recognized, of course, that his faithfulness was a conditioned one, but he saw the possibility here too of constantly drawing the demarcation line and setting limits to this relativizing: up to here and no farther! One can in one's own spirit put a stop to the politicization of truth, to the identification of truth with what is useful.

Franz Rosenzweig (1920).

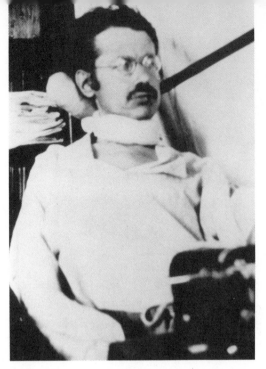

Rosenzweig at the
writing desk (1928).

Martin Buber
in the 1920s.

Buber on his first trip to Palestine (1927).

Buber around 1930.

Buber at the summer camp for
Jewish teachers in Lehnitz, Germany (1934).

Buber with
his German publisher,
Salman Schocken.

Buber with Leo Baeck,
leader of the German Jews under the Nazis.

Buber in
his study
in Jerusalem.

Buber in Palestine.

Buber with
Leo Hermann
of the former
Prague Bar Kochba
Union in Jerusalem
in the 1940s.

Buber in conversation.

Buber with students at the Hebrew University
on Mt. Scopus in Jerusalem (1940).

Buber at his Jerusalem bookdealer's (March 1946).

In his work as director of the Mittelstelle, Buber set as the goal of its educational program bringing groups with different world views into contact with one another in the experience of community. "Only in lived togetherness, indeed, do they really come to sense the power of the whole." Those teaching periods in which the leader united some youth groups according to a single *Weltanschauung* remained in the minority. As a rule several groups of varied orientations came together. Buber himself characterized these two types of groups as homogeneous and heterogeneous.

> The former was an idyll, bright and warm, uninhibited; in the first hour it grew to its full shape. The latter was a drama, hard and eventful. We enjoyed the otherness of the other person. We had something to develop to the full; we did so. We were at loggerheads and then we fell in each other's arms. On the third day, matters had reached a critical point. We had known all along that things couldn't go on like that . . . on the fourth morning sport and singing revealed a new impulse in our togetherness. The first of these two types of class belonged fully to the "Mittelstelle." I would not like to miss it. But only the second does the real work.

Here, even more than in *The Question to the Single One,* Buber pointed the way to what I have called the "community of otherness." The great community "is no union of the like-minded," Buber wrote, "but a genuine living together of men of similar or of complementary natures but of differing minds. Community is the overcoming of *otherness* in living unity." This is not a question of some formal and minimal understanding but of an awareness from the other side of the other's real relation to the truth—"inclusion." "What is called for is . . . a living answering for one another . . . not effacing the boundaries between the groups, circles, and parties, but communal recognition of the common reality and communal testing of the common responsibility." Vital dissociation—the sickness of the peoples of our age—is only seemingly healed through crowding men together. "Here, nothing can help other than persons from different circles of opinion honestly having to do with one another in a common opening out of a common ground." This is the andragogy (the adult pedagogy) of our educational work. "We live—one must say it again—in a time in which the great dreams, the great hopes of mankind, have one after another been fulfilled—in caricature!" This massive experience Buber saw as caused by the power of fictitious conviction, the uneducated quality of the man of this age. "Opposed to it stands the education that is true to its age and adjusts to it, the education that leads man to a vital connection with his world and enables him to ascend from there to faithfulness, to standing the test, to authenticity, to responsibility, to decision, to realization."

The Mittelstelle established contact with teachers and rabbis and with institutions devoted to instruction and study. One of these was the famous Hochschule für die Wissenschaft des Judentums (College for the Science of Judaism) in Berlin, where Leo Baeck had taught. At the Hochschule (now renamed the Lehranstalt by the Nazis, who took away its academic title) the Mittelstelle carried on a series of general cultural courses from 1935 to 1936 and later. Among its noted lecturers was the phenomenologist philosopher Fritz Kaufmann, who had been dismissed from his position at Freiburg by Martin Heidegger, a fellow disciple of Husserl, when Heidegger became the rector. There were also lectures on classical, medieval, and modern history, on Semitic languages, on the study of society, and on other types of philosophy. Buber's lectures on the problem of messianism in January–February 1935 were the link with the Mittelstelle. In addition, the Mittelstelle ran conferences in smaller Jewish communities which usually took place in a country hostel. These meetings (Lernzeiten) began with a cross-country run and breathing exercises (one can imagine that Buber, who outran all his fellow educators after a meeting at the home of Elisabeth Rotten when he was fifty, might have still taken part in these), and meals opened with a quotation from the Bible or a Hasidic story and ended with a saying of grace. The prominent American Jewish educator Meier Ben-Horin, who has written several highly critical articles concerning Buber's philosophy, has said how very deeply he was impressed at one of these conferences by the way in which Buber said the traditional grace, emphasizing every word and communicating the power of presence in such a way that all those attending felt bound together. The themes discussed at these conferences ranged from the Bible to the present day. Buber himself gave a course on the four basic types of biblical style: narrative, prophetic, psalms, proverbs.

In opposition to the spirit of the time, Buber taught the art of reading slowly, treating the meaning and content of holy text in a spirit that was far from orthodox yet possessed maximum fidelity to letter and word, particularly in sound and rhythm and the choice and repetition of words. Thus Buber brought to many who had never before been face to face with the Bible the fruit of his years of work in translating the Bible in the way that he and Rosenzweig pioneered. "It was an experience that has lived with them for decades," testifies Simon. The most important thing that Buber achieved was changing the Bible for his hearers from a book to a spoken teaching. "The biblical word cannot be detached from its spokenness," taught Buber. "Otherwise it loses its concreteness, its corporality. A command is not a sentence but an address." "My Bible course was received downright enthusiastically," Martin wrote Paula from Lehnitz, where a Teachers Training Week took place in the summer of 1934 under the guidance of Buber and Ernst Simon. "Anyone able and willing to learn could derive great benefit from the formulation of the problems and the stimulus received," writes Fritz Friedlander, who himself was a teacher at the First Elementary Boys' School of the Berlin Jewish Community.

A large proportion of the pupils in these Jewish schools were strongly influenced by radical Zionist youth groups which diverted their minds from everything German and led them uncompromisingly toward training farms for Palestine and Youth Aliyah (immigration to "the Land"). The students in the upper forms took it for granted that after learning a trade they would sooner or later leave the country. Despite schools suffering from lack of facilities and crowded classrooms of more than fifty children, the system of Jewish education in Nazi Germany succeeded in molding the whole existence of the individual and thereby laid the foundations for the growth of a generation of Jews capable of striking roots in Palestine or in the countries of the Diaspora. Thus Buber did find support from the Jewish youth of Germany, and his expectations of the Jewish schools were to some extent fulfilled. The Jewish youth joined Buber in refusing to believe—as so many of the older generation continued to—that a Judeo-German symbiotic relationship could exist any longer in Nazi Germany.

This context heightens immeasurably the meaning of the address "Teaching and Deed" which Buber delivered at the Frankfurt Lehrhaus in 1934, as it illuminates the subtitle of *Israel and the World: "Essays in a Time of Crisis."* Israel received both its life and its teachings at the same time and in that hour became a nation and a religious community. The spiritual transmission of the teachings is as vital to the continuation of Israel as bodily propagation. But a generation can receive the teachings only by renewing them; for in a living tradition it is not possible to draw a line between preserving and producing. Only when the older generation time and again stakes its existence in the act of trying to teach, waken, and shape the young does the holy spark leap across the gap. Buber clearly understood the integral connection between the human image and education: "The total, living, Jewish human being is the transmitting agent; total, living, Jewish humanity is transmitted . . . Israel is renewed, not by what they say but by the totality of their existence." Rabbi Leib, Son of Sarah, said that he did not come to the Maggid of Mezritch in order to hear him say Torah but to watch the way in which he laced and unlaced his felt boots. This tale Buber superscribed with the title "Not to Say Torah but to Be Torah!"

But if there can be no teaching apart from doing, neither can there be a doing independent of the teachings: a truly Jewish communal life cannot develop in Palestine if the continuity of Judaism is interrupted and the Jews settle for a mere biological perpetuation and a "civilization" springing from it. Nothing merely social, merely national, or merely religious will be strong enough to ward off decay, for it too will be involved in the "abysmal problematic of the hour." "In this crisis of humanity in which we stand at the most exposed point, the Diaspora cannot preserve its vital connection . . . without recognizing and renewing the power the teachings possess."

In July 1934, the Orientalist Martin Plessner wrote Buber from Haifa, to which he had immigrated from Germany the year before, that he had never read or heard a speech of Buber's, including the *Three Speeches on Judaism,* which he had experienced as so personally directed to him as "Teaching and Deed." Buber's 1920 phrase "to become human and in a Jewish way, as Jews" now gained new meaning for Plessner. Since coming to the Land, he had experienced an unanticipated turning to Judaism which enabled him to teach the Bible, along with Arabic, and contribute a little to that propagation of the spirit that is just as necessary in "the Land" as in the Diaspora.

The noted German scholar Heinz Politzer tells how he first met Buber in 1934 in Prague, where Buber had come to address a meeting of young Zionist socialists agitated by Hitler's rise to power. Politzer had come for comfort, but instead of the sermon he anticipated, Buber talked about the *kvutzot,* the village communes established by the pioneers in Palestine, and the relation of utopian socialism to the biblical teachings about social justice. Although there was neither comfort nor religious fervor in Buber's words, Politzer witnessed "the application of a living belief to the immediate needs of an existential situation."

I had come late, and Buber was already talking when I entered the hall. All I could see of him was his face, the forehead, the aquiline nose, the greying beard, the head of an Old Testament prophet. Gradually he warmed up and left his place behind the lectern; it became obvious that this mighty head was supported by a body smaller than average size and inclined, around the middle, towards a wholly unprophet-like fullness. I noticed his hands, very white, very delicate, and almost feminine. But there was also his voice, scooping the speech, as it were, from the depth of an ever present memory, and audibly reflecting the weight of responsibility which supported the speech without straining the words. Listening, I felt questions as well as objections arise in my mind, and I would like to think that they were not of the most obvious kind. Yet during the very time it took them to arise, Buber had already answered them in his speech. Similar experiences were had by several friends in the audience. This kind of rapport between Buber and his listeners has turned many of his lectures into dialogues with persons who were unknown to him, silent dialogue.

In 1934, Buber also went several times to Munich to help the Jewish youth there set up a mode of resistance of which until then they had hardly been aware. The situation of the dwindling minority of German Jews made impossible both the active resistance of revolution and the passive resistance of noncooperation, but there existed a third way of seemingly invisible resistance, and this is the one which Buber adopted. It was the resistance of the spirit that took inventory of itself and thus unfolded its own powers in confrontation with the power of the Nazis. Both praying and learning could embody such resistance, and of both of these Buber spoke in the great synagogue, not standing at the pulpit above but speaking from a simple table as one of the congregation which at that critical hour had become a community. "Service to God burns" were the last words of Buber's speech on one such occasion, and his words burned deeply into his hearers. "Through Buber's talk," recalls the well-known Israeli writer and journalist Schalom Ben-Chorin, "we sensed in this beautiful room of the chief synagogue of Munich the essential, so often misunderstood significance of this building over which stood the name of God. But we did not yet know that the days of this house were numbered and that this would be Buber's last speech in the synagogue, which shortly thereafter was burned to the ground through an order of the Führer." Buber's Mittelstelle created a new center, Ben-Chorin attests, through which the post-assimilated Jews could again experience what is essential in Judaism. The great and celebrated man, whom they had formerly heard read from his translation of the Bible in the celebrated Cherubin Hall of the Munich literary society the "Argonauts," now came and studied with the Jewish youth of Munich in the small communal hall. In the dialogue between master and pupils, the spoken nature of the Bible was opened to many, including Ben-Chorin, who through this found a way into the Bible for the first time. On these visits, Paula would usually accompany Martin, and the sight of the two of them, outwardly so unlike and inwardly so closely bound together, walking through the streets of his home city of Munich, became for Ben-Chorin an unforgettable symbol of how love between the Jew and the German could be stronger than all hate.

In October 1934, Buber gave a lecture, "The Power of the Spirit," at the Frankfurt Lehrhaus. Later he repeated this lecture at a large public gathering in the Berlin Philharmonie. Although the audience was predominantly Jewish, there were also quite a number of non-Jews, including some two hundred S.S. men, dispersed throughout the hall and especially in the gallery. In this remarkable setting Buber delivered an unmistakable challenge to the gods of the time by distinguishing among Christianity, which holds the elemental powers in subjection; paganism, which glorifies them; and Judaism, which sanctifies them. "Spirit is not a late bloom on the tree, Man," Buber stated, "but is what constitutes man." But this is so only if spirit is understood not just as one human faculty among others but as man's totality, "the totality which comprises and integrates all his capacities, powers, qualities, and urges." The spirit, therefore, has three possible relationships to the elemental forces: their glorification, their conquest, or that hallowing through which they are transformed. "Neo-paganism," by which Buber meant Nazism, couples Judaism with Christianity, arguing that both of them deny the great vital powers. Neo-paganism declares these powers holy as they are, thus creating a dualism between a spirit alien to the world and world alien to the spirit. "Blood and soil," the Nazi slogan, which the Nazi leader Alfred Rosenberg at the Nuremberg trials sought to link Buber with, is actually opposed to the true spirit of Judaism which proclaims: "Blood and soil are hallowed in the promise made to Abraham, because they are bound up with the command to be 'a blessing' (Genesis 12:2). 'Seed' and 'earth' are promised but only in order that . . . a new people may 'keep the way of the Lord to do righteousness and justice' (Genesis 18:19) in his land, and so begin building humanity."

The Christian desanctification of hunger, sex, and the will to power left the spirit holy and the world unholy. "Even when Christianity includes natural life in its sacredness, as in the sacrament of marriage, the bodily life of man is not hallowed but merely made subservient to holiness."

In contrast to both Christianity and Nazi neo-paganism, Judaism sees the spirit as taking possession of man for the sake of hallowing the world; for everything created, including all the urges and elemental forces of the body, has a need to be hallowed and is capable of receiving it. "Hallowing transforms the urges by confronting them with holiness and making them *responsible* toward what is holy." In this hallowing, "the total man is accepted, confirmed, and fulfilled. This is the true integration of man." Buber closed his speech with a ringing and unmistakable challenge to Nazism. If this spirit of Judaism which hallows the elemental urges "is given a new shape, it will be able to resist even in areas where the barely tamed elemental forces and urges are supreme."

As a result of this speech in the presence of the S.S. men, even after the lifting of the ban on Buber's teaching on February 21, 1935, he was no longer allowed to speak in public. When a ban on Buber's speaking at public functions and in closed sessions of Jewish organizations was announced, the Frankfurt Quaker Rudolf Schlosser offered Buber the opportunity of continuing his lectures at closed sessions of non-Jewish organizations, and in particular at the meetings of the Quakers, an invitation which Buber repeatedly accepted. In March 1935, another teaching ban was announced, although it was later qualified through the intervention of the Reichsvertretung so that Buber could continue his teaching, even if only on a limited scale.

This ever-tightening situation led to the creation of a "new Midrash," to use Ernst Simon's phrase, which, like the old Talmudic commentary, "created for itself, in its disputes with the outside world, an internal language, which was seldom understood by the enemy but almost always by co-religionists." The Jews of Nazi Germany consciously created a new Midrash or filled the old one with topical meaning. An example of this was the annual almanacs and the series of "little books" published by Schocken Verlag, founded by Salman Schocken. The series of Schocken "Buecherei," under the direction of Dr. Moritz Spitzer, began with the volume we have already alluded to, "The Consolation of Israel," in which Chapters 40 to 55 of Isaiah were published in the Hebrew original and in Buber's translation (Rosenzweig died in the middle of their work on this section). The more the oppression increased, the more allusive the language of spiritual resistance had to become until it focused mostly on the text of the Bible, leaving it to the reader to carry out the task of finding the topical meaning. A clear example of this was another Schocken "little book," Buber's selection of twenty-three Psalms under the title, "Out of the depths have I cried unto Thee" (Psalm 130). In his short Preface, Buber rejects all traditional theories as to who the "I" of the Psalms is in favor of the eminently topical assertion that all the individual sufferers and the "humbled" utter their heartfelt words as an outburst of the collective spirit of the community of Israel. The collected Psalms present an autobiography of the people (*Lebensgeschichtlich*), revealing thereby a clear continuity.

Ernst Simon has provided us with a partial deciphering of the allegory of spiritual resistance contained in these Psalms in the order in which Buber printed them. It begins with the cry out of the depths (130:1) for which the need is not yet objectified: "I await his speech" (130:5); complains about God's forgetting (42:10) and asks with the scornful word of the oppressor, "Where is your God?" (42:10); rises to its first consolation: "Yes, now I shall thank him" (41:12; 43:5); becomes impatient: "Thou, But THOU—how long?" (6:3); makes the diagnosis of the time: "For the faithful have vanished from among the children of Adam" (12:2), and "Vileness is exalted among the children of Adam" (12:8); again rises to consolation: "But all those who take shelter in thee will rejoice" (5:11); complains about the absence of prophetic leaders: "There is no longer any prophet" (74:9); yet is sure of its knowledge: "Yet God is my King from of old" (74:12); and one can therefore call to him and demand of Him: "Do not forget forever the life of the soul that is bowed down for thee! Have regard for thy covenant! . . . Arise, O God! fight your fight! remember how the mockers scorn Thee all the day!" (74:19, 20, 22). Yes, God will take vengeance: "All men must fear" (64:9), and save: "But Thou, THOU, dost laugh at them; thou dost hold all the nations in derision" (59:8); and will recognize why Israel suffers: "For it is for thy sake that I have borne reproach, that shame has covered my face" (69:7); will hearken to the prayer of his people: "Pull me from the mire, that I may never sink in it, rescue me from those who hate me, from the deep waters!" (69:14); therefore, one may praise Him (69:35, 36) and to those who deny Him: "The fool says in his heart, 'There is no God!' They are corrupt, they do abominable deeds, there is none that does good" (14:1) are given the answer: "He is the king of time and eternity!"

(10:16). In the face of this eternity the lords of the hour are but a passing show: "Their bellies are fat, they never feel the pain that other men do. They are not in trouble as other people are. Therefore pride is their necklace, violence covers them as a garment. Their eyes swell out with fatness, their hearts overflow with follies" (73:4–7). But God "tries the hearts and the reins, a true God" (7:9), and of those who oppress his people (94:5): "They slay the widow and the sojourner, and murder the orphans . . ." (94:6) because they imagine: "He does not see!" and "the God of Jacob does not notice!" (94:7)—of those it is said: "Blessed is the man whom thou dost chasten . . ." (94:13). If only David and his people will call out (4:2), God will answer, He will hearken to the prayer of those who turn back to Him, those who turn ever again: "Restore us, O God of hosts; let thy face shine, and we shall be liberated!" (80:7, 19). God will save this soul, which, like a liberated bird, slips out from the hands of the one who caught it, from the lying lips and deceitful tongues (120:2; 124:7). Those who return to Zion will be like dreamers (126:1), with laughs in their mouths, with jubilation in their songs (126:2), greeting the dawn with harps and lutes (57:9).

The first Almanac of the Schocken Verlag began with Buber's short essay "The Jewish Man of Today," who is described as "inwardly the most exposed man of our world," in whom the tensions of the epoch are concentrated in order to measure their strength against his. The Jew is a radical, special case of the anthropological situation as such. When Buber published his talks on education in a collected volume, he described the task of Jewish adult education as a task of spiritual resistance to the Nazis: "What was at stake in the work performed under such great difficulties was to oppose Hitler's wish to wear down Jewry; to give the Jews, and especially the young people, unshakable support."

Moritz Spitzer, the editor of the Schocken Almanac, had been connected with Buber since 1919. On May 1, 1932, he moved from Berlin to work with Buber as his personal secretary, and he remained there until late in 1934. Although the Nazis feared Buber in the beginning, they searched his house only once, at which time they received a spirited tongue-lashing from Paula Buber, and the foreign press reported the event. But they searched Spitzer's house in nearby Benz five or six times to find something incriminating on Buber. They even put Spitzer in solitary confinement and later issued a deportation order. He protested to the Ministry, and they let him stay until 1939. In the early years not only did no one anticipate the exterminations of the Jews but also no one could have predicted that wide circles of population would tolerate the anti-Jewish measures. In the beginning, in fact, most of the sympathies of the Germans were with the Jews. Although the S.S. men stood before Jewish shops on April 1, 1933, the beginning of the Jewish Boycott, most Germans did buy. But as time went on, brainwashing and fear changed them. On the day after *Kristallnacht*, in November 1938, Spitzer visited a famous New Testament theologian. Both the theologian and his wife had seen the smashed windows and felt very bad about what had happened. Yet they said to Spitzer, "Why are the Jews then so greedy? Why did they not go away long ago?"

Many converted Jews who had been baptized had a bad conscience when Hitler came, and they wrote to Buber to find their way back to Judaism. Buber gave these letters to Spitzer to answer. One such was Angelica Reckendorff, whose father had been baptized in order to become a professor of Islamics (even under the Weimar Republic the Jews did not enjoy full rights and equality). Angelica converted to Judaism and became strictly Orthodox under the guidance of the biologist Professor Bruno Kisch. Spitzer had a friend who was a very observant Catholic and whose uncle was a bishop. His wife was a Jewess who wanted to be baptized when she married, but he would not allow it. Like Franz Rosenzweig, he did not believe a Jew could convert to Christianity as a pagan but only as one who really understood Judaism from within. He asked Moritz Spitzer to give her teaching in Judaism. Since Spitzer was leaving Berlin to work with Buber at that time, he proposed Dr. Joachim Prinz in his place. In 1934, he came with Buber to a series of lectures in the Lehranstalt des Judentum in Berlin (the former Hochschule). Spitzer was late to one of the lectures, so he sat in the last row. In a pause, he noticed the Baroness Goldenberg sitting some rows in front of him. She had become an ardent Jewess. (When Spitzer related this incident to Professor Ernst Michel, who had simply declined to swear allegiance to the Nazis, Michel retorted: "That I can get everyday. But for that Schnözel [good for nothing] I must leave Germany!")

In 1934, Spitzer, who had been working part-time with Buber for the Schocken Verlag, left Heppenheim and went to Berlin to take over full charge of the publishing firm. Buber was closely connected with the Schocken Verlag, and he always gave Spitzer his advice. As a young man, as we have seen, Schocken had discovered Buber's *Tales of Rabbi Nachman* and venerated Buber. But when he became more and more successful with his department stores and other businesses, he suffered from a sense of dependence on Buber, spiritual and otherwise. "The real rub between Schocken and Buber," Spitzer claims, "was that Schocken was envious of Buber." Schocken always did what Buber wanted him to, but he was angry at him. "Is it a Schocken Verlag or a Buber Verlag?" Schocken used to say to Spitzer. Buber himself once said to me that Schocken wished to run a publishing house as he ran his department store.*

At a Jewish gathering at which Buber spoke in 1937 a gentleman arose at the beginning and disclosed, in a somewhat embarrassed tone, that he was an official of the Gestapo, a remarkable occurrence at the very least. He was invited to take a seat and participate in the proceedings. Buber and the other people present spoke for three hours about religious questions. The Gestapo official dutifully made notes, but he also gave Buber the impression that he listened with personal interest. At the conclusion he said, "We Christians can subscribe to that word for word." After further speech and answer, he seized Buber's right hand with both his hands and said: "Stay well!" On the journey from Leipzig back to Heppenheim, Buber asked Paula about her impression of this man and his parting words. "That was just a euphemism!" she replied. Buber translated this euphemism as "God grant that we do not have to kill you!"

At another time, Buber went walking in Heppenheim. A man stood on the path before him and said, "Na, you Jew!" "Na, you oaf!" Buber retorted, without hesitation. The man was nonplused. "I admired his presence of mind," comments Werner Kraft, to whom Buber told this story. We can also admire his courage. Many Germans of high standing were, unfortunately, cowardly, Buber remarked to Kraft and added, "I do not understand how one can live at all without courage."

In January 1935, Ernst Simon wrote Buber thanking him for all that his work with him during the previous half-year had given him. ",I believe it was a decisive time of my life." Of the most important, the human, he could not say much, but he could tell Buber that now, as a result of the place that the Bible had played in their work, he knew how he stood toward the Bible and how he could learn it. "For that and for all, my thanks always." Others have testified less directly and more publicly to what Buber meant to them at this time, such as the noted Israeli literary critic Baruch Kurzweil, who said that Buber's

---

*See Note to Chapter 11.

teaching of the Bible was so vital, so impressive, as to be imprinted indelibly upon all who were fortunate enough to study with him. At no yeshiva or seminary did the verses of the Bible take on such a deep significance, burningly convincing in their topicality. Although he had been familiar with literary interpretations of the Bible before he met Buber, when Kurzweil heard Buber lecture in a great hall in the winter of 1936–1937 he experienced what he described as a spiritual *teshuvah,* or turning of the whole being. "Buber's lecture opened to me a new method of reading the Bible, and of reading in general." In August 1935, Franz Rosenzweig's close friend Eduard Strauss wrote Buber expressing his fears that all of their educational work might be taken over by the compulsory organization for Jewish culture that the Nazis had established. But at the same time, he said that if a fateful moment in German-Jewish history had not been allowed to pass unnoticed, it was because at the top was the right, the decisive Jewish person, and "this man—*is you,* dear Martin! . . . I have from a wholly personal need the longing *to confess to you who have always confirmed it:* You are he, dear friend. And as I write this, Franz stands before me and I see his approving look."

Robert Weltsch testifies that since the days of the Mittelstelle a new path was opened on all sides for Jewish education and culture. This can be observed in many institutions in Israel, but also in the countries of the Diaspora. It is true where Buber's disciples have been directly at work, and, moreover, his influence has also penetrated in places where the name of the Mittelstelle is not even known. "Wherever Jewish culture is pursued in the world today, the name Buber cannot be ignored," writes Weltsch. "Directly and indirectly, many times diluted or totally misunderstood, the mighty stream that flowed from Buber's education of the people has reached and fructified even those who are far away."

On his sixtieth birthday in February 1938, Buber received a great many testimonials from those with whom he had worked during those years in Jewish adult education. One of these was from Ernst Kantorowicz, who succeeded him in the direction of the Mittelstelle when he immigrated to Palestine a month later. "When you summoned me to work with you," wrote Kantorowicz, "I did not know what difficulties we would encounter and what difficulties would arise precisely from the fact of my working together with you. The objectivity and the human trust that you displayed toward me, and that I responded to from my heart, made this work possible for me. . . . Such a human alliance of two such very different people seems to me to be a consolation for life, and I could only wish that it would endure over time and space." That it would not endure, Kantorowicz already knew, and he added, "With many who are bound to you in friendship, I feel the turn that your life is now taking as a tragic one."

In numerous demonstrations, communications, and congratulations, the Jewish public of Germany expressed the gratitude and respect of the Jews in Germany on the occasion of Buber's sixtieth birthday. All leading Jewish institutions, the Reichsvertretung, the Jewish community of Berlin and other great communities, the Jewish Cultural Union, the Lehrhäuser, and many unions and organizations sent to Buber their warm greetings and best wishes. The presidium of the Reichsvertretung, Leo Baeck and Otto Hirsch, personally presented Buber in his house in Heppenheim with congratulations in the name of the Jewish community of Germany. One of these, written in parchment and bound in leather, was a statement making Buber an honorary member of the Zionist Union of Germany. "Zionism in Germany in its development and at its height is unthinkable without you," it read. "You have taught us that to be a Zionist, to be a Jew, and to be a human being are for us a single unity. . . . Your call to awake is equally valid for the Zion of the world and the Zion of the soul. . . . Three generations of German Zionists are bound to you in love and gratitude." An issue of the *Jüdische Rundschau* contained a series of articles thanking and honoring Buber, including a number by close friends such as Hugo Bergmann, Robert Weltsch, and Hermann Gerson. The one that most aptly summed up this phase of Buber's life was that by Ludwig Feuchtwanger on "The Educator"; for Buber's central service during these trying and strenuous years had been, in all he did and said, to bring before the Jews of Germany a biblical humanism that gave them a new image of man.

After the Nazi passage, in 1935, of the still harsher set of restrictions on the Jews known as the Nuremberg Laws, Leo Baeck composed a special prayer for the Yom Kippur service (the Jewish Day of Atonement). This prayer exactly expresses the spirit of Buber's speeches of that period: the combination of self-knowledge and self-judgment, on the one hand, and the refusal to accept the judgment of the Nazis and their attempts to vilify, defame, and demoralize the Jewish people, on the other. "Every person should have two pockets to use as the occasion demands," said the Hasidic rabbi Bunam. "In one pocket is, 'For my sake the world was created,' and in the other, 'I am dust and ashes.' " This occasion demanded that both pockets be taken out. Baeck, like Buber, walked the narrow ridge between self-righteousness and self-abasement, the same narrow ridge walked by all the contenders with God and man from Abraham and Job on. Thus Baeck, who had already recognized in 1933 that "the thousand-year-old history of German Jewry is at an end," stood shoulder to shoulder with Buber, Hirsch, Simon, and many others in the work of spiritual resistance to the Nazis:

> In this hour every man in Israel stands erect before his Lord, the God of justice and mercy, to open his heart in prayer. Before God we will question our ways and search our deeds, the acts we have done and those we have left undone. We will publicly confess the sins we have committed and beg the Lord to pardon and forgive. Acknowledging our trespasses, individual and communal, let us despise the slanders and calumnies directed against us and our faith. Let us declare them lies, too mean and senseless for our reckoning.
>
> God is our refuge. Let us trust Him, our source of dignity and pride. Thank the Lord and praise Him for our destiny, for the honour and persistence with which we have endured and survived persecution.
>
> Our history is the history of the grandeur of the human soul and the dignity of human life. In this day of sorrow and pain, surrounded by infamy and shame, we will turn our eyes to the days of old. From generation to generation God redeemed our fathers, and He will redeem us and our children in the days to come. We bow our heads before God and remain upright and erect before man. We know our way and we see the road to our goal. At this hour the house of Israel stands before its God. Our prayer is the prayer of all Jews; our faith is the faith of all Jews living on the earth. When we look into the faces of one another, we know who we are; and when we raise our eyes heavenward, we know eternity is within us. For the Guardian of Israel neither slumbers nor sleeps. Mourning and desolation overflow our hearts. Devoutly and with awe let us look into the innermost depths of our souls, and let that which cannot be spoken sink into the silence of meditation.

On behalf of the Reichsvertretung, Otto Hirsch distributed copies of this prayer to all the synagogues in Germany to be read aloud on Yom Kippur. As a result, both he and Leo Baeck were arrested and confined in the S.S. prison in Columbia House. Both Hirsch and Baeck were frequently arrested, and Hirsch suffered intermittent tortures. In 1941, Hirsch was sent to the Mauthausen concentration camp, where he was murdered. In 1942, Leo Baeck voluntarily went to the concentration camp in Theresienstadt to be with his fellow Jews. There the famous author of *The Essence of Judaism* wrote the remarkable history of Israel that he titled *This People: Jewish Existence,* thus making the journey from nineteenth-century essentialism to twentieth-century existentialism! In 1943, on the occasion of Leo Baeck's seventieth birthday, Buber published in Palestine a little tribute titled "In Theresienstadt." There he recounted the story he had told in the *Jüdische Rundschau* on Baeck's sixtieth birthday of how a famous, noble man, until then personally unknown to him, had come to visit him at his house in Heppenheim and had responded to the question of what it really meant to be noble by the statement, "When I want to conceive of the noble, I think of Leo Baeck." Coming from this person, the statement made a special impression on Buber. But he did not attain an insight into its depths as long as the image that he bore in himself was, "Baeck in Berlin." Only since the image "Baeck in Theresienstadt" replaced it did he penetrate further. "And in night hours of a most intensive wakefulness between light sleep and light sleep, it becomes at times uncannily present to me that he is there and I am here. Ah, you who are at ease in Zion and who imagine all the virtues of the nation are concentrated here, cast your glance there toward where those in the innermost vortex stand true!" In conversation with Kraft, Buber asked whether the Nazis would also have sent him, Buber, to Theresienstadt and added, "If they did not, I would have had to go there when Baeck went." "A remarkable question to which I could not respond!" Kraft comments and adds, "It sounded like a belated shudder."

Writing the editors of the *Jüdische Rundschau* on its fortieth birthday in 1935, Buber averred that the greatest praise he could give it was the way it had represented Jewry and Judaism in the last two years: with pride and composure; upright, not sparing our lacks but showing them in their real dimensions; courageous, with a peaceful, matter-of-fact courage, without bravado and without emphasis; clever, giving to every report the right language and to every expression of opinion the right tone; unprejudiced, abstaining from all outbursts, irritation, and pettiness; able to adjust and wait, true to facts and ideas at once; significant, unforgettable, historic. In 1961, in a statement published for Robert Weltsch's seventieth birthday, Buber spoke of the *Jüdische Rundschau,* which Weltsch edited, and of the Mittelstelle, which he himself directed, as two fighting, spiritual institutions that had led to a concrete and independent Jewry that, instead of imitating the Nazis while using Jewish names, prepared a specific Jewish humanism.

In 1941, Buber placed the spiritual resistance to the Nazis within the context of the Maccabees' fight for monotheism which is commemorated on the Jewish festival of Hanukkah. In language reminiscent of *The Question to the Single One* and "Education and World View," he described this fight as one in which those who know about the *one* truth that is not dependent upon us but upon which, rather, we are dependent, are opposed by all those for whom the truth is nothing other than the changing product of psychological or social conditions. This was and is the battle of the one God against the many idols. "In our time this battle of Antiochus is being fought anew—by Hitler against Jewry." When Hitler says, "Conscience is a Jewish invention," and when he pictures his battle against Jewry as a battle for the destiny of the whole world, it becomes clear that here it is not two nations but two ultimate principles that contend. It is no wonder that in 1963, against Hannah Arendt and others, Buber defended those who led the German Jews at the time of the Nazis: "Our disposition in that time proved true in all essentials."

The choice which Buber made years before between Theodor Herzl the leader and Ahad Ha'am the teacher was embodied anew in the contrast that Ernst Simon made between the role of Leo Baeck and that of Martin Buber in the spiritual resistance against Nazism. Simon, who knew and worked with both men, declared that both "belonged among the outstanding and courageous leaders of German Jewry in its most critical hour." Baeck, however, "was forced to take responsibility for the organized Jewish community at the end of German-Jewish history, and thus faced the necessity imposed on men of action to make unavoidable compromises." Buber, who did not have that responsibility, taught "the meaning of spiritual resistance against identification with the aggressor . . . He was and remained our teacher, not a leader of men."

CHAPTER 12

·_____·

Last Years in Germany

·_____·

WRITING TO BUBER IN 1933 to thank him for his book of essays and speeches *Kampf um Israel,* "which has meant more to me even than the Hasidic Legends," Max Picard said that it was rare that as one grows older he becomes more of a person, something which is made possible only because a life is open to what comes "from above." "One of the paradoxes of eternity is that what is 'from above' needs time in order to become more." In 1934, the economist-philosopher Kurt Singer wrote Buber from Japan, also in response to books that Buber sent him, that a great dialogue, spoken and silent, had been going on between them underground since their first meeting and that the same stream bore them both.

Buber wrote to Albert Schweitzer on the occasion of his sixtieth birthday that for many years the knowledge that Schweitzer existed in this world had strengthened him, and in recent years had consoled him. "I am concerned about the helper, and you have been at all times and in many ways a great helper." Schweitzer responded by telling

Buber how often and with what love and respect he had thought of him since they last met, adding with pathos, "Ah, I had so much to do and was so dreadfully fatigued that I did not exist for acquaintances and friends." Another sad letter was that which Buber received in August of the previous year from his father Carl, who said that if the present uncertain times did not come to an end, there would be nothing left for Martin to do but go to Palestine. "I have grown very old," he said, "and cannot avoid discomforts. I understand that it cannot be otherwise and do not complain." In April 1935, Carl Buber died. Replying to Max Brod's letter of consolation, Buber wrote that he had acquired a new feeling of being bound to others "despite all." In the same letter Buber commented on the collected edition of Kafka that Brod had edited: "It shows how one can live with all honesty on the edge without falling into the abyss. The real refutation of Ivan Karamazov is hidden in it." Leo Baeck also wrote Buber expressing his sadness for the death of his father. "The flowing line between past and present becomes a decisive demarcation when one loses one's father."

"Friendship has become almost obsolete," Buber wrote his friend Eduard Strauss in 1936, "but where it still exists it is one of the few ties binding a humanity that has become disastrously fragmented. (Isaiah 24:19)" A remarkable example of a friendship which persisted through the Nazi period was that of Buber with the Catholic theologian and philosopher Ernst Michel. In May 1936, Michel wrote Buber a "confession" such as he probably could not make to any other person. "If to be a Christian means to believe in the sense of the Gospel of John," he stated, "then I am no Christian." At the same time he affirmed his vital connection with the Old Testament and with the early Jewish Christianity that preceded Paul and John. He saw himself as following Jesus but as belonging to the church only by destiny, not by faith. "I ask myself ever again whether my work within the framework of the Church is legitimate, whether it is permissible for me to speak out." To remain open to it, to wrestle with it, to learn from it how to live with Catholics—this he could do. But he was not a member of the Church in the sense of its self-concept and the demands it placed on its members. "With you and with the Judaism taught by you, Rosenzweig, and others, I know myself bound in faith, although the Law and the Talmud do not and could not have for me binding significance since I am not a Jew in the religious-ethnic sense and have to live by other presuppositions. I tell you all this in confidence," he concluded. One wonders to what extent the disgraceful performance of the

Church vis-à-vis the Nazis precipitated this loss of faith and his confession of it.

The end of 1936 was a period for Buber remarkably like the years immediately preceding his death, and for the same reason—the expectation of an imminent end to his creative and scholarly labors. In this period he completed book after book, even in the midst of the enormously demanding work for Jewish adult education. Yet he also found time to strengthen the bonds of friendship with many to whom he remained close. One of these was the writer Rudolf Pannwitz. At the end of one of his letters Buber confessed to Pannwitz in all candor that he could not find the same inner relation to his poetry as to the rest of his writings but suggested that he not cease sending it to him despite this criticism. Pannwitz replied with a remarkable letter indicating that Buber's dialogue with Paul Natorp over the use of the word "God" showed him how he and Buber were one in root and crown and offered to stand on a "Du" relation with him. To this, Buber responded with "my hand to your outstretched one" (and he used the *Du*—as to very few). "What is so needed in this hour as this!" Two months later Buber wrote Pannwitz that the last weeks had resulted in a crisis in his thought. "I have experienced something surprising that can only be reported orally." Four months after this, Buber wrote Hermann Hesse from Jerusalem upon the latter's sixtieth birthday. He spoke of what Hesse's works had meant to him and his wife, to his children, and even now to his grandchildren, for whom they were selecting appropriate readings. But he spoke even more of how often Hesse visited them in their thoughts and conversations, and of "how happy we are to exist with you in this time—despite all—and how we could not be without you in our world." Hesse responded by sending them two new collections of his reflections (Gedenkblätter) and poems. "My thoughts are often with you, often with sympathy and concern, often almost with envy; for you belong to and can serve a community even if at the cost of frequent suffering."

Buber's interest in psychology and psychiatry also persisted during this period, particularly through his friendship with Hans Trüb and Ludwig Binswanger. The impact of Buber on Trüb was shown by the latter's remarkable 1935 essay "Individuation, Guilt, and Decision: Beyond the Boundaries of Psychology." In this essay Trüb described how he went through a decade-long crisis in which he broke with his personal and doctrinal dependence on the great psychologist Carl Jung in favor of the new insights that his relationship with Buber had given him. The greatest influence on Trüb, according to his own testimony, was not Buber's philosophy but the personal meeting with him, and it was from this meeting that the revolutionary changes in Trüb's method of psychotherapy proceeded. Trüb found himself fully disarmed by the fact that in conversation Buber was not concerned so much about his partner's ideas as about the person himself. In such unreserved interchange, it is simply not possible to bring any hidden intention with one and to pursue it, wrote Trüb. One individuality did not triumph over the other, for each remained continually the same. Yet Trüb emerged from this meeting " 'renewed for all time,' with my knowledge of the reality of things brought one step nearer to the truth." "What gives Buber his imperishable greatness and makes his life symbolic," declared Trüb, "is that he steps forth as this unique man and talks directly to other persons."

> Martin Buber is for me the symbol of *continually renewed decision.* He does not shut the mystery away in his individuality, but rather from out of the basic ground of the mystery itself he seeks binding with other persons. He lets a soft tone sound and swell in himself and listens for the echo from the other side. Thus he receives the direction to the other and thus in dialogue he finds the other as his partner. And in this meeting he consciously allows all of his individuality to enter . . . for the sake of the need and the meaning of the world.

Trüb told how the closed circle of the self which predominated in his analysis was again and again forced outward toward relationship when, despite his will, he found himself confronting his patient as human being to human being. The secret meaning of the lost and forgotten things that the analyst helps bring to the light with the aid of his psychology first reveals itself *in the outgoing to the other* in which the psychotherapist seeks and loves the human being in his patients and allows it to come to him.

The personal experience which caused Trüb to break out of the security of Jung's system was an overwhelming sense of guilt—the guilt of a person who had stepped out of real relationship to the world and tried to live in a spiritual world above reality. Real guilt is the beginning of responsibility, said Trüb, but before the patient can become aware of it, he must be helped by the analyst to become aware of himself in general. This the analyst does through playing the part of both confidant and big brother. He gives the neurotic the understanding that the world has denied her or him and makes it more and more possible to step out of self-imprisonment into a genuine relationship. But to do this, the analyst must avoid the intimacy of a private I-Thou relationship with the patient, as well as the temptation of dealing with the patient as an object. This is that very dialogical relationship of concrete but one-sided "inclusion" which Buber had designated as proper for the teacher in his 1925 essay on "Education" and which in 1958 in the Postscript to *I and Thou* he explicitly applied to the world of the psychotherapist.

In September 1935, Buber responded to Trüb's question of what meaning the principle of "individuation" had for him by suggesting that it is a false term: "We *arise as* individuals, but we become *persons.*" The existential problem of becoming a person which Kierkegaard discussed is dealt with by Jung as a problem of *psychological development.* It does not at all set foot upon the dimension of existence. In a comment on the manuscript of Trüb's book *Psychosynthesis as Psychological-Spiritual Healing Process,* Buber remarked that every act of synthesis is a *factual* protest against the claim of psychoanalysis. It sets the right of reality against that of its symbolic substitute. Synthesis represents the whole, analysis brokenness; synthesis being, analysis its becoming questionable. When Buber himself used the term "psychosynthesis" fifteen years before, he did so in conscious opposition to Freud, whereas Trüb did so in conscious opposition to Jung. Trüb pressed Buber further as to whether the synthesis only became conscious of itself as the positive through the penetration of the analysis which negates it. Buber saw this as a very delicate question. "All becoming conscious is divisive, dangerous, only to be used for healing out of the depths of responsibility—and nonetheless the way goes only through this crisis."

In October 1936, Buber informed Trüb that he was working with intense concentration on a new book on the "place" of faith, a section of which would deal with madness. "Naturally, I am not concerned with theories." Trüb referred him to Ludwig Binswanger, the lifelong friend of Freud and founder of an important school of existential analysis, for literature on the subject. Trüb himself was much more oriented to practice than to theory, although he had the gift, which Binswanger did not at all possess, of writing simply, clearly, and intimately. "I am very happy that you now have many new patients," Buber wrote to him. "That is now just right for you. Henceforth believe your 'Thou' able to do it!" A week later, Buber inquired of Trüb if he had a French book on the doctor faced with grief and death, because he wanted to devote a section of his next book to death. Strangely enough, given his categorical refusal to discuss immortality, Buber also stated that a French book on the psychology of immortality would be of importance to him. "Despite all troubles," he added, "I am now in the midst of a period of great creativity of thought. I begin again with the simplest states of fact."

In the same month, Buber wrote Binswanger thanking him for his book on Freud's conception of man in the light of anthropology. "Your anthropological critique at last does full justice to Freud as I have not been able to." Expanding on his question concerning the literature on madness, he added that he was principally concerned with the relation of the "unreal" to the "real," more exactly of the special world of the schizophrenic and the paranoid to the common world. Here we can see the roots of Buber's important anthropological essay, "What Is Common to All," published thirty years later in *The Knowledge of Man.* Also in a letter to Trüb, Buber spoke of the double series of consciousness of the schizophrenic, treated by Eugen Bleuler (1857–1939), but not to Buber's satisfaction. This is a topic Buber spoke of at the private seminars of the Washington School of Psychiatry in 1957 but never wrote about.

In November 1936, Trüb sent Buber a remarkable letter telling him of a "setback in my practice." Trüb began by describing for Buber a fullness of demand and response for which he was truly grateful. "There happen daily in my meetings with my patients little miracles of true knowledge, real decision, turning and confirmation." But this very fullness of positive happening at times suffocated him. He discovered that he could not will to preserve this fullness and that, in consequence, he again and again found himself delivered over to a weakness in which he experienced *nothing more;* for he was fully locked in and shut off. He called his a "tunnel sickness" that had turned him away for the last twelve years from a general connection with mankind in order to break through to the solitary and hidden place of individual persons. Now he found himself increasingly unsure of the way back to the "common world" from these secret recesses of individuals. The exclusive "one on one" of the analyst's room had so taken over his soul that he feared indiscretion and shunned the light of day in which what he said in his therapy room might leak out to the larger community. To this he attributed his functional difficulty in hearing: by an act of force he was making himself deaf to his own deepest word because it threatened to get out to the great space of the outer world. He knew, of course, that what took place in the meetings with his patients in his office must be verified and confirmed in the sight of the common world. But he feared the way in which his own special world was shut off and felt the necessity of bringing it into the larger world for the sake of the many patients with whom he worked. "I must almost guard myself now against too much positive happening that I then allow to lie hidden until it attacks *me.* I must learn daily to accept and share it; otherwise it runs after me and finally hits me over the head for my blindness and deafness."

Buber's response to Trüb's letter was to advise him to the use of the It in the service of the Thou. "He who has to do with many people in such a way that he involves his own person must, if he does not want them to collapse into a single world, objectify every individual—despite all subjective ties," responded Buber. As an example of this, Buber suggested keeping a notebook for each patient in which all details are written down, the notebook itself to be divided into one part on material and one on interpretation. In the interpretation every meaning-insight should be entered. "That sounds crudely technical, but it simply bespeaks an ordered intellectual- and work-*world.*"

In December 1936, Rudolf Pannwitz wrote Buber at length about Trüb, saying that he was a practitioner and that he would not be able to accomplish the task he had set himself of making a theoretical and systematic exposition of his thought which would lead beyond Jung's analytical psychology. He also suggested that Trüb had a sort of Oedipus complex vis-à-vis Jung. "You are certainly right in your remarks about Trüb," Buber responded; "yet he now seems to have overcome his dependence on Jung." "What is most important to me about him," Buber added, "and what again and again transcends in significance the deficiencies in his conceptualization, is that in his living he does more than he promises in his thought."

In an exchange with Hermann Gerson concerning the significance of psychoanalysis in 1937 Buber said, "Naturally I am not 'against analysis as a therapeutic tool'—that would make no sense at all!" But Buber held that the concept of therapy concerning sicknesses of the "soul" was itself ambiguous, problematic, and in need of clarification. Buber was ready to leave room for criticism in all realms, but he also insisted on room for the criticism of the criticism. "There is no worse dogmatist than a critic who uses his criticism dogmatically. And many a psychoanalysis does that already with its claim, that ostensibly needs no scrutiny, that it can disentangle the psyche as if it were a spatial thing." "I too do not believe in the possibility of 'dialogicizing the impulses,'" Buber responded to a doubting theologian, "but I do believe in an occasional penetration of the dialogical element even into the impulses." Buber was not prepared to tolerate the limitation of life "in the Face" to what present-day man experiences merely as the *intervals* in his existence.

In 1936, Buber had a public exchange with Dr. Joachim Prinz, a rabbi and a Judaic scholar, on the subject of the Jewish law. Prinz, a leader of liberal Judaism in Germany and, later, in America, said in his attack that Buber demanded of others that they fulfill the Jewish law (Halakhah) while not living it himself. Buber, instead of dismissing this as a simple misunderstanding, replied at length because of the importance of the subject. "Not a week goes by," Buber responded, "without my being asked by people whom I know and whom I do not know why I do *not* demand it of others and complaining because I do not demand it." That he did not do so, despite great respect for and receptivity to the law, Buber saw not as a religious lack but as the seriousness of living in faith in which one has the "lonesome, hard duty of drawing a sharp line of demarcation between what one may believe and what one may not" and of not practicing what one cannot believe. That this position leads to misunderstanding is to be expected, but to say that he demanded of others what he did not of himself, *that* may not be said. Prinz said that his generation wanted to know "what religion is" in order to bring it to reality in life. But where an organically believing and living community no longer exists or does not yet exist, there can be no generally valid answer, but only the experiencing again and again in personal and communal life what any particular situation demands and makes possible. This too is not a religious lack but belongs rather to the crisis and test of an age. "He who does not have in mind 'religion' (a false and sterile designation which I never tire of fighting as the really false path) but believes with honest passion, be it 'much' or 'little,' does not ask how he must bring his faith to reality. That life itself teaches him . . . through all its occasions. . . . Certainly this is not a fixed communal life-form; even the realizing is only at first a waiting, but an active and fruitful one. Today there is no way that leads to a community believing and living organically, naturally, except through severe crisis and test."

Buber also pointed out that his understanding of tradition had changed since he wrote about the Law in "Herut," the last of his "Speeches on Judaism." Tradition does not allow contents and forms to be passed on unchanged from generation to generation; for what is passed down is not a fixed content but a way of existing. Living tradition is change and therefore renewal out of deep-seated spontaneity. What is demanded is listening to the call, and this, Buber witnessed, was the faith in which he lived and in which he would die as a Jew—and not the attempts of Moses Maimonides, the great twelfth-century Spanish-Jewish philosopher, to codify Judaism into a set of principles. From this it follows that if he could not say that acceptance of the traditional Law is the way, neither could he say that not accepting it is the way. For one must also be open to the voice that may speak to one through the Law. "More than this I cannot demand, but I may also not demand less than this."

Buber closed by expressing his thanks to Prinz, who had forced him to do what the softer promptings of his friends did not—to clarify his own stance toward the Law. And "in this hour"—the hour of the Nazi persecution of the German Jewish community—nothing soft is appropriate. Prinz responded by saying that if "liberalism" were not today so hopelessly confused a cause, Buber would be one of its most important spokesmen. It was probably this interchange that prompted Buber to make accessible to Moritz Spitzer the letters between himself and Rosenzweig, an exchange on the Law which Spitzer published in the 1936–1937 Schocken Almanac.

Given the central importance of the Bible in his work of spiritual resistance to the Nazis through Jewish education, it is not surprising that this was also for Buber a period of great productivity in biblical scholarship. In Hasidism, in contrast, he did almost nothing during this period except for the second half of the lecture "Symbolic and Sacramental Existence in Judaism" that he gave at the Eranos Conference in 1934 and later published. Although much in this essay repeats Buber's earlier emphasis upon *kavana*, or intention, Buber sharpens here the contrast between Hasidism and the Kabbala from which it took all its formal teaching, and claims that Hasidism rejects the *gnosis*, magic, and schematizing of the mystery that the Kabbala embraces. Given the composition of his audience—predominantly Jungian—and of his later controversy with Jung, on the one hand, and Gershom Scholem, on the other, over just these matters, this is a highly important development in Buber's thought. It is no accident that the mysterious character in Paula Buber's novel of this period, *Storm of Gnats*, the one who at first is close to the higher Nazis and later escapes the country, is himself unveiled as a Gnostic.

"Symbol" is the manifestation of the covenant between the absolute and the concrete, "sacrament" the bodily fulfillment of this covenant. "That the divine and the human join with each other without merging with each other, a lived beyond-transcendence-and-immanence, is the foremost significance of sacrament," a significance which is fulfilled even in marriage in which the "eternal wings" overshadow the two human partners. Here is a new way of understanding the "eternal Thou": "Everything conditional into which persons enter with each other receives its strength from the presence of the unconditional." But, like marriage itself as Buber spoke of it in *The Question to the Single One,* sacrament "is stripped of its essential character when it no longer includes an elementary, life-claiming and life-determining experience of the *other,* the otherness, as of something coming to meet one and acting toward one." In traditional religion, sacrament is founded upon the separation of the holy from the profane, and this easily misleads the faithful into feeling secure in a merely "objective" consummation without personal devotion, and into evading being seized and claimed in one's whole being. Hasidism changes this by rejecting a fixed distinction between the holy and the profane—the profane is simply what has not yet been hallowed—*and* by understanding hallowing as *kavana,* "the fulfilling presentness of the whole, wholly devoted person, through sacramental existence." Nothing known or learned or inherited can prepare us for our meeting with the unforeseen, unforeseeable moment. All we can do is to remain open to it and withstand it; we cannot determine what is to meet us and what not.

In the legends of the Hasidim, "the like of which in compass, many-sidedness, vitality, and popular wild charm I do not know," the sacramental person is shown as being what Buber might have said of himself, open to the world, pious toward the world, in love with the world. This is nothing esoteric: "the mystery is valid for all or none, to none or all the heart of eternity is open." The Kabbala, like all *gnosis,* tries to see through the contradiction of being and remove itself from it; whereas Hasidism seeks faithfully to endure the contradiction and redeem it. It is not concerned with objective knowledge that can be formulated and schematized, but with vital knowledge, the biblical "knowing" in the reciprocity of the essential relation to God. The faith and humor of Hasidism rejects any attempt to get "behind" the problematic: "The absurd is given to me that I may endure and sustain it with my life; this, the enduring and sustaining of the absurd, is the meaning which I can experience." Here, Buber anticipates what, in my work on Kafka, Camus, and Elie Wiesel, I have come to call the "Dialogue with the Absurd." The Kabbala almost never shudders and prostrates itself, whereas Hasidism stops short and lets itself be disconcerted. Hasidic piety has its true life in "holy insecurity"—the deep knowledge of the impotence of all "information" and possessed truth. Although Hasidism took over Kabbalistic theurgy, its true life as revealed in the legends is not *kavanot,* special magical and mystical intentions, but *kavana:* everything wants to be hallowed, to be brought *in its worldliness* into the *kavana* of redemption, to become a sacrament. It is this distinction between Hasidism and the Kabbala which Scholem was later to attack so bitterly.

The symbol, to Buber, is transitory, unique, corporeal—the true binding of the absolute and the concrete. It does not float timelessly above concrete actualities but "serves our born, mortal body." When it loses immediate validity, it can be renewed out of new human existence that fulfills anew.

> Every symbol is always in danger of changing from a real sign sent into life into a spiritual and unbinding image, every sacrament of changing from a bodily event between above and below into a flat experience on the "religious" plane. Only through the man who devotes himself is the strength of the origin saved for further present existence.

Such a person is the biblical prophet, or *nabi,* who does not foretell an unalterable future but appeals to the openness and the deciding power of the hour. "Not the word by itself has effect on reality, only the word that is set into the whole human existence." As the most powerful example of this, Buber takes Hosea's action of marrying a strumpet and giving to the children of this marriage names such as "You will not find mercy" and "not my people." "What is here represented in the human world is the marriage between God and the whore Israel." Israel's "whoring after strange gods" is not just a matter of idolatry but of failing to fulfill the covenant to make real the kingship of God in every aspect of personal and communal life. Thus the *nabi* does not give a sign but, while he acts, is himself a sign. "No symbol, in no timeless height, can ever attain. . . . reality otherwise than by becoming embodied in such a human existence."

In 1935, Abraham Joshua Heschel wrote Buber a letter criticizing this treatment of the biblical prophet on the curious ground that he made the life of the prophet into mere illustration and robbed it of any existential meaning. In the essay itself, it is unmistakably clear that it is only through the fact that it has existential meaning that the actions of the prophet have symbolic meaning. What really lies behind this misunderstanding is the sadness Heschel expressed in his letter that Buber could not confirm Heschel's own work on the prophets in his doctoral dissertation published in Cracow, Poland, in 1936. Behind this is the still deeper rift between Buber's understanding of the prophet as speaking the word of response to his own preverbal dialogue with God in the historical situation and Heschel's less dialogical but no less historical understanding of the prophet as identifying with God's pathos and expressing God's love and wrath in the historical situation.

In 1936, the German-Jewish philosopher David Baumgardt wrote Buber expressing his joy for Buber's rendition of the Book of Psalms, the fourteenth volume of his Bible translation, the continued publication of which was now taken over by Schocken. The "transparence" of one link in the chain of the translation to another is becoming "ever thicker," Baumgardt paradoxically exclaimed. "If Ernst Simon rightly always repeats the statement that only you have again shown the unity of the Hebrew Bible, then you have given a classic description of the How of this unity in your essay 'On the Translation of the Psalms.'" Emil Brunner also thanked Buber for his "splendid translation of the Psalms," the strange German of which reveals the secret of the language of the Psalms as no other translation. "God bless you and guard you wherever he leads you," Brunner concluded, fully aware of the uncertainty of Buber's future as a German Jew. Another Protestant theologian, Martin Dibelius, by implication connected the Buber-Rosenzweig translation with the Nazi incursion into history. "You have said so much that is important, even downright prophetic, about the unity of the biblical word and its ever-new demand on man. Today indeed, vexation and confrontation are made manifest in a new seriousness." In 1938 Leo Baeck praised Buber for his translation of the Proverbs. Hermann Herrigel, in contrast, told Buber that his book *The Bible and Its Translation* revealed an altogether different relation to the word than he, Herrigel, had. "For you the word is inexhaustible, whereas for me it is always the word that is insufficient and reality that is inexhaustible."

In 1937 in a letter to Hans Kosmala, Buber explained that when he interpreted the famous passage in Leviticus as "deal lovingly" instead of "love" he by no means meant a mere action but rather a turning oneself, a being turned toward with all that that entails. But Buber's most important biblical concern in these years, aside from the continuation of the translation which he and Rosenzweig began, was the revision of *The Kingship of God* along with a twenty-five-page, highly scholarly second preface and the preparation of a sequel, a book on the prophet Samuel which was never published as such because of the closing down of the Schocken Verlag in Germany. Buber was well into the revision of *The Kingship of God* by 1933, the year after its first publication. By 1935, he was also intensively working on *The Anointed,* as the sequel was to be called. In 1936, he published the second edition of *The Kingship of God,* enlarged by more than a quarter. In the Preface to the Second Edition he responded at length to all the scholarly critiques that had been written concerning the first, which had been sold out two years after its publication. He also attacked the famous "Kenite hypothesis," according to which Moses, through his contact with the Kenite peoples to which his father-in-law Jethro belonged, had converted the Israelite God of history into a nature god, more specifically the mountain god of Sinai. "Instead of an image which is only a god of nature and one which is only a god of history, there dawns the form of the One Who is the lord of nature *and* the lord of history."

Only five pages of *The Anointed* have been published in English, but one hundred twenty-five pages have been preserved in the second volume of Buber's collected works, that on the Bible. In this book, Buber sees Samuel as working together with a great religious popular movement of *nebiim,* or prophets, stretching over many generations and responsible for vigorous drives for independence, especially during the period of Philistine domination. Samuel supplants the ruined priesthood in a period without ark or sanctuary and bears the divine voice as an independent *nabi.* YHVH is no longer seen as bound to the ark or any other object but is himself the true vanguard, champion, leader, and king who speaks to the man of God who wanders from place to place. This is not a pseudo-king to whom one can dictate but the true *melekh* who leads the way to redemption for those who hearken to his voice, the way God wants them to go.

The anointing of Saul by Samuel meant the carrying out of God's command to dissolve the direct primitive theocracy in favor of the indirect. The majesty of the king still stood, nonetheless, under the judgment of the Lord, and the herald and guardian of the indirect theocracy was the *nabi,* who could call the king to account as the

prophet Nathan did to David. Under Solomon and in the two king-
doms that followed, this place of the prophet progressively deteriorated, giving rise to new rebellious types of *nebiim* who spoke the
powerless word of the spirit to the kings with power. The priests and
magicians were concerned with the realm of God; the *nabi* was concerned with the realm of man to which the divine had descended
through spirit and word, the spirit which storms the whole corporal
existence, and the word which addresses the human being and calls for
a response. Theocracy in the primitive sense recognized no other rule
than that of God alone. In it there was no firm succession of human
rule, only a seminomadic life with the necessary minimum power and
authority. The demand of the direct theocracy was that a rightly
formed human community arise. "Israel" came into existence as a
result of the response *and* the resistance to this demand. Eli, the father
of Samuel, attempted a centralization of power in the hands of the
priests, a materialization of the theocracry into a hierocracy through
the recognized authority of the oracle and the ark as powers in battle.
Samuel and the bands of prophets rejected this rule of priests in favor
of the leadership of God. But in the end they had to bow to the word
of God: to renounced the direct rule of God, which was no longer
historically possible, in order to preserve the reality of the rule of God
in indirect form. "This, it seems to me, is the spiritual-historical meaning of the 'Anointing,' " Buber concluded. That the importance of this
conclusion is not limited to the historical we can instantly recognize
when we recall that the Hebrew word for anointing is *meshiach*, from
which comes the word Messiah. The overall title that Buber chose for
The Kingship of God and *The Anointed* was *The Coming: The Origins of
Biblical Messianism.* Although the subsequent biblical interpretation
that Buber wrote in the forties—*Moses, The Prophetic Faith,* and *Two
Types of Faith*—did not formally stand under this title, they can be seen
as the continuation and fulfillment of Buber's original plan to write a
great work on the biblical understanding of messianism.

In 1938 in the Schocken Almanac, Buber published an essay, "The
Election of Israel: A Biblical Inquiry," which hints at this understand-
ing of messianism. Just as human history began with the fratricide of
Cain and Abel, so the history of nations began with the Tower of
Babel. We cannot return to the time before the division of nations, but
we can bind ourselves together in a single humanity which realizes
God's dominion upon earth if only one people were to set an example
of harmony in obedience to God for the others. From being a nation

whose members are connected merely by origin and common lot, Israel must become a true people bound by a just and loving participation in a common life. Israel is a special treasure to God only when and as long as it hearkens to God's voice and keeps His covenant. This is no "salvation by works alone." Jewish faith "teaches the mysterious *meeting* of human turning and divine mercy." Israel is elected only when it realizes its election, yet the Rejector can never cease being the Elector. The God who turns away in response to *our* turning away awaits our turning back. This is "the consoling paradox of our existence"—that which Jeremiah looks forward to with his prophecy of a new covenant which God will make with the house of Israel in which God will put His Torah in their inward parts and write it in their hearts. In the ever darkening time in which Buber wrote this, these words may have consoled those who later found their way to Palestine and those others whose way led only to the gas chambers.

PART III

Palestine and the Second
World War

(1938-1945)

CHAPTER 13

Ascent to the Land

IMMIGRATION TO PALESTINE OF GERSON AND THE WORK FOLK, RAFAEL, AND EVA

EVEN APART FROM his own negotiations with Hebrew University, an increasingly important part of Buber's attention during his last years in Germany was focused on Palestine. The immigration to Palestine of Hermann Gerson and his Werkleute (Work Folk) circle, of Buber's son Rafael, of his daughter Eva and her husband the poet Ludwig Strauss —and of many others to whom Buber was bound—made this inevitable, as well as the fact that much of the work of Jewish adult education in Nazi Germany was oriented toward preparation for settlement in Palestine.

With the rise of the Nazis to power it became impossible for the Werkleute to believe any longer than they could meaningfully live and work in Germany. In April 1933, they unanimously decided to emigrate to Palestine and to establish a Werkleute kibbutz. By April 1934, they had raised enough money to buy land in Palestine, and by the end of the month they set out without waiting to actually complete the purchase of the land. In his farewell letter to Buber, Gerson thanked him "for much more than I can say, for the basic direction into the human and the Jewish that I maintain only through you, for the whole way in which you have constantly been present for me in everything. . . . Now I shall try in another field to remain a true disciple." Buber responded with the hope "that in the midst of all the difficult problematic of the Land you will still experience afresh that genuine, imperishable joy in the human that of all earthly forces most helps us to live." Buber also gave Gerson a letter of introduction to Hugo Bergmann in which he characterized Gerson as the leader of the Work Folk and as the representative of "my youngest disciples." "I have always had few disciples, as you know, but almost always the right ones, and he belongs to these. From the Bar-Kochbans of 1903 to the Work Folk there runs a genuine, visible path, and this path I have walked, as you have walked it."

In a publication of 1935, Gerson explained their earlier failure to become Zionists as due to their having assumed that most Europeans were fated to live in the city, with all its rootlessness and alienation from nature and life, and to their belief that "there is no place that is empty of God." In Palestine, they tried to carry on Buber's spirit by taking seriously the problem of the relations of the Jews to the Arabs and by fighting the Revisionists who held that the only criterion was the development of the Jewish people. They saw themselves as taking part in a fight for the Jewish youth to help them avoid the double dangers of fleeing from the land out of a desire for the less restricted culture that the city offered, or of becoming so involved with practical problems as to have no time for the spiritual. The Werkleute were concerned with transforming their kibbutz, which they named Hazorea, from an economic unity to a real community, with overcoming the danger of collectivism, and with allowing the concern about the basic human task of giving meaning to life to penetrate into the community.

Kibbutz Hazorea is in the Jezreel Valley in the lower Galilee. What is now a cultivated farm and forestland was at the beginning of the kibbutz an inhospitable wilderness which exacted years of back-breaking labor, hazards, and even the lives of some of the Werkleute. These new conditions of life entailed a far-reaching change of the internal structure. In a kibbutz the influence of the rank and file is much greater than in a movement primarily based on spiritual values. Correspondingly, the influence of Gerson and the inner circle of the Werkleute progressively diminished. A new kind of leadership emerged in tune with the new consciousness of the collective. "I was a charismatic leader," Gerson said, "but the kibbutz had no need for a charismatic leader." Disputes between parties, such as existed in Germany, now became political and social struggles fought vehemently on both sides with little possibility of remaining neutral. The politicization against which Buber inveighed in *The Question to the Single One* permeated the whole kibbutz, and religion, which was once a positive life-stance for the Werkleute, was now frequently used and abused as a political weapon. Kibbutz Hazorea tried from its very beginning to give the Jewish festivals a secular—national and social—content. It was the first kibbutz which edited its own Haggadah (order of service) for Passover, a direction which eventually all the kibbutzim of whatever social and political persuasion followed. But the core of religious socialism, which underlay the Werkleute, disappeared, and simultaneously Buber's influence increasingly declined.

In 1935, Gerson wrote to Buber from Hadera, the city nearest Kibbutz Hazorea, "The whole time since we have not seen each other heavy things have happened to me here which I could not bring myself to write about. But now, when again something so bad has taken place, I cannot write to anyone but you. Once again a *Chaver* (comrade) of the Kibbutz has died." Even apart from this it was already very difficult, wrote Gerson. "Resistance to building the community is composed of so many small threads in the eventful life of the Kibbutz." Among these threads, Gerson pointed out the members' fear of anything religious, the tension that arose from their conscious attempts to attach themselves to the Jewish heritage, the mistrust of anything that required will power and did not come spontaneously, the flagging interest in questions that became complicated, the tendency to react to others superficially without grasping the whole person, the danger of "parties" arising between which direct speaking becomes difficult, the tensions revolving around Gerson himself and the tendency to be overcritical. Compared to other forms of social action, such as politics and teaching, this was like being in the front trenches from which no retreat was possible.

In the face of all this, Gerson fell at times into hours of deep despair, hours in which all sense of present reality disappeared and he felt cut off, cast into a heavy abyss. To find his way back to health was not easy, moreover, because what was at stake was not simply his personal feelings but the very meaning of the goals that he had come to Palestine to realize. He also found resources that sustained him and gave him "light for the seeing eye, strength for the working hand," as Buber put it in his Introduction to *The Great Maggid and His Followers*—above all his wife Lo, but also friends, individual meetings, and, since he had come to Palestine, nature as a "messenger." Despite all, he felt himself becoming more peaceful and more firmly grounded. "Something impels me to write all this to you," Gerson concluded.

"As I share all your experiences in my heart," replied Buber, "the bad ones naturally more strongly even than the good, so your new sadness has touched me deeply. I know how it is when young life is torn from young life. But one must transform this strong sadness into a strength of work and creation; one must, there is nothing else left for one to do. All that you have written me of the difficulties of community I have thought through and lived through in reading and then again in memory—which is not like the memory of what one has read but of events." Every Yes owes its existence and validity to a No, Buber added. "I myself learn through your report, not new objects of knowledge but a new heightening of the concrete clarity in the manner in which one learns through one's own fate. At times I actually feel a 'collective' I in my breast."

In December, Gerson again wrote to Buber—about the difficulties caused by not belonging to any of the kibbutz movements or other political affiliations among the Jewish settlement in Palestine, about the lack of clear vision in many important aspects, and above all the problem of the dominating type being the Jews from Russia and the East and the assumption that the German Jews should adapt themselves to this type. Gerson wished, in contrast, to show that the Western Jews brought special values with them suited to their situation. In June 1936, Gerson wrote Buber of discussions with the Marxist Hashomer Hatzaïr, or Kibbutz Artzi, movement that threatened to swallow the Werkleute up and put an end to "our movement." Buber replied that he was not concerned with the outcome of the discussions. " 'Community' has in common with sexual love the fact that too much consciousness is not conducive either to its growth or fruitfulness. By consciousness I mean, naturally, the discussing type—there is another, that of the whole being, but that lets growing take place, feels it, notices it and: is silent or sings."

In his next letter, Gerson announced the stunning news that his wife Lo intended to leave him for another member of the kibbutz. In the first despair over this, Gerson left the kibbutz and considered taking his own life. In his reply, Buber comforted and scolded Gerson at the same time. "Your letter has disturbed me," wrote Buber. "I am with you with my whole heart, but I do not merely grieve over you; I am also angry at you. This will not do, not for you! You have sworn yourself to a group of persons. All possible personal disappointments and defeats must be included and anticipated in your oath. Nothing that befalls you may any longer liberate you to dispose of yourself like a private individual. I know what it means when dying becomes easier for one than living, but responsibility is greater than death and life, and you have one that today you cannot yet fully comprehend but about which you know. If you forsake it, you will have debased all that you have ever said about leadership and laid waste the heart of the community that began under your leadership. It seems that you have not imagined concretely enough not merely Lo but also the band to which you have vowed yourself.

"As to what is happening between you and Lo, you have spoken most harshly, almost too harshly I feel. You are simply (I do not forget why, but that does not change anything) too bound to your I, and for your sake it is essential that you free yourself from this. . . . Open yourself to the world. The world with which you have to do you must really make present to yourself as the world, Lo as Lo, and not as a content of your soul. Abandon yourself to the grace! I embrace you, dear friend, I am vexed and pleased with you as never before."

After four years of intensive discussion, Kibbutz Hazorea decided to join Hashomer Hatzaïr. In the process of doing so, they adopted a Marxist ideology, looked back on their earlier position as bourgeois rationalization, and dismissed their ideals of religious socialism and community as "ideology" in the Marxist sense: a spiritual disguise for a materialistic interest. They accused themselves of not having wanted to become settlers in Eretz Israel (the land of Israel) but of wishing to remain well-to-do professional people in Germany. This process was hastened by the increasing terror of the Nazi regime, on the one hand, and the pressures of life in Palestine, on the other. They had not succeeded in transplanting their hopes for realization of community and at the same time remained apolitical in a highly politicized atmosphere. In Hashomer Hatzaïr they found a total commitment, similar to what they had demanded of themselves in Germany, and a common ideology embracing economy, cooperation, politics, culture, and education. Many of them even persuaded themselves that the views and motives which they had formerly expressed in religious language were identical with those that Hashomer Hatzaïr expressed in its Marxist language! Among these were the former leaders of the Werkleute, men like Eliyahu Maoz (formerly Mosbacher), who still appeared more like one of the Wandervögel than a kibbutznik, and Hermann Gerson himself, who now changed his first name to the Hebrew "Menachem."

Gerson now rejected Buber and his teaching as being sentimentally idealistic, unsuited to the harsh realities of kibbutz life. He still continued to write to Buber, but his critical position became more and more evident, as in his comments in February 1937 on *The Question to the Single One.* Gerson rejected Buber's whole debate with Kierkegaard as unnecessary, since the danger of injuring one's relation to the world through one's experience of God seemed unreal to him. "Intercourse with God is alien to me, today still more than before. I cannot truly say of myself: I believe in God." He also criticized Buber's 1936 essay on "The Halutz and His World." In this essay Buber put forward the *Halutz,* or pioneer, as the new human type that guaranteed the genuineness of a folk movement by leading to new community. The original, genuine *Halutz* is the person in whom the liberation of the people and of the self are actively equated. For the first time in the Diaspora, the general situation of the hour—that of Jewry—is answered by a personal, central stance: as a Jew. One can understand the *Halutz* only if one recognizes in him the full unification of the national and the social. The synthesis of people, land, and work is a social one: "the working Jewish 'society' in Palestine." And in the word "society" resounds fulfillment of the idea of community, realization of what is really meant by community but has been until now unrealized.

Of this really very simple speech, compared to those which he had earlier praised, Gerson complained that it used highfalutin words that did not always appear compelling and necessary. "I often ask myself: 'Is that really spoken seriously in the face of the reality such as I have come to know it in the last years?' " Gerson also criticized Buber's statement in *The Question to the Single One* that the person building community "has God's own time" as a form of self-redemption, claiming that Buber was driven to his action by his concern for the salvation of his soul and not because he sought the realization of community. He also "mistrusted" Buber's distinction between the "usual conscience" and the "conscience from the depths" as "somewhat empty" and its high-flown words as "out of tune." "What is important to me," wrote Gerson, "is that everything that is said is graspable in its reality; that the manner of speaking applies to all and not just a thin intellectual stratum." A book that by virtue of its theme treats difficult subjects must be written in as clear and simple language as possible. Gerson had in mind the language of the working person such as is found in the kibbutz, a type that "you have not come up against enough." Gerson conceded, midway through, that much of what he was saying might be "very subjective, grounded in my present life situation."

"For the transformation of *persons* one needs another tempo than the 'political,' " Buber responded, "but how can you think thereby of 'self-redemption' or the like?" On the subject of "conscience," Buber pointed out that he had sent the proofs to five competent people with the request that they point out passages difficult to understand, and not one of them had singled out this passage. "One only need to think of the . . . much discussed term of Meister Eckhart's, 'the spark,' to notice that here an ontological conscience that binds the person with being, and a merely moral conscience, are distinguished. I am convinced (since after all I still know you a little) that you need only consider it without prejudice to understand it. Instead of which you become 'mistrustful.' When I place trust in a person as person (or a book as his or her expression) and an action, a word, is incomprehensible to me or seems wrong, then I first of all mistrust myself: my knowledge, my understanding, but above all my attentiveness to it."

Beyond that, Buber pointed out that Gerson proceeded from an incorrect assumption, namely that different "languages" are possible for a certain thought that one has thought and that one could choose between them. "That is a misunderstanding of the event of original thinking both according to its manner and its dynamic. . . . What I can do to make it understandable I have already truly done—in that I describe, enlarge, simplify, explain. But I cannot thereby alter the original language of the thought. In this need to think thus and therefore of having to speak thus I do not find a trace of pride."

During this same period, the life of another kibbutznik from Germany, Buber's son Rafael, underwent profound changes. Separated some time since from his wife Margarete, who was later interned in a Nazi concentration camp and, despite her communism, in a Soviet slave-labor camp,* Rafael remarried and in 1934 immigrated to Pales-

---

*See Note A in Sources for Chapter 13.

tine, where he worked in Kvuza Geva, near Ain Harod. There he worked twelve hours daily in great heat but, as he wrote to his grandfather Carl, was very happy, in fact, downright delighted. Rafael intended to bring over not only Ruth, his second wife, but also Barbara and Judith, the children of his first marriage who had been living with Martin and Paula, as soon as he had successfully made it through this transition. "For you this will undoubtedly mean a great sacrifice," Carl Buber wrote Martin, "but it must be."

The injunction that Buber has God give to the prophet Elijah at the end of his "mystery-play" *Elijah*—" And when my day dawns, reconcile the sons with the fathers!"—was accomplished to some extent through Rafael's new life in Palestine. In response to a long letter that Rafael sent his parents in August 1936, Martin wrote: "Your letter has done your mother and me much good, above all because one constantly sees in it, joyfully, what one already knew, of course: what an excellent fellow you have become. Apart from you personally, this is for me a comforting sign in regard to your whole generation: it has had a difficult time of it and it has also gone seriously astray, but it is still granted to it to find the way."

Buber's son-in-law Ludwig Strauss had a more difficult time getting settled in Palestine. Finally, after a great inner conflict, he decided in January 1936 to join the Werkleute at Kibbutz Hazorea. He informed Buber of this decision in a long letter to which Buber did not respond until he learned from a letter from his daughter Eva, Strauss's wife, that Ludwig had taken it badly that he did not hear from Buber. In March, Buber wrote him a long letter in which he explained, in effect, that he had not written him because he could not confirm him in his decision. "Try to imagine that I have a strong feeling against it that seems to be connected with something basic in me, something that is mysterious even to myself. How shall I translate into argument what can in no way be put into words? . . . What can I legitimately do other than with a loving but silent heart let you try what you want to!"

There could be no question of trying to dissuade him, but Buber added a word of caution to make him particularly aware of a reality that he perhaps had not fully considered even though he wrote about it: "I take you quite seriously as an intellectual and spiritual person—but when you wish to take root in a kibbutz, you must forget to some extent who you are and take upon yourself the law of the commune, that of the full participation of everyone in manual labor. That will be more onerous than you imagine." Though Hermann Gerson and his circle would try to make things lighter for him, as a new member of a kibbutz he himself would not be able to allow that during the first years. This was not a question of the good will of the comrades but of an objective state of facts. "You will no longer be able to hold fast to the rhythm of activities and the leisure that you as a poet need. If you join a kibbutz, you must let yourself be swallowed hide and hair by the equal-and-common, by the command of the earth that needs to be plowed and only accord yourself the poet's breath when and if the situation of the kibbutz frees you for it." Buber was by no means as lacking in a concrete and realistic understanding of the worker's life as the disaffected Gerson liked to think!

The concern for good neighborly relations between the Jews and Arabs in Palestine that Buber voiced at the Zionist Congress in 1921 and earlier became ever more painful for him as the relations between the two peoples deteriorated into riots and internecine fighting from 1936 on. In February 1936, Buber received an anguished letter from a young man (whom he had talked with in Munich) questioning how one could build the "ideal" community, the community that would be a "blessing" and fulfillment, on the murder of men in war or on preparedness for war. This was a burning question for Paul Weinberger; for he had to decide soon whether to go to Palestine and he felt that if he did decide to go, he was affirming and participating in the killings that were taking place. He was not helped by the knowledge that history is full of power and killing and self-assertion, and it seemed that only through murder can states and cultures, and all that goes with them, arise. "Must the killing be intentionally increased by creating new conflicts as in the case of the Palestine settlement?" In his response Buber rejected Weinberger's either/or way of putting the problem as missing our true task. What is really essential is contributing to the actualization of what one has recognized to be of absolute value and in so doing taking on oneself no more guilt than the human predicament in general and the specific situation at any given time make indispensable. In this way we cease to be governed by principles and, instead, assume serious responsibility for the here and now, this moment and this situation.

In May 1936, commenting on the Arab uprisings in April, Buber wrote Gerson that one should *never* say that it is impossible to do something; for in the concrete situation *something* is always possible, and this something is at times enough. But in June, Buber confessed to Hans Trüb that both he and Paula were very depressed by the course of events in Palestine. "I have, indeed, always warned and foretold—the warnings have been collected into a little book in order to summon the conscience anew—but this makes the situation still worse." In 1936, Buber published the little book *Zion as Goal and Task* in which such admonitory essays as "And If Not Now, When?" appeared. In his Foreword to this book, Buber spoke of the sick understanding of the age that thought it necessary to "howl with the wolves" and expected to attain the building of Zion through the devious means common to the world. The genuine Zion can be attained as a goal only if one has brought into the way, into the task, as much as one can of the goal itself. No way leads anywhere else than to its own completion. Zion as a goal cannot be reached if the means to that goal are utterly unlike the end.

In August, Rafael wrote his parents describing the Arab attacks on his kibbutz and two other settlements in the Plain of Jezreel and of the measures taken by the settlers to defend themselves, including placing a special police guard in the fields they were cultivating. By day, Rafael worked on the tractors, but at special times and at night he served as a guard for his own and neighboring communities. In Palestine in general, the Arabs had attacked the Port of Haifa, the petroleum lines, and the trains, which had ceased to run between Haifa and Tel Aviv. Although the tension among the Jewish settlers was greatly heightened, the danger at that point did not seem serious. What gave Rafael particular cause for joy was the fact that, although they had to work their fields with weapons in their hands and almost every night had to fight against the Arabs who hid behind the rocks, no feeling of hatred for the Arab peoples existed. There were many men on both sides who wanted peace. His father responded: "Unfortunately, I do not see how in the immediate future the grave conflict can be overcome satisfactorily. What one might propose in this direction would not find a hearing with either of the two parties." In October 1936, Ernst Simon, who had returned to Jerusalem, wrote Buber that only those without conscience were doing well. Everyone else had a bad conscience. "Whatever one does—it is too little." But, like Buber, he held that he had found a position training teachers and that he could not consider returning to Germany to help with the work of Jewish adult education. "I belong now to Palestine: for long, uninterrupted years of continual work."

HEBREW UNIVERSITY NEGOTIATIONS AND PLANS

Buber too was to have "uninterrupted years of continual work" in Palestine, but like Jacob toiling for Rachel, his was a long period of waiting, frustration, and disappointment before he could arrive there. It took eleven years of negotiations plus years of complications with the Nazis and the British authorities in order for Martin Buber, co-originator of the movement to found the Hebrew University and world-famous scholar and philosopher, to take up residence in Palestine as professor at the Hebrew University! The negotiations with the university began in 1927 and repeatedly bogged down, despite every effort on the part of Judah Magnes, Hugo Bergmann (who became the rector of the university during this period), Gershom Scholem, and many others. On August 1, 1933, Judah Magnes, founder and then chancellor, extended Buber the invitation of the Hebrew University to become professor of the science of religion (*Religionswissenschaft*) and asked that he begin his work in November. At the end of October, Buber sent Magnes a schema for the study of religion, including such subdivisions as the phenomenology of religion (religious conceptions and expressions), religious typology (the personal bearers of religion), sociology of religion, general history of religion, and the history of religions. Despite all this, Scholem wrote Buber in February 1934 that Magnes, without leaving his own position in doubt, had held back, but that he was ready to fight the fight to the end if he only knew that Buber would really come if he were called to the position. They were afraid, Scholem explained, Buber might not be willing to give up the educational activities that he had begun in Nazi Germany. "Your friends in Palestine are convinced," Scholem urged, "that in this land and in the education of the young in Jerusalem there is something still more decisive at stake than in Mannheim. You must be here if you do not want to forgo having an effect in this growing land; anything else would be illusion. You remain far from the daily life, and nothing of yours has become part of it."

Two weeks later Scholem wrote Buber that it had been decided by a very significant majority to invite him as ordinarius for general science of religion and that everything now hung upon whether he would come that winter. On February 21, Magnes wrote Buber: "The Rubicon has been crossed and we are now expecting you to turn your face definitely towards Jerusalem." This was for a two-year chair in the science of religion. Buber replied on March 8, saying that he was honored and delighted by the summons, which he thought to accept, but he recommended in the strongest terms, in the interests of the university and its organic development, that with the funds available fewer professors be appointed for a term of five years each rather than more professors for a term of two years each.

Salman Schocken, hearing of Buber's intention, wrote him that their German publishing work seemed to him endangered if Buber were to go to Palestine. "I am and remain a German-Jewish author," Buber replied. "What I have to do in this sphere . . . cannot be set aside in favor of other tasks, no matter how important." He intended, indeed, to make his connection with the Schocken Verlag still more secure in the time to come. In a letter to Lambert Schneider, which began with condolences for the death of his wife from a fall while mountain climbing, Buber said that if the question became one of "Palestine or Germany," he would have to renounce Palestine and with it a new and most significant university affiliation.

In July, Hermann Gerson wrote Buber from Hadera expressing questions about his coming from the other side—the possibility of his influence in Palestine. It seemed to Gerson that the rejection of every historical connection on the part of the Jews in Palestine, the total formalization and perversion of nationalism, the dominant rationalism, mixed with sociologism, and the strong critical attitude of many in labor circles toward Buber all made his coming doubtful. Above all, he questioned whether any real effectiveness was possible for *Buber* there, since Buber's existence as a "professor," a "detached intellectual," would keep him removed from the milieu that might create a basis for that effectiveness. Nor did he think that at Buber's age and in his position he could easily tolerate the sort of tensions and hindrances that would arise from his being reduced to gradually influencing individuals and small groups without any important, official post. Finally, Gerson declared that the direct religious language of Buber's speeches would hinder everything there and was equally sure that Buber would not be prepared to renounce it. Buber would be met not merely with incomprehension but with hostile rejection. And added that, "the prejudice against the 'mystical and doubtful Zionist Buber,' who constructed an unreal, romantically transfigured Judaism" is very great. At the same time, Gerson expressed doubt concerning the reality of all Buber's activities in Germany and said that in Palestine intellectual thrusts worked in a real space. "To be Jewish is a thing of life," Gerson lectured his master; "but in Germany it easily becomes a spiritual construction." After which he ended by saying that, despite all, work in Palestine would be the best thing for Buber and that he *must* come!

To this Buber responded from the Dolomite Mountains in Austria, where he often went for vacation in August, that the question did not seem to him rightly put, or at any rate it was not *his* question. "I cannot concern myself at all with whether I shall be 'effective' somewhere. Something like that would go against modesty. When I think of a life in Palestine, I think only about whether I can live and work there, not whether I can have influence there (about which I have never had illusions)." Despite this, Gerson's questions would seem to have been prophetic *in the short run*, though not, it can be said in the long. Buber then informed Gerson that he had accepted the position even though serious private difficulties of an economic nature might affect the time of his going. He hoped to go the beginning of March 1935. But less than a week later Buber learned that the Board of Governors of the university had rejected the recommendation. The narrowly clerical clique did not find him Jewish enough, Magnes explained, and the specialists did not find this "gifted writer" scholarly enough!

While expressing disappointment in the outcome, Gerson accused Buber of quibbling when he did not include being effective in the idea of "working." Buber replied in somewhat Taoist fashion that one can only provide the "scaffolding" of life—the real building "comes to pass." "When am I really 'effective'? When I am not concerned about it." One can be concerned about a livelihood and a calling but not about the unforeseeable, the noncategorizable, what is outside one's will. "And as a German writer (I am not incidentally but basically a *German* writer) to be without a calling bound to the normal life of the people there, the needs there, the economy there, would be repugnant to me. . . . If I thought otherwise, I would be a gypsy; but I am a 'civic' man, son and father of the law. . . . To come as an immigrant without any proper settled civic ties would be to deny myself."

Buber approached Lambert Schneider about a book on Palestine, the honorarium for which should pay the expenses for a trip to Palestine in 1935. Schneider informed Buber that this proposal had annoyed Schocken, who wondered why Buber had not gone directly to him for help in planning a trip to Palestine. If a book on the trip came out of this, so much the better. Schocken was also stunned by Buber's alleged remark that the publisher would have to pay as the result of being chosen honorary treasurer and member of the Executive Council of the Hebrew University in Jerusalem. "That is the bitter experience that a rich man has," commented Schneider, "that the people who come to him almost all do so only with the intention of asking for money. From many conversations I know how painfully hard it strikes him." Schneider urged that Buber and Schocken meet more frequently, and he sent a copy of the letter to Schocken.

Buber immediately wrote to Schocken in the same vein: "The contents of this letter touches me so profoundly that I must write to you about it at once. There are so many conflicts that cannot be overcome in this brief life that we should do what we can to overcome those that can be overcome and should hurry in order that they not become intractable." "Especially in a time like this, the most precious thing that we have are the genuine relationships to other persons, and it is up to us from time to time to clear away the misunderstandings that threaten them. I shall try to do that in our case as far as I can." "You have *never* since I have known you," Buber went on to say, "been for me 'the rich man,' but always a man who concerns me, whose existence is important to me, who belongs to the structure of my life." While none of that had changed, Buber explained, since Schocken became his publisher it became more difficult to discuss money matters with him because he now had the obligation to produce books for him. Buber also explained that the people to whom he referred in his comment about Schocken's position in the university had nothing to do with the university and were not persons who would come to him asking for money. Rather they were people who said that Schocken's name would add to the financial security and general confidence in the university.

In August, Buber wrote Magnes his profound regret that he could not attend a meeting of the Board of Governors of the university because of an acute ear infection which made it necessary for him to be under the care of a doctor. The growing controversy within the university had made a painful impression on him. In the same letter Buber wrote Magnes of his dismay that the university had failed to appoint Ernst Simon, whom Buber characterized as "this unusually valuable force, this representative man of a German-Jewish generation." Buber testified from working with Simon in the Mittelstelle, and particularly at Lehnitz, to Simon's great gifts as teacher and seminar leader. "The university needs such a vital educational spirit." Eventually Simon was, in fact, appointed professor of education at the Hebrew University, a position which he held until his retirement.

It is an interesting comment on Buber's supposed lack of scholarship that he was ready and able to take on three different chairs in three quite different departments—history of religions, education, and social philosophy—and that, in fact, the position he finally held was the chair in sociology and the chairmanship of the Department of Sociology at Hebrew University. In a letter to Hugo Bergmann expressing his joy at Bergmann's being selected for the new position of rector of Hebrew University, Buber also commented on the sacrifice entailed in his switching over to a discipline which, while it had for many years been very important to him, was not in the final sense "his" discipline. He would have to spend so much time working up independent points of view and methods that he would have little time for scholarly work in areas with which he was more personally concerned. "I have the feeling that, with two or three exceptions, no one there knows how hard this decision is. Such a feeling had never been able to disturb me all my life; now for the first time I feel a burden laid upon my heart."

In April 1936, Buber sent Bergmann a long letter in which he pointed out that he had always made clear to both Magnes and Schocken that he would need a good while to settle in before commencing work at the university and that he would have to make this a precondition of his coming, whether in the form of a leave in advance or of not assuming the position officially until some time after his arrival in Palestine. His explanation of his stand gives us a deep glimpse into the state of his soul at this fateful moment of transition. "I am not a university person," he wrote. His acceptance of the appointment at Frankfurt University was connected in a tragic manner with his relationship to Rosenzweig and had the character of a sacrifice that he made for the sake of Rosenzweig. The Hebrew University position also had for him no absolute value, although the thought of a place being created for him to work in Palestine had affected him powerfully when Magnes first raised the question in 1927.

But for that work to be fruitful he needed time to become familiar with the land, people, language, and atmosphere. The statement that each person would find two months' preparation for lectures sufficient had a ring of public control to Buber that "at this relatively late hour of my life would be unbearable." He would rather change his course at the twelfth hour. Rest and relaxation was not the issue. "Probably because for three years I have devoted myself with the utmost intensity (of which you, of course, can only know little) to a situation, I find myself in a difficult spiritual (and presumably also bodily) crisis which I must allow myself to bear with all the composure that is necessary in such a case before I take on myself a new obligation with its responsible daily duties." Buber also pointed out that something had been germinating in him that he had to give a proper shape and bring to some conclusion. "It is not permitted me to endanger that." He could in no case give up Palestine, Buber concluded, but he was ready to give up the university plan as impracticable if this need was not met.*

In July, Scholem wrote Buber how much they hoped he would come soon and, referring to the Arab uprisings, said, "Your coming will fall at a difficult time in which many things may be discussed in which your voice will carry weight." However, Buber could not come then. He had to go to Poland in September to determine what could be done about his father's estate, since settling it was of special importance for dealing with the problems of their emigration. Only in April 1937, were the obstacles overcome to the extent that he could make a trip to Palestine from May to July and even then only by way of preparing for his future coming. But this trip made Buber certain that he wished to move to Palestine, whatever might happen with his position at the university. Meanwhile he continued the study of modern Hebrew which he had begun under the tutelage of Abraham Heschel and in which he made such remarkable progress that Heschel could not avoid wondering whether he had not sought help elsewhere as well. The difference between the biblical and talmudic Hebrew with which Buber was familiar from childhood and the modern, especially in its spoken form, was so great that he could envisage the first semester of his teaching as consisting only of reading from written texts and he would not venture on engaging in conversation except with his close friends.

He was ready to come, nonetheless, in the fall of 1937 but had to wait until April of 1938 before he could get the visas signed by the Mandate Government approving immigration that would make his departure possible, and this took place only with intervention from the outside. He had written Simon in November 1937 asking his help in finding someone who could translate his writings and thought into Hebrew. He was already working on his lectures, which took the form of laying the foundations of an anthropological system (to some extent

*See Note B in Sources for Chapter 13.

the anthropology of I and Thou) that he had so long postponed. It was these lectures that formed the basis for the next step in his philosophical anthropology *What Is Man?* He also started work at this time on his inaugural lecture on "The Demand of the Spirit and Historical Reality," in which he proposed to compare Plato's attempt to apply philosophy to politics in Syracuse with Isaiah's approach to the political.

In January, Buber wrote to David Werner Senator, the vice-president of the university, saying that he had received news that made him hope to be able to travel in February, but that if the certificate were still held up, he would telegraph him asking for a temporary labor certificate for himself and his wife. He did this latter, and Senator applied for such a certificate in his behalf. "You do not know and cannot perhaps foresee how much some persons here wait for your coming. For there are those here who believe that you . . . could bring together and make effective forces that today are unrecognized, ineffective. . . . We stand in the tragic predicament of attempting to realize our objectives in a transformed world that is no longer ours. Perhaps your wisdom and goodness can help us out of this confusion that has made a man like me, for example, deeply pessimistic about finding a way. Come quickly!"

In March 1938, Buber told Ernst Simon that when finally all the difficulties and obstacles had been overcome after the most troublesome months of his life, their moving plans had again been postponed because of Paula's falling down the cellar steps and not being able to move her foot for a week and his having come down with a bad case of the grippe. Now, however, they were really packed and would leave Frankfurt on March 13, stop in Zurich and Italy on the way, and sail on the nineteenth for Palestine, arriving in Haifa on the twenty-fourth. "The whole affair has been beyond belief."

"I was not 'driven out,' " Buber later corrected. They did not even want to let Buber emigrate because he could not pay 25 percent of the value of the land that he at that time possessed in Poland. Only after all sorts of intervention did they agree to his spending two-thirds of the year in Palestine on the condition that he live the rest of the time in Germany and maintain his house in Heppenheim in "inhabitable" condition. Paula took this condition so seriously that there really were possessions in the house for people to plunder in the *Kristallnacht* the following November.

A comic relief to this fantastic affair was provided by a bizarre incident at the very end. The most difficult part of the moving itself was packing Buber's library of 20,000 volumes into boxes and crates. The officials of the Third Reich were mistrustful and sent a Gestapo official to oversee the packing of the library. The officer stood inactive and bored in the midst of the chaos of books and finally turned to Buber with the request for a book that he might read. Buber invited his uninvited guest to choose any book that he wished. But the Gestapo official replied, "Herr Professor, I should like to read one of your books." Buber hesitated, since he was not at all clear as to which of his books would be appropriate for this minion of the Nazis. Finally he gave the official of the secret state police the collected edition of his Hasidic books. For three days the Nazi read with fascination the more than seven-hundred-page book until he had completed the whole thing. He then asked Buber if he might keep the book as a memento. When Buber assented, the Gestapo man asked him for a personal inscription. "I could not very well inscribe it, 'To my dear Gestapo man,' " commented Buber in telling this story. He solved the dilemma by simply writing his name in the book.

BUBER'S SIXTIETH BIRTHDAY

The celebration of Buber's sixtieth birthday, coming just a month before his departure, served in a very real sense as a *rite de passage*—from one homeland to another, from one type of work to another, from one language and culture to another, and from one phase of life to another. In addition to the public acknowledgments and thanks from the various segments of the German Jewish community for his leadership in establishing Jewish adult education, there were many individual testimonials that recognized the significance of this birthday for Buber's life as a whole. Hugo Bergmann sent Buber a thoughtful letter from Jerusalem in which he confessed that "we—your circle—have promised more than we have delivered up to this time. We have not shaped Jewish reality as we could and should have; we have not inserted ourselves simply and decisively enough into the Jewish and Palestinian reality." "Your true work lies before you," he added. "It must begin by definitely renouncing the German language and saying what you have to say to the Jewish people in plain, simple Hebrew. The richness of your German has often misled you and. . . . enormously injured your effectiveness, especially in these hard times." Buber himself at times explained that his style became simpler and more concrete in the last years of his life. The most often-told joke that one hears about Buber is that, interviewed by a radio station on his arrival in Palestine, he was supposed to have said that he did not know Hebrew well enough to obscure his thought in it!

Hans Trüb wrote Buber recalling how he was present ten years before when Franz Rosenzweig, "radiating joy," gave Buber *Aus unbekannten Schriften,* the book made up of a contribution from each of Buber's many friends from hitherto unpublished writings. "Today we cannot see ten steps ahead of us," Trüb contrasted. He himself could only approach Buber and firmly and hopefully shake his hand on this tragic occasion, because Trüb had imaginatively made his own Buber's experience of exile, affirming it for himself as the foundation of his own deepest human existence. Salman Schocken wrote Buber a touching letter quoting six pregnant lines from Goethe's *Faust* which began, "And so truly taught by change that the most precious is what never returns" and ended by saying that as man prepares man's way, it is the human that man contends with. Buber responded by saying that while he possessed no self-assurance, he was strongly confident because he knew that he had friends. Isaak Heinemann, the Jewish scholar, philologist, and researcher on Hellenism, professor at the Jewish Theological Seminary at Breslau, thanked Buber for the influence that the last decade of his life had had on scholars of all kinds, for whom he had been a model of bringing together basic life-experience and scholarly work. "I wish you long years of that astounding power of work and freshness with which you have accomplished that 'union of knowledge and life' . . . for which all of us long."

Hermann Hesse expressed similar sentiments, wishing that Martin and Paula preserve that elasticity and energy that he had so often admired and that a new source of lust for life and work would open for them in Palestine. "Despite all suffering it must strengthen and sustain you that you have a community and a direct, communal-building work." Hesse described himself, in contrast, as having "no community and no object of his concerns, cares, and life other than an indefinite, frightened diaspora of persons who, like myself, have no fixed place in the contemporary transformations and can only hope to leave our treasure of thought to some unforeseeable future." Ernst Simon gave a beautiful talk to the children of the Jewish settlement in Palestine on this occasion, asking them to picture what it was like for this man of sixty to begin a whole new life in the Land. Buber responded to this address as a "model" and added, "I feel myself *understood* by you as by very few. You see clearly the heart of the social theological paradox." Bergmann contributed a retrospective article for the *Jüdische Rundschau* recalling Buber's great importance for early Zionism and for the Third Aliyah of 1920 but saying that little of Buber's thought had been preserved in the Palestine of today. Hermann Gerson, in contrast, despite his own disaffection, penned a powerful testimonial to the importance of Buber for the youth of Palestine in his emphasis on personal as opposed to purely political realization. In the new situation of the kibbutz, basic thrusts of Buber's thought were still valid and important: taking the individual seriously, the undogmatic openness of the spirit, and the hallowing of the everyday that will unite present and past.

CHAPTER 14

Jerusalem and What Is Man?

ON THEIR ARRIVAL in Palestine, the Bubers found a house in Talbiyeh, one of the sections of the "new" (as opposed to the *really* old) city of Jerusalem. It was in the new sections of Jerusalem that the recent Jewish emigrants from Europe had mostly settled. The transition was a difficult one, but by May they were sufficiently settled so that Paula could get some rest after all the efforts and vexations she had undergone. Buber described himself as, if not tumbling in the ocean, at any rate still swimming in it with the aid of a life jacket. "Life here suits me well," he wrote Scholem. "I let the winds blow about my ears, and the atmospheric pressure that accompanied me everywhere in Europe I am free of—a proof that, despite all, there really is 'community.' " Both Paula and Martin suffered from the heat, which was bearable except during the notorious *hamsin,* or desert wind, the equivalent of the French mistral and the California Santa Ana. This was a dry, oppressive heat that Buber never got used to. On the contrary, with every year it became more difficult. Twenty-seven years later he died in the midst of a *hamsin*. In response to Eduard Strauss's question whether they were "safe," Buber replied that bombs (from the Arab terrorists) went off continually and in all parts of the city, including the part where they lived. "But with *this* unsafeness one can live remarkably well," he added, in an unmistakable contrast with the Nazi nightmare from which he had so recently emerged. Nor did the Nazis cease bothering Buber. They placed still further obstacles in his way in the form of taxes on the furniture from his father's Polish estate. There also remained the problem of selling the house in Heppenheim.

On November 5, Otto Hirsch informed Buber of the possibility of using him during the coming year for the work in Jewish adult education that he had left behind, although "our financial situation has deteriorated extraordinarily and the tasks grow ever greater." With the outbreaks accompanying *Kristallnacht* on November 9, any return to Germany on Buber's part became unthinkable. Buber's own house in Heppenheim was laid waste and plundered during this Nazi-organized pogrom. Arnold Berney, professor of modern history at Freiburg, wrote Buber from Switzerland, where he had fled, that he would gladly have saved some of Buber's remaining books from his house and brought them with him. However, he went over the border with only a small knapsack on his back. "But I discovered between heaven and the trackless undergrowth that the human voice never sounds truer and more directly than when a person is abandoned, wholly naked and stripped down, to every attack and every danger. Now I also understand for the first time (and one never understands this within the secure, furnished walls of a house, nor in the restful house of prayer) —I understood for the first time the crying need in the words: 'Let me not be put to shame.' " Not only could Buber not return to Germany but the Mittelstelle as such could no longer be continued. Ernst Kantorowicz informed Buber from Frankfurt that he had to liquidate his work as director of the Mittelstelle and emigrate during the middle of February without any idea of what might happen to that institution. Kantorowicz, who had seen Buber's immigration to Palestine as a tragic turn in his life, now had to ask Buber if he knew of any work that he himself might do in Palestine.

All of the furnishings of Buber's Heppenheim house were destroyed together with the 3,000 volumes remaining in his library there. At the same time the Nazi Office of Finance demanded 27,000 marks from Buber, which he could not, of course, pay. The Finance Office wrote Buber again, obviously wanting him to come to Germany to supervise the selling of his house, hoping to keep the affair strictly private in order to avoid the embarrassment of public disclosure of how much the house had been damaged and plundered. Because of Buber's fame, this too would undoubtedly have been reported in the foreign press. But Buber was not about to return to Germany under any circumstances.

Buber found life in Palestine difficult but more meaningful than in Europe. He experienced an incredible spate of creativity, both as a teacher and as a writer. Although he had written an enormous amount, it was only now that he settled down to being a writer in the real sense of the term. Before this, his writings were more occasional, with the exception of the Bible translation; snake skins which he needed to shed, as he expressed it. There could no longer be a question of German publications, and even Schocken wanted to continue only the Bible translation but did not want to take on anything new of his. However, Buber was already reaching out to Switzerland, England, and America, an effort which bore great fruit in the war years and after. In March 1939, Buber went to Poland with Paula for a strenuous lecture tour in behalf of the Friends of the Hebrew University in Jerusalem. In a little over two weeks, he spoke twenty-two times in as many different places. This set a pattern which continued in the years to come. When after the war Buber returned to Europe to lecture in Rome, Paris, Oxford, Stockholm, Zurich, Amsterdam, and other places, David Werner Senator saw this as a splendid opportunity for Buber also to take advantage of his ever-growing influence on behalf of the university. "He is a man who would admirably represent the university in intellectual circles," Senator proclaimed. Buber himself in a 1945 conversation with Senator said that having the professors of the Hebrew University visit the outside world to lecture ought to become a regular policy of the university. And, as in 1939, he insisted that his wife Paula had to accompany him. Paula was, indeed, the indispensable practical accompaniment to Buber's life. Without her, as he himself confessed, he would not have known how to tie a package. After her death, his daughter Eva or his granddaughter Barbara accompanied him on his lecture trips.

Over and above the enormous energy that the schedule of his trip to Poland demanded, both Martin and Paula found it a disturbing and painful experience. They encountered a great deal of war psychosis, especially in the German-speaking border districts, where he spoke several times. They also became acquainted at first hand with the dire need of many of Poland's population of three million Jews. And, in contrast to Nazi Germany, where demonstrations against the Jews were commanded and staged, they discovered a deep-seated hatred of the Jews such as Buber had never before experienced and from which they both returned literally sick. He took advantage of the trip to inquire into the affairs of his father's estate, but the limitations of the situation made it impossible for him to do very much about this.

In May 1939, Hermann Gerson sent Buber a book on fascism that he had written so that Buber might understand Gerson's present position and see it as a continuation of his earlier efforts. "It pains me when anyone tells me that you regard me as a 'lost son,' " he added, and claimed that the fundamental thing, which he learned from Buber—taking the individual person seriously—found expression in this book. He had remarried and had a son; he worked in the kibbutz to which he had returned, and he was content. Buber thanked Gerson for the book and found the social and political elements of it to be solid work. In contrast, he found the treatment of the ideologies of the French sociologist Georges Sorel and the German poet Stefan George to be inadequately grounded, and the unfaithfulness of the fascist movements to these ideologies was not even touched on. Nor could Buber accept Gerson's simple contrast between rationalism and irrationalism as illuminating fascism. "What is at stake today is already another, less simple contrast, less oriented to world-views." At the same time, Buber denied that he looked upon Gerson as a "lost son," despite Gerson's defection to Marxism from Buber's own religious socialism. "For *me* you are not lost, only (above all or in general, that remains to be seen) *for* a *cause.*"

At this very time, Buber wrote a remarkable letter to his old friend Franz Oppenheimer, a doctor and sociologist who espoused a liberal, non-Marxist, agrarian socialism somewhat akin to Buber's, and who was now a professor in Tokyo. This letter was literally a reclaiming of the past. Musing on the fact that the two of them, who had been neighbors in Germany, were now living at opposite ends of Asia, Buber turned back to Oppenheimer's 1919 book on capitalism, communism, and scientific socialism and discovered once again how it expressed what was in his own heart: "Today the fate of the largest part of mankind depends upon our willingness to risk true decision. We experience mankind's greatest need." "That has become even truer now," Buber commented. And even though the faith that a way exists to truth and righteousness was hardly perceptible, it was still ineradicable, as

Oppenheimer had written in 1919, and though the will to reach this goal today appeared weak, it was still irresistible. This faith and this will bound Buber to Oppenheimer for life. "We do not dwell in one house of the spirit, but we are neighbors. . . . The developing reality we strive for in our will is one." In his contribution to *Out of Unknown Writings* for Buber's fiftieth birthday, Oppenheimer had written, "God's mills may grind slowly but they grind surely." Now, for Oppenheimer's seventy-fifth birthday, Buber added: "Just as slowly and just as surely grows the seed of God." Oppenheimer saw this new saying as "the formula which our time needs"; for the earlier formula was one of retaliation and vengeance whereas the latter was concerned with "the new kingdom of righteousness in which we both, you and I, have lived from of old." Retaliation belongs to justice, to be sure, but it also demands that the judge not be an interested party. Oppenheimer confessed that when he thought about what had been done by the Nazis not only to the Jews but to the whole of mankind, his will fought against his spirit and he wished revenge. In this fight "Your good word will be of help to me."

The good spirit in the Buber household was his wife Paula, who determined the lifestyle of the house to a large extent, even when she remained somewhat unaware of the outside world. Buber preferred Arabic architecture, and all three of his houses in Jerusalem had high ceilings and thick walls which provided protection from heat and cold. The old European mahogany furniture in his relatively new Oriental house gave the impression of a synthesis of Orient and Occident. In his study there stood large glass cases in which, next to scholarly works, stood art books with reproductions of the old masters. There were also individual pieces of art from his early years in Florence and a splendid edition of Dante which Buber loved to read in the original Italian. The study was dominated by a large, foreign desk, on which there was always a large collection of pens but never a typewriter. The desk was covered with books and manuscripts and, above all, the notebooks in which Buber jotted down ideas that occurred to him from wholly different spheres, systematically entered into one notebook or another according to the topic. Buber did not smoke, but he always had pieces of sugar at hand which served to increase his energy and concentration when he was fatigued. In his first house in Jerusalem, he kept a complete edition of Goethe near his desk.

Buber always knew exactly where to go in his library to find the precise book or passage that he needed. He was able to read any book in a few hours and remember its contents entirely. Along with books, his study was never lacking in cats, which entered freely through the open window and lay on the sofa in his study. Buber spoke to the cats as if they were human beings, and they minded him in the same way. If he said to a familiar cat, "Ja, what are you doing? Lie down in the corner and don't disturb me," the cat obeyed.

By the time Buber settled in Palestine, he had already mastered spoken Hebrew. At first he wrote his lectures in German and then worked them through in Hebrew with the Hebraist Fritz Aronstein, with whom he also studied conversational Hebrew. In Hebrew as in German his handwriting was almost sheer calligraphy, so that he often gave his written manuscripts to the printer. When he gave his inaugural lecture in the great auditorium in Hebrew University on Mount Scopus overlooking Jerusalem, his Hebrew was so clear and rich that his hearer often did not know where Buber was citing the Bible or Plato and where he was speaking for himself.

Over the next few years, when most of his writing was in Hebrew and not in German, Buber became a unique Hebrew writer. He tried to do in Hebrew what he did in German. The result was somewhat strained because the language was not suited for such a close transposition. He had to create his own Hebrew as he had created his own German. But he expressed himself very forcefully in Hebrew. It was not true at all, as his detractors were wont to say, that he could not write a good Hebrew. When Theodor Heuss, the President of the West German Republic, came to Israel in 1960 for a lecture sponsored by Buber, Bergmann, Scholem, and Ernst Simon, David Ben-Gurion, the Premier of Israel, approached Buber in the lobby of a hotel where a banquet was being given for Heuss. Ben-Gurion sought to relieve his own embarrassment at feeling constrained to honor a high-minded statesman, who was nonetheless a German, by attacking Buber. "How is it that you have never written your books in Hebrew?" Ben-Gurion demanded. "I have written many in Hebrew," Buber replied, "including *Gog vMagog* [*For the Sake of Heaven*], which was published serially in your own party's newspaper!"

One might perhaps say of Buber's writing in both languages what he himself said of Ludwig Strauss's German and Hebrew poetry in the essay "Authentic Bilingualism" which he wrote as an introduction to the collected edition of Strauss's German work. It is "representative of a significant situation in the history of the spirit, of the exodus of the Jewish spirit from the German culture." At least in the case of the

Tales of the Hasidim and *For the Sake of Heaven*, both of which he wrote originally in Hebrew, if not of the more theoretical works such as *Moses, The Prophetic Faith,* and *Paths in Utopia,* one can speak of Buber as one of those Jews in Palestine who, again in the words of this essay, "did not speak Hebrew because they determined to do so but because the very tongue itself fatefully took possession of their corporeality, because it fatefully emanated from their brain and their throat." This is in no way contradicted by the fact that Buber continued to write his *philosophical* books in German. In abstract thinking and in poetry and drama, Buber continued to rely on German. Yet in important spheres of his life, such as the Hasidic, he became one of those "men who spontaneously thought in Hebrew." It was, if not the same task as writing poetry in two languages, nonetheless a work of the most intense concentration to write book after book for many years in both German and Hebrew. This was especially so because, as Buber himself pointed out, the two languages were not suited to say the same things. Hasidic legends had to be presented to the Hebrew reader in an essentially different way than to the German reader, and exegetical works, which in Hebrew proceeded naturally from the original text of the Bible, needed other formulations when they were published in German. This was particularly the case because of the many Christian readers familiar with very different versions of the Bible and almost not at all with the Hebrew original. Only in his last years did Buber undertake to correct the translations into the Hebrew and into English, and he often succeeded in finding more exact words than the translators.

Buber's lecture "The Demand of the Spirit and Historical Reality" was a remarkable combination of the old—Plato and Isaiah—and the new—the modern science of sociology—the academic and the spiritual, the timeless and the topical. In contrast to the "scientific" and statistically oriented sociologists who succeeded Buber in the department at Hebrew University, Buber saw the origin of modern sociology "in the meeting of the spirit with the crisis of human society, which the spirit accepts as its own crisis and which it undertakes to overcome through a spiritual turning and transformation." He by no means wanted to remake the sociologist into some sort of biblical prophet, but he saw sociology's true task, according to its development and its legitimate functioning, as placing a demand on the society that it studied. This demand extends to the direct relationships between persons and not merely to the institutions of society. "If the new house that man hopes to erect is not to become his burial chamber, the essence of living together must undergo a change at the same time as the organization of living." In contrast to Max Weber and others who held sociology to be "value-free," Buber insisted that philosophical treatment of social conditions, events, and structures includes valuation—criticism and demand when the situation calls for it. First, the sociologist involves himself in his subject and then he distances himself from it: "No one becomes a sociological thinker if his dream and his passion have never mingled with the dream and passion of a human community." But in the moment of thinking, the sociologist wills with all the powers of his spirit to achieve free vision. Only then may he value and decide, censure and demand, without violating the law of his science. This valuing is demanded of him by the heart of sick reality, which asks spirit to speak as its partner, not as its mere spokesman.

But it makes all the difference how the spirit tries to transform social reality. Plato imagined that he could assume power in Syracuse, but he could not found the Republic he projected. Plato's "glorious failure" is instructive; for it was founded on his imagining that he, the philosopher, possessed the truth and could impose it on reality. Isaiah also failed, but in a very different way; for failure was an integral part of the way he had to take. Isaiah did not imagine that he possessed either spirit or truth or power as Plato did. Plato believed his soul was perfect; Isaiah acknowledged himself as unclean, yet he was able, for all that, to speak the word of God in the historical situation. "The man of spirit . . . is one whom the spirit invades and seizes, whom the spirit uses as its garment, not one who contains the spirit." Spirit is an event that happens to man, a storm that sweeps him where it wills and then passes on.

Isaiah had no blueprint of a perfect and just state. He had only a message, a proclamation that was both criticism and demand. He was the powerless prophet who reminded both the people and the government of their *common* responsibility toward God's will for true community. His criticism was directed toward the lives of men in a society in which social inequality and the distinction between the free and the unfree split the community and made it impossible that there could be a true people able to fulfill the demands of the covenant. "When Isaiah speaks of justice, he is not thinking of institutions but of you and me, because without you and me the most glorious institution becomes a lie." When the mountain of the Lord's house is "established" on the reality of true community life, then, and only then, will the nations "flow" toward it (Isaiah 2:2), there to learn peace in place of war. Isaiah in his very failure in his historic hour instilled his vision in the people for all time so that that spirit is still effective in any new situation in which there is once again a chance to translate it into social reality. Just because he received a message for a particular situation rather than a universal and timeless ideal truth, his word still speaks after thousands of years to manifold situations in the history of peoples. He cannot withdraw into Plato's attitude of a calm spectator when he feels himself surrounded by wild beasts. He must speak a message that will be misunderstood, misjudged, misused, yet whose sting will rankle forever.

In an uncanny way, with these words Buber charted his own lonely and painful course in the years to come in Palestine and the State of Israel. If he might humorously be spoken of as the Rebbe of Zehlendorf or Heppenheim while he was in Germany, the image that fits his life in the Land is not that of the Hasidic leader surrounded by his community but of the lonely prophet bringing the hard word of the hour to deaf ears and hardened hearts. Not that Buber *was* a biblical prophet but, rather, a philosopher. He did not have a divinely inspired message but a teaching. Yet he too intended what was decisive for the transformation of social reality—the reality within the society and the reality between society and society. He too carried forward the prophetic task of criticism and demand within the present situation. He did not see the future on the basis of inspiration, as did Jeremiah, but of understanding, as did Isaiah. According to Aharon Shoshar, Buber was a prophet by way of philosophy. Although Buber himself repeatedly and emphatically rejected the designation of "prophet," there is probably some truth in Shoshar's claim that Buber sometimes considered Isaiah his best friend. "Once when I visited him," Shoshar said to me, "he stood and pointed out the window with his finger and said, 'When Isaiah stood here, what did he think?' Plato wanted the philosopher to become king or the king a philosopher. But we should ask, 'What does it mean to be a philosopher?' A philosopher is a person who penetrates into the inner reality of human life, examines the changing situations, understanding what leads to these situations and where these situations will lead."

This conversation is identical in tone with "The Demand of the Spirit and Historical Reality." The spirit cannot be the dictator of things to come, as Saint-Simon thought, but it can be the preparer and counselor that educates persons for what is to come. When men despair of power and its autonomous decisions as the crisis grows deeper, when power for power's sake goes astray and longs for direction, then the peoples may at least *listen* to the social philosophers who take up the prophetic task in modern times. Only then will knowledge become, if not powerful, at least effective. Resigned or unresigned, the spirit works. But at that moment, looking back on the Europe he had left and forward to the society and community still to be built in Palestine, Buber was emboldened to believe that an hour was near in which the people would become open to change and the impossible possible!

Buber's inaugural course of lectures as professor of social philosophy at the Hebrew University constitute a notable exception to that distraction from his own discipline that occasioned Buber's heartfelt complaint to Bergmann about accepting this position. *What Is Man?*— or *The Problem of the Human,* as it is called in the separate German edition and in the philosophy volume of Buber's collected works— represents a decisive step forward in the development of Buber's philosophical anthropology, Buber's most significant contribution to philosophy and to the history of Western thought. Although seemingly an objective survey of the history of philosophy from the standpoint of the problem of the human, there is much in this book that reveals its lived historical grounding in Buber's life.

What Buber said of the sociologist in "The Demand of the Spirit and Historical Reality," he here applies to the philosophical anthropologist in general: one can understand the human only from within, from full involvement and participation. A psychologist may split himself into two parts so that he can observe his anger while he is feeling it. A philosophical anthropologist must live anger or any other moment of existence with whole, undivided being in order that in recollection it is precisely the knowledge of human wholeness including the concrete self and subjectivity of the knower, which issues into thought. What Melville says of the whale in *Moby Dick*—that to know it you must go whaling yourself and risk being eternally "stove in"—Buber says of the philosophical anthropologist: "Here you do not attain to knowledge by remaining on the shore and watching the foaming waves, you must make the venture and cast yourself in, you must swim, alert and with all your force, even if a moment comes when you think you are losing consciousness." Melville points to the encounter with reality which can only be known in encountering it; Buber, no less dialogically, points to that human wholeness which can never be known through individual disciplines of philosophy or science or through the objective observer who leaves out the knower, the human, in her or his self as an indispensable and inextricable part of what is to be known. The philosophical anthropologist places man in nature but also sees the uniqueness of man that sets him apart from nature. No universal "human nature" is accessible to philosophical anthropology: "A legitimate philosophical anthropology must know that there is not merely a human species but also peoples, not merely a human soul but also types and characters, not merely a human life but also stages in life." Only through this duality of distinction and comparison—"the recognition of the dynamic that exerts power within every particular reality and between them"—can philosophical anthropology reach the whole, real human being who walks on the narrow ridge from birth toward death knowing and testing out what no other being can do for him, wrestling with destiny, rebellion, and reconciliation.

Even more than in *The Question to the Single One* Buber stressed the importance of solitude in *The Problem of the Human*—a solitude which he himself was to experience ever more keenly during the remaining years of his life. Only in a strict and inescapable solitude does the human problematic present itself as an independent reality to the thinker. "In the ice of solitude man becomes most inexorably a question to himself," and it is in the most solitary persons that anthropological thought has become fruitful in human history. Buber distinguishes here between epochs of habitation in which the human being lives in the world as in a house or a home and epochs of homelessness in which the person "lives in the world as in an open field and at times does not even have four pegs with which to set up a tent." Aristotle, building on the Greek world in which the visual sense dominated every other, saw man as a thing in a universe of things. Wonder at the world in general was the beginning of philosophy for him. But Augustine, who lived in a time in which this world view had broken down, had, as a result of experiences with his self, turned his eyes inward and demanded the same of all men. In Aquinas man is once more housed and unproblematic, but Pascal experiences the uncanniness of the starry heavens and knows what even a mystic such as Nicholas of Cusa, to whom man was a microcosm containing the whole, does not know: what it means to be exposed as a human being to infinity. It is striking that Buber, who had experienced the threat of the infinity of space and time so keenly at fourteen that he had almost committed suicide, had settled into the microcosmic security of Cusanus by the time he wrote his doctoral dissertation—only to lose it again and forever with the First World War.

After the discoveries of Copernicus and Einstein, the universe can still be thought—in mathematical theorems—but it can no longer be imaged or lived in as a home. Hegel's modern house of the universe did not overcome even for a moment in the actual life of man the great anthropological unrest first expressed in modern times by Pascal's question. An intellectual image of the universe built on *time,* such as Hegel's, can never give the same feeling of security as one built on space. Intellectual time is always *cosmological*—the time of the world seen as a whole—for which the future is just the past that has not yet unfolded. But actual human time is *anthropological* in which my decision and that of other persons affect the shape of the future historical hour and make it genuinely open. Marx's sociological reduction of Hegel's image of the universe into an image of society is still founded on *cosmological* time in that it posits an inevitable historical process and leaves out of consideration the problem of human decision as the origin of social events and destiny. It depends on the direction and force of the power of decision how far the renewing powers of life as such are able to take effect, and even whether they are not transformed into powers of destruction.

The crisis of Nazism, which drove Hermann Gerson and Kibbutz Hazorea to Marxism, for Buber shattered once for all Marx's claim that capitalist production breeds the antithesis which negates it "with the necessity of a natural process." For there is no doubt that this is what Buber is referring to when he speaks here of "a moment in history in which the problematic of human decision makes itself felt to a terrifying degree. I mean a moment in which catastrophic events exercise a frightening and paralysing influence over the power of decision, and repeatedly move it to renunciation in favour of a negative élite of men —men who, knowing no inner restraint, do not act as they do from real decision, but only in order to consolidate their power." Marx offered what Hegel did not: the real historical security of the inevitable rise to power of an actual class of men—the proletariat. Today *this* security "has perished in the ordered chaos of a terrible historical revulsion." A new anthropological dread has arisen: "the question about man's being faces us as never before in all its grandeur and terror—no longer in philosophical attire, but in the nakedness of existence." No dialectical guarantee, whether that of Hegel or of Marx, keeps us from falling. The strength to take the step which will lead us away from the abyss can arise only from those depths of insecurity in which, overshadowed by despair, we answer with our decision the question about man's being.

To an important extent *What Is Man?* or *The Problem of the Human* represents Buber's own dialogue with thinkers who exercised a decided influence on him in his youth; Kant, Feuerbach, Kierkegaard, and Nietzsche. Feuerbach's anthropological reduction of Hegel to *unproblematic* man had at least the virtue which Marx did not—understanding man in terms of the real relation between the truly different *I and Thou,* that "Copernican revolution of modern thought" (Karl Heim) which gave Buber a decisive impetus in his youth. Marx opposed an unreal individualism with a collectivism that was just as unreal. Nietzsche, in contrast, surpasses Hegel, Marx, and Feuerbach in his recognition of the problematic of man, the "unfinished animal." Nietzsche "endows the anthropological question with an unprecedented force and passion." For Nietzsche the problem of man is a problem of the *edge*—that perilous end of natural being where the dizzying abyss of nothing begins. Man is not a being but a becoming —"an attempt, a groping, a missing the mark." Nietzsche's question "How is it to be understood that such a being as man has emerged and stepped forth from the animal world?" is the question with which Buber himself was explicitly to start in *The Knowledge of Man* and which he was to attempt to answer with his concepts of "distancing" and "relating."

Buber's critique of Nietzsche's doctrine of "the will to power" as sick is not surprising in a philosopher who from his earliest writings stressed the necessity of making power responsible to meaningful personal, social, and national *direction.* What is new is what Buber says here about real greatness in the history of the spirit and of culture, as well as in the history of people and of states; for in this characterization we can perhaps glimpse something of Buber's self-insight:

> Greatness is an inner powerfulness, which sometimes grows suddenly and irresistibly to power over men, sometimes exerts its effect quietly and slowly on a company that is quietly and slowly increasing, sometimes, too, seems to have no effect at all, but rests in itself, and sends out beams which will perhaps catch the glance only of some far time.

... The great man, whether we comprehend him in the most intense activity of his work or in the restful equipoise of his forces, is powerful, involuntarily and composedly powerful, but he is not avid for power. What he is avid for is the realization of what he has in mind, the incarnation of the spirit.

When a great person desires power instead of his or her real goal, then a threat of senselessness ensues and a snatching after empty power which places a genius like Nietzsche on the same level as persons like Hitler—"those hysterical figures of history who, being by nature without power, slave for power, for an ever fresh display of power and an ever fresh increase of power, in order that they may enjoy the illusion that they are inwardly powerful, and who . . . cannot let a pause intervene, since a pause would bring with it the possibility of self-reflection and self-reflection would bring collapse." Power as an instrument is not evil, only power *in itself,* power withdrawn from responsibility. It is this power which betrays the spirit and corrupts the history of the world.

Only in our time has the anthropological problem reached maturity and come to be treated as an independent philosophical problem, because only in our time has homelessness in the universe been combined with the homelessness caused by the increasing decay of the old organic forms of the direct life between person and person. This double homelessness is intensified by man's lagging behind his works and finding himself dominated by the Frankenstein monsters which he himself has created in the form of machines, the economics of production, and incomprehensible political powers. Edmund Husserl, from whom the two anthropological attempts that Buber examines both stem—that of Martin Heidegger and that of Max Scheler—was a German Jew. As such he was the son of a people—the Jews—which had experienced the decay of organic forms of common human life more grievously than any other people. As such also he was the adopted son of another people—the Germans—which experienced more grievously and fatefully than any other people man's lagging behind his works. Behind Husserl, to be sure, stands the figure of Kierkegaard, who made possible modern philosophical anthropology. The philosophical anthropologist renounced Kierkegaard's theological presupposition without acquiring an adequate philosophical one that would retain the concrete person's bond with the absolute.

Heidegger sees the whole of human existence as "zum Tode sein"

—toward death. Buber, more realistically, recognizes that death is not just the end-point of our existence of which we must be aware in the present but is itself present at every moment as a force that wrestles with the force of life. We begin to die when we begin to live; destructive and disintegrative power is inseparable from constructive power. Our attitude toward our future death is determined by the reality of death's power in this very moment. Heidegger offers us instead of life a chess game, "whose rules we learn as we advance, deep rules which we . . . must ponder," but which exist only because a decision has been reached to play this intellectual game in this very way. Buber by no means sees this game as an arbitrary decision on Heidegger's part but one of necessity: "it is his fate."

Heidegger recognizes a primal, existential guilt, but he sees this guilt as arising out of one's relation, to one's *own* being, whereas Buber holds that "original guilt consists in remaining with oneself," hence out of an injury to our relation with *others.* The presence of the other appears by no rules and is often terrifyingly different from myself and from what I expected. But it is only in answering the call of present being which comes to me through the other and which I must respond to with the truth of my whole life that I can avoid existential guilt. "Heidegger's doctrine is significant as the presentation of the relations to one another of various 'beings' abstracted from human life, but it is not valid for human life itself . . ." His philosophy arises from that situation of modern solitary man in which, unable to stretch his hands out from his solitude to meet a divine form (Nietzsche's "God is dead"), there is nothing left for him but to seek an intimate communication with himself.

The difference between Heidegger and Buber is an ontological one. Despite Heidegger's insistence that *Dasein* ("being there") is *Mitsein* ("being with others"), his "existence" is monological—a monologue disguised as dialogue in which one unknown layer after the other of the human self answers the inner address. But the hour of stark, final solitude comes when the illusions of "calling" and "hearing" give way. Now everything depends upon whether the solitary person who can no longer say "Thou" to the "dead" known God can still say it to the living unknown God by saying "thou" with all his or her being to another living and known person. If one cannot do this, then one still has the sublime illusion of detached thought that one is a self-contained self: as a human being one is lost. This "exalted and unblessed game of the spirit" absolutizes the situation of the radically solitary man and tries to derive the essence of human existence from the experience of a nightmare. The person who can no longer really live with other persons now knows a real life only in communication with his or her self. In spite of his uniqueness, man can never find, when he plunges to the depth of his life, a being that is whole in itself and as such touches on the absolute. Yet two limited and conditioned beings can experience the absolute in being together in genuine dialogue.

Heidegger, to be sure, sees real life together as the first thing to arise out of the real self-being of resolution. But he does not actually acknowledge the relation to the other as essential; for he sees this relation as one of solicitude, and solicitude does not set one person's life in direct relation with that of another. In *mere* solicitude we remain essentially with ourselves, even when moved by extreme pity; whereas in an essential relation the barriers of self-being are breached and one experiences the mystery of the other being in the mystery of one's own. The two participate in each other's life existentially, not merely psychically. If we do not all know the reality of this mutual inclusion, we at least know the effects of its lack in our lives. When we do not use the opportunities that come our way to open ourselves to another, we "squander the most precious, irreplaceable and irrecoverable material." Our lives pass us by. Heidegger would perhaps reply that it is only the self which has become free that is really capable of love and friendship, but since self-being is here *the* ultimate which the existence is able to reach, "there is absolutely no starting-point for understanding love and friendship still as essential relations." "Heidegger's self is *a closed system.*"

If, in connection with Nietzsche, Buber characterized the great person, in connection with Heidegger he characterized the great relation. The child says Thou before it learns to say I; "but at the height of personal existence one must be truly able to say *I* in order to know the mystery of the *Thou* in its whole truth." Only the individual who has become a Single One, a self, a real person, is able to have a complete relation to the other self, "a relation which is not beneath but above the problematic of the relations between man and man, and which comprises, withstands and overcomes all this problematic situation." But one becomes a Single One in order to go out to the meeting with the *Thou.* "A *great* relation exists only between real persons. It can be strong as death, because it is stronger than solitude, because it breaches the barriers of a lofty solitude, subdues its strict law, and throws a bridge from self-being to self-being across the abyss of dread of the universe." Buber was not afraid of the nightmare any more than of the solitude or the abyss of dread. But, walking his narrow ridge, he went forth again and again to encounter the other that came to meet him, and this encounter on the narrow ridge was the starting point for his anthropology as for his life.

Only in *What Is Man?* did Buber begin the task of laying an adequate groundwork for his philosophy of community and society: with the recognition that alongside the essential *Thou* there is also an essential *We.* This *We* means the possibility of human directness among a group of persons. Thus it includes the *Thou* potentially. "Only men who are capable of truly saying *Thou* to one another can truly say *We* with one another." It is not in authentic resoluteness that we are saved from the impersonalness of the "one" *(das Man),* as Heidegger imagines, but in the essential *We.* "A man is truly saved from the 'one' not by separation but only by being bound up in genuine communion." Thus the critique which Buber made in *The Question to the Single One* of Kierkegaard's chariness in having to do with others returns here in sharpened form in his critique of Heidegger. If Kierkegaard has no relation to things other than as similes, Heidegger knows things only as a technical, purposive relation. Neither has that essential relation to things without which we cannot understand the fact of art. Neither thinker makes essential all three relations—those to the world, to other persons, and to the mystery of being. "Heidegger, influenced by Hölderlin, the great poet of this mystery, has undoubtedly had a profound experience of the mystery of being . . . but he has not experienced it as one which steps before us and challenges us . . . to come out from ourselves to meet with essential otherness." Even lyric poetry, Buber maintained, is not the completion and transfiguration of the human relation to one's own self but "the tremendous refusal of the soul to be satisfied with self-commerce." "Poetry is the soul's announcement that even when it is alone with itself on the narrowest ridge it is thinking not of itself but of the Being which is not itself," which is visiting it there, "perplexing and blessing it." "When I read Kierkegaard in my youth," Buber concluded, "I regarded Kierkegaard's man as the man on the edge. But Heidegger's man is a great and decisive step beyond Kierkegaard in the direction of the edge where *nothing* begins."

The second anthropological attempt with which Buber dealt in *The Problem of the Human* was that of his old friend Max Scheler, who had taken a very different direction from him, as we have seen, at the beginning of the First World War. When Buber met Scheler a few years after the war, after they had not seen each other for some time, Scheler had, unknown to Buber, passed through a phase of Catholicism. Scheler surprised Buber by saying, "I have come very near your narrow ridge." If there was anything Buber did not expect from Scheler it was that he would forgo the security provided by the sure knowledge of the ground of being. Yet this is exactly what the "narrow ridge" had come to mean to Buber since his own thoughts about ultimate concerns reached, in the First World War, a decisive turning point. When he described his standpoint to his friends as the narrow ridge, he meant that he did not rest on the broad upland of a system that includes a series of sure statements about the absolute, but on a narrow rocky ridge between abysses where one cannot have the certainty of metaphysical truths yet can have confidence in the genuineness of a meeting which yields the knowing of mutual knowing without the certainty of objective knowledge. His second statement to Scheler was, "But it is not where you think it is"; for in the meantime he had understood that Scheler had confused it with his early philosophy, influenced by German mysticism, in which he held that man is the being through whose existence the Absolute, while remaining eternal truth, can attain reality in time. Scheler's new philosophy of the becoming God was close, in fact, to this concept of the realization of God through man. Scheler too had had a shattering experience during the war, one so radically different from Buber's that instead of bringing him to a meeting with otherness and the recognition of the spirit as existing in the realm of the between, he became convinced of the essential powerlessness of the spirit.

Buber's critique of Scheler is essentially a critique of this conviction; for Scheler's divine image is really the transfigured likeness of a modern man in whom the sphere of the spirit and the sphere of impulse have fallen apart more markedly than ever before. Spirit as it is here can indeed hold ideas and values before the impulses, but it can no longer make them credible. The person in the modern world, in Buber's paraphrase of Scheler, "perceives with apprehension that an unfruitful and powerless remoteness from life is threatening the separated spirit, and he perceives with horror that the repressed and banished impulses are threatening to destroy his soul." Now spirit can arise only through repression and sublimation of the instincts, psychological categories which Scheler takes from Sigmund Freud. In the context of his critique of Scheler, Buber gives us a hint of his own anthropological critique of Freud, which occasioned his enthusiasm for Binswanger's study of Freud. The central position that Freud gives repression and sublimation, their dominating significance for the whole structure of personal and communal life, is not based on the general life of man but on the situation and qualities of the typical man of today who is sick, both in his relation to others and in his very soul. "I know no such deep-reaching and comprehensive crisis in history as ours," Buber commented; for it is a crisis of confidence that undermines human existence as such. Although the individual must often adapt his or her wishes to the commands of the community in any society, only if the organic community disintegrates from within and mistrust becomes life's basic note does the repression acquire its dominating importance.

> The unaffectedness of wishing is stifled by mistrust, everything around is hostile or can become hostile, agreement between one's own and the other's desire ceases, for there is no true coalescence or reconciliation with what is necessary to a sustaining community, and the dulled wishes creep hopelessly into the recesses of the soul. . . . Now there is no longer a human wholeness with the force and the courage to manifest itself. For spirit to arise the energy of the repressed instincts must mostly first be "sublimated," the traces of its origin cling to the spirit and it can mostly assert itself against the instincts only by convulsive alienation. The divorce between spirit and instincts is here, as often, the consequence of the divorce between man and man.

Buber criticized Scheler's "world's ground" as "only one of the countless attempts to strip the mystery from the biblical God," and in that sense anticipated his later critique of Jung's modern gnosticism as wishing to approach the mysteries of faith without the attitude of faith. At the same time, Buber rejected Scheler's seemingly religious claim that the ascetic is *the* basic type of spiritual man. The artistic genius of Rembrandt, Shakespeare, or Mozart carries out continual acts of renunciation and inner transformation. But the real conduct of its spiritual life is not based on asceticism, on endless negotiations between spirit and instinct. Rather each listens to the other, and even the daemonic realm of conflict which such persons experience is not one between spirit and instinct. The true negotiations and decisions in the life of great persons take place between spirit and spirit, between instincts and instincts, between one product of spirit and instinct and another product of spirit and instinct. Nor could Buber accept Scheler's category of "sympathy" as a basic anthropological one. The person who has really responded to the depth of the pain of others lives does so with great love. "Only then does his own pain in its ultimate depth light a way into the suffering of the world." Pain is like those early mysteries whose meaning no one learns who does not himself join in the dance. One discovers a mode of being in communion with it, and every philosophical idea springs from such a discovery. Even for the philosopher, contemplation is secondary to participation in existence. Therefore, philosophy must return to existence, fighting its way through already existing thoughts and systems. "All philosophical discovery is the uncovering of what is covered by the veil woven from the thread of a thousand theories. Without such an uncovering we shall not be able to master the problems of man at this late hour." For Buber, this also applied to religion: "If the religious man is something different from the existential actuation of all that subsists in 'non-religious' man as dumb need, as stammering dereliction, as despair crying out, then he is a monster. . . . There is no other spirit but that which is nourished by the unity of life and by unity with the world."

In opposition to Scheler, Buber pictured the arising of spirit in the child and peasant as happening become word. It begins *mythically* and then steps forth itself, independently, in the *word.* The instinct toward the word is the impulse to be present with others in a world of streaming communication. The old peasant staring at the clouds utters a saying that expresses his insight into the *grace* of things experienced, despite all contrariness, as participating in the being of the world. "Here too it holds true that the spirit arises from concord with things and in concord with instincts." The impulse to form in art is inseparable from the impulse toward the word: "the picture is shown with passion, the singer sings to the listeners with passion." In its most primal stage spirit already wished to express itself: "the picture itself strives to be painted on the roof of a cave, and some red chalk is at hand, the sound strives to be sung, and the lips are opening in a magic song."

In earlier ages, man thought with his whole body to the very fingertips; now he thinks only with his brain. For ours is the age of the sick man, cut off from the world and divided into spirits and instincts. "So long as we suppose that this sick man is *man,* the normal man, man in general, we shall not heal him." Individualism, which understands only a part of man, and collectivism, which understands man only as a part of a larger entity, can neither one give us the wholeness of the human; for they are the conclusion or expression of the same human condition, at different stages. "This condition is characterized by the union of cosmic and social homelessness, dread of the universe and dread of life, resulting in an existential constitution of solitude such as has probably never existed before to the same extent." And collectivism means a more terrible isolation than individualism. The collective whole aims logically and successfully at reducing, neutralizing, devaluating, and desecrating every bond with living beings: "That tender surface of personal life which longs for contact with other life is progressively deadened or desensitized." But the solitude takes vengeance in the depths and rises secretly to a cruelty which will become manifest with the scattering of the illusion. "Modern collectivism is the last barrier raised by man against a meeting with himself."

Buber detected on the horizon, "moving" with the slowness of all events of true human history, "the great disillusionment with modern collectivism" and the recognition of the "between" as the sphere of genuine community, "the real place and bearer of what happens between men." In the most powerful moments of dialogue, where "deep calls unto deep," the narrow ridge, on the far side of the subjective "inner" impression and on this side of the objective "outer" event, is the place where *I and Thou* meet, the realm of "between." Only from this knowledge of the eternal meeting of the One with the Other can we recover the genuine person again and establish genuine community.

> In the deadly crush of an air-raid shelter the glances of two strangers suddenly meet for a second in astonishing and unrelated mutuality. . . . In the darkened opera-house there can be established between two of the audience, who do not know one another, and who are listening in the same purity and with the same intensity to the music of Mozart, a relation which is scarcely perceptible and yet is one of elemental dialogue.

The philosophical science of man, which includes anthropology and sociology, must take as its starting point the consideration of "man with man."

The extent to which Buber had mastered modern Hebrew in this period is shown by the long introduction that he wrote in 1943 to the Hebrew translation of the French philosopher Henri Bergson's essays and lectures on "Spiritual Energy." In this introduction Buber focused on Bergson's concept of intuition, maintaining that "the main entrance to the lifework of a thinker is not the content of his thought but his manner and method of thought." Buber espied in Bergson a personalistic strain similar to his own, though much more concerned with the knowledge of the "inner life" than he himself was. Bergson deals, inadequately, with the basic metaphysical question of the relation between being and knowing, and Buber, in his appreciative criticism, gives us a glimpse into his own approach to this question, revealing the development of his philosophical anthropology. When Bergson identifies the intuition of one's inner duration with the intuition of the life of others, he makes a basic mistake, Buber claimed. Without the awareness of the primary reality of the Thou, all intuition is a patchwork; for it leaves out the essential distinction between empathic identification and "inclusion," or experiencing the other side of the relationship, on which Buber increasingly built his own philosophy. Bergson wishes to inflate the *contact* which the philosopher has into a *vision* that yields knowledge. Buber, in contrast, points to a difference between our *contact* with living beings and our apprehending a person through our knowing, a difference which our intuitive transportation of ourselves into the interior of the other can diminish but not abolish.

The artist and the genuine philosopher do not hold a fragment of being up to light. Theirs is a contact with being which brings forth what has never before existed, in the philosopher's case a symbol of the whole. Buber accepted Bergson's notion of the intellect as dividing the self and holding us apart from the world that it assists us in utilizing. But he rejected Bergson's claim that instinct is a form of sympathetic knowing—as when the wasp paralyzes the caterpillar—contending that instinct joins us to the world, but not as persons, and hence gives us no true knowledge. Against Bergson's claim that intuition gives us absolute knowledge, Buber defined intuition, in true dialogical fashion, as a knowing that binds us as person with the world that faces us without making us one with it, "through a vision that cannot be absolute." In the end Buber was not a metaphysician, like Bergson, but a philosophical anthropologist concerned with both general human and personal perceptions which are limited but which, in the case of intuition, afford "us an intimate glimpse into hidden depths."

The true teacher, for Buber, like the true sociologist and the philosophical anthropologist, is not a "value-free" scholar and imparter of knowledge. "Education worthy of the name is essentially education of character," Buber said at the opening of the address he gave to the

National Conference of Jewish Teachers in Palestine at Tel Aviv in 1939. "The Education of Character" was included, along with "Education" and "Education and World View" in the little book *The Educational (Der Erzieherische)* that Buber published in Germany after the war, and it is the latest of the essays included in *Between Man and Man*. Although the examples Buber used were chosen from Palestine, the life-experience that engendered this view of education was, predominantly, his work in Jewish adult education in Nazi Germany.

Because education of character is concerned with the person as a whole, both in present actuality and in what this person can become, it is problematic in a way that imparting of facts or theories, such as the idea of the quadratic equation, cannot be. The direct approach of giving instruction in ethics does not work at all. "I try to explain to my pupils that envy is despicable, and at once I feel the secret resistance of those who are poorer than their comrades. I try to explain that it is wicked to bully the weak, and at once I see a suppressed smile on the lips of the strong. I try to explain that lying destroys life, and . . . the worst habitual liar of the class produces a brilliant essay on the destructive power of lying." As soon as the pupils notice that the teacher wants to educate their characters, precisely those who show most signs of genuine independent character will resist it; just as those who are seriously laboring over the question of good and evil rebel when one dictates what is good and bad. The education of character is a goal, but it is not to be aimed at as a conscious objective. "Only in his whole being, in all his spontaneity can the educator truly affect the whole being of his pupil." If the teacher is vital and able to communicate himself directly to his fellow beings, that in itself will affect them more powerfully than if he had deliberately set out to influence them. But he can do this only if he has the *confidence* of his pupils; for only then will they accept him as a person, a person whom they may trust because he is not manipulating them but is taking part in their lives, accepting them before desiring to influence them. This is that *human* truth that enables the adolescent, frightened and disappointed by an unreliable world, to enter into a dialogue with the teacher: to ask and to respond. "It is not the educational intention but the meeting which is educationally fruitful."

When this is the teacher's standpoint, then everything that passes between him and his pupils can open a way to the education of character, including the conflicts which inevitably arise when there is genuine confidence. These conflicts are the supreme test for the educator:

He must use his own insight wholeheartedly; he must not blunt the piercing impact of his knowledge, but he must at the same time have in readiness the healing ointment for the heart pierced by it. Not for a moment may he conduct a dialectical manoeuvre instead of the real battle for truth. But if he is the victor he has to help the vanquished to endure defeat; and if he cannot conquer the self-willed soul that faces him . . ., then he has to find the word of love which alone can help to overcome so difficult a situation.

One example of such a conflict, offered by Buber, was from the time of the Arab terror in Palestine. When a young person insisted that the Ten Commandments do not apply to the life of a people, the teacher suggested that only through adhering to those Commandments had the Jewish people survived. Banging his fist on the newspaper report of the British White Paper restricting Jewish immigration to Palestine, the student burst out with, "Do you call that life?"

In our time the problem of the education of character lies even deeper; for today host upon host of people have everywhere sunk into the slavery of collectives, and each collective is the supreme authority for its own slaves. This is true not only of the totalitarian countries but also for the parties and partylike groups in the so-called democracies. No reference to absolute values can rescue a person from such slavery. Only that pain experienced in the hours of utter solitude can lead to a rescue of one's real personal self from the enslavement of collectivism. In this connection, Buber referred for the first time to what he later called the "eclipse of God": "To keep the pain awake, to waken the desire—that is the first task of everyone who regrets the obscuring of eternity. It is also the first task of the genuine educator in our time." The way he or she can fulfill this task is, again, not to aim at, but to have as a final goal, the education of great character; for only through pointing to the great character can the educator awaken or keep alive the pain in the individual pupil, who becomes aware of the contrast between what she is and what she might be. The "great character" forms the link between the "great person" and the "great relationship" as Buber treated them in *What Is Man?* The great character responds with the whole of her or his being to the uniqueness of every situation which challenges her or him as an active person. The great character is thus one who lives the life of dialogue in the face of the utter newness of every moment:

In spite of all similarities every living situation has, like a newborn child, a new face, that has never been before and will never come again. It demands of you a reaction which cannot be prepared beforehand. It demands nothing of what is past. It demands presence, responsibility; it demands you. I call a great character one who by his actions and attitudes satisfies the claim of situations out of deep readiness to respond with his whole life, and in such a way that the sum of his actions and attitudes expresses at the same time the unity of his being in its willingness to accept responsibility.

It would be a mistake to regard this emphasis on uniqueness and presentness as excluding the past. Those deep-seated attitudes which we bear with us from the past are a vital part of our response to the present. "No responsible person remains a stranger to norms," but the norms do not operate through maxim or habit but through those commands that remain latent until they reveal themselves to us concretely. As illustration, Buber told of a man whose heart was struck by the lightning flash of "Thou shalt not steal" in the very moment when he was moved by a very different desire from that of stealing, and whose heart was so struck by it that he not only abandoned doing what he wanted to do, but with the whole force of his passion did the very opposite. "*I* was that man," Buber told me, "only the command to me was not, 'Thou shalt not steal,' but 'Thou shalt not kill!' " "I was not about to kill anyone," he added; yet in this prohibition Buber discovered the positive direction that he had to take. In a similar way, the prohibition of Buber's conscience against telling the teacher about the sexual pantomine of his schoolfellows in his childhood experience of "The Two Boys" contained a direction, a "yes," that made him put aside the teacher's maxim that "A good boy is one who helps *us*" in favor of the command of the situation that addressed him as a unique *Thou*. Maxims, in contrast, command only the third person, the each and the none.

The teacher can awaken in young persons the courage to shoulder life again by bringing before them the image of a great character who denies no answer to life and the world, but accepts responsibility for everything essential that he or she meets. Today the great characters are still "enemies of the people" whose love for society includes the desire to raise it to a higher level. "Tomorrow they will be the architects of a new unity of mankind," born from the longing for personal unity. This is a reciprocal process. A great and full relationship can exist only between whole and responsible persons, but they become this precisely through the life of dialogue.

Buber criticized the Hebrew University chiefly because it did not fulfill the original aim of being a center for adult education, and he repeated this criticism and demand again and again after he came to Palestine. But when he himself taught at the Hebrew University he was a professor and not in very close contact with his students. Distinguished students like Shmuel Eisenstadt, who eventually was to succeed Buber as chairman of the Department of Sociology, have attested to the reality of dialogue that Buber evoked in the classroom. Buber raised issues and got the students to ask questions, but he was too "charitable" to students who would break in, Eisenstadt reported. "He was a great stage actor in the best sense of the word. He could listen within the framework of the drama he was directing." Eisenstadt also greatly admired Buber's knowledge of the whole range of modern sociology in which he had read everything important, including what did not particularly interest him. "He could read three hundred to four hundred pages in an hour, could do in an afternoon what it would take an ordinary person a week to read." When Eisenstadt became a young teacher in sociology at the university, Buber was cooperative and understanding; he always gave him full protection and help and offered him the free use of his library. But this did not mean that he entered into close relationship with his students. One graduate student of sociology, who later became a professor of sociology before her early death, turned bitterly against him because of this and said he did not live his own theory of dialogue. Professor Jacob Katz of the Hebrew University, who knew Buber since the reopening of the Frankfurt Lehrhaus in 1933, said that "he always found Buber very pleasant to work with but that he never expected of him a close relationship nor demanded of him what he could not give." Aside from the natural aristocracy, to which Arnold Zweig referred when Buber was fifty, the lack of intimacy with his students arose, most likely, less from any incapacity (since Buber had had many close relationships throughout his life, including those with younger disciples), but from a residue of the European conception of what it meant to be a professor, something shared by most of his colleagues at the Hebrew University. When Walter Goldstein remarked to Buber in 1942 that he saw something tragic in the life of Hermann Cohen, Buber smiled and said, "What do you expect? The man was for forty years a professor!"

CHAPTER 15

Prewar Palestine

BUBER CAME TO Palestine in a time of great unrest. For two years there had been continual attacks by Arab terrorists on out-of-the-way Jewish settlements, on travelers in autos and trains, and on solitary walkers. The press carried almost daily accounts of bloodletting. Whereas Haganah, the organization of Jewish self-defense, continued to follow its policy of self-restraint and refused to carry out reprisals on those who did not take part in the terror, the radical Jewish groups, such as the Stern Gang and the Irgun Zwai Leumi, who stood outside the discipline of the Haganah, believed it necessary to fight terror with terror. Against this policy Buber raised his voice in the first article that he had published in Palestine, "Against Betrayal" (July 1938). "The confusion in the country has intensified to an unbearable degree," Buber began. Buber called on his fellow Jews in Palestine to unite against the internal treason of those who did not want to obey the authorities of the Jewish settlement and attacked both British and Arabs. "Factions which cannot reach power as long as confidence exists stimulate this betrayal in order to win through it." "We should have supported those among the Arab population with good intentions, thus isolating the Arab terrorists. If blind violence replaces the fulfillment of justice on which the Zionist movement was built, contradiction, the wretched daughter of exile, will aspire to the status of the ruling law of Zion." By "blind violence" Buber meant the Jewish terrorists' professed principle of killing any Arab, no matter how innocent, in reprisal for the murder of Jews by Arab terrorists. "In the life of our nation there has never been an hour of affliction *or* of temptation like the present one."

In the same month, Buber joined the League for Human Rights in its appeal against the death sentence for Arab terrorists. They were particularly grateful for Buber's support, since they suddenly found themselves accused of being a "small band of traitorous Jews." In August, he wrote Hans Trüb, "Here all is more frightening, confused, crueler, and more innocent than one could imagine . . . What one can experience here of human reality and of the indwelling [of God] 'in the midst of our uncleanness' [Isaiah] can perhaps be experienced nowhere else."

In Nazi Germany, Buber had awakened the Jews to faithfulness to Jewish peoplehood. In the reverse situation in Palestine, where the politically overheated atmosphere favored a fanatical nationalism, he tried to awaken them to humanity. Nowhere is this walking of the narrow ridge clearer than in Buber's famous letter to Gandhi, in which, in order to remain faithful to his witness to the covenant of peace *and* to Zionism, Buber took to task the man he admired more than any living person in public life.

In the November 26, 1938, issue of his paper *Harijan* (The Untouchable)—the same issue in which he counseled the Jews of Germany to use *satyagraha*, nonviolent resistance, against the Nazis—Gandhi said that Palestine belonged to the Arabs and that it was therefore "wrong and inhuman to impose the Jews on the Arabs." Declaring sympathy with the Jews as "the untouchables of Christianity," Gandhi set in opposition "the requirements of justice" and the Jewish cry for a national home, which "does not much appeal to me." "Why should they not, like other peoples of the earth, make that country their home where they are born and where they earn their livelihood?" "What is going on in Palestine today cannot be justified by any moral code of conduct," Gandhi pronounced in a curiously one-sided assessment of the situation on the part of the great exponent of a nonviolent direct action which meets the opponent with love and understanding. The nobler course, Gandhi suggested, with equally remarkable naïveté considering the situation of the Jews at that very moment, "would be to insist on a just treatment of the Jews wherever they are born and bred." "Surely it would be a crime against humanity to reduce the proud Arabs so that Palestine can be restored to the Jews partly or wholly as their national home." Gandhi imagined that as a consequence the Jews might be forced out of other parts of the world where they were settled and suggested that "this cry for the National Home affords a plausible justification for the German expulsion of the Jews." "The Palestine of the biblical conception is not a geographical tract," he added, "it is in their hearts." If the Jews must look to the geographical Palestine, they should realize, as Buber himself had often said, that "it is wrong to enter it under the shadow of the British gun." But Gandhi proposed that they should win Arab hearts and good will and the sympathy of world opinion by offering themselves to be shot or thrown into the Dead Sea without raising a finger against the Arabs. "There are hundreds of ways of reasoning with the Arabs, if the Jews will only discard the help of the British bayonet. As it is, they are co-sharers with the British in despoiling a people who have done no wrong to them."

In April 1939, the Jerusalem group known as "The Bond" published, as the first of a proposed series of pamphlets, two letters to Gandhi from Martin Buber and Judah L. Magnes, together with Gandhi's statement from *Harijan.* It is characteristic that Magnes addressed the great Indian leader as "Dear Mr. Gandhi," whereas Buber began with "Mahatma," the expression of a reverence which took birth in Buber when he read Gandhi's statement in 1922 that "our nonviolence is skin-deep. . . . due merely to our helplessness." This reverence remained so great in Buber that even Gandhi's injustice to the Jews in Palestine could not destroy it. For this reason, Buber's reply to Gandhi is a deeply personal response as well as a political action, one written slowly with repeated pauses, days sometimes elapsing between short paragraphs: "Day and night I took myself to task, searching whether I had not in any one point overstepped the measure of self-preservation allotted and even prescribed by God to a human community, and whether I had not fallen into the grievous error of collective egoism. Friends and my own conscience have helped to keep me straight whenever that danger threatened."

In his reply, Buber pointed out that the 150,000 Indians in South

Africa were nourished by the more than 200 million in India, and he asked Gandhi whether "the India of the Vedic conception is not a geographical tract but a symbol in your hearts?" A land is in men's hearts because it is in the world; it is a symbol because it is a reality. A mere idea cannot be holy, but a piece of earth can. Dispersion is bearable, even purposeful, if somewhere there is an ingathering, a growing home center where there is the life of a community which dares to live today because it hopes to live tomorrow. Otherwise dispersion becomes dismemberment. But, as in *The Kingship of God* and later in *Israel and Palestine,* Buber insisted on the indissoluble unity of people, land, and task. "Decisive for us is not the promise of the Land —but the command, the fulfillment of which is bound up with the Land, with the existence of a free Jewish community in this country. For the Bible tells us and our inmost knowledge testifies to it, that once, more than three thousand years ago, our entry into this Land was with the consciousness of a mission from above to set up a just way of life through the generations of our people, such a way of life as can be realized not by individuals in the sphere of their private existence but only by a nation in the establishment of its society." In this connection Buber set forth the laws in Exodus and Leviticus that call for communal ownership of the land, recurrent leveling of social distinctions, guarantee of the independence of each individual, mutual help, a common Sabbath embracing serf and beast as beings with equal claim, and a Sabbatical year in which, by letting the soil rest, everybody is admitted to the free enjoyment of its fruits. This command, unfulfilled when the Jews went into exile, has become more urgent than ever. "It may not be that the soil and the freedom for fulfillment be denied us."

At this point, with characteristic honesty, Buber denied that he spoke for the Jewish people as a whole, in whom the contemporary world's lack of faith finds its concentrated expression. But he did speak for those whom Isaiah called the "remnant," those who remained faithful to the covenant to make real the kingship of God: "I speak only for those who feel themselves entrusted with the commission of fulfilling the command of justice delivered to the Israel of the Bible . . . the ancient mission of the nation lives on in them as the cotyledon in the core of the fruit." But he was not talking about those who professed a belief in God as opposed to those who did not: "The true solution can only issue from the life of a community which begins to carry out the will of God, often without being aware of doing so, without believing that God exists and that this is His will." The innermost truth of the Jewish life in the Land is not found in directing or demanding, urging, or preaching, but in sharing the common life. That is why Buber's concern was never with the religious kibbutzim but only with the socialist kibbutzim that made some real, concrete progress toward the realization of community and justice.

In order to clarify his own position to Gandhi in the Arab-Jewish conflict, Buber told him that he belonged "to a group of people who, from the time when Britain conquered Palestine, have not ceased to strive for the concluding of genuine peace between Jew and Arab." In his explanation of what he meant by this statement, Buber gave classic expression to the life of dialogue, the "community of otherness," and to the encounter on the narrow ridge that eschews all either/ors in favor of holding the tension of *both* points of view in any conflict:

> By a genuine peace we inferred . . . that both peoples should together develop the Land without the one imposing its will on the other. . . . Two vital claims are opposed to each other, two claims of a different nature and a different origin, which cannot be pitted one against the other and between which no objective decision can be made as to which is just or unjust. We considered . . . it our duty to understand and to honour the claim which is opposed to ours and to endeavor to reconcile both claims. We cannot renounce the Jewish claim; something even higher than the life of our people is bound up with the Land, namely the work which is their divine mission. . . . Seeing that such love and such faith are surely present also on the other side, a union in the common service of the Land must be within the range of the possible. Where there is faith and love, a solution may be found even to what appears to be a tragic contradiction.

Gandhi's axiom that a land belongs to its population implied that the Arab settlement by conquest was justified whereas the Jewish settlement by buying the land and working it was not. "Ask the soil what the Arabs have done for her in 1300 years and what we have done for her in 50! Would her answer not be weighty testimony in a just discussion as to whom this land 'belongs'?" But it seemed to Buber that God does not give away any portion of the earth but lends it and waits to see what even the conqueror will make of it. "I believe in the great marriage between man (Adam) and earth (Adama). This land recognizes us, for it is fruitful through us." The Jewish settlers did not come to Palestine as colonists with natives to do their work for them but set their shoulders to the plow and made the land fruitful with their strength and their blood, and they were ready to teach their brothers, the Arab peasants, to cultivate the land more intensively so that together they might "serve" it.

A note which already appeared in *The Question to the Single One* and which appeared increasingly in Buber's thought and utterances in the years to come was the politicization which exaggerates the real needs of people into claims of principle and political watchwords. The serpent of politics "conquers not only the spirit but also life." That was certainly Buber's own experience and fate in the highly charged political atmosphere of Palestine and, later, Israel, from his immigration there in 1938 to his death in 1965. Yet this never deterred him from holding to the "lived concrete" as much as possible in any given situation. Though he had protested from the beginning against the tie between Zionism and British imperialism implicit in the Balfour Declaration, he pointed out to Gandhi that the Jews began to settle in Palestine anew thirty-five years before the "shadow of the British gun" was cast upon it and that this shadow appeared and remained to guard British interests and not Jewish ones.

Gandhi's statement also evoked from Buber his most profound and deeply personal testimony of his attitude toward violence and force, and this too was not because of any "ism" but an affair of the narrow ridge. Buber reminded him that in March 1922 Gandhi himself wrote, "Have I not repeatedly said that I would have India become free even by violence rather than that she should remain in bondage?" To Buber this implied that nonviolence to Gandhi was a faith and not a political principle *and* that the desire for the freedom of India was even stronger in him than his faith. "And for this, I love you." "We have not proclaimed, as you do and as did Jesus, the son of our people, the teaching of nonviolence," Buber added. "We believe that a man must sometimes use force to save himself or, even more, his children. But from time immemorial we have proclaimed the teaching of justice and peace; we have taught and we have learned that peace is the aim of the world and that justice is the way to attain it. . . . No one who counts himself in the ranks of Israel can desire to use force." Although Buber would not have been among the crucifiers of Jesus, he would also not have been among the supporters of his absolute nonviolence. "I am forced to withstand the evil in the world just as the evil within myself," and although he strove not to have to do so by force, if there were no other way of preventing the evil destroying the good, he trusted that he would "use force and give myself up into God's hands." In an echo of his poem "Power and Love," Buber confessed: "We should be able even to fight for justice—but to fight lovingly."

Rudolf Pannwitz, to whom Buber sent his "Letter to Gandhi," wrote that he had been deeply gripped by it: "it has alongside the tenderness of soul the growth of the reality lived by the self and the background-tone of solitude-conscious history." Ludwig Binswanger, to whom Buber also sent it, wrote how interesting it was to him to learn Buber's political position. "That you find the synthesis between the philosopher Buber and the political actionist Buber in 'loving conflict' made an especially deep impression on me, all the more since *my* double existence demands a similar synthesis. At any rate, you shall become as God when you attain such a synthesis! But to have such a goal in view touches on eternity!"

One of the reasons for the Arab unrest was the high immigration for three years running which led to fear that the Jews might become a majority in Palestine within the near future. Arab violence, British royal commissions, unsuccessful plans for partition, and proposals for strict curtailment of immigration finally culminated in a new White Paper of May 1939, which foresaw the establishment within ten years of an independent state in Palestine in which the Arabs would be a permanent majority; 75,000 Jewish immigrants would be allowed to enter Palestine during the following five years, but after that Jewish immigration would depend on Arab consent, which was unlikely to be given. The White Paper also envisaged very strict limits to Jewish land purchase. The Jews saw in the White Paper a death sentence for the National Home, which had no hope of development under an Arab government. The Mandates Commission in Geneva declared the new policy to be opposed to the letter of the Mandate, but the British were unconcerned about the sensitivities of the Jews and world opinion and wanted a relatively calm Middle East and the pacification of the Arabs, whom the Italians and Germans were trying to win over to the side of the Axis. In the face of this situation, mass illegal immigration of Jews began and the hand of the anti-British and anti-Arab nationalists among the Jews in Palestine was strengthened.

In June 1939, Buber published a paper titled "Pseudo-Samsonism" in which he suggested that there were youths in the Jewish settlement who imagined that they were Samson and that their acts of terrorism were the deeds of a Samson. "When we first returned to the Land after a long series of centuries, we acted as if it were empty—no, still worse, as if we did not need to be concerned about the population that we saw there. . . ." Reliance was placed on the Balfour Doctrine and the League of Nations, instead of on building a genuine security through the reality of common work and common interests with the population of the Land. "We have, for the most part, been able to distinguish between the terrorist bands and the Arab people," Buber stated, but it could not be hoped that the Arabs would do the same in relation to the Jews. Those Jewish youths and "illusion politicians" who imagined that the Jewish Settlement could persevere indefinitely without a peaceful community with the Arabs fall into blind rage at a critical time, threatening to tear down the very bricks and walls of the Settlement. What they were really carrying out was suicide—and not the suicide of a Samson who took down three thousand Philistines with him but senseless destruction of all that devoted generations have built on this soil for which they sacrificed even their lives. "Who murders as they do, murders his own people." The fight of the Jewish Settlement against the White Paper should be a responsible one, not one that would make a future understanding with the Arabs impossible and thus endanger the life of the Settlement. "The implements of our fight remain now as before: spades, unfrightened spades. We need diggers in the earth who will not yield, not bomb throwers whose chief art is running away. . . . We do not need disturbers of the order—the order which they disturb is the order of our own work."

CHAPTER 16

The Second World War and For the Sake of Heaven

THE SECOND WORLD WAR

BUBER EXPERIENCED the Second World War with all its drama and tragedy in the relative isolation of Palestine. The Nazi invasion of Poland in 1939 resulted in the final loss of Buber's Polish possessions. This made it impossible for him to repay in the foreseeable future a loan from Hans Trüb that had enabled him to sell his house in Heppenheim. In the face of this situation, Buber fell into a depression that for a long time prevented him from writing personal letters. Although outer circumstances occasioned the depression, by Buber's own testimony to Trüb, it reached deep within. His not being able to take care of his debt to Trüb was "a burden that not only bowed the neck but also choked the throat." "You must try to imagine," Buber wrote Trüb in a play on the story of Jonah, "that for seven months I have lain in the belly of the monster and only just now have been spewed forth on to land."

A less gloomy note is sounded in a letter Buber wrote to Agnon two years after the war began in which he told of many interesting discussions which he had had with Princess Irene of Greece during her stay in Jerusalem. Born a grand duchess of the Russian house of Romanov and married to the ethnographer Prince Peter of Greece and Denmark, she lived in exile during the Second World War. She had been three years in India and Tibet, where she had learned a good deal about their religions, and she was very much interested in the Jewish religious customs to be found in Jerusalem. Buber proposed to Agnon, who was an observant Jew as Buber was not, that he acquaint her with the many different Jewish religious practices to be found among the Orthodox and Hasidic Jews from all over the world who now lived in Palestine, adding, "She will certainly interest you."

In November 1941, Buber received an invitation from the poet Else Lasker-Schüler to come to the Kraal, a circle that included Werner Kraft and other distinguished literary figures in which readings of poetry and lectures were held periodically. She proposed to invite up to thirty poets and artists to her living room. Buber responded immediately that he was glad to fulfill a wish of hers, something he had long wanted to do. Years before they had known each other and found a rapport for a short while in Berlin before Buber moved to Heppenheim. But, Buber added, he would not be happy about speaking alone and without interruption in a small closed group. He found that unnatural—something entirely different from reading a work aloud. What he would prefer would be to lead a discussion on a topic proposed by her and her friends or to answer questions but also to pose questions himself.

On another, more public occasion, the meeting between Else Lasker-Schüler and Buber was not so harmonious. In the years of the Second World War, Buber held an "open forum" devoted to questions and issues of the time on Saturday afternoon in the Jerusalem synagogue of German Jews, Emeth v'Emunah. The occasion for these discussions was the threat in 1942 of the Nazis' breaking through the line at El Alamein, in which case there was no way Britain could defend Egypt or Palestine. As a result, the atmosphere of the time was marked by defense measures, discussions among the Jews of mass suicide, and proposals that the British remove all the Jews from Palestine to India. The very first one of these forums took on a tragicomic aspect through an unexpected bit of dialogue. Buber began in a reserved, judicious, and even skeptical manner: "If anyone should say to me today: I have revelations, or: I know exactly what history will bring us—I would deeply mistrust him." He could not get further; from the corner of the small prayer hall the voice of a woman proclaimed: "But, Herr Professor, I have continual revelations." This was the poet Else Lasker-Schüler. With great calm and patience Buber asked her about the nature of her revelations, intending to point out to her that poetic inspiration is not identical with prophetic revelation. But Lasker-Schüler was not to be pacified by any kind of compromise. She insisted on her revelations and actually claimed that no one less than King David himself had personally visited her in the Hotel Koschel in Berlin to reveal to her the mysteries of the spirit world and of the future. Buber stroked his beard thoughtfully while glancing at the ecstatically trembling poet whose diminutive figure stretched to its full height as she finally threw her parting shot: "Herr Professor, I revere you very much!"—and left the synagogue.

But that was not the end of the story, as related by Schalom Ben-Chorin. Barely had Else Lasker-Schüler left the room when another person arose, Frau J. N. from Munich, a pious but eccentric woman who was known in Jerusalem through her slogan "Kesher l'Echad" (Union with the One), which she incessantly repeated and made into her battle cry. Now she also spoke up and declared roundly that she knew exactly what the future would bring, and was ready on the spot to foretell the chain of events to come. The audience murmured, and Buber resignedly motioned them to be silent. Finally the rabbi of the synagogue, Dr. Wilhelm, intervened as host and proposed that "Kesher l'Echad" make her disclosures of the future to Buber sometime in private.

Ben-Chorin accompanied Buber to his house and said on the way, "Today I really suffered for you from the heart that you had to endure these two women." Buber stood amazed and said, "How can you compare these two, or even name them in one breath? Lasker-Schüler is a real poet to whom everything may be forgiven, but the other is not worth powder and shot." Although Ben-Chorin feels that Buber's judgment was too harsh, he suggests that Buber's response was symbolic of his own distinction between the prophetic and the apocalyptic. Else Lasker-Schüler was not a prophetess in the popular sense of one who foretells the future, but she was perhaps one in Buber's sense of the biblical prophet who bore in himself a speech of God that came to him during a prophetic vision. Buber himself at times jokingly remarked, "The prophets were no prophets," by which he meant that the biblical *nabi* was no clairvoyant but the bearer of a "word" of God that he spoke as an alternative placed before the people in a concrete situation.

Once Lasker-Schüler visited Buber in Heppenheim, and they talked of the poet Stefan George. Lasker-Schüler advanced the completely senseless theory that Stefan George (who came from a strictly Catholic family) was a Jew. This error arose because two important disciples of the master, Gundolf and Wolfskehl, were really Jews. Else Lasker-Schüler, indignant because Buber would not credit George's Jewish descent, rode away incensed. A few days later she sent Buber a post-card on which she wrote in her bold and hard-to-decipher handwriting: "You will not grant Stefan George to the Jews, and you want to be the King of Zion?!"

But such occasional differences of opinion could not injure the mutual high regard in which they held each other. Buber honored Else Lasker-Schüler as a true poet, and she spoke of him as the "Rabbi from the Odenwald," the forest on whose borders Heppenheim was located. Buber's admiration for Lasker-Schüler was not unqualified, however. At one of the meetings of the Kraal in her living room he heard her dramatic poem "I and I" read aloud and was very troubled by it, particularly by her familiarity with God. When he later read the play, he opposed its publication, and it was, in fact, never published in full.

When the "Kesher l'Echad" had finally followed Else Lasker-Schüler out of the synagogue and Buber was free to continue his speech, he used this first meeting of the "Open Forum" to discuss issues of the world war about which both he and his hearers were intensely concerned. The Satanic quality of the ruling fascist systems already documents itself in their speech, Buber said. Speech should primarily serve dialogue, but the speech of the dictators is a monological bellowing that expects and allows no reply at all, seeking only to be accompanied by a chorus of enthusiasm. But where speech is devoid of its dialogical character, the lie becomes a system, and the possibility of protest is eliminated a priori. The lie holds itself to be the truth and seeks to suffocate the conscience (that "Jewish invention," as Hitler said in conversation with Hermann Rauschning). But even Hitler could not suffocate his conscience entirely, Buber held, and in his most lonely hours was surely exposed to its judgment.

Buber expanded on this theme in a Hebrew essay, "People and Leader," which he published in 1942. Recalling that in 1927 he had written that our time believes it can get rid of the teacher in every realm and manage with the leader alone, Buber declared that what had happened in the world during the last fifteen years "has confirmed the truth of my words to a degree that at that time I could barely have had a presentiment of. Successful leading without teaching has come near to destroying all that makes human life seem worth living." Mussolini held that "illusion is perhaps the unique reality of life," commenting at the age of twenty-seven on that very book of Stirner's, *The Ego and His Own,* that Buber criticized in *The Question to the Single One,* and now Buber was able to make this connection explicit. In Mussolini, one can see how Stirner's gospel of individualism, in Mussolini's words "the greatest poem that has ever been sung to the glorification of the man who has become God," is transformed into the role of the dictator of the totalitarian stage. However far bolshevism may have removed itself, through its tendency to accumulate power, from the objective common to all genuine socialist thinking, it remains bound to an idea as its goal, whereas fascism, in contrast, basically acknowledges nothing but "the firm will to retain power." Mussolini characterized his mood in marching into Rome as that of the artist commencing his work rather than that of the prophet obeying a summons. In a truly prophetic comment on this statement, Buber observed, "I do not believe, as is related of an authentic Roman, Nero, that Mussolini, in the hour of defeat, will also succeed in feeling like an 'artist.' "

Hitler is no pathetic cynic, like Mussolini, nor is he an actor. "He is honest before the microphone and honest in intimate conversation, but the contents of the two honesties contradict each other." When he surrenders to the intoxication of public address, he is a possessed man, but when he explains himself to an intimate he can lay bare motives of which he is not conscious when in the grip of the hysterical muse that inspires his raging rhetoric. Mussolini is a consummate actor of the demonic; Hitler really becomes demonic. "When one considers Mussolini, one can be astonished and frightened by what man is; but when one looks at Hitler, one is seized by dizziness."

What distinguishes man as man, that he himself may judge concerning what he does and what he leaves undone, has been superseded in Nazism. Hermann Goering, Hitler's famous second-in-command, said that Hitler was his conscience, and Hitler himself insisted he had no conscience. "Conscience is like circumcision, a mutilation of the human being." He restores the mutilated member through becoming the conscience for all while himself remaining the man without conscience. Ever since people have existed there has existed the ever-renewed self-confrontation of the person with the image of what he was destined to be and what he has relinquished. Only in our time has this tension between what one is and what one should be been dissolved in favor of the complete and fundamental lack of restraints that is the secret of Hitler's effectiveness. Buber saw the exact parallel to Hitler not in Machiavelli, who believed in the state and in power only for the sake of the state, but in the peculiarly Jewish eighteenth-century product of disintegration, the antinomian gnostic and pseudo-messiah Jacob Frank. Frank proclaims the leader who is without belief, who believes in nothing other than himself, and boasts of himself as having come "in order to abolish all laws and all doctrines . . . to bring life into the world." "You shall rid yourself of all laws and doctrines and follow after me, step by step."

In Hitler's world, only the leaders are persons, only they are the "superior race," while the "people" stand opposite them as a mass of the spiritually castrated. "What need have we of the socialization of banks and factories?" boasts Hitler. "We socialize men." Hitler blends the people into masses through the common absence of restraint. But the will to power for the mere sake of power leads from the self-aggrandizement of the individuals to the self-destruction of the people. Frank and Hitler eminently perfected the skill of avoiding the self-encounter that might reveal the inner emptiness of those who find the being of the Unconditioned empty. "Probably both have experienced what it is to stand at midnight staring at one's own naked face. But that is a mystery into which no other person can penetrate." Walther Rathenau in 1921, a year after the National Socialist party received its name and a year before his own assassination, declared frivolous the belief that the Lord God is on the side of the bigger battalions. "The truth is that destiny is with the deeper responsibility." Twenty years later, in a situation in which the Allied Powers and many of the members of the Yishuv joined the fascist states in believing that the bigger battalions need no Lord God, Buber, again prophetically, claimed them mistaken: "Power without genuine responsibility is a dazzlingly-clothed impotence. . . . Their powerlessness will become manifest in the hour when they must vie with a strength born of belief. Those who depend upon empty power will be dragged down in its collapse."

In great epochs of history, important work was done by important persons, but in our age, powerful transformations are accomplished through individuals who are not equal to their deeds, exploiters of the situation of despair in which the people find themselves. Another feature of the age, Buber wrote, is that it leers. Barbarian hordes inundated civilized land, but they did not say, like Hitler, "Yes, we are barbarians!" Those who ruled with ruthless brutality did not ogle their brutality. "An age that stands before the mirror and admires its greatness lacks greatness."

BUBER'S LIFE IN PALESTINE

In November 1942, Buber was very upset by the sickness of his half-sister, who was brought, more dead than alive, from Teheran to the Hadassah Hospital in Jerusalem. Seeing her after all those years greatly excited Buber. The following month he was forced to move from his dwelling in Talbiyeh, which belonged to a consulate. Not only was the task of packing the more than 20,000 books an overwhelming one for Buber, but there was also the difficult problem of where to move. Paula preferred the far-lying hill of Dir Abu Tor. The fact that this was a purely Arab neighborhood at that time did not disturb Buber, but he himself would have preferred a house somewhat less far removed from the university. At the end of the year, the Bubers settled on a place in Dir Abu Tor known as the house of Jussuf Wahab Dajani. Dir Abu Tor is a hill exactly opposite Mount Moriah, divided from it only by the valley of Kidron. The house has old-fashioned timbering, large rooms with high ceilings, and it is situated high up on the hill visible from afar. It has, especially from the roof, a fantastic view of the Temple Square, which is almost never the case in new Jerusalem. The El Aksa Mosque is also visible, and even the Dome of Rocks above the stone on which Abraham is supposed to have been ready to sacrifice his son Isaac until the divine command prohibited it. The view from the study was "truly worthy of a Martin Buber," as Walter Goldstein puts it. This house was the most beautiful and spacious, if also the most old-fashioned, in which Buber lived in Jerusalem.

The Hebrew poet Lea Goldberg, who translated much of Dostoevsky into Hebrew, tells of how she met Paula Buber in this house in Dir Abu Tor. She had already come to know her daughter Eva and Eva's husband Ludwig Strauss at Ben Shemen, where she came to lecture, and she spent three months with the Strausses every summer in Beit Hakerem, a kibbutz on the northern side of Galilee that is a center for music and the arts. But she came to know Eva's father through her book on the Russian writer Nikolai Gogol. Buber was particularly interested in Gogol's pilgrimage to Jerusalem, and she had translated a chapter from the Gogol book for him. After this he invited her to visit him in his house on a hot summer day. When she arrived, she had the impression that Paula Buber was not particularly happy about her presence. "She was very suspicious of Buber's friends," Professor Goldberg commented, in addition to which she was tired and did not like all the people who came to see him. To Lea Goldberg, she was not at all friendly, in fact was highly reserved. Buber spoke of the view from their window and said to Paula, "Please open the door to show Miss Goldberg the view." "No," Paula replied, "it is too much bother." Then she remarked to Lea Goldberg in the presence of Eva and Ludwig, who were also present, about how large the house was. "My children think I should have a smaller one." To this Lea Goldberg responded, "I cannot imagine you in a smaller house." At that Paula suddenly became most friendly and proceeded to open the window and show her the view. This friendship lasted until the end of Paula's life.

"Paula Buber was a very difficult, unbalanced person," Lea Goldberg has said of her friend. "She was very hard on her children and her grandchildren. I used to call her Maria Theresa."

Martin Buber had a special relationship to the landscapes of Jerusalem, especially the Old City. The new one, he said to Eugenia and me, "is only a suburb." Although he once referred to it as asymmetrical, he called the Temple Square the finest square that he knew: "Rome cannot compare to it." In 1927, he had visited it with Masaryk, the President of Czechoslovakia, and had crawled under the stone to look at it from below. It is a *pre-*Israelite holy place which David had inherited. This feeling for the Jerusalem landscape is mingled with his understanding of art in his little essay on the landscapes of Jerusalem painted by his late friend Leopold Krakauer. Krakauer was so powerfully devoted to the natural phenomenon of these landscapes that he was able to grasp it from its inwardness, in the dynamic of its solitude that corresponded to his own: "The inner tension that works out of the restless and yet wholly finished form of the thistle, the great inner trembling that is etched into the limbs of the olive tree as the lifetime pain of a man is etched into the lines of his face, yes even the immeasurable movement that hides behind the apparent deadness of a heap of stones but that lets a strange knocking penetrate to us—all that is intensified in Krakauer's pages to the language of a solitary torment at the very base of each creature."

Sometimes Krakauer's drawing of an olive tree so appeared like a human shape to Buber that he told him, to his surprise, of the West Manichean conception of Jesus *patibilis*, a tellurian Christ figure which, imprisoned in the plants of nature, suffers its forsakenness by hanging in every tree. In his vision, Krakauer *suffered* the turning into wood and the grasping of the roots into the earth. "Certainly, in today's forlorn-ness it may at times appear as though we had been deprived of the meeting with nature," Buber remarked, but "we stand in a changing world," affected by our will and our repugnance. "Our senses are not sufficient by far to withstand what moves toward us," Buber con-cluded, in an anticipation of "Man and His Image-Work." "Nature too moves toward us, even in the most extreme motionlessness; it has to do with us."

Although Buber had written a great deal in the first half of his life, it was only in the second half that he settled down and became an ordered and disciplined writer. In 1942, the original, Hebrew edition of his important book *Prophetic Faith* appeared, which carries forward the study of the origins of messianism of *The Kingship of God* and *The Anointed.* He also worked at that time on the Hebrew original of *Israel and Palestine, Paths in Utopia,* and *The Origin and Meaning of Hasidism.* In response to a book that Leonard Ragaz sent to him, Buber wrote: "I am receptive only to living books, such as yours, but to these with my whole heart." On the other hand, he refused in 1944 to lend Walter Goldstein the support which he asked for his books interpreting Buber's thought. "I have no Archimedean point outside myself from which I might testify to any sort of interpretation of my thought," he wrote Goldstein. "On this point I must be intransigent. Otherwise I would go astray in my relation to the spirit, which grants me only the word, but not also this or that interpretation of it."

In September 1939, after the outbreak of the war, Buber told Ragaz that the geographic distance between them had become all too appar-ent in the last weeks. In November 1939, Abraham Heschel wrote Buber from London, "In this life on the narrow border of misery and trust . . . the pain over what has happened and what is happening is so acute that one must make a mighty effort not to fall prey to the torment." When Buber left Germany for Palestine, Heschel had taken over the directorship of the Frankfurt Lehrhaus. In the same year, he left Frankfurt and went to Warsaw because of an edict driving all Polish citizens out of Germany. In 1940, he founded in London an Institute of Jewish Learning modeled after the Frankfurt Lehrhaus. There he tried to educate about 1,500 Jewish refugees destined for Palestine. But, he informed Buber, he did not succeed in any concentrated work and was called by Hebrew Union College in Cincinnati, the seminary for Reform rabbis, to come there as a member of its faculty. "The end cannot be foreseen. There are no signs of a reversal. How will it turn out? What is to be done?" Heschel cried.

In February 1941, there was still no end in sight and no sign of reversal. "The fate of Jewry often oppresses us beyond the limit of the endurable," Ragaz wrote Buber. "It is also the subject of a great part of our work, namely my wife and daughter, here in our house, where we have a 'help center,' but also over all the world, especially France and America." In September 1941, Buber corresponded with Leopold Marx about the creation of a memorial place for Otto Hirsch, Buber's co-worker in Jewish education in Germany who had been murdered by the Nazis in the Mauthausen concentration camp. "How can you imagine that anything in my heart has changed toward you?" Buber wrote Marx. "It is only that here writing personal letters is only done, as it were, with a violent effort. Just imagine please (it is that way to a certain degree with all of us) that here I have to do almost twice the amount of work as in Germany without being able to afford any assistance." After this preamble he informed Marx that Robert Weltsch was skeptical whether during the war any memorial could be achieved, but that he, Buber, felt strongly that at least the collecting of money should be begun as a symbol and was ready to do everything possible to further this cause which lay close to his heart. "The death of our friend has hit me very hard. I can even now barely take it in."

In September 1941, Buber appealed to Thomas Mann, the great German writer, who, as a representative of the free and liberal Germany, immigrated to Switzerland in 1933 and to the United States in 1939. Mann, at this time, was traveling around the United States speaking on "The Coming Victory of Democracy." "I am turning to you with an extraordinary request, unique in my life, as the bearer of the true German spirit in the present world." The request was to help find a publisher for Paula's novel *Muckensturm,* which Buber characterized as of extraordinary comprehensiveness. "In this swarm of gnats the great community with its pathology is mirrored. This work, in which the pain and rebellion of a strongly rooted German has found expression, directly concerns the present world, but it is also an historical novel which preserves the meaningful connection of a place and an hour." "I know that this request to you to read an extensive manuscript is a presumption," Buber concluded, "but I hope that you find that the circumstances justify it . . . and that you know, although we met each other only fleetingly, that I would make such an unusual request only for something for whose sake it must be made."

In December 1941, Mann wrote Buber from Pacific Palisades, California, that it was an honor and a joy to receive his letter. Recently back from a lecture tour, he had read only the opening pages of Paula's novel. But already he sensed its significance and wanted Buber to know how thankful he was for his confidence and how seriously he took the matter. Although it was difficult to find a publisher for an untranslated German narrative, he promised to do all he could. As it turned out, the novel was not published until 1951 and then only in Germany.

In October 1941, Ragaz wrote Buber that his journal *Neue Wege* (New Ways) was about to fall victim to a Nazi action against it and to an unquenchable hatred against him on the part of the German Embassy —which, in fact, was the highest government in the German part of Switzerland. To submit it to the Nazi censor would have meant moral suicide and would have provided his enemies with a still greater victory than letting the journal die. In any case, he felt as if he had received a powerful and malicious thrust of the knife in his work and in his heart. "The worst of it is that it is a sign of our Swiss situation," Ragaz said. "We are, in fact, already a 'protectorate' of Hitler's. For the time being still somewhat disguised." In January 1942, Ragaz reported that the suspension of *Neue Wege,* on grounds that it had violated neutrality, gave him time to work on two books long put aside, adding, "My own existence fluctuates between bright light and deep shadows; it is now again especially heavy because of the sad spiritual condition of my country." At the same time, he was convinced that the new danger that threatened the Holy Land, the German-Italian advance into Cyrenaica, in northeastern Libya, would pass away like the earlier ones. Buber responded to Ragaz that his letter had again been a restorative for him. "We feel cut off from the world, and a voice like yours, when it reaches us, does much to deliver us from this exile." In June 1942, Ragaz expressed his concern for the safety of Palestine, because the German Africa Corps under General Erwin Rommel had taken Tobruk. In December 1942, Buber wrote Ragaz asking his help in interesting the children's help organization Pro Juventute in Switzerland in the rescue of Jewish refugee children and bringing them into Switzerland.

In March 1942, two Russians paid a visit to Jerusalem through the Turkish Embassy, and a banquet and an evening at the Edison Theater were arranged in which Buber took part. In response to Walter Goldstein's remonstrations that this was a dreadful political error, Buber explained that, although he was an opponent of the strict regimentation of life and a true socialist (in contrast to the seeming socialism of Russia), he met with the Russians in the hope that by so doing some loosening of the regime in the Soviet Union might take place that might bring it closer to the Anglo-Saxon countries. Too, there was the hope of making contact with the three million Russian Jews. If the Anglo-Saxon–Russian bond did not last beyond the war, Buber saw nothing ahead but the cessation of spiritual life on the planet, which would then be in the overpowering grip of an unchallenged capitalism. "The massive Russian atheism frightens me less than the Western seeming-Christianity," he said to Goldstein. He was not interested in the question of religion and *Weltanschauung*. "All fixed world-views are abominable to me." He greeted (prematurely) the crumbling of the walls as the beginning of a new dialogue, the very lack of which characterized the politicization of the cold war of which he later complained.

Like most of the other Jews in Palestine, Buber could not at that time credit the reports of the mass murder of Polish Jews. He conceded that 10 to 15 percent of what was reported might be true, which was frightful enough, but he saw that as a consequence of the war and deplored any political exploitation of these reports. "For a long while afterward he did not perceive the cruel reality," comments Goldstein. "His whole being resisted 'accepting' what exceeded his imagination and was incompatible with any of his basic views." When verified reports of the extent of the Holocaust began to arrive in Palestine in 1945 and 1946, he finally had to believe, even though he still could not picture the unimaginable horror. For the rest of his life, he once said, not an hour passed in which he did not think of the Holocaust.

On March 24, 1943, Wilfrid Israel, one of the noblest of the German Jewish immigrants to Palestine and a comrade of Kibbutz Hazorea, left Palestine on a mission for the Jewish Agency which took him to Portugal and Spain, where he hoped to arrange for the speedy transfer of Jewish refugees, mostly children from the occupied countries, to Palestine. After successfully accomplishing this task, as he had so many others, the unarmed passenger plane in which he traveled on June 1 was shot down in broad daylight over the Gulf of Biscay by Nazi fighters; all its seventeen occupants, including Wilfrid Israel and the English movie actor Leslie Howard, perished. This was the first time a noncombatant airplane had been attacked. Buber, who had known him well, wrote a short piece on "Traits in Wilfrid's Portrait" for a memorial volume published in 1944. This portrait gives us a glimpse of Buber's relation to this remarkable person and of Buber himself at this moment. It was, like Arnold Zweig's portrayal of Buber at fifty, a series of paradoxes:

> He was solitary as a star, and believed unshakably in community.
> He lived with us as in a strange country, and was still the truest friend.
> Deeply shy and yet infinitely decisive.
> Wounded and whole at the same time . . . he was exposed to life like a sacrifice yet mastered it with a light hand. . . .
> The melancholy in his heart was not bitter, it had the clarity of the ultimate . . . in his heart was the will to offer himself and do what is to be done.
> His gestures were Eastern, his knowing glance Western, and his voice? *vox humana,* wholly simple.
> Here humanity became nature. . . . Thus arises genuine virtue.
> In a world in which no one could help him, helping became for him a passion. We recognize the noble man in what he makes out of his most painful experience.
> Zealously and tenderly he served the land of Israel, as one serves a homeland. Yet it never became a homeland for him. There always lay a drawn sword between him and what he loved.
> He died a symbol as helper and as solitary man. We see him fall like a star.
> But when we look upward to the mighty heaven of our memories, among the most illuminating that are there for us, pure and comforting, there shines his inextinguishable image.

In his 1942 poem "Rachman, A Distant Spirit, Speaks," which he selected just before his death to be preserved in his "Gleanings," Buber likens the conflict between the powers in the Second World War to the opposition in ancient Germanic mythology of the Ases, the light, heavenly Nordic gods, and Hel, the shelter place of the world of the dead, and he sees "trembling Israel" as caught up in their conflict, and himself, in a striking image, as holding it in his hands like a wounded bird, a responsibility he did indeed feel. The title, "Rachman," may be a play on the Hebrew word *rachmones,* or mercy, the merciful attribute of God in the Kabbala.

Already in the cracking All
The gods and the phantoms fight,
There flew to me, the flight is a fall,
A gray little bird into the window.

From heaven the fires rain,
The earth ground bursts already smoldering.
On the bench I see it bleed,
O my little bird, how you are wounded!

Over the shuddering world confusion
A fallow shadow lays itself.
The eye of the little bird glances waveringly,
Its heart is near exhaustion.

And however it ends,
The fight between Ase and Hel,
I cherish in trembling hands
The trembling Israel.

In Hermann Hesse's last great novel *Magister Ludi*, the rainmaker sacrifices himself because he is unable to bring rain and save his people. After the war, Buber confessed to Hugo Bergmann that he felt compelled to identify himself with this rainmaker!

By 1944, the reality of the extermination of the European Jews was beginning to be known among the Jews of the Yishuv. Buber's impassioned article, "Silence and Outcry," in the spring of 1944 showed that he was fully capable of responding to what was happening despite his inability to grasp it fully. In a situation in which the masses of the Jewish people were abandoned to the violence of their worst enemies in a catastrophe the extent of which was still unknown, but which was undoubtedly immeasurably greater than any other in Jewish history, the Yishuv identified with what was happening only in terms of individual relatives or friends, but it failed to "imagine the real"—to comprehend the reality "there." To those who held this to be just as well, since anyone who encompassed it could not possibly carry on his life as before, Buber replied that it is "our duty to display a sufficient amount of imagination. . . . to weave whatever happens into the fabric of our lives—not in order to emit the customary roar of revenge in which there is a mere relief of tension, but rather in order to be effective, to co-operate where it is possible to do something."

It is incomprehensible to me, Buber wrote, that the well-informed in the Jewish Settlement knew what was happening months before and kept it a secret from the rest of the community. Still more incomprehensible was the fact that when the community heard what was going on, it kept silent. After the silence came the outcry, but even this was vitiated by the mixture of the spontaneous clamor with organized protests that wished to use the catastrophe and the rescue as means to furthering political aims for a Jewish majority in Palestine, thereby harming the rescue effort itself. Worst of all were the particular political parties that tried to exploit the catastrophe in order to radicalize the situation, knowing full well that this would not help the rescue. "I have sometimes wondered," wrote Buber, "whether a front could be formed in some extraordinary hour which might cut across all party lines—the front of those who want the salvation of their people with all their hearts and who want to work together for that worthy cause." The lives of the nameless ones to be saved should not be jeopardized by partisanship and playing politics. What is needed, at this late hour, Buber contested, is "to save as many Jews as possible by treating realistically the various practical questions with all means at our disposal, wherever and whenever there is still someone to be saved."

FOR THE SAKE OF HEAVEN

It was his strong personal response to the Second World War that enabled Buber finally to write the Hasidic chronicle-novel *For the Sake of Heaven* that he had tried unsuccessfully to complete for more than twenty years. In his early work of retelling Hasidic tales and finding the right form for them, Buber came upon a powerful complex of stories that were connected by content. Together they formed a great cycle, although they were narratives from two different traditions and tendencies that were in opposition to each other. This complex of stories could not be ignored; especially the events that stood at their center were highly significant. They were often looked at from a legendary perspective, but their real substance was unmistakable. Some *zaddikim* had tried through theurgical acts (the so-called practical Kabbala) to make Napoleon into the "Gog of the Land of Magog" from the Book of Ezekiel, whose war, as some eschatological texts announce, will be followed by the coming of the Messiah. Other *zaddikim*, opposed to these attempts, warned that the advent of redemption is not to be prepared through external actions but only through the turning of the whole person. What was most remarkable, that all, those who dared and those who warned, died within a single year.

Buber was convinced that the sphere into which they had entered, if from different sides, had consumed their earthly life. It was not an image or legend, but a simple fact, that here in a battle both sides had been annihilated. In this battle what was at stake, first of all, was the question of whether it is permissible to try to compel the divine power to effect what we desire, whether the way to fulfillment is through magical procedures or through inner transformation. The events were so concrete and their significance so far-reaching that Buber felt that he could not evade the task of organizing them into an organic whole. In his book *The Great Maggid* (1921), it was these related tales that Buber was referring to when he said he had omitted such tales from that book because "the narrative of a whole must be itself a separate story."

His task now was not, as with the rest of the legendary material, to place anecdote next to anecdote; for what he had to represent was precisely their external and internal connection. But since this connection was given only in fragments in the written and oral tradition, Buber had to bridge the gaps in what had been handed down in order to restore the continuity of the chronicle.

In addition to this, Buber found another obstacle in the way of his completing the book. The two traditions that he found before him, that of Lublin with its magical, and that of Pshysha with its antimagical, tendencies, were, like the tradition of the party of Saul and that of David, the residue of a long battle. Both traditions clearly related to actual events, but each selected those that were important to it, and each reported what it selected the way it saw it. Buber had to try to penetrate to the core of the happenings from both sides. That could, of course, succeed only if he did not proceed in the service of one of the two tendencies. The only satisfactory approach was that of tragedy, where two persons oppose each other, each just as he or she is, and the true opposition is not one of the "good" will and the "bad" will but the cruel antitheticalness of existence itself. "Certainly, I was 'for' Pshysha and 'against' Lublin; from my youth on, the life and teaching of Rabbi Bunam had won my sympathies for Pshysha. But I had to relate only what happened if I wished to do justice to the reality of both. Nothing that the tradition offered that was positive about Lublin might be neglected, and nothing that the tradition of Pshysha asserted in criticism of Lublin could be used if it was not confirmed by the opposing tradition in essentials." Buber felt that this difficult task was lightened by the fact that, in his opinion, anyone who immersed himself or herself in the tradition of Lublin would discover that it secretly bowed itself before the opponent, the "Holy Jew." This is just the sort of "unscientific" comment that has led Buber's own opponents, such as Gershom Scholem and Rivka Schatz-Uffenheimer, to see red!

Buber also found his task made easier because during the last years of the First World War, when he felt most pressed to deal with this theme, he took a journey to visit his son Rafael in the Polish steppes and on the return journey became acquainted with the environs in which the battle played itself out. "Now for the first time I could *see.*" But the attempt to write down the narrative failed two different times, and he put the work aside, without confidence that it would yet be completed but also not without hope. "My whole writing experience has taught me that books that are conceived by one ripen slowly, and then most strongly if one does not concern oneself with them, and that they finally announce their inner completedness to one so that, so to speak, one only needs to transcribe them."

What finally brought this book to its final maturity was the beginning of the Second World War, "the atmosphere of the tellurian crisis, the dreadful weighing of forces, and the signs both on the one side and the other of a false messianism." What gave Buber the decisive impetus was a half-dream in which unexpectedly there appeared that false messenger, of which the first chapter tells, as a demon with batwings and the traits of a Judaized Goebbels (Hitler's propaganda minister). "I wrote—now no longer in German but in Hebrew (the German version was written only later)—very quickly, as though I really needed only to transcribe. Everything now stood clearly before my eyes; the interconnections came to view as though of themselves."

It is clear from the above that *For the Sake of Heaven* was tied up profoundly with Buber's concerns with tragedy, with messianism, with the Nazis, and with the Second World War. This link is reinforced by Buber's view of Hitler as a would-be Napoleon. Buber spoke, in his story of Herzl's attack on his friend and fellow Zionist Davis Trietsch, of how at the age of twenty-four, he stood for the first time on the soil of tragedy. His years of searching for the proper standpoint from which to tell the story of *For the Sake of Heaven* were deeply connected with what he came to understand then about "the grave of right and wrong," with his much later understanding of how, out of the grave of right and wrong the right is resurrected, and, perhaps most significantly of all for Buber's own life, with his personal opposition to Theodor Herzl—the leader to whom he nonetheless remained loyal in his heart—as the Yehudi remained faithful to the Seer. The Yehudi's affirmation of the oneness of God in his refusal to cut himself off from the Seer entirely or see him as simply evil and wrong has a powerful association with one of the most painful events of Buber's early life, as with his understanding of genuine dialogue as confirming the other in a human way even in opposing him.

In January 1941, Buber wrote to Agnon asking him to go through the tenth to eighteenth chapters of *For the Sake of Heaven* (or *Gog and Magog,* as it is called in both the Hebrew and the German editions) so as to preclude any essential difference between the two parts. "There is no one else in the country who can help me in this," he wrote, a striking statement, since Scholem was thoroughly familiar with all the texts that were involved. Scholem could not, of course, give the sort of advice about writing a novel that Agnon could. *For the Sake of Heaven* was first published serially in the Hebrew daily *Davar,* and the Hebrew book edition was published in 1943. Yet by November 1941, Buber had already written the book a second time—in German; for at that time he sent the German manuscript to Ragaz with the request that he try to find a Swiss publisher for it. "In this narrative I have written from the heart something most essential and not expressible in any other way." His heart was particularly set on a German edition, he wrote Ragaz. "A book of this kind I have never written before . . . and even if God grants me a long life, I shall never write such again." He also suggested to Ragaz that he would not be unhappy if the book came into the hands of Hermann Hesse.

After Ragaz read the manuscript, he replied that the book was not really a novel and could not be read like one, but something *sui generis* to which no category applies. Without knowing Buber's "Nachwort," published for the first time in the 1949 German edition, Ragaz wrote Buber that he again and again had the feeling that Buber had simply elaborated on reports that were already at hand. He also had the experience that most readers of *For the Sake of Heaven* have had, namely, that the book had to be read at least twice before it could be grasped. The theme of the book seemed to him of the greatest possible significance for "Christians" as well; for the problem of "Gog and Magog" was current and central. He found so much else that deeply moved him and so much profound knowledge and wisdom that he could not put it into words. He felt that the book contained much that was "personal" for Buber and felt himself grasped by it in a way that only a *living* work could effect. He found it, finally, "a wonderful new representation of that Hasidic world in which I feel myself so strangely at home and which is so important to me. The book will find its way, though possibly slowly. . . . I feel it a *great honor* that you have entrusted it to me."

The Swiss classicist and authority on myth Karl Kerényi later singled out *For the Sake of Heaven* as *the* work which won for Buber a secure place in the ranks of classical authors, in the deepest sense of the term. Buber told me that he regarded *For the Sake of Heaven* as his most important book. By this he did not, of course, mean the most influential, like *I and Thou,* or the most culturally significant, as one might say of his translation of the Bible, but that in which his heart had found its fullest and most significant expression in response to the world in which he lived. In his first telling of Hasidic tales, he was, as he later recognized, too free. In the form of the "legendary anecdote" that he developed for the later telling of the Hasidic tales, he found the proper format for the crude originals. But only in *For the Sake of Heaven* did he discover how to combine freedom and faithfulness to the spirit of the tales.

"Every controversy that takes place for the sake of heaven will endure," we are told in the "Sayings of the Fathers" in the Talmud. Even though the opponents in such a controversy present irreconcilable convictions, both are witnesses for the only human truth we have, that of our relation to the reality that accosts us at any concrete historical moment. It is just such a controversy that stands at the core of Buber's Hasidic chronicle-novel. Although it is set in the time of the Napoleonic wars and focuses on the struggles of obscure Hasidic communities, *For the Sake of Heaven* is in many respects Buber's most profound and concrete image of the human. The heart of the novel is the simultaneous closeness and conflict between Jaacob Yitzhak of Lublin, the "Seer," and his namesake, the "holy Yehudi," or "holy Jew." At the beginning of the novel, we discover that the Seer has been tormented for a year by the presence of another namesake, a sinister and demonic "double." Even the Seer's power of vision was disturbed when this Jaacob Yitzhak came to him and demanded that he accept him as a pupil. The young man was condescending and insolent toward his fellow pupils, and to the Seer he proposed problems "which must lead even the sagest master on and on in a coil of endless speculation." Worst of all were his hours of private conversation with the Seer in which he told him stories of his life.

It seemed to the Rabbi that these stories were the events of his own youth or, rather, the evil distortion and caricature of these. What he remembered as the arch face of a child was transformed into a stealthy grimace; there was no path so smooth but that it was not now pockmarked with holes and crevices.

At the end of a year, when the demon double demands that the Seer announce that it is this younger Jaacob Yitzhak that will be his successor, the Seer finally frees himself of this incubus.

It is then that the Yehudi comes, drawn by the report that the Seer deals with questions of good and evil. He is not disappointed in the profundity of the Seer, yet he cannot go along with his desire to use evil means for good ends. In *Tales of the Hasidim, The Later Masters*, Buber said that the Yehudi (who is an actual historical figure like all the characters in the novel) once formulated the teaching which took shape in his life in the terse saying, "We ought to follow justice with justice and not with unrighteousness." This saying is the very one with which Buber opens the Preface to his book of Hasidic sayings *Ten Rungs* (1947) and of which he writes, "The use of unrighteousness as a means to a righteous end makes the end itself unrighteous. . . . What knowledge could be of greater importance to the men of our age, and to the various communities of our time?"

The Yehudi is tremendously impressed with the Seer. He follows the Seer's advice to give up his concern with "spiritual planes" in favor of "the way," which, like the building of a road, proceeds step by step from where one is. But he is troubled from the first by the fact that the disciples of the Seer are concerned with miracles. Love, the turning, and liberating good from evil are important, he tells the Seer's disciples, but the miracle is not so important, for it "merely bears witness." The Yehudi finds himself in conflict with the Seer himself when he ministers to a sick man who has been told by the Seer that he is destined to die. The Yehudi insists that the man forget what he thinks he knows and turn to God. The Seer is displeased with this action and relieves the Yehudi of his post as the teacher of the younger disciples. Here is a concrete embodiment of the tension between the "prophetic," which calls the hearer to turn with his whole being, and the "apocalyptic," which predicts a fixed future that needs only to unfold. This tension runs throughout the novel and forms its core. A similar conflict comes when the Yehudi's very presence destroys the effectiveness of some magical mystical intentions (*kavanot*) which the Seer is practicing with his disciples in order to influence the course of the Napoleonic wars. Although the Yehudi was in another room and knew nothing of what was going on, he says when it is later explained to him, "I can possess truth only by fighting for it." The narrator, who heard these words, says of them, "I had never heard any mouth of mortal speak with such clean sincerity," and he adds that truth was the Yehudi's "one and only concern."

At the Seer's suggestion, the Yehudi leaves him and founds a congregation of his own. Yet he remains a loyal disciple of the Seer's despite the Seer's growing hatred and distrust of him, fostered by the malicious tale-bearing of the Seer's disciples. The Yehudi's opposition to Lublin takes the form of a congregation which is described as "a dwelling place of the spirit." The Yehudi teaches his congregation that the periods of darkness and the eclipse of God are themselves trials which make possible repentance and the turning; for through them despair shatters the prison of our energies and enables us to turn them to God. The fight against evil is not a fight against the evildoers; for they are the very people who most need to be redeemed. It is the fight within ourselves, and it succeeds only through serving God with our "evil" urges. The man who has purified himself can take hatred on his own shoulders and not be corrupted by it, and he can transform the passion of hatred into love. But he must confine himself to helping individual lives and not attempt to use evil for the sake of the good or he may become the unwitting servant of evil. Although evil is terribly real, the redemption of evil can take place through the love with which one person meets another. To believe that evil is incapable of redemption and to permanently exclude the evildoer from the kingdom of God is to divide the world forevermore between God and Satan, and this is a division which the Yehudi will not admit. God's exiled Glory, his Shekinah, dwells in all places, even the most evil, and it can be served wherever it is met.

Thus the Yehudi's struggle with the Seer is a part of affirmation of the oneness of God—his insistence that redemption must be *of* evil and not just *from* it. It is this that prevents us from seeing the conflict of the story as one between good and evil. Rather it is tragedy in that special sense in which Buber defines it—the fact that each is as he or she is and that there are not sufficient resources in the relationship to bring the opponents into genuine dialogue so as to prevent the relationship from crystallizing into fixed opposition. Elsewhere Buber wrote of the Seer and the Yehudi:

The Seer lived in the world of his own spiritual urges, the greatest of which was his "seeing." His humility—though passionate like all his other qualities—impelled him time and again to strike a compromise between his personal world and the world at large, yet he could not really understand a human being like the Yehudi or the premises of his nature, for he lacked the one essential to such a man: the confidence of one soul in another. The Yehudi, in turn, could never realize this failing in the Seer's personality. That was why the relationship between the two was one of both intimacy and remoteness.

Even this tragic conflict is not left entirely unredeemed. Though the Yehudi cannot remove the tragedy itself, he brings it into his relationship with God. He refuses to allow the contradictions of existence to cut him off from a faithful relationship with the teacher whom he acknowledges even while he opposes him.

The Seer asks the Yehudi to die so that through him the Seer might learn from the upper world what next step to take in the great messianic enterprise. Despite its unusual nature, the reader is not unprepared either for this request or its fulfillment. After the Seer advises the Yehudi to come to Lublin no more because "there is no way of checking the power of hatred," the Yehudi says to his friends: " 'His influence has permeated me and can be separated from me no more. If the need arises to bear witness for God without respecting any man, I must oppose his word and his action. But no mortal power can separate me from him; only death can do that.' " Although the Seer knows well that the Yehudi is following an entirely different spiritual path from his own, he demands of him his life, and the Yehudi, through a loyalty to the Seer which transcends the merely personal, complies.

The Epilogue of *For the Sake of Heaven* gives evidence of a growing internal conflict in the Seer and of a belated recognition of the evil into which he has fallen. To this extent, one may speak of some redemption of evil from his side of the tragic conflict too. The Seer finally comes to the realization that he has identified his own will with the will of God and has demanded that others follow his will as if it were the will of God. Although the Seer's disciples and his second wife carry on an active hostility against the Yehudi, in which evil manifests itself in its least attractive forms—envy, malice, dishonesty, narrowness, and pettiness—there are instances of the redemption of evil even in the Yehudi's foes. One of the most striking of these is that of the brothers Meier and Mordecai, to whom the Yehudi seemed "an alien element which had penetrated the sanctuary and was boldly in revolt against the whole realm of mystery." Both brothers have on the same night a dream in which the Yehudi, and he alone, is able to drive away the goblinlike Jaacob Yitzhak, the Seer's double, after which they lead the disciples against the Yehudi and hew off his hands. Shamed and stricken, the two brothers go to Pshysha, where they are received with kindness by the Yehudi. Equally striking is the conversion of Rabbi Naftali. For years Naftali leads the slander against the Yehudi and is particularly effective in arousing the suspicion and hatred of the Seer. Called on to witness against the Yehudi by Rabbi Manahmen Mendel, a *zaddik* whom he had turned against the Yehudi, Naftali feels within him a mighty presence which commands him to speak the truth. With a new clarity of thought and a sudden loss of fear, he realizes that the truth is the very contrary of what all these years he has told the Rabbi of Lublin "as a matter of course." He experiences a great sense of freedom, and he testifies, "According to my knowledge the Rabbi of Pshysha has incurred no guilt toward the Rabbi of Lublin." Later he goes on a journey to try to counteract the forces that the Seer has set in motion.

The Yehudi does not believe that the redemption of evil is something that can take place quickly and easily; for the return to the good is born out of the depths of suffering and despair. He advises Menachem Mendel (later the Kotzker Rebbe), a young disciple of an intense and somewhat misanthropic disposition, to be a friend to Rabbi Bunam, whose wisdom is his love of the world. And he adds,

> "The world will make you suffer, even as it has made me suffer, only in an even more somber way. There is nothing that can be said in this matter, nor anything that can be done. Only try not to be angry at the world. The world and all of us who are in it exist by grace."

In the profundity of its insights into evil, *For the Sake of Heaven* is comparable to Dostoevsky's novel *The Brothers Karamazov*. The conflict between the Seer and the Yehudi is paralleled in *The Brothers Karamazov* by the contrast between the Grand Inquisitor, the hero of a dialectical poem composed by Ivan Karamazov, and Father Zossima, a holy monk, or *staretz*, whose life and teaching have a determining effect on Alyosha Karamazov. The Grand Inquisitor is like the Seer in that he is willing to use any means to attain his end, in that he relies upon "miracle, mystery, and authority," and in that he takes upon his own conscience the responsibility for other men's souls. As the Seer represents the degeneration of the institution of the *zaddik* within Hasidism, so the Inquisitor represents the degeneration of spiritual authority within Christianity. On the other hand, the Seer actually possesses a measure of true holiness, humility, and sincerity, whereas the Inquisitor admits that he is serving Satan rather than Christ.

Like the Yehudi, Father Zossima teaches joy in life as the creation of God, and like him he experiences rapture and ecstasy through the feeling of God's presence. Like him too, he is humble and does not judge others, and he teaches that the right attitude to evil is to love the evildoer and to take the responsibility of the evil upon oneself. He too cannot dissociate the love of God from the love of men and teaches the concrete love of particular persons rather than the abstract love of humanity. Both men deemphasize miracle, magic, and asceticism in favor of humble love, and both have an unswerving faith in the redemption of evil and of the evildoer. Both men stand, moreover, for a concrete and active mysticism that is essentially oriented toward the world and toward the cherishing of the particular.

In the essay with which he introduced *The Great Maggid* in 1921, Buber suggested a contrast between the Russian *staretz*, as he is portrayed by Dostoevsky, "with the transfiguring fidelity of a great poet," and the Hasidic *zaddik*. The *staretz* mediates between the people and God on the basis of an already accomplished redemption; the *zaddik* works along with others toward a redemption that has not yet taken place:

> The zaddik is not a priest or a man who renews in himself an already-accomplished work of salvation or transmits it to his generation, but the man who is more concentratedly devoted than other men to the task of salvation that is for all men and for all ages. . . . the man in whom transcendental responsibility has grown from an event of consciousness into organic existence. He is the true human being.

This contrast is illuminated by the different way in which the two novels treat the redemption of evil. In *For the Sake of Heaven*, it means serving God with the "evil" urge—turning with *all* of one's passion to the good—and it means bringing the tragic conflicts of existence into one's faithful dialogue with the everyday. In *The Brothers Karamazov*, on the other hand, evil is not so much *transformed* through real events between persons as it is *accepted* through a subjective attitude that the author conveys to the reader. Whereas the "man-god," Ivan, presses to the extreme of isolated consciousness and absolute self-affirmation, the "god-man," Zossima, presses to the extreme of an already existing perfection of mutual love, or one that is easily and directly attainable. If Ivan's Euclidean mind loses sight of the interconnections of human existence, Zossima's mystic mind fails to take note of its contradictions and tragic cleavages. The "active love" of which Zossima talks often appears as more of an emotion *within* the person than a concrete reality *between* persons. Although the affirmation which encloses the opposites in *The Brothers Karamazov* removes some of their terror, the evil which Dostoevsky portrays remains evil in the hearts and lives of most of the persons who bear it—untransformed and unredeemed.

To contrast the *redemption* of evil in *For the Sake of Heaven* with the *affirmation* that accepts both good and evil in *The Brothers Karamazov* is not to imply that in Buber's view evil can always be redeemed. The conflict between the "prophetic" and the "apocalyptic," between the Yehudi's way of working for redemption and the Seer's, has behind it the tragic fact that our human existence is compounded of hope for man's turning and despair over his being able to turn. This is exactly what William Blake portrays in the contrast between the first "Song of Experience," in which the bard-prophet calls man to turn back, and the second, in which earth answers that first the heavy chain that binds it must be broken by a force outside itself.

This dialectic is poignantly expressed in the Hasidic tale "Turning and Redemption":

> The rabbi of Rizhyn laid the fingers of his right hand on the table after the morning meal, and said: "God says to Israel: 'Return unto me . . . and I will return unto you.'" Then he turned his right hand palm up and said: "But we children of Israel reply: 'Turn Thou us unto Thee, O Lord, and we shall be turned; renew our days as of old.' For our exile is heavy on us and we have not the strength to return to you of ourselves." And then he turned his hand palm down again and said: "But the Holy One, blessed be he, says: 'First thou must return unto me.'" Four times the rabbi of Rizhyn turned his hand, palm up and palm down. But in the end he said: "The children of Israel are right, though, because it is true that the waves of anguish close over them, and they cannot govern their hearts and turn to God."

"The cruel antitheticalness of existence itself" is inherent in the fact that in order to communicate we must be "over against" each other —distant from and opposite to, and only then and through that "face to face." Tragedy arises from the fact that we do not and often cannot respond to the address that comes to us from what is over against us. We thereby crystallize this over-againstness into simple opposition and prevent the realization of its possibilities of relationship. "We cannot leave the soil of tragedy," Buber said in 1951 when he first visited America. "But in real meeting we can reach the soil of salvation after the tragedy has been completed." Tragedy can be experienced in the dialogical situation; the contradiction can become a theophany.

According to Karl Kerényi, *For the Sake of Heaven* stands on the peak of epic prose next to such masterworks as Thomas Mann's *The Holy Sinner* and Pär Lagerkvist's *Barabbas.* Buber's great achievement in his Hasidic chronicle-novel "is the evocation of fighters of the spirit who are without comparison in the whole of epic world literature in the ardor and exclusiveness of the unfolding of their religious powers." There is nothing more shattering in the history of the spirit than the overbearing on the part of the Seer. This "height" of humanity does not appear in classical Greek tragedy, Kerényi points out, but is reserved for later ages, "and no work of our time speaks of it so unambiguously and clearly as the 'Chronicle' since Buber wanted to communicate this shattering to us as no one else has." A *zaddik* such as the Seer can no longer correspond "to the idea of the perfected man," as Buber wrote in *My Way to Hasidism,* but "only to an image of man, to whom such genius also belongs, but which can also become tragic in its turn." "Martin Buber has also accomplished this great achievement," concludes Kerényi: "he has allowed the good *and* the evil, the holy *and* the dangerous to appear in his own and his most beloved sphere. His 'Chronicle' transcends time and people as does every work which is a 'classic.' "

In the Buber volume of The Library of Living Philosophers, Rivka Schatz-Uffenheimer, a disciple of Scholem's, devoted the last part of a long critique of Buber's interpretation of Hasidism to *For the Sake of Heaven.* Although Buber wished to set forth a "messianism without eschatology," Schatz-Uffenheimer held that Buber's own presentation of the Yehudi's death lies in the mystic "unification" which he performs, and which is not to be performed except in the land of Israel. "He seeks truth in heaven, and joins himself to those who are 'forcing the end.' " Nor is this merely submission to the Seer, in her opinion. "In the sources there appears more prominently the personal tragedy of one who wanted to 'work'—and to 'work' is a technical term reserved for one who strives with the upper world." She held that there is anecdotal and biographical material in the sources that Buber did not use that shakes one to the depth. "The most extravagant elements, elements of the abyss, found a place in this personality who was called 'the holy Jew' " whom even his own disciple Simha Bunam of Pshysha likened to " 'a drunkard and good-for-nothing' whom everyone drives away, but in the end they realize that salvation depends only on him." She concluded with a positive assessment:

> Every conversation in *For the Sake of Heaven* is a chapter of life in the spiritual world of Hasidism, a chapter sifted free of all banality and sentimentality, all of it polished by the masterful use of adumbration, so that if you have not read it several times, you have not read it at all. Here we are taught by Buber how man should face the world and God.

In his "Replies to My Critics" in the same volume, Buber reasserted his claim that "the 'holy Yehudi,' without giving up the basic Kabbalistic teaching, essentially set a simple human 'existence' " in opposition to the magical actions of the Seer in behalf of Napoleon. In so doing, the Yehudi "reaches back to the cry that one can already hear in the prophets of Israel, that we must first 'turn' before God 'turns' from the 'flaming of his wrath,' " and to the talmudic teaching that all eschatological combinations have passed by and it now depends on the human turning alone. The Yehudi himself reliably said, "Turn, turn, turn quickly in the turning, for the time is short and there is no longer any leisure for further wanderings of the soul; for redemption is near." In the oral tales that Buber heard in the Galician villages in his youth, this was the kernel of the sermon that the Yehudi time after time repeated on his "great journey" through those villages.

Of the three versions of the Yehudi's death, Buber chose the most problematic precisely because here the ambivalence of the Seer toward the Yehudi related to the wish to use magic and the Yehudi's "personal obedience, undiminished despite all essential opposition, finds unsurpassable expression." "For me," Buber added, what divided "the two schools is not to be seen in a difference of doctrines but in one of 'existence': in Lublin, the teacher imposed himself on his disciples, in Pshysha, he helped them to become themselves." In an age in which the propagandist and the leader dominated to the almost total exclusion of the teacher, Buber dared to elevate the teacher, and he did so because of the need of that age, the age of the greatest and most terrible war that human history has known. He who in the highest and most dispassionate seriousness dares to carry over that controversy between 'metaphysics' and 'existence' into the problematic of our own world-hour will recognize that all attempts to know the mysteries in order to use them for human ends means an attempt to flee before the command of our human reality into the darkness above the abyss.

Perhaps the most important critique of *For the Sake of Heaven*— because it is the one that led Buber to write the "Nachwort" that he added to the German edition of his novel in 1949 and as a "Foreword" to the revised English and Hebrew editions that appeared in the 1950s —is that by Baruch Kurzweil published in 1947 in the important Tel Aviv newspaper *Ha-aretz*. "One could find whole chapters in this book which could occupy an honorable place in a novel of world-stature," wrote Kurzweil. "But this chronicle is not a story, nor a novel, nor a scientific investigation." Kurzweil saw it, rather, as an expression of what was closest to Buber's heart, a conscious or unconscious attempt to give a summary of his teaching, pointing the way of life through the story itself without preaching abstract moral doctrines. "Behind the Hasidic world of this chronicle there stands the teacher and the guide Buber entering once again into dialogue with his contemporaries through reading to them the chronicle of days which are apparently past." Kurzweil compared Buber to a great wizard or magician who hides behind the story and makes pass before our eyes all sorts of details, dreams full of poetic beauty, conversations, and hints which are breathtaking. "The artistic climax of the book is the description of the last trip of the Yehudi to Lublin before his death," and here a strong epic power overshadows and transforms the pathos and rhetoric of the style.

If Buber endowed the Seer with the demonic grimness of the personality of King Saul, the Yehudi, so far from being David, is, according to Kurzweil, in many respects interchangeable with Jesus. Kurzweil charged Buber with portraying the Yehudi as having a hidden Christian tendency and asserted that, not participating in the observance of the Jewish law that characterized the Hasidim, Buber could not, in fact, faithfully present the atmosphere of their world.

> Only he can reach this unity of literary presentation and doctrine who stands with his whole being in that world from which he brings the mission. This was the position of the figures of the Bible. This was the position of Hasidic story-tellers in past generations. Buber lacks this precondition. . . . Buber once again manifested his amazing talents, but

once again his pupils were disappointed who wanted to receive from him a pointing of the way.

Although Buber does not mention Kurzweil by name, the whole of his Foreword (published in the second hardback and the original paperback editions of *For the Sake of Heaven* and, utterly incomprehensibly, omitted from the Atheneum paperback!) is, aside from the details related above of the stages of his writing the book, devoted to the questions Kurzweil raises. In contrast to Kurzweil's criticism that Buber stood outside of the world from which he brought his mission, Buber asserted that he stood at a point of very vital oneness with those men. "When, in my youth, I came in contact with my earliest Hasidic document, I accepted it in the spirit of Hasidic enthusiasm. I am a Polish Jew." His background was that of the Enlightenment, of course, "but in the most impressionable period of my boyhood a Hasidic atmosphere had a deep effect on me." This we already know, but nothing in Buber's earlier Hasidic writings prepares us for the statement that follows: "Had I lived in that period when one contended concerning the living Word of God and not concerning its caricatures, I, too, like so many others, would have escaped from my paternal home and become a Hasid." Although this was forbidden in the epoch into which Buber was born "according to both generation and situation," Buber identified himself with those in Israel who, equally opposed to blind traditionalism and blind rebellion, continue the Hasidic striving to renew the forms of both faith and life. Only now this striving "takes place in an historic hour in which a slowly receding light has yielded to darkness." Although Buber's entire spiritual substance did not belong to the world of the Hasidim, his foundation was in that realm and his impulses were akin to it. In this connection Buber made an oblique reference to Kurzweil's assertion that Rosenzweig's question to Buber about the Jewish Law in "The Builders" remains unanswered: " 'The Torah warns us,' a disciple of the Holy Yehudi and Rabbi Bunam, namely, Rabbi Mendel of Kotsk, said, 'not to make an idol even of the command of God.' What can I add to these words!"

Ernst Simon has pointed to a conversation between the Yehudi and his friend Yeshaya in which the latter reproaches the Yehudi for not praying until he was overcome by enthusiasm rather than praying at the appointed times, like the rest of the community. This, according to Simon, is an autobiographical reference to Buber's own interchange with Franz Rosenzweig on the Law. "This is a point which even

Buber's latest biographer [meaning me] has missed," Simon remarks in a footnote. Actually I had thought of the same thing and wrote Buber concerning it, but Buber categorically stated that he did not have himself in mind. The basis of Yeshaya's reproach cannot be applied to Buber, because Buber, in contrast to the Yehudi, turned away from mystic ecstasy in his youth. But the argument of Yeshaya in favor of the congregation is one that has been used again and again in criticism of Buber:

> We do not pray according to the inspiration of the individual heart. We join an ordering of the word of prayer which generations of our fathers organically built. We subordinate ourselves to and within this ordering not as this *I* or this *you*, but as part of that congregation. ... the order of prayer has its place and its appointed times, which you should respect.

The Yehudi replies that what a hundred generations have built up a single generation can ruin. All the stress on intention from the Baal-Shem to the present would not prevent this ruin if the living word of prayer deteriorates into a communal droning in which one individual, Simon, thinks of a grain deal while another individual, Reuben, considers his chance of being elected to the board of directors, and so on. "The word, that it may be a living word, needs *us*," and those who neglect appointed times and seasons do so because they want to wait until they can enter wholly into the spirit of the praying and thus prepare in their aloneness the rebirth of the congregation. Yeshaya objects that this way is not communicable nor can it be handed on, which the Yehudi does not deny. "But we dare not spare ourselves," he says. "God marches to His victory by the path of our defeats." We are reminded of Rosenzweig's statement that Buber's No may be more important for the tradition than "your or my or Ernst Simon's Yes."

To Kurzweil's charge that he had changed the figure of the Yehudi under the sway of a "Christianizing tendency," Buber replied that he had not described a single trait of his which did not exist in the tradition. Both the Yehudi and Jesus stood in a common tradition—the reality of the suffering "servants of the Lord," as we find it in Deutero-Isaiah. Only Jesus emerged from the hiddenness of the "quiver" (Isaiah 49:2), while the Yehudi remained within it. Here, more powerfully than in Hofmannsthal's play *The Tower*, the "suffering servant" is inextricably linked with tragedy in the deepest and most modern sense of that term.

Buber denied, finally, that he wrote *For the Sake of Heaven* as an expression of his "teaching." What is more, he held Kurzweil mistaken in expecting from him a teaching. "He who expects of me a teaching other than a pointing to realities of this order will always be disillusioned," Buber stated. In fact, what is crucial in this hour of history, which Buber for the first time, in *For the Sake of Heaven,* explicitly called that of the "eclipse of God," is not possessing a fixed doctrine but recognizing eternal reality and out of its depth facing the reality of the present. "No *way* can be pointed to in this desert night." All that one can do is "to help men of today to stand fast, with their soul in readiness, until the dawn breaks and a path becomes visible where none suspected it."

Notes and Sources

SOURCES FOR CHAPTER 1:
Zionism in the Twenties

. ————————————————————— .

Hebrew University and Palestine Folk School

MB to Franz Rosenzweig, June 13, 1924; February 8, 1925; March 27, 1925; Undated #578; Undated #600; July 19, 1929, in Archives of Leo Baeck Foundation, New York City; Martin Buber, *Briefwechsel aus sieben Jahrzehnten*, Vol. I—*1897–1918*, with a Foreword by Ernst Simon and a Biographical Sketch by Grete Schaeder (Heidelberg: Verlag Lambert Schneider, 1972), Schaeder, "Biographischer Abriss," p. 79; *Buber Briefwechsel* II, #144. Leo Kohn to MB, London, February 15, 1924, pp. 180–86; #152. Robert Weltsch to MB, London, June 23, 1924, pp. 194 f.; #161. MB to Paula Buber-Winkler, London, July 23, 1924, pp. 203 f.; #176. Chaim Weizmann to MB, London, February 2, 1925, p. 217; #201. MB to Hans Kohn, January 31, 1926, pp. 241 f.; #248. Hugo Bergmann to MB, Jerusalem, August 31, 1927, pp. 289 f.; #251. MB to Judah L. Magnes, September 8, 1927 (?), pp. 292 f.; #252. MB to Hugo Bergmann, September 11, 1927, pp. 293 f.; #253. Hugo Bergmann to MB, Jerusalem, September 29, 1927, pp. 294 f.; #254. MB to Hugo Bergmann, October 5, 1927, pp. 295 f.; #288. Gerhard Scholem to MB, Jerusalem, November 15, 1928, p. 325; #295. MB to Chaim Weizmann, May 30, 1929, pp. 332 f.; #297. Judah L. Magnes to MB, Jerusalem, July 4, 1929, pp. 335 f.; #300. MB to Franz Rosenzweig, Zurich, August 15, 1929, p. 338; #301. MB to Paula Buber-Winkler, Zurich, probably August 15, 1929, pp. 339–41; #302. Paula Buber-Winkler to MB, Heppenheim, August 17, 1929, pp. 341 f.; #303. Franz Rosenzweig to MB, Frankfurt a. M., August 18, 1929, pp. 342 f.; #304. MB to Paula Buber-Winkler, Zurich, August 20, 1929, pp. 343 f.; Buber, *Der Jude und sein Judentum*, "Universität und Volkshochschule" (letter to the Executive Committee of the Zionist Organization in London, January 22, 1924), pp. 684–88; "Volkserziehung als unsere Aufgabe" (speech given to the twenty-first conference of German Zionists, 1926), pp. 674–84.

Buber's Visit to Palestine

MB to Franz Rosenzweig, Jerusalem, May 4, 1927 in Archives of Leo Baeck Foundation, New York City; *Buber Briefwechsel* II, #171. MB to Gerhard Scholem, December 13, 1924, pp. 212 f.; #201. MB to Hans Kohn, January 31, 1926, pp. 241 f.; Hugo Bergmann, "Zur Ankunft Bubers in Palästina," *Selbstwehr. Jüdisches Volksblatt* (Prague), Vol. XXI, No. 17, April 22, 1927, p. 3.

Zionism, Socialism, and Community

Buber, *Der Jude und sein Judentum*, "Selbstbesinnung" (1926), pp. 488–500; "Drei Stationen" (1929), p. 751; "Zwei Hebräischen Bücher" (1928), p. 771; "Arbeitsglaube" (1929), p. 357; "Warum muss der Aufbau Palästinas ein sozialisten sein?" (1929), pp. 376–87; "Wie kann Gemeinschaft werden?" (1930), pp. 358–75; Buber, "Die Frage nach Jerusalem" (from a speech to the German Conference for the Working Palestine), *Das werdende Zeitalter*, Vol. VIII (1929), No. 2, pp. 65 f.; Ernst Simon, "Nationalismus, Zionismus, und der jüdischer–araber Konflikt"; Ernst Simon, "Martin Buber and German Jewry" in *Leo Baeck Institute Year Book* (London: East and West Library, 1958), p. 19.

The Arab Question

Martin Buber, *Briefwechsel aus sieben Jahrzehnten*. In 3 vols, ed. & introduced by Grete Schaeder in counsel with Ernst Simon and in cooperation with Rafael Buber, Margot Cohn, and Gabriel Stern, Vol. II: *1918–1938* (Heidelberg: Verlag Lambert Schneider, 1973), #142. Robert Weltsch to MB, Berlin, November 29, 1923, pp. 177–80; #221. MB to Franz Rosenzweig, Jena, June 19, 1926, pp. 261 f.; #297. Judah L. Magnes to MB, Jerusalem, July 4, 1929, p. 335; #298. Georg Landauer and Gershom Chanoch to MB, Berlin, July 11, 1929, pp. 336 f.; #299. Robert Weltsch to MB, Berlin, July 17, 1929, pp. 337 f.; #305. Hans Kohn to MB, Between Dresden and Berlin, August 26, 1929, p. 345; #307. Hans Kohn to MB, Zurich, September 2, 1929, pp. 347 f.; #309. Robert Weltsch to MB, Berlin, September 13, 1929, p. 349; #311. Hans Kohn to MB, Vienna, September 25, 1929, p. 351; #312. Hans Kohn to MB, Trieste, September 26, 1929, p. 352; #313. MB to Paula Buber-Winkler, October 3, 1929, p. 353; #315. Ernst Simon to MB, Jerusalem, October 10, 1929, pp. 354 f.; #316. Chaim Weizmann to MB, Meran, October 30, 1929, pp. 355 f.; #317. MB to Chaim Weizmann, November 24, 1929, pp. 356 f.; #334. Gerhard Scholem to MB, Jerusalem, May 22, 1930, pp. 380 f.; Martin Buber, *Der Jude und sein Judentum: Gesammelte Aufsätze und Reden*, with an Introduction by Robert Weltsch (Köln: Joseph Melzer Verlag, 1963), "Selbstbesinnung" (1926), pp. 495 f.; "Rede auf dem XVI. Zionisten-Kongress in Basel (August 1, 1929), pp. 520–26; "Jüdisches Nationalheim und nationale Politik in Palästina" (from an address given in Berlin, October 31, 1929), pp. 330–42; Martin Buber, *Israel and the World: Essays in a Time of Crisis,* 2d, enlarged ed. (New York: Schocken Books, 1963), "And If Not Now, When?" (address delivered at a convention of Jewish Youth representatives in Antwerp), 1923, pp. 234–39; Ernst Simon, "Nationalismus, Zionismus, und der jüdische-arabische Konflikt," in "Martin Bubers Theorie und Wirksamkeit," *Bulletin des Leo Baeck Instituts,* Vol. IX, No. 33, 1966 (Tel Aviv: Verlag Bitaon Ltd.), pp. 60 f., *passim;* Ernst Simon, "Buber's Political Way" (Hebrew), Introduction to Martin Buber, *Am v'Olam* (People and World) (Jerusalem: Sifriah Zionit, 1961), trans. for me by Uri Margolin; Judah L. Magnes, "Al Harz Hazophim" in *Der Jude,* Vol. X, No. 5 (March 1928), *Sonderheft zu Martin Bubers fünfzigstem Geburtstag,* p. 50.

Siegfried Lehmann, "Das Kinder- und Jugenddorf Ben-Schemen," *Das werdende Zeitalter,* Vol. VIII, No. 2 (1929), pp. 90–98.

Norman Bentwich, *Ben-Shemen. A Children's Village in Israel, Études Pédagogiques. Federation Internationale des Communautes D'Enfants* F.I.C.E., No. 7, Published with the Financial Assistance of UNESCO (Jerusalem: The Jerusalem Post Press, 1959?), pp. 18 f., 25–27, 29–32, 51, 55 f., 62–64, 90.

Aharon Cohen, *Israel and the Arab World,* abridged ed. (Boston: Beacon Press, 1976), pp. 79–81, 133, 38.

Norman Bentwich, *For Zion's Sake. A Biography of Judah L. Magnes* (Philadelphia: The Jewish Publication Society, 1954), pp. 185, 196–201.

Susan Lee Hattis, *The Bi-National Idea in Palestine during Mandatory Times* (Haifa: Shikmona Publishing Co., 1970), pp. 24 f., 38–47, 57 f., 61, 64 f., 70, 72, 74, 86–100, 136–38, 141 f., 144 ff.

SOURCES FOR CHAPTER 2:
Education

•——————————————————————————•

Martin Buber, *Rede über das Erzieherische* (Berlin: Lambert Schneider Verlag, 1926), "Vorwort."

Martin Buber, *Between Man and Man,* 2d, enlarged ed. with an Introduction by Maurice Friedman and an Afterword by the Author ("The History of the Dialogical Principle," trans. by Maurice Friedman), trans. by Ronald Gregor Smith (New York: The Macmillan Co., 1965), "Education," pp. 83–103.

Martin Buber, *Israel and the World: Essays in a Time of Crisis* (New York: Schocken Books, 1963, 2d ed.), "Imitatio Dei," trans. by Greta Hort, pp. 71–77.

Maurice Friedman, "Martin Buber's Concept of Education," *The Christian Scholar,* Vol. XL, No. 2 (June 1957), pp. 109–16. See also Maurice Friedman, "Existential Man: Buber" in Paul Nash, Andreas M. Kazamias, and Henry J. Perkinson, eds., *The Educated Man. Studies in the History of Educational Thought* (New York & London: John Wiley & Sons, 1965).

D. H. Lawrence, *Sons and Lovers* with an Introduction by Alfred Kazin (New York: The Modern Library, 1962), p. 366.

Letters from Martin Buber to Franz Rosenzweig in the Archives of the Leo Baeck Foundation, New York City: undated, #10, #491, #671; February 8, 1923; December 29, 1923; August 1, 1924.

Karl Wilker, "Religion, Politik, Erziehung" in *Das werdende Zeitalter*, Vol. VII, No. 2 (February 1928), pp. 35–38.

Buber Briefwechsel II, #90. Franz Rosenzweig to MB, undated, pp. 108 f.; #95. MB to FR, August 15, 1922, pp. 112 f.; #135. MB to Ernst Simon, Sonnenholz, July 30, 1923, p. 168; #138. Rudolf Hallo to MB, August 20, 1923, pp. 169–71; #141. Ernst Simon to MB, November 2, 1923, pp. 172–76; note 6, p. 176 f.; #139. Ernst Simon to MB, August 29, 1923, p. 171; #120. MB to Franz Rosenzweig, January 18, 1923, pp. 153 f.; #123. MB to Franz Rosenzweig, February 10, 1923, p. 158; #117. Franz Rosenzweig to MB, January 12, 1923, pp. 146–49; #118. MB to Franz Rosenzweig, undated, pp. 105 f.; #129. MB to Franz Rosenzweig, March 22, 1923, pp. 162 f.; #129. MB to Franz Rosenzweig, March 22, 1923, pp. 162 f.; #150. MB to Franz Rosenzweig, June 13, 1924, p. 192 f.; #151. Franz Rosenzweig to MB, June 17, 1924, p. 193; #306. MB to Paula Buber-Winkler, Pontigny, September 2, 1929, pp. 345–47; #308. MB to Paula Buber-Winkler, Abbaye de Pontigny, September 8, 1929, pp. 348 f.; #139. MB to Leopold Marx, August 8, 1925, pp. 233 f. & note 1; #530. MB to Hugo Bergmann, z. Zt. Berlin, April 16, 1936, p. 589.

Nahum N. Glatzer, *Franz Rosenzweig: His Life and Thought* (New York: Schocken Books, 1953), pp. 106, 108–10, 125–28; 138–42, from Dr. Richard Tuteur's notes; letter of May 27, 1925, to Martin Buber, p. 150.

Nahum N. Glatzer, "The Frankfurt Lehrhaus" in *Year Book I of the Leo Baeck Institute*, ed. by Robert Weltsch (London: East and West Library, 1956), pp. 109–18, 122.

Grete Schaeder, "Biographischer Abriss" in *Buber Briefwechsel* I, pp. 83 f.

The stories of the response of Ahad Ha'am to Buber's lectureship at Frankfurt University and of Buber's proposal to Agnon to take up the *Corpus Hasidicum* again in Palestine were related to me by Shmuel Y. Agnon at his home in Talpiyoth in Jerusalem, July 15, 1966.

The testimony of Nahum Glatzer concerning the *Corpus Hasidicum* was told to me by him in New York City, December 1969.

NOTE

Originally the plan was to have not one but *three* theological faculties at Frankfurt University. This proved to be impractical, since the Hochschule für die Wissenschaft des Judentums could not be moved from Berlin to Frankfurt as had been hoped. Instead three lectureships were established for the Protestant, Catholic, and Jewish religions. The Jewish community of Frankfurt nominated Rabbi Nehemiah Nobel for the Jewish chair, but the official appointment reached him the day before his death. Then Rosenzweig was chosen, and he had to reject it because of his illness. Thus it moved by steps from the more official and observant to the less. Robert Weltsch, "Nachwort" to Hans Kohn, *Martin Buber: Sein Werk und seine Zeit. Ein Beitrag zur Geistesgeschichte Mitteleuropas 1880–1930*, "Nachwort: 1930–1960" by Robert Weltsch (Köln: Joseph Melzer Verlag, 1961), pp. 418 f.

SOURCES FOR CHAPTER 3:
Rosenzweig and the Law

Franz Rosenzweig, *On Jewish Learning*, ed. with an Introduction by Nahum N. Glatzer (New York: Schocken Books, 1955), Nahum Glatzer, "Introduction," p. 23; Buber-Rosenzweig letters on the Law, pp. 109–18; "The Builders," pp. 75, 77, 79, 82–87, 91 f.; "The Commandments: Divine or Human," pp. 119–24.

Martin Buber, *Reden über das Judentum* (Frankfurt am Main: Rütten & Loenin, 1923), "Cheruth" (1919), pp. 202–09, 217–24; "Der heilige Weg" (1919), pp. 65, 71 (my translation, quoted from Maurice Friedman, *Martin Buber: The Life of Dialogue*, p. 262). See Martin Buber, *On Judaism*, ed. by Nahum N. Glatzer (New York: Schocken Books, 1968, paperback 1972), "The Holy Way," pp. 108–48, "Herut: On Youth and Religion," pp. 149–74, trans. by Eva Jospe.

Jakob Rosenheim, *Beiträge zur Orientierung im jüdischen Geistesleben der Gegenwart* (Zurich: Verlag "Arzenu," 5680, 1920), pp. 10, 19–23, 27–29.

Almanach des Schocken Verlags auf das Jahr 5696, ed. by Morris Spitzer (Berlin: Schocken Verlag. Jüdischer Buchverlag, 1936/1937), pp. 147–54.

Buber Briefwechsel II, #112. MB to Franz Rosenzweig, October 1, 1922, pp. 141 f.; #136. MB to Franz Rosenzweig, August 10, 1923, pp. 168 f.; #137. Franz Rosenzweig to MB, August 12, 1923, p. 169; #153. MB to Franz Rosenzweig, June 24, 1924, p. 196; #154. Franz Rosenzweig to MB, June 29, 1924, pp. 197 f.; #155. MB to Franz Rosenzweig, July 1, 1924, p. 198; #156. Franz Rosenzweig to MB, July 4, 1924, p. 199; #157. MB to Franz Rosenzweig, July 5, 1924, pp. 199 f.; #158. Franz Rosenzweig to MB, undated, p. 200; #159. MB to Franz Rosenzweig, July 13, 1924, pp. 200 f.; #160. Franz Rosenzweig to MB, July 16, 1924, pp. 201–03; #182. MB to Franz Rosenzweig, June 3, 1924, p. 222; #183. Franz Rosenzweig to MB, June 5, 1925, pp. 222 f.; #213. MB to Franz Rosenzweig, May 7, 1926, p. 254.

Letters of May 20 and May 26, 1924, from MB to Franz Rosenzweig in the Archives of the Leo Baeck Institute, New York City.

Franz Rosenzweig, *Briefe*, selected and ed. by Edith Rosenzweig in cooperation with Ernst Simon (Berlin: Schocken Velag, 1935), #399. To Martin

Buber, July 16, 1924, p. 504 (as in all other cases, my translation); #408.
To Ernst Markowicz, November 11, 1924, p. 514; #413. To those speaking in the Lehrhaus, "Göttlich und Menschlich," end of November, 1924, pp. 518–21; #414. To Jakob Rosenheim, December 2, 1924, pp. 521 f. See the illuminating discussion of Buber's position on the law in comparison with both Rosenzweig and the nineteenth-century Orthodox theologian Samson Raphael Hirsch in S. Daniel Breslauer, *The Chrysalis of Religion: A Guide to the Jewishness of Buber's I and Thou* (Nashville, Tenn.: Abingdon Press, 1980), Chapter 2 "*I and Thou* and Jewish Ritual," pp. 68–97. I follow Nahum Glatzer in holding Buber to be an "anomian" rather than an "antinomian," as Breslauer dubs him.

NOTES TO CHAPTER 4:
The Buber-Rosenzweig Bible

• ─────────────────────────────────── •

Note 1

It is Franz Rosenzweig who in his essay on "The Bible and the Word" gave the fullest explanation of the significance of Buber's discovery of the cola and of colometry. All word is spoken word, said Rosenzweig. The book stands originally in its service. But the chain that holds all written German in bonds of muteness is the system of signs in which words lie embedded: punctuation. Martin Buber found a sharp instrument for breaking these chains—the basic principle of natural, oral punctuation: respiration. Breath is the stuff of speech and the drawing of breath its natural articulation. It stands under its own law: one cannot speak more than twenty or at most thirty words without drawing a deep breath, and usually only five to ten. But within these limits the breath-renewing silence follows the inner traits of speech which are only occasionally determined by their logical structure, rather for the most part mirroring the movements and excitations of the soul itself in its strengths—and above all in its measures of time. The cola breaths are not identical with poetry, although at times there breaks through the breathing movement of natural speech the bound dance step of poetry. In most cases, the rhythmical speech of words triumphs over the measured song, prose over poetry. Poetry is indeed the mother language of the human race, as both Johann Georg Hamann and Johann Gottfried Herder, the eighteenth-century German philosophers of literature, maintained, but only of the race. This is still true today: the speech of every child is originally lyrical and magical; yet when this child grows up the nonlyrical and nonmagical fullness of the word breaks through this primordial language. In similar fashion, one day there also breaks through the primordial speech of the human race the speech of the mankind in man, the speech of the word. The Bible is the shelter of this human speech because it is prose—prose even in the enchanting song of the prophets. As writing it is the precipitate of the event of the breakthrough of the word which in the history of the race stands precisely where it does in the history of the individual: at the moment of his becoming human. All poetry that has arisen since then in its luminous circle—indeed poetry more than prose, Yehuda Halevi more than Maimonides, Dante more than Thomas, Goethe more than Kant—is inspired by its spirit of prose. Since then a gateway has been breached in the gloomy silence that surrounded the human race in its origins, separating each from each and all from without and within—a gate that will never again be wholly shut: the gateway of the word.

Note 2

Everett Fox expounds the Jewish biblical significance of this bold rendering in authentically Buberian terms:

The Hebrew Bible speaks of *ruah* in several different contexts: as the "spirit of God" which comes over a charismatic leader; as simply a natural phenomenon—wind; and as the *"ruah* of God" which hovers over the waters of chaos and confusion at the beginning of Creation. The first two usages are actually mirror-images of the third. *Ruah* does not speak of two separate spheres; rather, it speaks out of a unity which has two aspects. That this is intended may be seen from the function of *ruah* in Numbers 11:29 and 31, where the statement of Moses

Would it were given
that all HIS people were Proclaimers
that HE would give the rush-of-his spirit *(ruah)* over them

is juxtaposed with the narrator's

Now a rushing-wind *(ruah)* went forth
from HIM which drove quail from the sea.

The teaching here points back to the usage in the Creation story, and posits that both spirit *and* nature originate in God. As such it represents a view basic to the Hebrew Bible, one which the West has yet to learn. Ancient Israel knows of no realm called the "spiritual" or the "religious," as opposed to the "physical" or the "worldly." Man is placed in the world before God; either he lives his life under His aegis or he does not. But a fragmented life such as we find in the modern world—where private and public morality do not necessarily have to coincide—cannot be an authentic one in Biblical terms. . . . In this context, there is no internal struggle of man against "the desires of the flesh" and for "the world of the soul"; there is only man as a totality, who must struggle with reality and with the totality of its claim upon him.

Another example that Buber himself cites of the recovery of the original metaphor in the new translation by getting at the root meanings of terms by way of sound is that of the Hebrew word *qorban,* or *korban,* which is commonly rendered as "sacrifice." *Qorban* is a concept of relationships, wrote Buber; that is, it includes the presence of two persons, one of whom seeks to diminish the distance between the two of them by drawing the other near through the *qorban.* Therefore, *qorban* is rendered in German by *Darnahung,* or *Nahung,* in English by "bringing near." Whoever reads the story of the rebellion of Korah and his band (Numbers 16) and pays attention to the weight that "nearing" and "letting come near" has, can judge the central significance of distancing and coming near for the biblical concept of "sacrifice." Similarly, Buber points out that *torah* is not correctly rendered by the static "law" but by the dynamic "teaching," or "instruction." *Nabi* is not "prophet," which leads one to think of foretelling the future, but "proclaimer," the "mouth" of God who speaks out the word of God spoken to him. *Malakh* is not an "angel," hence a being of a special nature, but simply a messenger, who, for our biblical knowing, does not exist otherwise than in his message, or mission, as is captured by the Hagadic image of emerging from the stream of fire and returning into it. *Kabod* does not mean "honor" or "glory" or any Western equivalent but a "weight," the substance and power of a being, not as thought of in itself but as manifesting itself, as shining forth, as *appearing.* God's *kabod* should therefore be called his "appearing," not his "majesty"—the becoming visible of the invisible *majestas,* its *becoming apparent*—glory, but glory just as the shining forth of the "weight." *Zaddik* is not the "righteous" or "just" but the "proven" person whose personal conduct of life has been confirmed as true. *Emeth* and *emunah* almost never mean truth in any absolute sense but reliability and confidence between being and being, hence "faithfulness" and "trust," rather than "belief."

Note 3

A somewhat parallel change takes place in the Buber-Rosenzweig translation of proper names in the text of the Bible. The emphasis on sounds brings forth significances of names that are tied in with the real presence and the real life-situation of those spoken about. Everett Fox supplies two striking examples of this from Genesis, one in the case of Noah and the other in the case of Nod, the land in which Cain settles after his exile because of the murder of Abel. Thus Genesis 5:25 reads:

> *He called his name Noah*
> *saying*
> *This one will comfort-our-sorrow* (yenahamenu)
> *in our doing and in the trouble of our hands*
> *in the ground*
> *which HE cursed*

and again in Genesis 6:5–8:

> *HE was sorry* (vay-yinahem)
> *that he had made man on earth*
> *and he was troubled in his heart . . .*
> *for I am sorry* (nihamti)
> *that I made them*

Thus "Noah, the one who was to 'comfort,' becomes the ironic symbol of God's 'sorrow' over the impending end of the world." Similarly, in Genesis 4:12, 14:

> HE said . . .
> *wavering and wandering* (na va-nad) *must you be on earth*
>
> ....
>
> *Kayin said to HIM*
> *I must be wavering and wandering* (na va-nad) *on earth.*

Thus Nod is not necessarily a real place but is rather the condition and fate of a man who must settle in the land of no-settling—the land of Nod/Wandering east of Eden. In perfect consonance with this, Elie Wiesel in his novel *The Oath* portrays the narrator Azriel as a man doomed to be a *Na-venadnik* in order that he may carry about with him throughout his wanderings on the earth the terrible secret of the Holocaust which has destroyed the village (world) of Kolvillag—a survivor, a messenger, and a perpetual exile.

Note 4

The Hebrew Bible is essentially stamped and joined by the language of a message, Buber asserted. The "prophecy" is only the most distinct, the openly proclaimed message. But there is hardly any part, hardly any style-form of the Bible, that is not directly or indirectly bound to the message and borne by it. The narrative preserves untroubled by its epic completeness, the prescriptions their stern factuality, but within these forms there takes place in modified fashion the working of the message. The principle of formation through which this takes place is that of rhythm. By rhythm here is not meant movement of the parts but a meaningful order of connections appearing between something that remains the same and something that is manifold. What remains the same can be either purely structural—the repetition of an emphasis, an intensity of movement—or of a measure, or phonetic, the repetition of sounds, of sound-connections, of words, of phrases. One example that Buber gave of this is the pointing to the covenant relationship between man and the earth, between the people and the land of Israel, through the medium of the repetition of the same word with twofold meaning.

The great translators of the Bible were sufficiently inspired to see that the word of God is valid for all ages and places; but they failed to recognize that through such an insight the importance of starting from their particular age in all its national, personal, and physical conditions is not diminished but heightened. Completed revelation is always human body and human voice, and that means always: *this* body and *this* voice in the mystery of its uniqueness. To the proclamations of the prophets belong not merely their symbols and their parables, but also the ground-stream of ancient Hebraic sensuousness still preserved in the spiritual concepts, the taut span of the ancient Hebraic architecture of sentences, the ancient Hebraic manner of linking words that stand next to, but also those far removed from, one another through related roots or similar sounds, the powerful course of ancient Hebrew rhythm pushing beyond all meter. Buber called this type of linking of words through sounds or roots the style of "paronomasy." These words are thereby taken out of their immediate context and set in a special relationship in which often what is expressed in the text becomes strengthened and more impressive; something then is expressed in a peculiar manner that the text wishes to express in just that way. There are, accordingly, alliterations and assonances in the Bible, and repetitions of words, phrases, and sentences that are not to be comprehended through aesthetic categories alone. They belong for the most part to the content and character of the message itself, and their proper rendering is one of the central tasks of the translation. It is a matter often of very important connections when we strive to render the same Hebrew word-root through the same German ones within a section, not seldom also within a whole part, a whole book, indeed a majority of the books.

There is no room for some transcendental religious content in the narrative. It must obey the laws of the epic. Yet through the rhythmization of the leading word, there is a ring of similarity through which the higher message rustles. The leading-word rhythm is neither rhetorical nor lyrical; it is a genuinely epic rhythm, the legitimate artistic sign of a mystery enclosing and transcending the world of form. Therefore the interpretation of the leading-word style can only be of the nature of a pointing, a hinting, an indication of something which can be perceived in its reality but not described and conceptualized. Such an interpretation may appear to discover a primordial Midrash hidden in the biblical text, and that can lead one to doubt it. Yet the correspondences are so exact and they supplement one another so fully and without remainder that one is compelled to take upon oneself the insight: the roots of the "secret meaning" reach back into the depths of the earliest forms of the tradition. One might protest, Buber conceded, that he has ascribed to the biblical narrator an all too rational way of proceeding. But all genuine poetry is in this sense rational—i.e., it orders and forms the elemental under a formative law of reason. What matters alone is in whose service this reason stands. Or, in other words, whether it is the real, the perceiving reason.

The biblical narratives, unlike epics, cannot be comprehended in a single glance, but are meant to be received one after the other. Where a narrative or a sequence of narratives is brought together through a recurring formula, then the formula resounds ever more strongly with each recurrence. One example that Rosenzweig cites is when the angel with the sword repeats the same words in forbidding Balaam to go forward that Balaam had used in trying to force his donkey to move. Another is from Genesis when the aging Isaac tells Esau how his brother Jacob has deceived him and taken from Esau his birthright and, in a later chapter, when Jacob uses the same word to complain to his uncle Laban, who gives him Leah in marriage after he has worked seven years for the hand of Rachel: "Why have you deceived me?"

Note 5

Yaakov sent messengers from before his face to Esav his brother to the land of Seir, in
Edom's field,
and commanded them, saying:
Say thus to my lord, to Esav:
Thus says your servant Yaakov:
I sojourned with Lavan and have tarried until now,
ox and ass, flock-animal and servant and maid have become mine.
I have sent to tell it to my lord, to find favor in your eyes. . . .
For he said to himself:
I will cover his face with the gift that goes before my face,
afterwards I will see his face,
perhaps he will lift up my face.
The gift passed over before his face,
but he spent the night on that night in the camp.

On that night he arose,
he took his two wives, his two maids and his eleven children
and went over the ford of the Yabbok,
he took them, had them go over the river and had that which was his go over.
Yaakov remained behind alone.
A man wrestled with him until the dawn rose.
When he saw that he could not prevail against him,
he touched the socket of his hip,
and the socket of Yaakov's hip was dislocated as he wrestled with him.
Let me go,
for the dawn is rising.
But he said:
I will not let you go
unless you bless me.
Then he said to him:
What is your name?
And he said:
Yaakov.
Then he said:
Not Yaakov/Heel-Sneak shall your name be said henceforth,
rather Yisrael/Fighter of God,
for you fought with Godhood and with mankind
and prevailed.
Then Yaakov asked, he said:
Now tell me your name!
But he said:
Why then do you ask after my name!
And he blessed him there.
Yaakov called the name of the place Peniel/God's-Face, for:

I have seen God,
face to face, and my soul is delivered. . . .

Yaakov lifted up his eyes and saw:
here, Esav was coming and with him four hundred men. . . .
He bowed seven times to the earth, until he had stepped up to his brother.
And Esav ran to meet him,
he embraced him, fell upon his neck and kissed him.
And they wept.
Then he lifted up his eyes and saw the women and the children and said:
Who are these to you? . . .
What do you mean by all this camp which I have met?
And he said:
To find favor in the eyes of my lord.
Esav said:
I have much, my brother, let what is yours remain yours.
Yaakov said:
Now no!
Now may I have found favor in your eyes,
so that you take my gift from my hand.
For I have, after all, seen your face, as one sees God's face,
and you were gracious to me.
Now take my blessing that has been brought to you!

This "leading-word" method was known to classical Jewish exegesis, writes Everett Fox, but is virtually ignored in modern times. Fox points out how the first part of the story of the Tower of Babel introduces all the leading words—"all the earth," "tongue," "Come-now," "building," "city-and-tower," "name," and "scattered," and how in the second part of the story God answers the defiance of man in the *very terms* of the rebels (just as he does in the Flood story where man's "wrecking" of the earth through injustice leads to God's decision to "wreck" it).

All over the earth was one tongue and one kind of speech
they found a cleft-place in the land of Shinar and settled there
They said each man to his companion
Come-now
Let us bake bricks and let us burn them to burning
So the brick-stone was to them instead of building-stone
and the raw-asphalt was to them instead of red-mortar
They said
Come-now
let us build ourselves a city and a tower
its head up to heaven
and let us make ourselves a name
else we will be scattered over the face of all the earth. . . .
HE went down to see the city and the tower which the sons of men built

HE said
Lo one people is this and one tongue for all of them
and this is only the start of their doing
henceforth will nothing be too steep for them of all that they devise to do
Come-now
let us go down and there baffle their tongue
so that no more will a man hearken to the tongue of his companion
HE scattered them from there over the face of all the earth
so that they had to cease building the city
Therefore its name was called Bavel/Baffle
for there HE had baffled the tongue of all the earth
and from there HE had scattered them over the face of all the earth.

"Let us make a name for ourselves, lest we be scattered over the face of the earth!" Buber repeated from the text, and commented: " 'Name' signifies in the pregnant biblical speech the time and witness of a might that lasts beyond mortal man. But now a name comes into being for this work: the name of the antigodly world city, named after the mixed-up, confused speech of the jumble —Babel. And those who, devoted to and concerned about human unity, built a heaven-touching tower in order not to be scattered are just for that reason 'scattered over the face of the earth.' The perversity of man in its own turn underwent perversion."

Note 6

Isaak Heinemann found the Buber-Rosenzweig translation no less scientific than the one that Harry Torczyner was preparing and added that the scholar could learn an extraordinary amount from their way of rendering the Bible.

Harry Torczyner's response, as might be expected, was much more critical. Although admiring the courage and energy Buber put into this new work, Torczyner could not go along with Buber's method. Torczyner confined himself more and more to the biblical text itself, rejecting all accretions of tradition, either Christian or Jewish, naïve or scholarly. Buber, in contrast, allowed the Midrash, early talmudic commentaries on the Bible and elaborations of its stories, to have a very strong influence. Torczyner also held that Buber was led astray by apparent roots of words which actually grew up without any logic. In particular, he regretted that Buber had not discussed his translation with someone of a philological critical bent. He wished, indeed, that he had known of Buber's planned translation when he undertook his own; for he would have much preferred to work with Buber and felt that Buber might find his criticism of their translation useful. In his reply Buber thanked Torczyner for his candor and declared that, despite their different methods, he was united with him in the desire to win for Judaism a scientific exegesis of its Bible. Buber declared himself, in fact, an eager and grateful reader of Torczyner's writings and said that both he and Rosenzweig *had* profited from his textual criticism. He further declared himself one with him in his desire to build a serious scientific hermeneutic on no other ground than the biblical text, even though what that is might be debated. "All in all," Buber concluded, "the conditions for building a 'community in the midst of differences' were not unfavorable."

That a number of critics saw the translation as affected, "arty," and straining for effect is evident by the way in which some of its praisers defended it against these attacks. "Buber's translation at first gives the impression of a rare sublimity," wrote the German Protestant thinker Walter Nigg. It is wrong to call it "hieratic" and "aesthetic," Nigg insisted, or to regard it as a poetic re-creation. "On the contrary, the greatest faithfulness to the original predominates, because of which every trace of arid prosiness and bombastic grandiloquence was avoided." At the same time, Nigg conceded that the translation was not free from contrived word formations that did violence to the German language precisely because it was reaching back for the sensual basic meaning of the words. But Nigg rejected emphatically the reproof of a "tendency toward elegence." Buber succumbed to no self-aggrandizement; he produced no highfalutin language. On the contrary, he translated the "eternal words" with fear and trembling. At the foundation of each translated verse lie many considerations and a pronounced consciousness of responsibility. "With a splendid newness," Nigg concluded, "Buber's translation inserted the Bible into the world of the present in order that its timeless power show itself to the men of today. . . . The word opens itself to man with unexpected freshness, as Eastern as the first rays of the sun. Only in this way will he again hear the eternal voice of the Bible which, like a hammer, shatters the rocks and is able to break through the hard crust of the human heart. This is undoubtedly the finest thing that one can say in praise of the Buber translation."

SOURCES FOR CHAPTER 4 AND FOR NOTES TO CHAPTER 4:
The Buber-Rosenzweig Bible

Ernst Simon, "Martin Buber and German Jewry," in *Year Book III of the Leo Baeck Institute of Jews from Germany* (London: East & West Press, 1958), pp. 37 f.

Lambert Schneider, "Beginnen. 1925–1932," in Lambert Schneider, ed., *Rechenschaft über vierzig Jahre Verlagsarbeit 1925–1965. Ein Almanach* (Heidelberg: Verlag Lambert Schneider, 1966), pp. 10–12, 18–20.

Lambert Schneider, "Meine erste Begegnung mit Martin Buber," in *75 Jahre Sachse & Heinzelmann. Ein kleiner Almanach zum 1. November 1955*, ed. by Margarete Jockush (Hanover: Buchhandlung Sachse & Heinzelmann), pp. 21–24.

Martin Buber and Franz Rosenzweig, *Die Schrift und Ihre Verdeutschung* (Berlin: Schocken Verlag, 1936), Martin Buber, "Aus den Anfängen unserer Schriftübertragung: (February 1930), ("Aus den Anfängen" is not included in the Bible volume of Buber's *Werke*), pp. 316–21, 327 f.; Martin Buber, "Aus einem Brief an Hermann Gerson" (also not in Bible vol. of

Werke), pp. 350 f.; Buber and Rosenzweig, "Die Bible auf Deutsch. Zur Erwiderung" (1926) (also not in *Werke*), p. 291, my translation; Buber, "Eine Übersetzung der Bibel," pp. 307–09; Franz Rosenzweig, "Die Schrift und das Wort. Zur neuen Bibelübersetzung" (1925), pp. 76, 80 f., 83–87; Franz Rosenzweig, "Das Formgeheimnis der biblischen Erzählungen" (1928), pp. 249–54, 257–61; Rosenzweig, "Letter to Martin Goldner of June 23, 1927," pp. 335–37.

Franz Rosenzweig, "Jehuda Halevi, 92 Hymnen und Gedichte. Deutsch. Aus dem Nachwort, 1926" in Schneider, ed., *Rechenschaft,* pp. 26 f., 29–32.

Martin Buber, *Meetings,* ed. & trans. with an Introduction and Bibliography by Maurice Friedman (LaSalle, Ill.: Open Court Publishing Co., 1973), p. 21.

Franz Rosenzweig, *Briefe,* #421. To Martin Buber, January 25, 1925, p. 527; #430. To Buber, beginning of May, 1925, p. 533; #431. To Martin Buber, May, 1925, p. 533; #456. To Eugen Mayer, December 30, 1925, pp. 551 f.; #459. To Jacob Horovitz, January 3, 1926, p. 553; #442. To Martin Buber, June 29, 1925, p. 542; #446. To Martin Buber, August 2, 1925, p. 545; #537. To Martin Buber, August 18, 1929, p. 629; #447 To Martin Buber, September 21, 1925, p. 545 f., my translation. To Martin Buber, September 29, 1925, p. 546; #509. To Robert Arnold Fritzsche, September 5, 1927, p. 607; #485. To Ludwig Strauss, April 10, 1927, p. 579; #517. To Robert Arnold Fritzsche, April 18, 1928, p. 612; #538. To Gertrud Oppenheim, September 30, 1929, p. 650; #463. To Buber, January 28, 1926, pp. 557 f.; #455. To Buber, December 29, 1925, p. 551; #444. To Buber, July 29, 1925, p. 544; #469. To Buber, August 1926, p. 562; #508. To Buber, September 2, 1927, p. 606; #522. To August Mühlhausen, June 12, 1928.

The original German of the poem Rosenzweig sent Buber after the completion of "Im Anfang" reads:

> Dass aller Anfang Ende sei,
> ich habs erfahren.
> "Ins Leben" schrieb ich, schreibpflichtfrei,—
> nach knapp zwei Jahren
> ward lahm die tatgewillte Hand,
> die wortegewillte Zunge stand,
> so blieb mir nur die Schrift.
>
> Doch Anfang ward dies Ende mir:
> was ich geschrieben,
> ist kein—ich dank es, Lieber, dir—
> Geschreib geblieben.
> Wir schreiben Wort vom Anbeginn,
> Urtat die bürgt für Endes Sinn.
> Und so begann Die Schrift.

p. 544; #469. To Buber, August 1926, p. 562; #508. To Buber, September 2, 1927, p. 606; #522. To August Mühlhausen, June 12, 1928.

Hans Tramer, ed., *"Die Schrift"—Zum Abschluss ihrer Verdeutschung*, special printing of *"Mitteilungsblatt" (MB) des Irgun Olej Merkas Europa* (Tel Aviv: Bitaon Publishing Co., 1961), Eugen Mayer, "Der menschliche Hintergrund," p. 3; Gershom Scholem, "An einem denkwürdigen Tage," pp. 1 f.; Ernst Simon, "Ssijum—Schlusslernen," pp. 4 f.

Letters from Martin Buber to Franz Rosenzweig in Archives of the Leo Baeck Institute, New York City; Innsbruck, September 26, 1925; August 28, 1923; #676. undated.

Ernst Simon, "Martin Buber und das deutsche Judentum," in Robert Weltsch, ed., *Deutsches Judentum: Aufstieg und Krise: Gestalten, Ideen, Werke* (Stuttgart: Deutsche Verlags-Anstalt, 1963), p. 81.

Buber Briefwechsel II, #124. Franz Rosenzweig to MB, February 22, 1923, p. 159; #125. MB to Franz Rosenzweig, February 25, 1929, p. 159; #187. MB to Franz Rosenzweig, July 5, 1925, pp. 226 f.; #202. MB to Franz Rosenzweig, January 31, 1926, p. 242; #326. Alfred Mombert to MB, April 1, 1930, pp. 368 f.; #212. Gerhard Scholem to MB, Jerusalem, April 4, 1926, pp. 251–53; #216. MB to Gerhard Scholem, May 24, 1926, pp. 257 f.; #238. Gerhard Scholem to MB, April 10, 1930, pp. 371 f.; #331. MB to Gerhard Scholem, April 23, 1930, pp. 375 f.; #200. Rafael Buber to Martin and Paula Buber, Cottbus, January 2, 1926, p. 240; #224. MB to Samuel Joseph Agnon (Czaczkes), July 28, 1926, p. 266; #228. Benno Jacob to MB, September 28, 1926, pp. 269 f.; #241, #242. Rudolf Hallo to MB, March 19 and April 11, 1927, pp. 282 f.; #250. Alfred Jeremias to MB, September 5, 1927, p. 29; #332. Isaak Heinemann to MB, May 12, 1930, pp. 376 f.; #346. MB to Rudolf Borchardt, December 26, 1930, pp. 391–94 and note 9, pp. 394 f.; #379. Harry Torczyner to MB, May 23, 1932, pp. 428–31; #380. MB to Harry Torczyner, May 27, 1932, pp. 431 f.; #417. MB to Harry Torczyner, March 14, 1933, p. 472.

Karl Thieme, "Die Schrift-Übersetzung von Martin Buber und Franz Rosenzweig," *Freiburger Rundbrief*, Vol. XIV, No. 53/56 (September 23, 1962), pp. 35 f.

Benjamin Uffenheimer, "The Faith of Singularity" (in Hebrew), *Molad*, 1966.

Everett Fox, "We Mean the Voice: Toward a New Translation of the Bible," *Response: A Contemporary Jewish Review*, No. 12 (Winter 1971–72), pp. 32–38.

Ernst Simon, "Martin Buber and Judaism" (Hebrew), *Iyyun*, February 1958.

Martin Buber, *Werke*, Vol. II—*Schriften zur Bibel* (Munich: Kösel Verlag, Heidelberg: Lambert Schneider Verlag, 1964), "Über die Wortwahl in einer Verdeutschung der Schrift" (to the memory of Franz Rosenzweig), pp. 1112–14, 1116 f., 1119, 1121–29; "Die Sprache der Botschaft," pp. 1095 f., 1101; "Leitwortstil in der Erzählung des Pentateuchs," pp. 1132, 1134 f., 1139–41, 1149; "Das Leitwort unter der Formtypus der Rede. Ein Beispiel," p. 1157; "Zur Verdeutschung der Preisungen," p. 1159.

Martin Buber, *Tales of the Hasidim. The Later Masters*, trans. by Olga Marx (New York: Schocken Books [paperback], 1961), "Everywhere," p. 170.

Elie Wiesel, *The Oath*, trans. from the French by Marion Wiesel (New York: Random House, 1973).

In the Beginning. An English Rendition of the Book of Genesis by Everett Fox, based on the German version of Martin Buber and Franz Rosenzweig, with an Introduction by Nahum N. Glatzer, printed as the whole of issue No. 14 of *Response: A Contemporary Jewish Review* (Summer 1972), pp. 88–92.

The Portable Nietzsche, selected and trans., with an Introduction, Prefaces and Notes by Walter Kaufmann (New York: The Viking Press, 1945), p. 5.

Alfred Mombert Briefe, 1893–1942, selected and ed. by B. J. Morse (Heidelberg/Darmstadt: Verlag Lambert Schneider, 1961), Letter #96. To Martin Buber, Heidelberg, February 11, 1926, p. 70; #114. To Buber, November 1, 1927, pp. 80 f.; #117. To Buber, January 20, 1928.

Solomon Liptzin, *Germany's Stepchildren* (Philadelphia: The Jewish Publication Society, 1944), p. 256.

Emanuel bin Gorion, *Ceterum Recenseo. Kritische Aufsätze und Reden* (Tübingen: Alexander Fischer Verlag, 1939), pp. 28–38.

Walter Nigg, "Stelle Dein Wort sich ein, so verschlang ich es. Zu Martin Bubers Bibelübersetzung," in Hans M. Jürgensmeyer, ed., *Rückschau und Ausblick. Jakob Hegner zum achtzigsten Geburtstag* (Köln: Jakob Hegner Verlag, 1962), pp. 86–88.

Ernest M. Wolf, "Martin Buber and German Jewry," *Judaism,* Vol. I, No. 4 (October 1952), pp. 349 f.

Martin Buber, *A Believing Humanism: Gleanings,* trans. with an Introduction and Explanatory Comments by Maurice Friedman (New York: Simon & Schuster, 1967; Clarion Books-Touchstones, 1969), p. 33. For the German original of my translation see p. 32.

Maurice Friedman, *Touchstones of Reality: Existential Trust and the Community of Peace* (New York: E. P. Dutton, 1972; Dutton Paperbacks, 1974), Chap. 18, "Existential Trust: The Courage to Address and the Courage to Respond."

Martin Buber, *Israel and the World. Essays in a Time of Crisis,* 2d, enlarged edition (New York: Schocken Books, 1963), "The Man of Today and the Jewish Bible," pp. 89–102.

Buber, *Werke II—Schriften zur Bibel,* "Der Mensch von Heute und die jüdische Bibel," pp. 860–69. (This section of the essay is not included in the translation of "The Man of Today and the Jewish Bible" in *Israel and the World.*)

NOTE TO CHAPTER 5:
Tragedy, the "Suffering Servant," and Rosenzweig

In his note to the 1925 version of *The Tower,* T. S. Eliot wrote: "If *The Tower* is unplayable, we must attribute this not to failure of skill but to the fact that what the author wished here to express exceeded the limits within which the man of the theatre must work." Hamburger expresses himself very similarly: "Dramatically the earlier and richer version of *The Tower* almost exceeds the capacities of the stage as well as the capacities of most audiences. Yet in recent years it is the earlier version that has tempted producers, despite the technical difficulties." This delight in complex symbolism and dreamlike settings may explain, along with concern for preservation of the motifs of Sigismund's vulnerability, Hamburger's choice of the 1925 version of *The Tower* for translation in the volume of Hofmannsthal's *Selected Plays*. This does not mean that either he or Eliot regard *The Tower* merely as dramatic literature and not as theater. "Though the play may never become popular or frequent on the stage," Hamburger writes, " 'the fascination of what's difficult' should save it from being finally banished to the printed page."

Fortunately, the 1927 version of *The Tower* has since been published in English translation by Alfred Schwarz. Schwarz, like Buber, sees the 1925 version as raising "a historically conceived situation into the realm of myth." Again like Buber, Schwarz indicates how unbelievable the solution of the Children's King is following the terrors of the play up to that point. But unlike Buber, he finds a kind word for this sort of symbolic and allegorical nondrama as "a powerful gesture of faith, born out of a sense of despair." Hofmannsthal's own confession, which Schwarz quotes, "that it has something about it of a castle built over a bottomless void," seems a more honest recognition that *symbolic* faith born of *real* despair is not a powerful gesture but a weak one! Yet Schwarz recognizes that Hofmannsthal's thorough revision of the play for the theater might have been occasioned but not fundamentally motivated by Max Reinhardt's encouragement to shorten the tragedy and render it playable, and he recognizes the superior nature of the 1927 version as drama and as tragedy:

> He must first have yielded to a more radical voice of persuasion coming from himself. The play before us answers to a new mandate of poetic justice; it is an unflinching, historic testimony and a moving personal confession that the gathering night cannot be shut out. A more austere dramatic economy informs the revised version, and the action moves relentlessly to its stark conclusion.

What he does not recognize is that the "more radical voice of persuasion" of which he speaks did not come first from Hofmannsthal himself but from Buber, and that it was Hofmannsthal's carefully considered assent to Buber's criticism of the 1925 version that enabled him to go along with Max Reinhardt's suggestions for a radical revision of the play.

Martin Buber and the Theater, ed. and trans. with three introductory essays by Maurice Friedman (New York: Funk and Wagnalls, 1969), pp. 89–91. Since this book seems to be permanently out of print, it may be of help to the scholar if I repeat here the footnote that appears on page 42 after the statement: "What he does not recognize is that the 'more radical voice of persuasion' of which he speaks did not come in the first instance from Hofmannsthal himself but from Buber, and that it was Hofmannsthal's carefully considered assent to Buber's criticism of the 1925 version that enabled him to go along with Max Reinhardt's suggestions for a radical revision of the play."

The footnote reads: "Wishing to check further on the validity of these conclusions, I wrote to Dr. Rudolf Hirsch of Frankfurt am Main, Germany, who has the custody of Hugo von Hofmannsthal's papers. In a letter of May 1969 from Mallorca, Spain, Rudolf Hirsch replied:

" 'I published the Hofmannsthal-Buber correspondence in the *Neue Rundschau* really in order to show Buber's share in the second version of *The Tower* through his encouragement of changes which Hofmannsthal, although he perceived their necessity, found so difficult to make. A certain paradox, of course, lies in the fact that Buber, who must have had the greatest sympathy for the "Children's King," had now furthered the "darker mirror of time," as Hofmannsthal called the second *Tower* in a dedication to Thomas Mann. But Buber's dramaturgical sense, which Hofmannsthal prized—in an earlier letter Buber had characterized Hofmannsthal's play *Oedipus and the Sphinx* as the one great drama of the new century—felt that the way in which the play terminated— Sigismund still almost a saint, a martyr, and already replaced by a new *salvatio*—did injury to the tragedy. Hofmannsthal's complaints during the coming months over the formation of the fifth act (He called it a kind of return to an earlier version of the drama) are enormous. Yet he perceived the need of changes, then also sacrificed in consequence the gypsy.

" 'You comment rightly, that the expression "dramatic version," hence the form influenced by Reinhardt (who then *never* produced the play, not even after Hofmannsthal's death) is false and insufficient.

" 'I have not found a direct expression by Hofmannsthal to a third person about Buber's influence—but at that time Buber was important to him. The "Letter to Someone of the Same Age" printed in the volume of Hofmannsthal's Collected Works entitled *Aufzeichnungen* (Sketches), pp. 204 f., is directed to Martin Buber. And the end of February 1924 Hofmannsthal wrote to Buber, after the latter had congratulated him on his fiftieth birthday: "I thank you from my heart, dear Martin Buber, that you remember my birthday—as I never forget yours." ' " I am indebted to the Hofmannsthal scholar Professor Richard Exner of the University of California at Santa Barbara, who, being familiar with Dr. Hirsch's handwriting, kindly provided me with a typewritten transcript of this letter, and to Carl Burckhardt and Grete Schaeder.

In a letter to me of July 31, 1982, Grete Schaeder, who is probably the only person in the world with a comprehensive scholarly mastery and deep intuitive understanding of *both* Hugo von Hofmannsthal and Martin Buber, has written a comment on the relationship of the two men to *The Tower* that is so pregnant with meaning that I feel compelled to quote it here in full (in my translation from her German):

"Hofmannsthal and Buber: The general presupposition for both from their youth on is something Jewish-Austrian, then the way from the easy to the hard word [a reference to my chapter of that title in *Martin Buber's Life and Work: The Early Years*], from literature to genuine humanity. The young Buber enthusiastic over myth and saga felt Hofmannsthal's *Oedipus and the Sphinx* to be genuine tragedy although it remained with the bounds of Greek antiquity and did not belong to his world and time. By the time of *The Tower* both men were already simply concerned for the human: in *I and Thou* Buber had discovered something fundamental to all human beings. In *The Tower* Hofmannsthal brought the human into the full tension between the animal and spiritual greatness. With Sigismund, who is robbed of all human activity yet whose spirit remains indestructible, Buber must first of all have thought of Rosenzweig. Each tragedy must be seen within a spiritual order: for Buber this was the Bible and the destiny of the suffering servant. Hofmannsthal wanted to portray in his tragedy at once the human as such and the historical powers that manipulate it—the absolute kingship, the Church, which stands on the side of power but can also let it fall again, in Julian the great individuals for whom spirit and power are inseparable, and the rising revolution. Hofmannsthal was himself in the highest measure sensitive to the spiritual atmosphere of his time; he sensed something dark, threatening, revolutionary arising. He did not, to be sure, want to write a Christian tragedy, but he stood constantly in a Christian tradition and had earlier written the *Everyman* and the *Great Salzburg World Theater* in which allegorical figures symbolize the powers that determine the human. In a historical drama he could not employ allegorical figures, but he did not want to leave the play without hope. Buber, coming from his point of view, overestimated the messianic element in the first version, through his general Jewish sensitivity vis-à-vis the Christian messianic. Sigismund is also not in the first version the "messianically intended figure"—his tragedy is precisely, indeed, that what is bound to the situation wins the upper hand in him. In the military encampment he remains locked up in the solid tower of his inwardness, reads Plutarch and Marcus Aurelius; he remains the pupil of Julian, who had taught him: nothing is outside his own I, he cannot unite himself with the world, and so he succumbs to the 'vengeance of the material, maternal, timebound.' Even the children's king is not so unconditionally messianically intended: he is the new beginning who begins with each generation: 'Who still dwells in me whom I do not know,' says Sigismund. He is 'Christian hope,' as Eliot says (I have besides also worked on Eliot, who after 1945 was *the* poet for many of us and have also come to know him personally)—but it is, despite this, clear that he cannot be the redeemer—who will not think in connection with a children's king of the children's crusade of the Middle Ages? That the play in its first version is not entirely unsuited to be staged I have myself experienced in a performance in Göttingen. The state of balance of the first version was far closer to Hofmannsthal's nature than the second version in which Sigismund is only a sacrifice. Here, despite all the spiritual closeness that stands out in their exchange of letters, two religious traditions stand opposite each other in Hofmannsthal and Buber. One cannot, indeed, put that into bold enough relief."

Buber's central concern with the understanding of biblical messianism can be seen from a partial list of lectures that he noted around this time in a letter to Rosenzweig:

The Nameless Servant of God (Lehrhaus lecture)
The Messianic Mystery (Berlin address)
Messianism (university lecture)
The End-Time (Lehrhaus lecture)
The Messianic Promise of Our Life (address)
The Baal Shem (Lehrhaus lecture) I (about the messianic movement)

SOURCES FOR CHAPTER 5 AND FOR NOTE TO CHAPTER 5:
Tragedy, the "Suffering Servant," and Rosenzweig

Martin Buber, *Israel and the World*, "Biblical Leadership," pp. 1∠5–27, 130 f., 133; "The Faith of Judaism," p. 26.

Martin Buber, *Pointing the Way: Collected Essays*, ed. & trans. with an Introduction by Maurice Friedman (New York: Harper Torchbooks, 1963; Schocken Books, paperback, without my Introduction, 1974, "China and Us," pp. 124 f.; "Drama and Theater," pp. 63–66.

Letters from Martin Buber to Franz Rosenzweig #39–40; undated, #498; undated, #583; undated in Archives of the Leo Baeck Institute, New York City.

Buber, *Meetings*, "The Cause and the Person," pp. 37 f.

"Hugo von Hofmannsthal/Martin Buber. Briefe 1926–1928," *Die Neue Rundschau*, Vol. LXXIII (1962), pp. 757–61, my translations.

Buber Briefwechsel II, #210. MB to Hugo von Hofmannsthal, April 11, 1926, p. 250; #214. Hugo von Hofmannsthal to MB, Rodaun bei Wien, May 8, 1926, p. 255; #215. MB to Hugo von Hofmannsthal, May 14, 1926, pp. 255 f.; #219. Hugo von Hofmannsthal to MB, June 8, 1926, p. 260; #234. Hugo von Hofmannsthal to MB, December 19, 1926, pp. 274 f.; #235. MB to Hugo von Hofmannsthal, December 25, 1926, p. 276; #273. MB to Hugo von Hofmannsthal, February 21, 1928, pp. 311 f.; #226. Hans Trüb to MB, August 31, 1926, pp. 267 f.; #326. Alfred Mombert to MB, April 1, 1930, pp. 368 f.; #319. Hans Kohn to MB, Jerusalem, December 12, 1929, p. 360.

Hugo von Hofmannsthal, *Selected Plays and Libretti*, trans., ed., and introduced by Michael Hamburger (New York: Pantheon Books, 1936), Introduction by Michael Hamburger, pp. xvi, xxi f., xlviii, 1–liv; T. S. Eliot, "Note on 'The Tower,' " pp. lxxiii f.; pp. 173–378; Biographical Note by Herbert Steiner, pp. 827 f.; Textual Notes, p. 835.

Hugo von Hofmannsthal, *Dramen IV* (1958), Vol. XIV of Hofmannsthal, *Gesammelte Werke in Einzelausgaben*, ed. by Herbert Steiner (Frankfurt am Main:

S. Fischer Verlag), earlier version, pp. 7–208; later version, pp. 321–463.

Hugo von Hofmannsthal, *Three Plays: Death and the Fool, Electra, The Tower (1927)*, trans. with an Introduction by Alfred Schwarz (Detroit: Wayne State University Press, 1966), pp. 38 f. For the reader who enjoys cultural-historical connections, it is interesting to note that Schwarz acknowledges that in his introductory essay he follows the lead of Grete Schaeder, who wrote a long essay on the development of Hofmannsthal's understanding of tragedy in the stages of *The Tower*. Cf. Grete Schaeder, "Hugo von Hofmannsthal's Weg zur Tragödie (Die drei Stufen der Turm-Dichtung)," *Deutsche Vierteljahrschrift für Literaturwissenschaft und Geistesgeschichte*, Vol. XXIII (1949), pp. 306–50.

Martin Buber, *Daniel: Dialogues on Realization*, ed. & trans. with an Introductory Essay by Maurice Friedman (New York: Holt, Rinehart, & Winston, 1964; McGraw-Hill Paperbacks, 1965), IV. "On Polarity. Dialogue after the Theater," pp. 112–15.

Nahum Glatzer, *Franz Rosenzweig: His Life and Thought*, pp. 175 f.

Letter from Martin Buber to Maurice Friedman, December 1954.

Ernst Simon, "Martin Buber and Judaism" (Hebrew), *Iyyun*, February 1958.

Buber, *Der Jude und sein Judentum*, "Für die Sache der Treue" (end of 1929), pp. 816–18; "Rosenzweig und die Existenz" (December 1956), pp. 825–27.

Buber, *A Believing Humanism: Gleanings*, "After Death" (1927), p. 231.

Rosenzweig, *Briefe*, #478. To Martin Buber, end of December 1926, p. 571; #543. To Martin Buber, December 9, 1929, p. 633. See also p. 633, note 5, and p. 634.

Martin Buber and the Theater, ed. and trans. with three introductory essays by Maurice Friedman (New York: Funk and Wagnalls, 1969), Chap. 1: "Martin Buber and the Theater," by Maurice Friedman; Chap. 2: "Drama and the Theater: Buber and Hofmannsthal," by Maurice Friedman; Chap. 5: Buber, "Drama and the Theater"; Chap. 6: Buber, "Reach for the World, Ha-Bima!"

NOTE TO CHAPTER 6:
Religious Socialism and *Die Kreatur*

Note 1

The "signs of address" of which Buber speaks must not be understood as fixed signs with fixed meaning. They are simply the "speech" of the event to the unique person who receives it in unique presence. Of course, each person encases his or her self in an armor intended to ward off all signs—that is, to reassure himself that nothing that happens really concerns *him* as a person. The breaking through this armor to becoming aware of what addresses us as just the person that we are in this situation at this moment is the beginning of real faith: "Real faith—if I may so term presenting ourselves and receiving —begins when the dictionary is put down"; for what occurs to and speaks to me is a unique address that cannot be interpreted, explained, isolated, because it has never happened before, because "it is not a *what* at all, it addresses my very life. The true name of concrete reality is the creation which is entrusted to me and to every man." This voice cannot be heard above or alongside the every-day life but only in it. A man who comes to the gates of mystery to have direct contact with the God whose praise he has proclaimed in vain to mortals is told: "Turn back. . . . I have sunk my hearing in the deafness of mortals." Our meeting with God may come out of our mismeeting with persons: "True address from God directs man into the place of lived speech, where the voices of the creatures grope past one another, and in their very missing of one another succeed in reaching the eternal partner."

A new conception of ethics and responsibility emerges from this. Responsibility is brought out of the rarefied air of abstract morality into the place of lived speech where becoming aware is completed by responding, as the German succession of *Wort, Antwort,* and *Verantwortung* (word, answer, and responsibility) makes even more clear. If we do not wrap silence about us—"a reply characteristic of a significant type of the age"—if we dare to stammer a reply, however inarticulately, through our doing and our letting be, then we take our awareness and response into the substance of lived life in such a way that our existence is no longer a mere sum of disconnected moments but something on whose behalf we respond. A newly created reality has been laid in your arms; you take responsibility for it. A dog has looked at you, you take responsibility for its glance; a child has clutched your hand, you take responsibility for its touch; a host of people move about you, you take responsibility for their need.

SOURCES FOR CHAPTER 6 AND FOR NOTE TO CHAPTER 6:
Religious Socialism and *Die Kreatur*

• ——————————————————————————— •

Florens Christian Rang

Buber Briefwechsel, I—Grete Schaeder, "Martin Buber: Ein biographischer Abriss," pp. 85 f.
Briefwechsel, II, #146. Florens Christian Rang to MB, Braunfels, March 14, 1924; #169. MB to Emma Rang, Rome, October 12, 1924; #400. MB to Ernst Simon, Heppenheim, December 2, 1932.
MB to Franz Rosenzweig, June 13, 1924 in Archives of Leo Baeck Institute, New York City (The paragraph on Rang was not published with the rest of this letter in *Briefwechsel* II.).
Florens Christian Rang, *Deutsche Bauhütte. Ein Wort an uns Deutsche über mögliche Gerechtigkeit gegen Belgien und Frankreich und zur Philosophie der Politik. Mit Zuschriften von Alfons Paquet, Ernst Michel, Martin Buber, Karl Hildebrandt,*

Walter Benjamin, Theodor Spira, Otto Erdmann (Sannerz and Leipzig: Gemeinschafts-Verlag Eberhard Arnold, 1924).
MB to Florens Christian Rang in *ibid.*, pp. 182–84.
Personal conversation with Werner Kraft, Ph.D., Jerusalem, Israel, 1966.
Alfons Paquet, "Florens," *Die Kreatur*, Vol. I, No. 1 (Spring 1926), pp. 131–34.
Bernhard Rang, "Der katholische Protestant. Zeugnisse eines ökumenischen Christen," *Kunstwart* (February 1928), pp. 301–07.

Religious Socialism

Paquet, "Florens," p. 131.
Schaeder, "Martin Buber," *Briefwechsel* I, pp. 86 f.
Briefwechsel II, #121. MB to Leonhard Ragaz, Heppenheim, February 1, 1923, pp. 155 f. and note 2, p. 156; #131. MB to Leonhard Ragaz, Heppenheim, March 28, 1923, pp. 165 f.; #133. MB to Ernst Simon, Heppenheim, May 31, 1923, pp. 166 f.; #272. MB to Leonhard Ragaz, Heppenheim, February 20, 1928, p. 311; #364. MB to Hermann Gerson, Heppenheim, November 2, 1931, p. 413; #365. Hermann Gerson to MB, Berlin, November 4, 1931, p. 414; #366. MB to Hermann Gerson, November 21, 1931, p. 415; #399. MB to Leonhard Ragaz, Heppenheim, November 26, 1932, p. 451.
Ernst Simon, "Bridgebuilder: The Problem of Buber's Influence" (Hebrew), *Molad*, No. 115 (February or March 1958), trans., for me by Uri Margolin, revised, and paraphrased by me, Sec. III.
MB to Franz Rosenzweig, September 27, 1923, Archives of Leo Baeck Institute, New York City.
Martin Buber, "Religion und Gottesherrschaft, Besprechung von Leonhard Ragaz, *Weltreich, Religion und Gottesherrschaft,*" *Frankfurter Zeitung*, "Literaturblatt," No. 9, April 27, 1923.
Martin Buber, "Three Theses of a Religious Socialism" (1928), *Pointing the Way*, pp. 112–14.

Jewish-Christian Dialogue and Encounter before *Die Kreatur*

Schaeder, "Martin Buber," *Briefwechsel* I, pp. 88–91.
Ernst Simon, "Aufbau in Untergang," (See Sources for Chap. 11 below), pp. 5–7.
Briefwechsel II, #115. MB to Friedrich Gogarten, Heppenheim, December 20, 1922, p. 145; #116. MB to Friedrich Gogarten, December 22, 1922, p. 146 and note 1, p. 146; #165. MB to Eduard Strauss, Heppenheim, August 8, 1924, p. 207; #166. Eduard Strauss to MB, Frankfurt a. M., August 13, 1924, pp. 207 f.; #167. MB to Eduard Strauss, Ascona, August 15, 1924, p. 208; #168. Eduard Strauss to MB, August 26, 1924, pp. 209 f.; #172, Eugen Rosenstock-Huessy to MB, Breslaus, December 13, 1924, pp. 213–15; #174. MB to Chaim Weizmann, Heppenheim, January 12, 1925, pp. 215 f. and note 1, p. 216; #194. Hans Trüb to MB, Beinwil am See, August 12, 1925, p. 235; #195. MB to Hans Trüb, Heppenheim, August 14, 1925, pp. 235 f.; #196. Hans Trüb to MB, Zurich, September

9, 1925, pp. 236–38; #211. MB to Eduard Strauss, Heppenheim, April 16, 1926, p. 251; #356. Elisabeth Rotten to MB, Dresden, April 9, 1931, p. 404 and note 1, p. 404.
MB to Franz Rosenzweig, October 23, 1925, Archives of the Leo Baeck Institute, New York City.
Buber, *Der Jude und sein Judentum,* "Pharisäertum" (1925), pp. 221–30.

Die Kreatur

Schaeder, "Martin Buber," *Briefwechsel* I, pp. 91–96.
Viktor von Weizsäcker, *Begegnungen und Entscheidungen* (Stuttgart: K.F. Koehler Verlag, 1949), Chap. 1, "Nach dem ersten Weltkrieg," pp. 25–30.
Eugen Rosenstock-Huessy, "Rückblick auf 'Die Kreatur' " (1952), in *Rechenschaft über vierzig Jahre Verlagsarbeit 1925–1965,* pp. 95–105.
Simon, "Bridgebuilder: The Problem of Buber's Influence," Sec. III.
Die Kreatur. Eine Zeitschrift viermahl in Jahr erscheinend, ed. by Martin Buber, Joseph Wittig, and Viktor von Weizsäcker (Berlin: Lambert Schneider Verlag, 1926–1930, I-1926/1927, II-1927/1928, III-1929/1930).
Ibid., Vol. I, No. 1 (Spring 1926), pp. 1 f.
Eugen Rosenstock, "Lehrer oder Führer. Zur Polychronie des Menschen," *ibid.,* I, 1, pp. 52–68.
Joseph Wittig, "Das Geheimnis des 'Und,' " *ibid.,* II, 4, pp. 419–25.
Joseph Wittig, "Der Weg zur Kreatur," *ibid.,* III, 1 (1929), pp. 140–50.
Willy Haas and Martin Buber, "Ein Briefwechsel über die Zehn Gebote," *ibid.,* III, 3 (1929), pp. 290–92.
Briefwechsel II, #189. Viktor von Weizsäcker to MB, Heidelberg, July 12, 1925, pp. 229–31; #190. Joseph Wittig to MB, Breslau, July 28, 1925, pp. 231 f.; #192. MB to Joseph Wittig, August 3, 1925, pp. 232 f.; #206. Joseph Wittig to MB. Breslaus, February 26, 1926, p. 247 and note 1, p. 247; #209. Viktor von Weizsäcker to MB, Heidelberg, April 5, 1926, pp. 249 f. and note 3, p. 250; #217. Viktor von Weizsäcker to MB, Heidelberg, May 31, 1926, pp. 258 f.; #218. MB to Viktor von Weizsäcker, Heppenheim, June 1, 1926, pp. 259 f. and note 3 to p. 260; #220. MB to Ludwig and Eva Strauss, Heppenheim, June 12, 1926, p. 261; #223. MB to Franz Rosenzweig, Heppenheim, July 5, 1926, pp. 264 f.; #235. MB to Hugo von Hofmannsthal, Heppenheim, December 25, 1926, p. 276; #244. Viktor von Weizsäcker to MB, Heidelberg, June 20, 1927, pp. 285 f.; #245. Walter Benjamin to MB, Paris, July 26, 1927, pp. 286 f.; #330. Joseph Wittig to MB, Schlegel/Kr. Neurode, April 18, 1930, pp. 374 f. and note 1 to p. 374.
MB to Franz Rosenzweig (in Leo Baeck Archives, New York), June 19, 1925; July 21, 1925; July 31, 1925; undated, #604; December 16, 1926; June 4, 1927.
Die Kreatur, Vols. 1–3 (all publ.), Heidelberg, 1926–1930, 3 vols., clothbound has been reprinted by Kraus-Thomson Reprint, a Division of Kraus-Thomson Organization Ltd. Fl-9491, Nendeln, Liechtenstein, $70.00. The first paragraph of the notice in a catalog titled *German Expressionism, 20th Century* (reprinting 24 little magazines) reads: "*Martin Buber, Viktor*

von Weizsäcker and *Joseph Wittig* were the editors of this periodical which was published by *Lambert Schneider*, then still in Berlin. This timeless magazine carries on a conversation or dialogue about human life; it is a monument of communication between the Jewish, Protestant and Roman Catholic minds which was abruptly destroyed in 1933. Reading this fastidious magazine opens up an immediate picture of Germany's philosophical, religious and cultural problems between the two wars."

Jewish-Christian Dialogue during and after *Die Kreatur*

Briefwechsel II, #280. MB to Hans Trüb, Heppenheim, May 28, 1928, pp. 317 f. and note 1 to Brief 280, p. 317; #282. MB to Albert Schweitzer, Heppenheim, July 1, 1928, pp. 319 f.; #283. Ernst Michel to MB, Frankfurt a. M., August 7, 1928, p. 320; #290. Jakob Wilhelm Hauer to MB. Tübingen, December 31, 1928, pp. 326–28; #291. MB to Jakob Wilhelm Hauer, Heppenheim, January 3, 1929, pp. 328 f.; #292. MB to Theodor Bäuerle, Heppenheim, January 18, 1929, pp. 329 f. and note 1 to Brief 292, p. 329; #375. Hans Kosmala to MB, Bad Dürrenberg, April 18, 1932, pp. 425 f.; #276. MB to Hans Kosmala, Heppenheim, April 23, 1932, p. 427; #401. Albert Schweitzer to MB, December 3, 1932, p. 453; #402. MB to Albert Schweitzer, Heppenheim, December 5, 1932, p. 454; #403. MB to Hermann Gerson, December 23, 1932, pp. 454 f.; #405. Gertrud Bäumer to MB, Berlin, January 7, 1933, pp. 458 f. and notes 1 and 2 to p. 458; #407. MB to Hans Trüb, Heppenheim, February 15, 1933, p. 468.
Simon, "Buber as Bridgebuilder: The Problem of Buber's Influence."
Buber, "The Two Foci of the Jewish Soul" (1930), *Israel and the World*, pp. 28–40.
Buber, *Zwiesprache* (Berlin: Schocken Verlag, 1932).
Buber, *Between Man and Man*, "Dialogue," pp. 1–39.
Buber Briefwechsel I. Schaeder, "Abriss," pp. 98 f.
Buber Briefwechsel II, #393. Joseph Wittig to MB. Schlegel-Neusorge, September 6, 1932, pp. 445 f.; #398. MB to Ernst Simon, November 26, 1923, p. 450; #400. MB to Ernst Simon, December 2, 1932, pp. 451 f.
Ernst Simon, "Nationalismus, Zionismus and der jüdisch-arabische Konflikt in Martin Bubers Theorie und Wirksamkeit," *Bulletin des Leo Baeck Instituts*, Vol. IX, No. 33 (Tel Aviv, 1966), p. 36.

SOURCES FOR CHAPTER 7:
Martin Buber at Fifty

•————————————————————•

Buber at Fifty

Martin Buber, *The Origin and Meaning of Hasidism*, ed. and trans. with an Introduction by Maurice Friedman (New York: Horizon Press, 1972), "Spinoza, Saabatai Zvi, and the Baal-Shem," pp. 99, 104 f.

Men of Dialogue: Martin Buber and Albrecht Goes, ed. by E. William Rollins and Harry Zohn, Preface by Maurice Friedman (New York: Funk & Wagnalls, 1969), Albrecht Goes, "Martin Buber, A Living Legend," pp. 185 f.

Buber Briefwechsel II, #263. Hugo Bergmann to MB, Jerusalem, January 31, 1928; #265. Nelly Braude-Buber to MB, Lodz, February 5, 1928, pp. 303–06; #267. Lambert Schneider to MB, Berlin, February 7, 1928, p. 307; #268. Ernst Simon to MB, Frankfurt a. M., February 7, 1928, pp. 307 f.; #269. Ernst Joël to MB, Berlin, February 8, 1928, p. 308 f.; #270. Arthur Ruppin, Jerusalem, February 15, 1928, p. 309; #271. Mosche Y. Ben-Gavriêl to MB, Jerusalem, February 16, 1928, p. 310; #272. MB to Leonhard Ragaz, February 20, 1928, p. 311; #275. MB to Ernst Simon, February 28, 1928, p. 314; #278. MB to Hugo Bergmann, March 30, 1928.

Buber, Between Man and Man, "What Is Man?" p. 159.

Ernst Simon, "Martin Buber and German Jewry," loc. cit., pp. 8–10.

Der Jude. Sonderheft zu Martin Bubers 50. Geburtstag, 1928, Arnold Zweig, "Martin Buber, ein Mann von fünfzig Jahren," pp. 1–5; Adolf Böhm, "Idee und Organisation," pp. 20 f.; Markus Reiner, "Die Biologie des Zionismus," pp. 22–32; Robert Weltsch, "Zionismus als unenliche Aufgabe," pp. 37–40; Ernst Simon, "Zum Problem der jüdischen öffentlichen Meinung," pp. 49 f.; Siegried Lehmann, "Über die erzieherischen Kräfte von Erde und Volk," pp. 59, 67 f.; Hugo Bergmann, "Begriff und Wirklichkeit. Ein Beitrag zur Philosophie Martin Bubers und J. G. Fichtes," p. 101; Max Brod, "Zur Problematik des Bösen und des Rituals," p. 109; Friedrich Thieberger, "Die neue Gläubigkeit," pp. 111–13; Hermann Hesse, "Verwandtes," p. 166; Alfons Paquet, "Über Buber," p. 166.

Karl Joël, ed., Aus unbekannten Schriften. Festgabe für Martin Buber zum 50. Geburtstag (Berlin: Verlag Lambert Schneider, 1928), Karl Joël, "Vom Unbekannten," pp. 11–13; Joseph Wittig, "Aus dem Fragenbuche des Ambrosiasters," pp. 49 f.; Elisabeth Rotten, "Aus den Offenbarungen der Schwester Mechtild von Magdeburg," pp. 65 f.; Leonhard Ragaz, "Richard Rothe über Verweltlichung des Christentums," pp. 162–67; Max Brod, "Aus Franz Kafka Tagebüchern," p. 231; Franz Rosenzweig, "Aus Bubers Dissertation," p. 244.

S. Y. Agnon on Buber's fiftieth birthday in Davar (Hebrew), Literary Supplement, February 2, 1928. Quoted and paraphrased in Rivka Horwitz, Buber's Way to "I and Thou": An Historical Analysis and the First Publication of Martin Buber's Lectures "Religion als Gegenwart," Vol. VII of Phronesis: Eine Schriftenreihe (Heidelberg: Verlag Lambert Schneider, 1978), p. 201, note 15.

Das werdende Zeitalter (the German organ of the world union for renewal of education [International Circle of Workers]), ed. by Elisabeth Rotten and Karl Wilker), Vol. VII, No. 2 (February 1928). "Martin Buber zum fünfzigsten Geburtstag" (February 8, 1928), p. 33; Karl Wilker, "Religion, Politik, Erziehung," pp. 35–38; Martin Buber, "Kraft und Richtung, Klugheit und Weisheit" (from a letter), p. 98.

Wilhelm Michel, Martin Buber: wein Gang in die Wirklichkeit (Frankfurt am Main: Rütten & Loening, 1926).

Buber's Family and Friends

MB to Franz Rosenzweig, undated, #618, Archives of the Leo Baeck Institute, New York City.
Buber Briefwechsel II, #171. MB to Gerhard Scholem, December 13, 1924, p. 213; #198. Carl Buber to MB, Lvov, December 22, 1925, p. 239; #399. MB to Salman Schocken, November 11, 1930, p. 385; #362. MB to Hermann Gerson, October 7, 1931, p. 412; #119. MB to Ernst Elijahu Rappeport, January 14, 1923, p. 152.
MB to Franz Rosenzweig, April 7, 1928; December 16, 1926, Archives of the Leo Baeck Institute, New York City.
Buber Briefwechsel II, #170. MB to Louise Dumont-Lindemann, November 15, 1924, p. 212.
Buber Briefwechsel I, Grete Schaeder, "Abriss," pp. 82–84.
MB to Franz Rosenzweig, August 15, 1927, Archives of the Leo Baeck Institute, New York City.
Martin Buber, "Gedenkworte an Charlotte Kronstein geb. Landauer," gesprochen in Karlsruhe im Breslau am 16. August 1927. Written down by her husband Max Kronstein and presented to Buber in bound, handwritten booklet of fifteen pages on December 3, 1927. In Martin Buber Archives, National and Hebrew University Library, Jerusalem, Israel.
Buber Briefwechsel II, #258. MB to Hermann Hesse, December 12, 1927, p. 298; #264. MB to Hermann Hesse, February 2, 1928, pp. 302 f.; #377. MB to Hermann Hesse, May 3, 1932; #378. Hermann Hesse to MB, undated, p. 428; #230. Max Brod to MB, Prague, December 1, 1926, p. 272; #232. MB to Max Brod, December 4, 1926; #236. MB to Max Brod, January 22, 1927, p. 27 (selections from these last two letters were reprinted by Max Brod in his contribution to *Aus unbekannten Schriften*, p. 231); #233. Max Brod to MB, Prague, December 8, 1926, p. 274; #237. Max Brod to MB, January 25, 1927, pp. 277 f.; #350. Max Brod to MB, Prague, February 4, 1931.

Note A

Martin Buber, *Werke*, Vol. I—*Schriften zur Philosophie* (Munich: Kösel Verlag, Heidelberg: Verlag Lambert Schneider, 1962), p. 172. The original dedication of "Dialogue" (*Zwiesprache*) to Paula reads in German:

An P.
Der Abgrund und das Weltenlicht,
Zeitnot und Ewigkeitsbegier,
Vision, Ereignis und Gedicht:
Zwiesprache wars und ists mit dir.

Buber Briefwechsel II, #203. Hans Trüb to MB, Zurich, February 3, 1926, pp. 242–44; #285. MB to Hermann Gerson, z. Zt. Sils (Engadin), August 30, 1928, p. 322; #286. MB to Hans Trüb, October 2, 1928, pp. 322 f.; #287.

Hans Trüb to MB, Zurich, October 5, 1928, p. 323; Ludwig Binswanger to MB, Kreuzlingen, Switzerland, February 7, 1933, p. 462; #193. MB to Leopold Marx, August 8, 1925, pp. 233 f. and note 1; #204. MB to Leopold Marx, February 9, 1926, pp. 245 f.; #207. MB to Leopold Marx, March 21, 1926, pp. 247 f.; #337. MB to Robert Weltsch, October 21, 1930.

Judaism, Biblical and Modern

MB to Franz Rosenzweig, July 19, 1929, Archives of Leo Baeck Institute, New York City; *Buber Briefwechsel* II, #208. MB to Paula Buber-Winkler, March 25, 1926, pp. 248 f.; #339. MB to Salman Schocken, November 11, 1930, pp. 384 f.; #373. MB to Eduard Strauss, March 30, 1932, p. 423; #377. MB to Hermann Hesse, May 3, 1932, p. 427; #381. Joseph Wittig to MB. Schlegel/Kr. Neurode, June 1, 1932, pp. 433 f.; #382. Markus Ehrenpreis to MB, Stockholm, June 2, 1932, pp. 434 f.; #383. Emil Brunner to MB, Zurich, June 6, 1932, p. 434; #386. Leo Baeck to MB, Berlin, June 14, 1932, p. 437; #388. Hugo Hahn to MB, Essen, June 19, 1932, pp. 438 f.; #389. Gerhard Scholem to MB, Parma, June 29, 1932, pp. 439–41; #390. MB to Gerhard Scholem, July 1, 1932, pp. 441–43; #391. Arnold Zweig to MB, Berlin-Grunewald, July 1, 1932, pp. 443 f.; #392. Joseph Klausner to MB, Jerusalem, August 2, 1932, pp. 444 f.; #397. MB to Hermann Gerson, October 23, 1932, pp. 449 f.; Buber, *Israel and the World*, "Imitatio Dei," pp. 66–77; "The Faith of Judaism," pp. 13–27; "Why We Should Study Jewish Sources," pp. 146–48; Buber, *Der Jude und sein Judentum*, "Das Judentum und die neue Weltfrage," pp. 234–238; Alfons Paquet, "Martin Buber," in *Juden in der Deutschen Literatur*, ed. by Gustav Krojanker (Berlin: Sonderdruck für den Heine-Bund, 1926), pp. 165–78; Martin Buber, *The Kingship of God*, 3rd enlarged ed., trans. by Richard Scheimann (New York: Harper & Row, 1967, also Harper Torchbooks); Ernst Simon, "Nationalismus, Zionismus, und der jüdisch-arabische Konflikt in MB's Theorie und Wirksamkeit," *loc. cit.* 1924, p. 36.

Jewish Mysticism and Hasidism

Buber Briefwechsel II, #148. Gerhard Scholem to MB, Jerusalem, April 15, 1924, pp. 189–91; #149. MB to Gerhard Scholem, May 12, 1924, pp. 191 f.; #384. MB to Gerhard Scholem, June 10, 1932, pp. 435 f.; #173. Alfred Mombert to MB, Heidelberg, December 28, 1924, p. 215; #175. Shmuel Joseph Agnon to MB, Jerusalem, January 24, 1925; pp. 216 f.; #224. MB to Shmuel Joseph Agnon (Czaczkes), June 28, 1926, pp. 265 f.; #247. Shmuel Joseph Agnon to MB, Jerusalem, August 27, 1927, pp. 288 f.; #256. Agnon to MB, Jerusalem, November 14, 1927, p. 297; #277. MB to Agnon, March 30, 1928, p. 315; #355. MB to Simon Dubnow, April 3, 1931, p. 403; #374. MB to Agnon, April 12, 1932, pp. 424 f.; Martin Buber, *Hasidism and Modern Man*, ed. & trans. with an Introduction by Maurice Friedman (New York: Harper Torchbooks,

1960), Book V, "The Baal-Shem-Tov's Instruction in Intercourse with God," pp. 180 f., 196 f.; MB, "Ein Wort über den Chassidismus," *Theologische Blätter* (Marburg), ed. by Karl Ludwig Schmidt, Vol. III, No. 7 (July 1924).

Note B

Max Brod was deeply moved that to Buber too Kafka said something essential. The meaning of which Buber spoke Brod felt to be included in Kafka's works. The scurrilous form in which the "Court" or the "Castle" appears ought not blind us to the fact that they mean the highest world order—seen from a great distance, to be sure, or rather only sensed. Kafka was so reserved in his depths that the divinity that he so infinitely felt and witnessed in every trait of his being —making it perceptible to those around him as only a *zaddik* could do—he dared to describe only as something very distant, ungraspable, as something "not of our kind." That the hero of *The Trial* subjects himself to the Court, even though he disparages it and believes he has pushed it aside, is characteristic of Kafka's *humorous humility* (a witness also made by Kafka's close friend Felix Weltsch, who in 1960 gave me in Jerusalem the English manuscript of his book *Religion and Humor in the Life and Work of Franz Kafka*, published in German three years before).

SOURCES FOR CHAPTER 8:
Hermann Gerson and the Work Folk

• ——————————————————————— •

Ben Shemen

Siegfried Lehmann, "Das Kinder-Und Jugenddorf Ben-Schemen," *Das werdende Zeitalter*, Vol. VIII (1929), #2, pp. 90–98.

Youth Movements

Walter Z. Laqueur, *Young Germany. A History of the German Youth Movement* (London: Routledge & Kegan Paul, 1962), pp. 48, 81, 87, 115–18, 121.
George L. Mosse, *The Crisis of German Ideology. Intellectual Origins of the Third Reich* (New York: The Universal Library, Grosset & Dunlap, 1964), pp. 66, 182 f.; Victor Freud, A. H. Verband des Vereines Jüdischer Hochschüler "Bar Kochba" (Prague and Spolek Zidovskych Studentu "Theodor Herzl," V. Parze, in Israel, Tel Aviv, published by R. G. Pacovsky), p. 15; Eliyahu Maoz (Mosbacher), "The Werkleute," *Year Book V of the Leo Baeck Institute* (London: East & West Library, 1959), pp. 166–169.

Hermann Gerson and the Werkleute

Martin Buber, *Der Jude und sein Judentum*, "Volkserziehung als unsere Aufgabe," pp. 674–84.

Eliyahu Maoz, "The Werkleute," pp. 168–77; *Vom Werden des Kreises* (Werkleute Bund jüdischer Jugend, April 1934, Hermann zugeeignet), pp. 45–55, 71–77, 93–95, 100, 104–06, 109 f.; Menachem Gerson (Kibbutz Hazorea), "Encounter with Martin Buber," *AJR Information,* February 1963, p. 8; Menachem Gerson, "Martin Buber's Werk im Deutschen Judentum," *AJR Information,* August 1965, p. 9; personal conversations with Menachem Gerson and Eliyahu Maoz (Kibbutz Hazorea), Israel, Spring 1966; *Buber Briefwechsel* I, Schaeder, "Biographische Abriss," pp. 99 f.; *Buber Briefwechsel* II, #229; Hermann Gerson to MB, Berlin, November 25, 1926, pp. 270–72; #231. MB to Hermann Gerson, December 2, 1926, p. 272; #238. Hermann Gerson to MB, Berlin, January 29, 1927, pp. 278–80 and note 1, p. 279; #240. MB to Hermann Gerson, March 7, 1927, p. 281; #274. Moritz Spitzer to MB, Berlin, February 24, 1928, pp. 312 f.; #276. MB to Moritz Spitzer, March 3, 1928, pp. 314 f.; #285. MB to Hermann Gerson, z. Zt. Sils (Engadin), August 30, 1928, p. 322; #293. Hermann Gerson to MB, Stuttgart, March 28, 1929, p. 331; #294. MB to Hermann Gerson, April 4, 1929, pp. 331 f.; #300. MB to Franz Rosenzweig, Zurich, August 15, 1929, p. 339; #314. MB to Hermann Gerson, October 7, 1929, pp. 353 f.; #322. Hermann Gerson to MB, Berlin January 10, 1930, pp. 362–64 and note 4, p. 364; #324. Hermann Gerson to MB, Berlin, February 6, 1930, pp. 365–67; #340. Hermann Gerson to MB, Berlin, November 26, 1930, pp. 385–87; #341. MB to Hermann Gerson, November 27, 1930, p. 388; #342. MB to Hermann Gerson, November 29, 1930, pp. 388 f.; #343. Hermann Gerson to MB, Berlin, December 11, 1930, pp. 189 f.; #344. MB to Hermann Gerson, December 13, 1930, p. 390; #357. Hermann Gerson to MB, Berlin, May 3, 1931, pp. 405 f., #358. MB to Hermann Gerson, May 10, 1931, p. 407; #360. MB to Hermann Gerson, July 6, 1931, p. 410; #361. MB to Hermann Gerson, August 15, 1931, pp. 410 f.; #362. MB to Hermann Gerson, October 7, 1931, pp. 411 f.; #368. Hermann Gerson to MB, Berlin, November 29, 1931, pp. 418 f.; #385. Hermann Gerson to MB, Berlin, June 13, 1932, pp. 436 f.; #387. MB to Hermann Gerson, June 16, 1932, p. 438; #394. MB to Hermann Gerson, September 8, 1932, pp. 446 f.

SOURCES FOR CHAPTER 9:
The Hour and Its Judgment

•———————————————————————•

Nora Levin, *The Holocaust. The Destruction of European Jewry 1933–1945* (New York: Schocken Books, 1973), Chap. 4, "The Jews of Germany: 1933–1938," pp. 62–73.

Georg Munk (Paula Buber), *Muckensturm. Ein Jahr im Leben einer kleinen Stadt* (Heidelberg: Verlag Lamberg Schneider, 1953).

Newsweek Archives, "Forty Religion Woodward," June 17, 1965, 2:02 P.M., by courtesy of Kenneth Woodward, Religion Editor.

William L. Shirer, *The Rise and Fall of the Third Reich: A History of Nazi Germany* (New York: Simon & Schuster, 1960), p. 251.

Robert Weltsch, "Nachwort" to Hans Kohn, *Martin Buber*, p. 491.

Shmuel Y. Agnon, "For the Sake of Those Who Should Know Buber and Do Not Know Him" (in Hebrew), *Ha–aretz* (Tel Aviv), February 7, 1958.

Buber Briefwechsel II, #411. MB to Ernst Simon, February 14, 1933, pp. 465–67; #421. MB to Ernst Simon, March 28, 1933, p. 475; #422. Nikolaus Ehlen to MB, April 2, 1933, p. 476; #424. Emil Brunner to MB, April 10, 1933, p. 477; #427. Nahum Glatzer to MB, April 27, 1933, p. 479; #428. Max Picard to MB, May 1, 1933, p. 480; #429. MB to Nahum Glatzer, Zurich, May 4, 1933, p. 481; #430. Gustav Lindemann to MB, May 15, 1933, pp. 481 f.; #433. Joachim Ungnad to MB, May 31, 1933, p. 484; #439. Nahum Glatzer to MB, June 18, 1933, p. 490; #442. MB to Hans Trüb, June 22, 1933, p. 493; #461. Elisabeth Rotten to MB, December 31, 1933, pp. 514 f.; #464. Elisabeth M. to MB, January 6, 1934, pp. 532 f.; #478. MB to Hugo Bergmann, April 27, 1934, p. 563; #488. Albrecht Goes to MB, August 4, 1934, pp. 547 f. and p. 549, note 2; #503. Ernst Michel to MB, March 26, 1935, pp. 563 f.; #509. MB to Hans Trüb, Zurich, July 24, 1935, pp. 567 f.; #512. MB to Hans Trüb, August 2, 1935, p. 570; #550. MB to Hans Trüb, October 9, 1936, p. 611; #554. MB to Hans Trüb, p. 615; #562. MB to Hermann Hesse, Lvov, December 1, 1936, pp. 626 f.; #565. MB to Rudolf Pannwitz, January 1, 1937, p. 629 and note 1; #566. MB to Hermann Gerson, January 5, 1937, p. 631; #571. MB to Rudolf Pannwitz, February 4, 1937, p. 638.

Grete Schaeder, ed. and Introducer with the advice of Ernst Simon and in cooperation with Rafael Buber, Margot Cohn, and Gabriel Stern, *Martin Buber: Briefwechsel aus sieben Jahrzehnten*, Vol. III—*1938–1965* (Heidelberg: Verlag Lambert Schneider, 1975), #16. MB to Eduard Strauss, Jerusalem, January 8, 1939, p. 19.

Martin Buber, *Der Jude und sein Judentum*, "Der jüdische Mensch von Heute" (April 1933), p. 557; "Die Kinder" (May 1933), pp. 583–85; "Gericht und Erneurung" (September 1933), pp. 586–88; "Der Jude in der Welt" (January 1934), pp. 216–20; "Worauf es Ankommt" (June 1934), p. 591; "Erkenntnis tut Not" (Spring 1935), pp. 594–96; "Das Ende der deutsche-jüdischen Symbiose" (January 1939), pp. 644–46; "Brief an Gandhi" (February 1939), pp. 629–31; "Sie und Wir" (November 1939), pp. 648–54.

E. William Rollins and Harry Zohn, eds., *Men of Dialogue*, Martin Buber, "The Children" (1933), pp. 225–28; Albrecht Goes, "Martin Buber: Our Support," pp. 12 f.; MB, "The End of the German-Jewish Symbiosis" (1939), pp. 232–35; MB, "They and We" (on the first anniversary of *Kristallnacht*, November 1939), pp. 236–40, 42.

Buber, *Israel and the World*, "In the Midst of History" (Summer 1933), pp. 78–82; "The Jew in the World," pp. 167–72; "The Prejudices of Youth" (1937), pp. 47–52.

The account of Buber's defense of Christianity at Ascona was told me by Professor Fredric Spiegelberg of Stanford University in 1961.

Buber, *Die Stunde und die Erkenntnis. Reden und Aufsätze 1933–1935* (Berlin: Schocken Verlag, 1936), "Vorwort" (Spring 1936), pp. 7–9.

Aus Tiefen Rufe Ich Dich. 23 Psalmen in der Urschrift mit der Verdeutschung von Martin Buber. Bücherei des Schocken Verlags/51 (Berlin: Schocken Verlag, 1936), "Vorwort" by MB, pp. 6–8.

Buber, *Between Man and Man*, "Dialogue," pp. 32 f.

Buber, *Pointing the Way*, "Letter to Gandhi," pp. 139–41.

Konstantin Prinz von Bayern, *Die Grossen Namen. Begegnungen mit bedeutenden Deutschen unserer Zeit* (Munich: Kindler Verlag, 1956), pp. 75–78.

Werner Kraft, *Gespräche mit Martin Buber* (Munich: Kösel Verlag, 1966), pp. 13, 23, 110 f.

Max Picard, *Hitler in Ourselves* (Chicago: Henry Regnery, 1947), p. 125.

Paul Arthur Schilpp and Maurice Friedman, eds., *The Philosophy of Martin Buber* volume of The Library of Living Philosophers (LaSalle, Ill.: Open Court Publishing Co. and Cambridge University Press, 1967), Maurice Friedman, "The Bases of Buber's Ethics," p. 198; Martin Buber, "Replies to My Critics," trans. by Maurice Friedman, pp. 725 f.

Martin Buber, "Erinnerung an die Katastrophe," *Der Zeitgeist. Halbmonats-Beilage des "Aufbau" für Unterhaltung und Wissen*, No. 208, December 20, 1963, p. 18.

Ernest M. Wolf, "Martin Buber and German Jewry, Prophet and Teacher to a Generation in Catastrophe," *Judaism*, Vol. I, No. 4 (October 1952), pp. 351 f.

SOURCES FOR CHAPTER 10:
Jewish-Christian "Dialogue"

• —————————————————————————— •

Friedrich Hielscher, *Fünfzig Jahre unter Deutschen* (Hamburg: Rohwolt Verlag, 1954), pp. 222–24.

Eugene Jolas, ed., *Transition 1932*, No. 21 (March 1932) (The Hague: The Servire Press).

Maurice Friedman, "Introductory Note" to Martin Buber, "Church, State, Nation, Jewry," in David W. McKain, ed., *Christianity. Some Non-Christian Appraisals* (New York: McGraw-Hill Paperbacks, 1964), p. 175.

Buber, *Der Jude und sein Judentum*, "Kirche, Staat, Volk, Judentum," pp. 558–70. Cf. Buber, "Church, State, Nation, Jewry," trans. by William Hallo in McKain, *Christianity. Some Non-Christian Appraisals*, pp. 176–88.

Karl Ludwig Schmidt and MB, "Kirche, Staat, Volk, Judentum, Zwiegespräch im jüdischen Lehrhaus in Stuttgart am 14. Januar 1933," *Theologische Blätter*, Vol. XII, No. 9 (September 1933), columns 257–74.

Nora Levin, *The Holocaust*, pp. 70 f.

Buber, *Briefwechsel* II, #405. Gertrud Bäumer to MB, January 7, 1933, pp. 458 f.; #406. Karl Ludwig Schmidt to MB, January 12, 1933, pp. 460 f.; #407.

Karl Ludwig Schmidt to MB, January 28, 1933, p. 461; #416. Karl Ludwig Schmidt to MB, February 23, 1933, p. 471; #415. MB to Hermann Gerson, February 18, 1933, p. 470.

Buber, *A Believing Humanism*, "On the Ethics of Political Decision," pp. 205–10.

Briefwechsel II, #420. Jakob Wilhelm Hauer to MB, March 23, 1933, pp. 472 f.; #436. Gerhart Kittel to MB, June 13, 1933, pp. 486 f.; #437. MB to Gerhart Kittel, pp. 487 f.; #446. Karl Ludwig Schmidt to MB, June 26, 1933, pp. 496 f. and note 4, p. 497; #450. Ernst Lohmeyer to MB, August 19, 1933, pp. 499–501; #451. Gerhard Scholem to MB, August 24, 1933, p. 502; #545. Karl Ludwig Schmidt to MB, September 14, 1936, pp. 607 f.; #546. MB to Karl Barth, September 16, 1936, p. 608; #547. Karl Barth to MB, pp. 608 f.; #548. MB to Karl Barth, September 21, 1936, p. 610; #557. Wilhelm Michel to MB, November 15, 1936, pp. 619 f.; #559. Hermann Herrigel to MB, November 19, 1936, pp. 623 f.; #560. MB to Hermann Herrigel, November 20, 1936, pp. 624 f. and note 1 to p. 624 and note 3 to p. 625; #561. Albert Schweitzer to MB, November 27, 1936, pp. 625 f.; #563. Emil Brunner to MB, December 10, 1936, p. 627.

Buber, *Der Jude und sein Judentum*, "Brief an Ernst Michel," pp. 619 f.; "Offener Brief an Gerhard Kittel," pp. 621–24; "Zu Kittels 'Antwort,'" pp. 625–27.

Martin Buber, *Briefwechsel aus sieben Jahrzehnten*, ed. by Grete Schaeder, Vol. III: *1938–1965* (Heidelberg: Verlag Lambert Schneider, 1957), #89. MB to Adolf Sindler, Jerusalem, July 19, 1946, p. 111.

Werner Kraft, *Gespräche mit Martin Buber*, pp. 44 f.

Buber, *Between Man and Man*, "Foreword," p. xi; "The Question to the Single One," pp. 40–82.

NOTE TO CHAPTER 11:
Jewish Education as Spiritual Resistance

The Schocken Verlag under Spitzer's direction brought out the first four volumes of Franz Kafka's collected works. Klaus Mann, the son of the great German writer Thomas Mann, wrote a review of these volumes, saying that they came from the "ghetto" of Jewish publishing that was happy not to belong to the general trend of Germany at that time. Then a Nazi interdiction came. From then on, Kafka had to be published by a publisher in Prague, but a personal agreement with a Prague lawyer enabled Schocken to bring out the rest clandestinely in the original edition. After *Kristallnacht*, Spitzer went to London to meet father Schocken and told him that the time had come to liquidate and save what stock he could. Schocken said, "Look for a man who can continue. You are a pessimist." When Spitzer got back to Germany, the order to liquidate had already arrived. When Spitzer left Germany for Palestine in 1939, he brought with him 155 tons of stock. He sold the books to a clandestine organization for very little money. This remarkable transaction was made possible by the Nazi Propaganda Ministry. Spitzer was *persona grata* with the Jewish Department of the Ministry, for Buber and Rosenzweig had very good moral standing with the young intellectuals in the Jewish Ministry. It was they who helped Spitzer. But Schocken complained about having to pay for the transportation of books and for warehouses!

SOURCES FOR CHAPTER 11 AND FOR NOTE TO CHAPTER 11:
Jewish Education as Spiritual Resistance

• ——————————————————————— •

Buber Briefwechsel II—#418. Robert Weltsch to MB, March 22, 1933, p. 472; #419. MB to Hermann Gerson, March 24, 1933, pp. 472 f. and note 2, p. 473; #426. MB to Nahum Glatzer, April 24, 1933, p. 479; #431. MB to Hermann Gerson, May 29, 1933, p. 482; #432. MB to Ernst Simon, May 30, 1933, p. 483; #434. MB to Hermann Gerson, June 1, 1933, p. 485; #435. Hermann Gerson to MB, June 13, 1933, p. 486; #438. MB to Hermann Gerson, June 15, 1933, p. 489; #440. Leo Baeck to MB, June 21, 1933, p. 491; #441. MB to Leo Baeck, June 22, 1933, p. 491 f.; #456. MB to Otto Hirsch, December 5, 1933, pp. 507–09; #458. Leo Baeck to MB, December 14, 1933, p. 510; #459. Ismar Elbogen to MB, December 15, 1933, pp. 511–13; #460. Otto Hirsch to MB, December 26, 1933, p. 513; #462. Leo Baeck to MB, December 31, 1933, pp. 515 f.; #463. Chaim Weizmann to MB, January 4, 1934, p. 516; #471. MB to Otto Hirsch, March 1, 1934, pp. 527–29; #485. MB to Paula Buber-Winkler, Lehnitz, July 5, 1934, p. 541; #487. Martin Plessner to MB, July 29, 1934, pp. 545 f.; #502. Ernst Simon to MB, January 20, 1935, p. 562; #513. Eduard Strauss to MB, August 18, 1935, pp. 570 f.; #591. Ernst Kantorowicz to MB, February 7, 1938, p. 656.

Robert Weltsch, "Tragt ihm mit Stolz, den gelben Fleck!" *Jüdische Rundschau,* April 4, 1933.

Werner Kraft, "Gedenkrede auf Martin Buber," *MB (Mitteilungsblatt). Wochenzeitung des Irgun Olej Merkas Europa* (Tel-Aviv), Vol. XXIV, No. 24 (June 17, 1966), p. 10.

Menachem Gerson (Kibbutz Hazorea), "Martin Buber's Werk im deutschen Judentum," *AJR Information,* August 1965, p. 9.

Ernest M. Wolf, "Martin Buber and German Jewry," *Judaism,* Vol. I, No. 4 (October 1952), pp. 351 f.

Buber, *Der Jude und sein Judentum,* "Entwürfe und Programme. Zwei Vorschläge" (May 1933), pp. 608–10; "Unser Bildungsziel" (June 1933), pp. 597–601; "Programmerklärung des Frankfurter Lehrhauser" (November 1933), pp. 616–18; "Aufgaben jüdischer Volkserziehung" (November 1933), pp. 604 f.; "Jüdische Erwachsenbildung" (May 1934), pp. 604 f.; "Zwei Briefe an Dr. Otto Hirsch" (December 5, 1933; March 1, 1934), pp. 611–15.

Fritz Friedlander, "Trials and Tribulations of Jewish Education in Nazi Germany," in *Leo Baeck Yearbook III—Men and Epochs in German Jewry* (London: East & West Library, 1958), pp. 189–201.

Max Gruenewald, "The Beginning of the 'Reichsvertretung' " in *Leo Baeck Yearbook I*, ed. by Robert Weltsch (London: East & West Library, 1956), pp. 57–67.

Robert Weltsch, "Nachwort" to Hans Kohn, *Martin Buber*, pp. 424–26.

Ernst Simon, *Aufbau im Untergang. Jüdische Erwachsenbildung im national-sozialistischen Deutschland als geistiger Widerstand.* Schriftenreihe wissenschaftlicher Abhandlungen des Leo Baeck Institute of Jews from Germany, #2 (Tübingen: J. C. B. Mohr [Paul Siebeck], 1959), pp. ix–103.

Ernst Simon, "Jewish Adult Education in Nazi Germany as Spiritual Resistance," in *Leo Baeck Yearbook I*, pp. 68–104.

Ernst Simon, "Martin Buber and Judaism" (Hebrew), *Iyyun*, February 1958.

Buber, "Education and World View" in *Pointing the Way*, pp. 98–105.

Buber, "Teaching and Deed" in *Israel and the World*, pp. 137–45.

Heinz Politzer, "The Humanism of Martin Buber" (unpublished mimeographed ms., Oberlin College, 1955), p. 3.

Schalom Ben-Chorin, "Martin Buber in München. Erinnerungen," in *München ehrt Martin Buber* (Munich: Ner-Tamid-Verlag, 1961), pp. 41–45.

Buber, "Die Tugend der Propaganda, zum 50. Geburtstag Kurt Blumenfelds," *Jüdische Rundschau*, Vol. XXXIX, No. 43 (May 29, 1934).

Buber, "The Power of the Spirit," in *Israel and the World*, pp. 173–82.

Baruch Kurzweil, "Buber: The Great Teacher" (in Hebrew), *Ha-aretz* (Tel Aviv), February 7, 1958.

Personal conversation with Dr. Moritz (Moshe) Spitzer, Jerusalem, Israel, 1966.

"Martin Buber schreibt Uns," *Jüdische Rundschau*, Vol. XL, No. 31/32. 40 Jahre Sonder-Ausgabe (April 17, 1935).

Robert Weltsch, "Martin Buber zu seinem 60 Geburtstag" and Ludwig Feuchtwanger, "Der Erzieher. Bubers Wirksamkeit unter den Juden in Deutschland seit 1933," *Jüdische Rundschau*, Vol. XLIII, No. 17 (March 1, 1938), pp. 3 f.

Buber, "Robert Weltsch zum 70. Geburtstag," *MB (Mitteilungsblatt)*, Vol. XXIX, No. 24 (June 16, 1961), p. 3.

Nora Levin, *The Holocaust*, pp. 71 f.

Werner Kraft, *Gespräche mit Martin Buber*, pp. 30 f., 45, 83, 87.

Buber, "In Theresienstadt. Leo Baeck-Siebzig Jahre," *MB (Mitteilungsblatt)* Vol. VII, No. 21 (May 1943), p. 1.

Ernst Simon, "Einst and Jetzt. Martin Buber über den Makkabäerkampf," *MB (Mitteilungsblatt)*, Vol. V, No. 1 (January 3, 1941), p. 3.

Buber, "Erinnerung an die Katastrophe," *Aufbau-Zeitgeist*, No. 208 (December 20, 1963), p. 18.

Roy Oliver, *The Wanderer and the Way: The Hebrew Tradition in the Writings of Martin Buber* (Ithaca, N.Y.: Cornell University Press, 1968; London: East & West Library, 1968), p. 8.

Ernst Simon, "Lerntag," quoted in Leonard Baker, *Days of Sorrow and Pain: Leo*

Baeck and the Berlin Jews (New York: The Macmillan Co., 1978; London: Collier Macmillan Publishers, 1978), p. 176. For further discussion of Buber's and Baeck's work together at this time, see pp. 176–80, 184, 195.

SOURCES FOR CHAPTER 12:
Last Years in Germany

• ———————————————————————— •

Buber Briefwechsel II—#428. Max Picard to MB, May 1, 1933, p. 480; #468. Kurt Singer to MB, February 16, 1934, p. 523; #500. MB to Albert Schweitzer, undated, p. 561; #501. Albert Schweitzer to MB, January 15, 1935, p. 562; #504. Max Brod to MB, May 3, 1935, p. 564; #505. MB to Max Brod, undated, pp. 564 f.; #506. Leo Baeck to MB, May 21, 1935, p. 565; #509. MB to Hans Trüb, Zurich, July 24, 1935, p. 568; #515. MB to Hans Trüb, September 30, 1935, pp. 573 f.; #510. Abraham J. Heschel to MB, July 24, 1935, pp. 568 f.; #522. David Baumgardt to MB, January 29, 1936, pp. 580 f.; #524. MB to Eduard Strauss, February 13, 1936, p. 583; #525. Emil Brunner to MB, February 14, 1936, p. 584; #533. Ernst Michel to MB, May 2, 1936, pp. 594 f.; #535. MB to Hans Trüb, June 13, 1936, p. 596; #536. Hans Trüb to MB, June 17, 1936, p. 597; #538. MB to Hans Trüb, June 25, 1936, p. 598; #542. Martin Dibelius to MB, August 5, 1936, p. 602; #421. MB to Ernst Simon, March 28, 1933, p. 475; #537. MB to Hermann Gerson, June 18, 1936, p. 598; #551. MB to Ernst Simon, October 13, 1936, p. 612; #550. MB to Hans Trüb, October 9, 1936, p. 611; #552. MB to Ludwig Binswanger, October 23, 1936, pp. 613 f.; #554. MB to Hans Trüb, October 31, 1936, p. 615; #555. Hans Trüb to MB, November 3, 1936, pp. 616–18; #556. MB to Hans Trüb, November 7, 1936, p. 618; #559. Hermann Herrigel to MB, November 19, 1936, pp. 621 f.; #563. Emil Brunner to MB, December 10, 1936, p. 627; #565. MB to Rudolf Pannwitz, January 1, 1936, pp. 630 f. and note 5 to p. 630; #567. MB to Hans Kosmala, January 27, 1937, p. 623; #569. MB to Erwin Reisner, February 1, 1937, p. 634; #571. MB to Rudolf Pannwitz, February 4, 1937, p. 637; #573. Rudolf Pannwitz to MB, February 20, 1937, pp. 641 f. #574. MB to Rudolf Pannwitz, February 26, 1937, p. 642; #577. MB to Hermann Gerson, April 23, 1937, pp. 644 f.; #578. MB to Hermann Hesse, Jerusalem, June 27, 1937, p. 645; #579. Hermann Hesse to MB, August 2, 1937, pp. 645 f.; #585. Leo Baeck to MB, January 22, 1938, p. 651.

Martin Buber, *The Origin and Meaning of Hasidism*, ed. and trans. with an Introduction by Maurice Friedman (New York: Horizon Press, 1973), "Symbolic and Sacramental Existence in Judaism," pp. 152–81.

Martin Buber, *Kingship of God*, 3rd, newly enlarged ed., trans. by Richard Scheimann (New York: Harper & Row, 1967), "Preface to the Second Edition," pp. 21–46.

Martin Buber, *On the Bible. Eighteen Studies*, ed. by Nahum N. Glatzer (New York:

Schocken Books, 1968), "Samuel and the Ark (I Samuel)," pp. 131–36; "The Election of Israel: A Biblical Inquiry (Exodus 3 and 19; Deuteronomy)," pp. 80–92.

Martin Buber, *Werke* II. *Schriften zur Bible*, "Der Gesalbte," pp. 724–846.

Martin Buber, "Ein Wort an Dr. Joachim Prinz," *Israelitisches Familienblatt*, Vol. XXXVIII, No. 32 (August 6, 1936), and Buber, "Auf den Ruf hören (Schlusswort im Gespräch Martin Buber–Joachim Prinz)," No. 33 (August 13, 1936).

NOTE TO CHAPTER 13:
Ascent to the Land

Because of the objections of the Orthodox to Buber's being appointed as professor of religion, it had been proposed instead that he be given a professorship in the philosophy of education. At the meeting of the Board of Governors in Lucerne in September 1935 this proposal was rejected because the most important persons were absent. But in the evening session the fight was taken up again by Magnes, Schocken, and Felix Warburg, the American philanthropist. Schocken, in particular, made a speech about Buber as a person that made a great impression. The strong opposition to this particular appointment did not prevent the Board of Governors from agreeing unanimously that Buber should be appointed to some post, with the question as to the designation left open. Magnes wanted to go back to comparative history of religion, whereas others suggested ethics and social philosophy or social and cultural philosophy. At the same time, there was a shakeup in the power structure of the university. From being the chancellor of the university, Magnes was "kicked upstairs" to the less powerful position of president, after Chaim Weizmann had declined to take it. Schocken became chairman of the Executive Committee and took over the business of governing, and it was agreed that every two years a rector and deacon should be chosen by the university itself. About this development, Martin commented in a letter written to Paula from Lucerne, "Weizmann at any rate is now again wholly the politician, as I had foreseen."

The next day Buber wrote Scholem a description of the University chair as he saw it. He had no objection, he said, to expanding the term "social philosophy" into "general sociology." Whatever the designation, he saw the task of the discipline as including:

1. The essence, structure, and dynamics of societal life and of individual societal forms,
2. the relationships of persons to one another in the different orderings and formations of the society,
3. the reciprocal relationships between the persons and the social orderings and formations,
4. the relationships of the social forms among one another, whereby also

especially to be studied are the intermediate groups, on the one side, and the institutions, on the other,

5. the reciprocal relation between social facts and social norms,
6. the reciprocal relation between the society and the intellectual life, including its individual spheres:
   a. the societal strata and orderings and the national culture,
   b. the pedagogical problems of the society,
   c. religion and society,
   d. the social and political moment in public life.

While Schocken informed Buber that he had proposed that he receive 500 pounds salary a year plus an additional 50 pounds for traveling expenses, what took place behind the scenes was by no means smooth sailing. There were protracted and angry interchanges between the American Friends of the Hebrew University, Magnes, and others as to whether general funds of the AFHU could be earmarked for German professors and specifically for Buber's salary. There was also an unpleasant interchange between Magnes and Schocken as to whether Magnes was, in fact, obliged to raise half of the proposed salary. Finally, Schocken agreed to raise the whole salary from German funds over and above the budgeted contribution from Germany. In 1936, Buber received a letter from Hebrew University confirming that the Board of Governors of the Hebrew University had named him as professor for a temporary chair in social philosophy beginning the winter semester of 1936/1937 academic year. In September, Bergmann wrote Buber that the Executive Council had ratified the decision at Lucerne so that it had now become a fact—"for us a great event desired for long years."

SOURCES FOR CHAPTER 13 AND FOR NOTE TO CHAPTER 13:
Ascent to the Land

• ———————————————————— •

Immigration to Palestine of Gerson and the Work Folk, Rafael, and Eva

Vom Werden des Kreises (Berlin: Werkleute Bund jüdischer Jugend, April 1934), dedicated to "Hermann."

Hermann Gerson, *Werkleute. Ein Weg jüdischer Jugend,* ed. by the Bundesleitung der "Werkleute" Bund jüdischer Jugend (Berlin: Komissionsverlag Kédem, 1935), "Unsere innerjüdische Stellung," pp. 13 f., 22–27; "Probleme jüdischer Jugend," dedicated to "my teacher Martin Buber," pp. 51, 81 f., 87–90, 93.

Eliyahu Maoz (Mosbacher), "The Werkleute" in *Year Book IV of the Leo Baeck Institute* (London: East & West Library, 1959), pp. 172–82.

Buber Briefwechsel II, #475. Hermann Gerson to MB, April 23, 1934, p. 534, #477. MB to Hermann Gerson, April 27, 1934, p. 535; #478. MB to Hugo Bergmann, April 27, 1934, pp. 535 f.; #489. Carl Buber to MB,

August 5, 1934, p. 549; #517. Hermann Gerson to MB, Hedera, October 25, 1935, pp. 575–77; #519. MB to Hermann Gerson, November 14, 1935, p. 578; #520. Hermann Gerson to MB, December 10, 1935, p. 579; #523. Paul Weinberger to MB, February 5, 1936, pp. 581–83; #526. MB to Paul Weinberger, February 21, 1936, pp. 584 f.; #527. MB to Ludwig Strauss, March 9, 1936, pp. 585 f.; #528. MB to Hermann Gerson, May 1, 1936, pp. 592 f.; #534. Hermann Gerson to MB, June 4, 1936, p. 595; #541. MB to Hermann Gerson, July 29, 1936, pp. 601 f.; #543. Rafael Buber to Martin and Paula Buber, August 8, 1936, pp. 603 f.; #544. MB to Rafael Buber, Flims-Waldhaus, August 20, 1936, p. 605; #553. Ernst Simon to MB, October 30, 1936, pp. 614 f.; #570. Hermann Gerson to MB, February 3, 1937, pp. 635–37; #572. MB to Hermann Gerson, February 10, 1937, pp. 638 f.

Buber, *Zion als Ziel und als Aufgabe. Gedanken aus drei Jahrzehnten. Mit einer Rede über Nationalismus als Anhang.* Schocken Bücherei #62 (Berlin: Schocken Verlag, 1936), "Zum Geleit," p. 5.

Hebrew University Negotiations and Plans

Briefwechsel II, #466. Gerhard Scholem to MB, February 2, 1934, pp. 520–22; #467. Gerhard Scholem to MB, February 15, 1935, pp. 522 f.; #469. Judah Magnes to MB, February 21, 1934, pp. 525 f. and note 2, p. 525; #472. MB to Judah Magnes, March 3, 1934, pp. 529 f.; #482. MB to Salman Schocken, May 19, 1934, p. 539; #483. MB to Lambert Schneider, May 20, 1934, pp. 539 f.; #486. Hermann Gerson to MB, July 24, 1934, pp. 542–45; #490. MB to Hermann Gerson z. Zt. San Vigilio di Marebbe (Dolomiten), August 14, 1934, pp. 550 f.; #491. MB to Gerhard Scholem, August 20, 1934, p. 551; #492. Hermann Gerson to MB, August 28, 1934, pp. 551 f.; #493. MB to Hermann Gerson, September 7, 1934, pp. 552 f.; #498. Lambert Schneider to MB, October 2, 1934, pp. 558 f.; #499. MB to Salman Schocken, October 3, 1934, pp. 559–61; #508. MB to Hermann Gerson, June 27, 1935, pp. 566 f.; #514. MB to Paula Buber, Luzern, September 10, 1935, pp. 571–73; #516. MB to Gerhard Scholem, October 10, 1935, pp. 574 f.; #518. MB to Hugo Bergmann, November 13, 1935, pp. 577 f.; #521. Hugo Bergmann to MB, January 9, 1936; #530. MB to Hugo Bergmann, April 16, 1936, pp. 588–91; #531. Hugo Bergmann to MB, April 23, 1936, pp. 591 f.; #540. Gerhard Scholem to MB, July 16, 1936, p. 600; #544. MB to Rafael Buber, Flims-Waldhaus, August 20, 1936, p. 605; #576. MB to Gerhard Scholem, April 19, 1937, pp. 643 f.; #580; MB to Ernst Simon, November 5, 1937, pp. 646–48; #572. MB to Hermann Gerson, February 10, 1937, p. 639; #581. MB to Hugo Bergmann, November 12, 1927, p. 650; #586. MB to David Werner Senator, Berlin, January 28, 1938, pp. 651 f.; #587. David Werner Senator to MB, January 29, 1938, pp. 652 f.; #594. MB to Ernst Simon, March 2, 1938, p. 658.

Martin Buber Files of the Hebrew University Archives, Jerusalem, Israel— Letter from Judah Magnes to MB, August 1, 1933; Universitätes Schema der Religionswissenschaft, November 30, 1933 (sent by Buber to

Magnes); letter from Judah L. Magnes to MB, February 21, 1934; letter from J. L. Magnes to MB, March 16, 1934; letter from MB to Magnes, March 26, 1934; cable from Magnes to MB, April 5, 1934; letter from Magnes to MB, April 3, 1934; letter from MB to Magnes, April 16, 1934; letter from MB to Magnes, May 22, 1934; letter from MB to Magnes, San Vigilio di Marebbe (Prov. di Bolzano, Italien), August 10, 1934; Agenda, Section II (4) (A) (a)—memo on appointment of Prof. M. Buber from February 14, 1934, by the University Council of the Hebrew University; letter from MB to University (Magnes?), August 14, 1935; letter from Dr. A. S. W. Rosenbach, President, American Friends of the Hebrew University, to Salman Schocken at Hebrew University, October 23, 1935; letter from S. Ginzberg to Buber, Lucerne, September 13, 1935; letter from Schocken to Rosenbach, November 21, 1935; page in Buber's handwriting titled "Gesellschaftphilosophie" (Social Philosophy); letter from Charles J. Rosenbloom to American Friends of the Hebrew University, January 30, 1936; letter from the secretariat and financial officer of the Hebrew University to MB, August 12, 1936; letter from M. Ben-David to Magnes, February 24, 1937; application by David Werner Senator to Commission for Migration and Statistics, Jerusalem, for certificate under Labour Schedule for MB, June 9, 1937; letter of David Werner Senator, administrator to Magnes, June 22, 1937; comments made by Magnes in margins of Senator's letter of June 22, July 9, 1937; resolution re: appointment of Professor Buber, June 30, 1937; two letters of David Werner Senator to Magnes, July 13, 1937; letter from Magnes to Senator, August 2, 1937; letters from MB to Senator, September 11 and 30, October 14 and 23, November 3, 10, 17, 25, 29, 1937; letter of Magnes to Senator, December 19, 1937; letter of Senator to Magnes, December 20, 1937; letter of MB to Senator, December 23, 1937; letter of Senator to MB, January 2, 1938; letter of MB to Senator, January 5, 1938; letter of Senator to MB, January 13, 1938; letters of MB to Senator, January 15 and 30, March 16, 1938.

Buber Briefwechsel III, #496. MB to Albrecht Goes, Jerusalem, December 21, 1962, p. 559.

Buber's Sixtieth Birthday

Briefwechsel II, #588. Hugo Bergmann to MB, February, 4, 1938, pp. 653 f.; #589. Hans Trüb to MB, February 6, 1938, pp. 654 f.; #590. Salman Schocken to MB, February 6, 1938, p. 655; #592. Isaak Heinemann to MB, February 7, 1938, pp. 656 f.; #593. Hermann Hesse to MB, February 11, 1938, p. 657; #594. MB to Ernst Simon, March 2, 1938, p. 658; #596. MB to Salman Schocken, March 9, 1938, p. 659.

Note A

Margarete Buber-Neumann was with Kafka's friend Milena Jesenska when the latter died in a concentration camp, and she survived to write a book *Under Two Dictators* under the name Margarete Buber-Neumann (which both Martin and

Paula strenuously objected to when I made the mistake of mentioning her to them: "She has no right to use that name!" they exclaimed).

Note B

Bergmann responded sympathetically that it had pained him extremely that his letter had caused Buber so much concern while it was intended only as a proposal tailored to the customs there and not taking into consideration Buber's personal situation. He advised him to write to Schocken saying he would come to Palestine in the fall but would begin his lectures only in the summer semester (after Passover). He strongly advised him against mentioning his idea of laying the groundwork for an adult folk school during that time, as he had declared himself ready to do, since it was not directly connected with his teaching activities, and advised him instead to spend most of his energy in preparing himself to lecture in Hebrew.

SOURCES FOR CHAPTER 14:
Jerusalem and *What Is Man?*

• ——————————————————————— •

Buber Briefwechsel III, #2. MB to Gerhard Scholem, May 13, 1938, p. 10; #7. MB to Eduard Strauss, July 31, 1938, p. 13; #8. MB to Hans Trüb, August 1, 1938, p. 14; #9. MB to Hermann Gerson, October 22, 1938, pp. 14 f.; #10. Otto Hirsch to MB, November 5, 1938, p. 15; #12. Abraham J. Heschel to MB, Warsaw, November 25, 1938, p. 16; #13. Arnold Berney to MB, Baden, November 28, 1938, p. 17; #14. Eduard Strauss to MB, on board the *Rex,* December 5, 1938, p. 18; #15. Ernst Kantorowicz to MB, December 30, 1938, pp. 18 f.; #16. MB to Eduard Strauss, January 8, 1939, pp. 19 f.; #17. MB to Franz Oppenheimer, beginning of 1939, pp. 20 f.; #18. MB to Hans Trüb, February 5, 1939, pp. 21 f.; #19. Franz Oppenheimer to MB, Yokahama, April 1, 1939, p. 22; #21. Hermann Gerson to MB, May 2, 1939, p. 23; #22. MB to Eduard Strauss, May 7, 1939, p. 24; #23. MB to Hermann Gerson, May 12, 1939, p. 25; #69. Kurt Singer to MB, Melbourne, July 8, 1944.

Schalom Ben-Chorin, *Zwiesprache mit Martin Buber* (Munich: List Verlag, 1966), pp. 22 f., 26–30, 109–12, 127 f.

Buber, *A Believing Humanism: Gleanings,* "Authentic Bilingualism," pp. 80–82.

Buber, *Pointing the Way,* "The Demand of the Spirit and Historical Reality," pp. 177–91; "Bergson's Concept of Intuition," pp. 81–86.

Buber, *Between Man and Man,* "The Education of Character," pp. 104–17; "What Is Man?" pp. 118–205.

The Martin Buber File of the Hebrew University Archives, Jerusalem, File II —1944–1952, letter of David Senator to Walter Zander of the English Friends of the Hebrew University, 1945; notes by David Senator on a conversation with MB, June 16, 1945.

Martin Buber, "Bergson and Intuition" (Hebrew), Introduction to Henri

Bergson, *Spiritual Energy (Energia Ruhanit). Essays and Lectures* (Hebrew), Part 1 (Tel Aviv: Massada, 1944), pp. 7–16. (This is the large first part of Buber's essay that was not included in *Pointing the Way*, or *Hinweise*. It was translated for me from the Hebrew by Uri Margolin.)

Conversation with Professor Jacob Katz of the Hebrew University, Jerusalem, Israel, Spring 1966.

Conversation with Aharon Shoshar at the Hebrew University, Jerusalem, Spring 1966.

Conversation with Shmuel Eisenstadt, Jerusalem, Spring 1966.

SOURCES FOR CHAPTER 15:

Prewar Palestine

• ———————————————————————— •

Ernst Simon, "Nationalismus, Zionismus und der jüdisch-arabische Konflikt in Martin Bubers Theorie und Wirksamkeit," *loc. cit.*, pp. 67–71.

Martin Buber, *Am V'Olam* (Hebrew) (Jerusalem: Hasporiah Hazionit, 1964), Ernst Simon, "Buber's Political Way" (Introductory essay) and "Against Betrayal," trans. for me by Uri Margolin.

Buber, *Der Jude und sein Judentum*, "Gegen die Untreue" (July 1938), pp. 527–30; "Pseudo-Samsonismus" (June 1939), pp. 530–35.

Two Letters to Gandhi from Martin Buber and J. L. Magnes. The Bond, Pamphlets of the Group "The Bond," Jerusalem, No. 1 (Jerusalem: Rubin Mass, April 1939), Buber's letter, pp. 1–22, Gandhi's statement from *Harijan,* November 26, 1938, pp. 39–44.

Buber, *Pointing the Way,* "A Letter to Gandhi," pp. 141–47.

Buber Briefwechsel III, #6. Mordechai Avi-Sch'ul to MB, July 29, 1938, pp. 12 f.; #8. MB to Hans Trüb, August 1, 1938, p. 14; #24. Rudolf Pannwitz to MB, May 23, 1939, pp. 25 f.; #26. Ludwig Binswanger to MB, June 3, 1939, pp. 27 f.

SOURCES FOR CHAPTER 16:

The Second World War

and *For the Sake of Heaven*

• ———————————————————————— •

The Second World War

Briefwechsel II, #28. MB to Leonhard Ragaz, September 29, 1939, pp. 29 f.; #30. Abraham J. Heschel to MB, November 22, 1939, p. 31; #39. Leonhard Ragaz to MB, February 26, 1941, p. 43; #43. MB to Leopold Marx, September 8, 1941, pp. 46 f.; #44. MB to Thomas Mann, September 30, 1941, pp. 47–49; #49. Thomas Mann to MB, December 14, 1941, p. 55; #45. Leonhard Ragaz to MB, January 21, 1942, pp. 57 f.; #52. MB to Leonhard Ragaz, June 2, 1942, p. 60; #53. Leonhard Ragaz to MB, June

15, 1942, p. 62 and note 4; #57. MB to Leonhard Ragaz, December 12, 1941, p. 66.

Schalom Ben-Chorin, *Zwiesprache,* pp. 77, 142.

Walter Goldstein, *Martin Buber, Gespräche, Briefe, Worte,* pp. 96–99, 103.

Martin Buber, "Züge in Wilfrids Bild," in *Wilfrid Israel, July 11th, 1899–June 1st, 1943* (London: Marlsand Publications, Ltd., 1944), pp. 6 f.

Buber, *A Believing Humanism: Gleanings,* "Rachman, A Distant Spirit, Speaks," p. 223. (For the German original see p. 222.)

Buber, *Der Jude und sein Judentum,* "Schweigen und Schreien" (Spring 1944), pp. 655–58.

Buber, "Silence and Outcry" (1944) in E. William Rollins and Harry Zohn, eds., *Men of Dialogue: Martin Buber and Albrecht Goes,* pp. 244–48.

Buber's Life in Palestine

Buber Briefwechsel III, #34. MB to Hans Trüb, April 14, 1940, pp. 37 f.; #42. MB to Samuel Joseph Agnon, September 3, 1941, p. 46; #47. Else Lask-er-Schüler to MB, November 13, 1941, p. 54; #52. MB to Leonhard Ragaz, June 2, 1941, pp. 60 f.; #54. MB to Leonhard Ragaz, November 3, 1942, pp. 62 f.

Schalom Ben-Chorin, *Ich Lebe in Jerusalem* (Munich: Paul List Verlag, 1972), p. 145.

Schalom Ben-Chorin, *Zwiesprache mit Martin Buber,* pp. 75–77, 113.

Werner Kraft, *Gespräche mit Martin Buber,* pp. 37, 131, 149.

Walter B. Goldstein, *Martin Buber. Gespräche, Briefe, Worte* (Jerusalem: Rubin Mass Verlag, 1967), pp. 76, 100 f., 113, 121.

Conversations with Lea Goldberg in Jerusalem, Spring and Summer 1966.

Buber, *A Believing Humanism: Gleanings,* "An Example: On the Landscapes of Leopold Krakauer," pp. 106–08.

For the Sake of Heaven

Briefwechsel III, #38. MB to Samuel Joseph Agnon, January 1941, p. 41 and note 2 to p. 41; #46. MB to Leonhard Ragaz, November 17, 1941, pp. 52 f.; #50. Leonhard Ragaz to MB, April 21, 1942, pp. 55–57; #54. MB to Leonhard Ragaz, November 3, 1942, p. 63.

Martin Buber, *Gog und Magog, Eine Chronik* (Heidelberg: Verlag Lambert Schneider, 1949), "Nachwort," pp. 401–08.

Buber, *For the Sake of Heaven,* trans. from the German by Ludwig Lewisohn, 2d ed. (New York: Harper & Row, Philadelphia: Jewish Publication Society, 1953), "Foreword to the New Edition," pp. vii–xiii (this "Foreword" is not reprinted in the Atheneum Books paperback edition), pp. 101–03, *passim.*

Maurice S. Friedman, "Martin Buber: Mystic, Existentialist, Social Prophet— A Study in the Redemption of Evil" (University of Chicago dissertation, June 1950, The University of Chicago Library, Microfilm #T809), Chap. 15, "The Yehudi and the Seer: Dialectic of Good and Evil."

Maurice Friedman, "Martin Buber's *For the Sake of Heaven* and Dostoievsky's *The Brothers Karamazov,*" *Comparative Literature Studies* (May 1966).

Martin Buber, *The Origin and Meaning of Hasidism,* Chap. 4, "Spirit and Body of the Hasidic Movement," pp. 129–31.

Paul Arthur Schilpp and Maurice Friedman, eds., *The Philosophy of Martin Buber,* The Library of Living Philosophers (LaSalle, Ill.: The Open Court Publishing Co., 1967), Karl Kerényi, "Martin Buber as Classical Author," pp. 635–38; Rivka Schatz-Uffenheimer, "Man's Relation to God and World in Buber's Rendering of the Hasidic Teaching," pp. 424–34; Martin Buber, "Replies to My Critics," trans. by Maurice Friedman, pp. 737–41.

Baruch Kurzweil, "Buber's Gog and Magog," *Ha–aretz* (Hebrew, Tel Aviv) November 24, 1944, trans. for me by Uri Margolin.

Index